NATIONALISM AND EMPIRE

NATIONALISM AND EMPIRE

THE HABSBURG EMPIRE AND THE
SOVIET UNION

Edited by

Richard L. Rudolph and David F. Good

St. Martin's Press
in association with the Center for Austrian Studies,
University of Minnesota

For information write:
Scholarly & Reference Division
St. Martin's Press, 175 Fifth Avenue
New York, N.Y. 10010

First published in the United States of America in 1992

Printed in the United States of America
ISBN   0-312-06892-1

Library of Congress Cataloging-in-Publication Data

Nationalism and empire: the Habsburg Empire and the Soviet Union /
    edited by Richard L. Rudolph and David F. Good.
        p. cm.
    Rev. and expanded versions of papers presented at a symposium held
    Apr. 26-28, 1990, sponsored by the Center for Austrian Studies at
    the University of Minnesota.
    Includes bibliographical references and index.
    ISBN 0-312-06892-1
    1. Austria—Politics and government—1848-1918—Congresses.
2. Nationalism—Austria—Congresses. 3. Austria—Ethnic relations
—Congresses. 4. Soviet Union—Politics and government—1945-
—Congresses. 5. Nationalism—Soviet Union—Congresses. 6. Soviet
Union—Ethnic relations—Congresses. I. Rudolph, Richard L., 1935-
. II. Good, David F. III. University of Minnesota. Center for
Austrian Studies.
DB48.N35 1992
305.8'009436—dc20   91-39433
                                                          CIP

TABLE OF CONTENTS

REFLECTIONS ON NATIONALISM AND EMPIRE

PREFACE

Can the past illuminate the present? This age-old question guided historians and social scientists as they gathered for the symposium "Great Power Ethnic Politics: The Habsburg Empire and the Soviet Union" sponsored by the Center for Austrian Studies at the University of Minnesota, April 26-28, 1990. This volume contains revised and expanded versions of the papers from the conference, which ensures that the findings will have the wide audience they deserve.

The idea behind the symposium was simple. The Habsburg Empire dissolved in 1918 in part because it could not contain the growing conflict among its nationalities. In the same period, the Soviet Union stabilized its multinational empire on the heels of the Russian Revolution. The year 1989 marked the early rumblings of ethnic discontent in the Soviet bloc, which rapidly brought on a political crisis of major proportions. Our goal was to examine the current Soviet crisis in light of both the Habsburg experience and the Soviet experience in the early twentieth century. Of course events quickly outran our ability to absorb them as violence and calls for independence reverberated throughout Eastern Europe and within the republics of the Soviet Union. By spring 1990, the academic gathering that we had been conceived as a fascinating intellectual exercise had assumed major policy significance. As of this writing (August, 1991), the Soviet Union has all but disintegrated as a centralized state.

No single conference, of course, can yield conclusive answers to such a complex issue, so it is not surprising that participants failed to reach a consensus on the likely course of events in the Soviet Union. Some predicted an imminent disintegration of the Soviet Union similar to the dismemberment of the Habsburg Empire after World War I. Others predicted a more protracted period of decline during which many of the Soviet republics would negotiate and win varying degrees of autonomy from Moscow. All left with a strong sense that comparing these three cases of empire had been a valuable exercise, despite the vast differences in time and space.

The papers offer rich insights into the pressures faced by the central authority in a multinational state as it tries to hold together its territories and peoples. Subsequent events have taught us the more general importance of the papers and the symposium that generated them. The end of the cold war and the dawn of the new Europe have brought both the promise of unity and the reality of rising ethnic tensions. How to accommodate demands for cultural diversity in the face of increased pressures for economic and political integration may well be *the* central issue faced by Europeans in the next century. In this sense, the themes discussed here transcend both the Habsburg and the Soviet cases.

With a gift of $1 million from Austria to the University of Minnesota, the Center for Austrian Studies began in 1977 to serve as the focal point in North America for the study of Austria across disciplines. The symposium marked the entry by the Center into discussions on the shape of the new Europe. The theme symbolizes Austria's historic and geographic position in the heart of Central Europe, which gives it and the Center a unique and significant role in these discussions.

The editors thank Professor William O. McCagg, Jr., for his intellectual contributions in planning the symposium and for arranging some of the financing. Suzanne Sinke skillfully and patiently served as symposium coordinater and worked with Barbara Krauss-Christensen, the Center's executive secretary, to organize on-site logistics. Several other participants contributed to the success of the symposium and therefore indirectly to the volume: from Minnesota—Evelyn Davidheiser, Edwin Fogelman, Helga Leitner, Norma Noonan, Leonard Polakiewicz, and R. John Rath; and from outside Minnesota—Peter Hanák, Jan Havranek, Andrew Janos, Charles Jelavich, Andreas Moritsch, Drago Roksandic, Arnold Suppan, and Robert Wistrich. Major funding was provided by the Winton Chair of the College of Liberal Arts, University of Minnesota. The symposium was cosponsored by the Austrian Cultural Institute in New York and received generous support from several other sources: the College of Liberal Arts, the Department of Political Science, the Department of History, and the Western European Studies Center at the University of Minnesota; the Russian and East European Studies Center at Michigan State University; and the Institute on East Central Europe at Columbia University.

The chapter by Valery Tishkov is reprinted with slight editorial changes by permission of Kluwer Academic Publishers from *Theory and Society* 20 (October 1991) 603-629.

The Editors wish to thank Barbara Jelavich for her advice and encouragement. Mary Beth Ailes did outstanding work preparing the manuscript as assistant editor and Mary Byers copyedited the manuscript with exceptional care and thoroughness.

The editors gratefully acknowledge generous subsidies from the Austrian Cultural Institute in New York and the Center for Austrian Sutdies at the University of Minnesota.

David F. Good
Minneapolis, Minnesota
August, 1991

INTRODUCTION

1

Nationalism and Empire in Historical Perspective

Richard L. Rudolph

The specter that is haunting Europe at the end of the twentieth century is no longer communism but nationalism, the force which some have called the most important historical factor in the twentieth century. There are two immense struggles taking place in Europe at the present time, and they both involve the enormous force of nationalist movements. One is the battle of one of the last great Leviathans, the Soviet empire, to hold on to its political and territorial power. In this struggle, a multinational empire must deal with ethnic movements that threaten to tear it apart. At the same time, both within the Soviet Union and within the former members of its bloc, there is a contest between, on the one side, those who envision a common economic and political entity for all of Europe, and those who strive for autonomy or independence for smaller ethnically based units.

These broad struggles are central to an understanding of modern European history, but they are in no way clear-cut or simple. The essays in this book are in essence attempts to deal with various aspects of these historical processes. The authors, a distinguished group of scholars from different countries and disciplines, have sought to deal with both the theory and practice of imperial rule and nationalist strivings. The task undertaken has been to examine the problems of governance of multinational empires and the varieties of experience of nationalist movements within these empires in the context of comparing the Soviet case with the Habsburg and Russian imperial experience.

Three overarching themes are dealt with in the following pages. First, there is the problem of the nature of empires and their ability to sustain themselves. In looking at this question, as in surveying the others, the propitious mixture of political scientists, sociologists, and historians allows us first to examine the theory of empire, or what theory in reality offers us, namely, the range of logical possibilities inherent in the nature of empires. To begin, Alexander J. Motyl, in "From Imperial Decay to Imperial Collapse: The Fall of the Soviet Empire in Comparative Perspective," examines the theory and practice of empire in the Soviet Union and argues that the origins of change must be viewed in the light of "the dynamics of empire in general and of imperial decline in particular." Motyl contends that empires contain within them the seeds of their own dissolution and will inevitably decline. He states further that, as in the Soviet and Habsburg cases, "absolutism engenders pathologies that lead to its own degeneration." What is involved is an overextension of rule and the need for the decentralization of power. When power is decentralized, however, in whatever way, constituencies are formed that vie with the center for power, and in the long run the center cannot hold. Eventually, according to Motyl's schema, the center implodes and the subordinate parts are left to fend for themselves. To what extent Motyl's thesis is valid may be judged in reading through the other chapters that shade in the actual histories of the regions and that offer their own particular views of the historical processes involved. Also important in this regard is the chapter written by William O. McCagg, as well as the comments of others, with respect to the degree to which the Soviet Union and Habsburg empires are comparable.

The second major question concerns the development of nationalist movements within the various empires. In part the studies deal with the problem of understanding exactly what is meant by nationalism.[1] Nationalism itself, undergoing a powerful renaissance in Central and Eastern Europe, is an awesome phenomenon. Both political and cultural nationalism stem from movements in the late eighteenth century, flowing at times then, as now, from earlier local or tribal consciousness. The timing of the birth of these movements is most significant. They arose in the period when the age of rationalism and science was gradually replacing theology as the predominant European worldview. In essence, nationalist ideology has elements of both worlds: it belongs to a period when folk beliefs, religious fervor, and romantic philosophy combined with scientific and pseudoscientific arguments as to the nature of human society. These ideas spoke of mystical national destinies and the special particular identities of each national group, the *Volk*. In many instances the nationalist movements were mixed with the new ideas of racism, born, as well, in the eighteenth century from some of the same sources, as well as from the infant science of anthropology. The rationalists and Marxists argued, then as now, that nationalism was an aberration, was irrational; that it was merely a way for rulers to keep their subjects divided and eventually, in a rational society, would wither away. Yet what they did not grasp was that nationalism has been a fundamentally religious movement. Already in the 1930s the inveterate scholar of nationalism, Hans Kohn, in his study of nationalism in the Soviet Union, discussed the religious qualities of nationalism. He saw nationalism serving, as it were, as a functional equivalent of religion in the modern secular world. In discussing the various contentions of the new Marxist ideology with those of the nationalists, Kohn argued that economics were important, but that

> this economic fear for his livelihood is not man's only mortal fear. His creaturely fear proceeds from more fundamental depths in the human soul. In modern times the religious conception of the world with its sheltering God had broken down. The individual had become master of himself, and at home amid his natural world and the laws which it observed, but no longer felt assured of the continuance of his existence in any purely transcendental sense. Under the stress of his isolation he sought for association, for permanence, for immortality: for a bond, for 'religion.' Here we have the basis of the significance of nationalism as the religious force of modern times. In community with his compatriots, with whom he forms a living and organic whole, the individual finds companionship on his way and a removal of the limitations of his influence; it is thus in our times that he attains an extension and multiplication of his personality amid the national mass-emotions, as the individual of the past did amid the ecstasies of worship.[2]

This is not to say that nationalism does not fulfill actual needs in the real world. In many cases it has become the battle cry of economically and psychically oppressed ethnic groups, and in fact, as nationalism grew and nationalist states came to power, national differences increasingly became a reason for oppressing people, thus leading to an even greater rationale for ardent nationalist strivings.

Like other religious or semireligious movements, nationalism has more than one sect, and as one reads through the chapters here one quickly learns that there are many varieties of nationalism, as well as many responses to it. In this respect Helmut Konrad's contribution, "Between 'Little International' and Great Power Politics: Austro-Marxism and Stalinism on the National Question," is most instructive. In dealing with the debate over Austro-Marxism, and particularly Stalin's critique of it, Konrad touches on the varying attempts to understand the meanings and ramifications of the concept of nation. He then comments on the working out of the concept of nationality in the incipient Soviet state and notes in passing the significant question of fascist ideas of nationalism. Konrad's essay is essential for an understanding of the Soviet views and practices with regard to nationality. Konrad is followed by the Czech scholar Miroslav Hroch, who develops a powerful argument concerning the degree to which language and language rights are integral to nationalist movements; he contends that they are a vital integrating factor of community and provides arguments as well as warnings concerning the consequences of such struggles over language.

The chapter by John-Paul Himka, "Nationality Problems in the Habsburg Monarchy and the Soviet Union," is a particularly helpful one, because it essentially shades in the actual historical processes referred to by Alexander Motyl in his theoretical posing of the dynamics of imperial rule. Himka traces the history of the nationality question both in the Habsburg domains and in the Soviet Union, and in many regards he demonstrates the validity of Motyl's ideas concerning the interaction between center and periphery, between imperial rulers and nationalist governed. He contends that in contrast to the case of the Soviets, in the Habsburg lands national differences tended to coincide with social differences, and holds that this is one of the reasons that one finds less antagonism between the peoples of the Soviet Union during the revolutionary period. He also points out that although the Bolsheviks had initially strongly supported the nationalist groups in "Russia, the Prison of Nations," still, already in early 1923, Stalin had begun his attacks on the nationalists. In a later section, which deals with alternative paths for empire, the essay by Valery Tishkov elaborates on the dialectic of center versus the nationalities as it has worked itself out throughout the Soviet period both before and since the inauguration of *perestroika*.

From this overall treatment of the nationalities problems, the essays turn to enlightening case studies. Paul Magocsi examines the experience of the Ukrainians in Eastern Galicia, which provides us with an opportunity to view the same ethnic group under both the Habsburgs and the Soviets. Magocsi distinguishes between two types of nationalism. The first is inspired by the intelligentsia and emanates from below, while the second type is imposed by the state. In the first type leaders tried to convince people that they formed a distinct nationality and as such deserved cultural or political autonomy or even independence. In the second case, the state attempts to use nationalism to obtain the allegiance of the people. In the Ukrainian case, the intellectual-led popular movement was met by activities on the part of both the Habsburgs and the Soviets to impose their own versions of state-oriented nationalism upon Galicia's Ukrainians. For the Habsburgs it was loyalty to an imperial dynasty, whereas for the Soviets it was loyalty to a "classless and eventually nationless Communist state." This generated multiple loyalties, which Magocsi contends are the basis of the particular nature of Ukrainian national aspirations in both the past and present. One of the most important conclusions one might reach after reading Magocsi's discussion is the degree to which one may view nationalism, as well as attempts to create various types of nationalist loyalties, as an artifice; one begins to see nationalism as an ideology formed by human beings, rather than as an innate human trait. This, I think, is vitally important, for although nationalism is a powerful historical force, and appears to reflect special psychic and cultural needs, it is at the same time an artificial and time-bound construct with its own not-too-ancient history.

This historical aspect of nationalism is further elucidated by Tofik M. Islamov, who in subtle and elaborate fashion points out the many versions of the concept of "nation" in differing historical contexts, using the Hungarian experience as a case study. A vital element in his essay is his treatment of the different nuances in national movements as they reflect different political, class, and cultural influences. In particular, he traces the formation of the Hungarian nation from the origins of the *natio*, which was a non-national entity, the nobility, to its later manifestation, still with a mixed nature, in light of the fact that to be considered a Magyar patriot one need not have had Magyar ethnic origins.

Islamov's essay is followed by that of Sergei Romanenko, who compares movements for national autonomy in the Habsburg and the Russian empires as reflected in the experiences of the Finns, Croatians, and Slovenians. Here again one sees still other variants. Romanenko argues that within both the Austro-Hungarian Monarchy and Russia the focus of these national movements was on ways of attaining degrees of self-determination *within* the framework of the existing multinational empires. In dealing with this topic, Romanenko demonstrates the degree to which, as Motyl argued, the individual parts of the empire begin acting on their own, with, for example, the Croatian tendency at the turn of the century to conduct its own foreign relations, while the Finns developed their own military policy. At the same time, there are parallels with the present in the degree to which imperial policy was complicated by interethnic rivalry, such as that of the Finns and Swedes or the Croatians and Serbs.

Henryk Szlajfer discusses the relationships between the Soviets in the early revolutionary period and the Asian nationalist and revolutionary movements. He describes the degree to which the interests of the Asian revolutionaries and the Russian Bolsheviks for a time merged and then parted. The dynamics of this relationship are a rarely discussed topic and are particularly germane for understanding current developments within the Soviet Union. In contrast to Himka, who stresses Stalin's attacks on the nationalists beginning in 1923, Szlajfer traces an earlier beginning, noting that as early as 1918 there were no Communist parties independent from the center. Already from this time the Bolsheviks began to take up the mantle as heirs to the imperial tradition, adopting the "theory of the historical superiority of large state organisms," and continuing Russia's historical mission toward the east. The dominant view of the center was that the revolution would solve the national question and that "any disintegration or territorial weakening of Russia would constitute a historical setback—from the point of view of the further development of 'civilization' in the backward areas." Under these circumstances the interests of the Kirghiz, Kazakhs and other groups that had joined in the revolution were now subordinated to the leadership of the Russian Communists.

The third major theme of the book is that of the methods of rule, and in particular, questions as to the degree to which nationalities of the empire can or should stay together. Dennison Rusinow offers a unique and stimulating analysis of the national question in the Habsburg Monarchy and its successor states and offers a variety of solutions to the problems of nationalism. Among other things, he poses the vital question as to whether or not the national state is the only basis for a modern polity, for a modern legitimate state. This question very clearly points up the importance of not confusing what could be with what is, or with what is possible. That is to say, the question is raised as to the historical inevitability of the predominance of the nation-state system into the future. Rusinow discusses three possible answers or solutions to the national question and takes a cost-benefit approach to degrees of heterogeneity versus homogeneity within states. A number of the essays in this volume, including that of Rusinow, raise the question of various forms of federation. Already in the mid-nineteenth century the Czech historian and nationalist František Palacký argued for a continued federation of Central European nations within the framework of the Habsburg Monarchy, with the elemental rationale that if the small nations were to pursue their own independent paths they would fall prey to the larger states on their borders. Similar ideas were put forth by the Hungarian revolutionary leader Lajos Kossuth, among others, and were to be raised periodically in the twentieth century, particularly in the interwar period and during the period of Soviet hegemony over the region following World War II. At the time of the Soviet invasion of Czechoslovakia in 1968 the slogan "FSN" or "Federation of Central European Nations" was written on the walls of buildings in Prague.[3] After 1989 the theme of close cooperation has again emerged in the region, and this theme is developed in Erhard Busek's contribution to this volume.

István Deák brings out an important aspect in terms of the methods of rule of the two empires. Deák describes the government's policy toward the military and discusses what he sees as a major difference between the Habsburgs and the Russian and Soviet empires. According to Deák, while the Habsburg policy increasingly moved in the direction of ethnic neutrality and decentralization within the military, the Soviets increased the weight of Great Russian and Slavic nationalism as well as centralized control. Deák suggests that this Soviet policy may have contributed to the current crisis in the Soviet army and hence in the Soviet empire. From the perspective of Alexander Motyl, the two different policies in reality would merely be different inevitable phases of imperial rule, in the sense that the centralized empire must eventually try to decentralize in order to hold on to power and in so doing creates peripheral groups that will do battle against the center. However, Deák's contribution leads one to consider whether bureaucratic decentralization might not have been an asset in terms of maintaining ethnic loyalties, and hence in maintaining imperial cohesion.

Erhard Busek in his turn discusses the variations on the theme of holding the region together. In his article, "Concepts of Cooperation in Central Europe," he deals with the concept and historical reality of a *Mitteleuropa*. He notes that there were not only ideas of cooperation, such as those of Palacký, but also ideas of domination by Germany of the Central and East-Central European area. All of these ideas were to have echoes in the period of intense nationalist rivalry of the 1920s and 1930s and again in the present. The ramifications of these ideas will be discussed later. The concluding section of the book contains remarks by Teresa Rakowska-Harmstone and Walter Leitsch, who were asked to analyze the various contributions as a whole. Their remarks also serve to enhance a comparative view of the Habsburg and Soviet experiences.

Teresa Rakowska-Harmstone speaks of two themes that predominate in the essays: the emergence of modern nationalism and its immediate and inevitable corollary, the decline and disintegration of the imperial structures within which the new nations appeared. She stresses that the new nations are seen as part of natural law, as it were, and that loyalty to them overrides all other competing loyalties. "It inevitably follows, therefore, that a community's destiny is fulfilled only when its nationhood converges with a statehood or, in other words, when it emerges into the international arena as a sovereign nation-state. Nationalism is thus the only true source of political legitimacy." While some might debate this, it is an important view, particularly in that it raises the question of the inexorable and necessary development of nationalist movements to the point where they develop the singular goal of attaining national independence. To put this another way, in the nineteenth century, and in many cases up to World War I, one could speak of nationalist demands for various degrees of autonomy, but since that time the call was primarily for outright national-political independence and sovereignty.

It is Rakowska-Harmstone who touches the heart of the problem of empire and nationalism when she states that among the features held in common by the various imperial systems, "none was able to develop a common identity that would override new burgeoning political loyalties based in particular nationalisms. All failed in developing policies that would neutralize and counteract nationalist claims." Essentially, nationalism was an ideology that withstood or superseded all others. Neither the idea of a supranational loyalty to the Habsburgs or Romanovs nor the promise of a socialist utopia could surpass the psychic and social value of nationalism. The question arises as to whether the promise of economic and social progress on a vast scale, as promised now by the "market system," will have any more success in lessening the potency of nationalist and separatist movements.

Although it has been remarked here that nationalism has a semireligious character, it should be noted that nationalism also has extremely real functions in the political and economic spheres as well. Once the nationalist movements develop, they play a vital role in legitimizing particular political leaders. The birth of the idea of nationalism in politics came with political leaders of the early modern period who utilized local and regional loyalties to marshal forces for centralization and conquering neighboring enemies. In turn, once national sentiments had been unleashed, various political leaders could harness these sentiments to further their own careers. In the period after World War I, as in the present period, one of the strongest weapons in political campaigns in Eastern Europe has been the waving of a national banner. We have often seen the rise of increasingly nationalist leaders, as politicians vied with each other as to who was the most ardent representative of the true national destinies of the people. Thus nationalism became the major legitimizing factor for Central and Eastern European governments. It was also true that one of the chief factors inhibiting cooperation between the nationalities in Eastern Europe was this wedding of political leadership to strong nationalist programs. In a broader sense, nationalism was the cry taken up by the peripheral powers against the imperial center, and as such served to rally support for local leaders against the center, a phenomenon much in evidence in the Soviet Union today. Nationalism is reinforced within the economic sphere as well. In difficult times the theme of economic nationalism has supported the view that if only a nation had sovereignty and complete economic independence, or autarky, then its economic development would be much greater. Historically, since the mid-eighteenth century, cries against foreign capital, colonial treatment, or alleged influence of particular nationalities have been a strong part of nationalism. While economists with rare exception hold that economic cooperation and economies of scale are the path to economic progress, nevertheless, the virulence of nationalist views makes the economic nationalist arguments sound convincing. All in all, political, cultural, and economic nationalism have proved to be mighty forces against centralized imperial rule.

Having said, however, that the elemental force of nationalism is great, one must raise the question as to the alternatives available to the imperial powers, and it is in this regard that one finds major differences of opinion. What choices do the imperial powers indeed have? In 1914, facing the growth of demands for national autonomy of various sorts within its borders, the leaders of the Austro-Hungarian Empire reasoned that if they taught the Serbian nationalists a lesson, the nationalist strivings of other groups within the Empire would be quelled. However, when the dust had settled after the invasion of Serbia and the subsequent worldwide conflict, all that was left of the Empire was the small, decapitated Austrian head, and the often contentious successor states. When one views some of the statements and policies of Mikhail Gorbachev with respect to the Baltic republics, one senses that the same kind of reasoning of holding back nationalist movements by opting for a quelling of the smallest protester is occurring. Yet the question arises as to what alternatives leaders may take if their goal is that of holding together an empire. The first alternative, that of maintaining it by force, seems, by the Habsburg example, to merely foment more strife. The idea of autonomy, however, either by revolt or by agreement, means giving power to the periphery and signals the end of empire. The third alternative, federation, is more promising, and yet the success of this alternative is based largely on what the center has to offer to counter nationalist dreams. It is probably not accidental that several of the Austrian contributors to this volume, notably Walter Leitsch and Erhard Busek, suggest that the gains for the nationalities who deserted the Empire after 1918 were not so great, and that they might well have done better within the Empire or at least within a federative framework. In his remarks at the conference Tofik M. Islamov argued that it is wrong to say that nationalist strivings were the element that destroyed the Habsburg Empire; in his opinion it was rather the overwhelming power of the Great Powers' military and diplomatic victories. In other words, it is too easy to say that the Empire, in a federative form, could not have held together. Valery Tishkov, too, discusses the alternatives facing the Soviet empire and weighs the possibility of success of federation.

Whether or not the decline of empire is inevitable, as scholars from Toynbee to Deutsch and Motyl have contended, is an issue to be debated. What is certain is that nationalism, for all the discussion of it as illogical and irrational, is so closely entwined with current views of political sovereignty that it will remain a key force to be studied and reckoned with. In a passing remark Busek comments on the "artificial" nations set up after World War I, just as people speak of the "historic" nations within the Habsburg Monarchy. In fact, however, all nations are "artificial" in a sense, for they are all products of romanticism. The paradox, however, is that the idealistic philosophy of Hegel is wreaking its revenge on the materialism of Marx in our age of reason. For it is these artificial and semireligious creations that are one of the strongest forces in political and social life in this century and that have destroyed one empire after another.

NOTES

1. For discussion of the various theories of nationalism see Karl W. Deutsch and William J. Foltz, eds., *Nation-Building* (New York, 1963); Anthony D. Smith, *Theories of Nationalism* (New York, 1971); Hans Kohn, *The Idea of Nationalism* (New York, 1948). For a description of nationalism as it developed in Eastern Europe see Peter Sugar and Ivo J. Lederer, eds., *Nationalism in Eastern Europe* (Seattle, 1969); and Emil Niederhauser, *The Rise of Nationality in Eastern Europe* (Budapest, 1982).
2. Hans Kohn, *Nationalism in the Soviet Union* (London, 1933), 18-19.
3. In Czech: "Federace středoevropských narodů."

THEORY

2

From Imperial Decay to Imperial Collapse: The Fall of the Soviet Empire in Comparative Perspective

Alexander J. Motyl

A puzzling development occurred in 1989. The Communist regimes of Eastern Europe collapsed quickly, simultaneously, and—with the exception of Romania—peacefully, while the Soviet Union itself approached systemic prostration. In Eastern Europe, protracted struggles were absent, regimes fell within weeks of one another, and for the most part violence, and even force, was eschewed. The USSR, a former superpower, proved incapable of containing nationalist demands and preventing regional fragmentation. It is no exaggeration to say that little in the past behavior of these states prepared scholars for such an ignominious performance.

Although no explanation of this remarkable string of events would be complete without a detailed look at the structure both of the states that weakened and of the societies that asserted themselves,[1] the simultaneity and universality of decline and fall suggest that a *common* external factor or set of factors may have been a necessary, and perhaps even a sufficient, condition of these internal upheavals. Placing these regimes in an international context is therefore imperative; seeing them as part of a larger system may be the *conditio sine qua non* of explaining the internal developments of 1989.

What sort of international system is most appropriate as a unit of analysis? As I shall argue in greater detail below, the concept of *empire* is especially suitable for the countries of Eastern Europe and the republics of the Soviet Union. Like the non-Russian republics, the former Soviet bloc countries were, I argue, part of a Soviet empire. Consequently, the collapse of Communist regimes in Eastern Europe and the self-assertion of the republics cannot be explained only in terms of state-society relations and their effect on regime transformation or transitions to democracy. Rather, these changes must be viewed as having had their origins in the dynamics of empire in general and of imperial decline in particular.

Although the collapse of Soviet imperial rule in Eastern Europe is not tantamount to the collapse of the Soviet empire, it will be worth our while to ask whether or not the former event heralds the latter and to compare both developments with other instances of imperial collapse. Two empires with comparable trajectories immediately come to mind, those of the Habsburgs and the Romanovs. Like the Soviet empire, they were continental and European; unlike the Soviet case, they had capitalist or semicapitalist economies, religiously grounded ideologies, propertied elites, and formal emperors. Indeed, just as the Romanov realm seems to have shared some of the Soviet empire's salient features—a point emphasized by Richard Pipes[2]—so, too, it is hard to imagine two imperial domains more outwardly dissimilar than those of the Habsburgs and the Soviets. In sum, not only are these three entities manifestly comparable, but they also appear to be sufficiently different from one another to allay fears that the "deck" is being "stacked." It is all the more significant, therefore, that a conceptually informed look at the historical development of these so similar, yet so different, political entities reveals uncanny uniformities as well as significant differences.

The most striking uniformity is the fact that the process of imperial decay and the reasons for imperial collapse appear to be identical in all three cases. Thereafter, the path of the Habsburg and Soviet realms diverges radically from that taken by the Romanov territories. Like Eastern Europe in 1989, the Habsburg lands embarked on simultaneous transitions from absolutism to various forms of democracy or authoritarianism within independent states. In sharp contrast, the Romanov realm fell under the sway of the absolutist rule of the Bolsheviks who proceeded to establish an empire of their own. Why such different outcomes? As we shall see, the nature of the center-periphery relations characterizing the Habsburg Empire and the Soviet domain on the one hand and the Romanov Empire on the other hand holds the answer to this question.

My approach in this essay is "comparative historical." My goal is not simply to compare the histories of several entities and draw appropriate lessons. That would be natural history, a method of which I am extremely skeptical as it assumes—quite wrongly, I believe—that history exists independently of the concepts we use to apprehend it.[3] As I am persuaded that history can be given meaning only by scholars and other interpreters, natural history becomes an impossibility and the only logical approach is to construct conceptual—that is, causal—schemes and then to impose them quite explicitly on the historical "record." Thus, I shall not be interpreting history, as such an act assumes that history exists prior to our interpretation. I shall, however, be constructing history by means of the rigorous examination of concepts—specifically, those of empire, imperial decay, absolutism, state decline, and crisis—and the assignation of causality to conceptual chains. In this sense, my approach, although nominally the same as Theda Skocpol's, differs fundamentally from her casual attitude toward conceptual clarity and from her belief that "facts" precede understanding.[4]

One final point. This study forms the basis of a larger work in progress on imperial decline, one that discusses theoretical approaches to this question in some detail. So as not to be redundant as well as due to limitations of space, I shall not refer extensively to the existing literature on the rise and fall of empires. Suffice to say that my own approach differs from the economically, sociologically, or ideologically grounded theories of Robert Gilpin, Joseph A. Tainter, Arnold Toynbee, and others in its aspiration to be explicitly political. In this sense, this study draws most on the work of S. N. Eisenstadt, Michael Doyle, Johan Galtung, Herbert Kaufman, and George L. Cowgill for inspiration.[5]

EMPIRES AND IMPERIAL DECAY

The starting point of my analysis is the concept of empire. According to Michael Doyle, "Empire . . . is a relationship, formal or informal, in which one state controls the effective political sovereignty of another political society."[6] George Lichtheim concurs, defining empire as the "relationship of a hegemonial state to peoples or nations under its control."[7] Two definitions suggest three questions. What sort of relationship does empire entail? What sort of entity is the subject of this relationship? And who or what is the object of the imperial relationship?

As Doyle and Lichtheim argue, the relationship is one of control, hegemony, or domination. These concepts have a common denominator—power—but the concept of power, as Jan-Erik Lane and Hans Stenlund show, has two different connotations. According to the first, the "concept of power is to be understood as a causal relation in which a power subject's behavior is the effect of the power holder's behavior." Alternatively, "power stands for the capacity of an actor to be able to change the outcomes of a decision-making situation in which there may not be any power subject in the proper sense as the power holder, being pivotal or decisive, may not cause any other actor to do something."[8] Not only did the Soviet, Habsburg, and Romanov empires involve both forms of power, but the distinctive characteristic of these entities is that both forms of power were so closely intertwined in them. In all three instances, de facto or de jure emperors possessed the capacity to make a pivotal difference in the decision-making process, and metropolitan centers, which were also the bailiwicks of the emperors, exercised decisive control over peripheral regions.

We require an entity with a bureaucratic and coercive apparatus for the relationship that it maintains with the periphery to be genuinely based on power. As Doyle and Lichtheim suggest, the center is best characterized as the *state*, which, in Anthony Giddens's words, is "a political organization whose rule is territorially ordered and which is able to mobilize the means of violence to sustain that rule."[9] Only the state—and not, say, the *political system*[10]—possesses this capacity.

In turn, three characteristics define a genuine imperial periphery. First, it is necessary for the periphery to be populated by a population distinct from that of the center. Second, the periphery must be either a distinct polity or a distinct society. And third, the periphery must be located in a distinct territory. I insist that populations be distinct—in ethnic, religious, class, or other terms—as otherwise it would be impossible to distinguish between center and periphery, between ingathering and extension, between empires and unitary states. It is also necessary that the center dominate at least one distinct polity or society. After all, if empires are relationships of power, then two partners must be involved. Territorial compactness is an associated characteristic and a necessary condition of the continued existence of distinct polities and societies.

The object of the relationship between center and periphery in an empire is apparent. On the one hand it may be, as Doyle suggests, the political sovereignty of a polity; on the other hand, it may be the self-regulating capacity of the incorporated society. In both instances, the imperial relationship transforms both entities into politically subordinate civil societies.[11] That is to say, distinct societies with autonomous institutions and regional elites must continue to exist, but their capacity for self-governance must have been extinguished.

We know now what imperial decay must be. Empires decay as empires (and not as states on the international arena, a point I consider below) when the relationship of dominance, control, and hegemony between center and periphery is no longer stable. Decay sets in, not when the relationship has been terminated (that would be imperial collapse), but when the absolute power of the center over the periphery can no longer be effectively maintained and the periphery can, and does, act contrary to the will of the center. For this requirement to be meaningful I insist that only those actions concerning the periphery's potential reacquisition of political sovereignty or, minimally, the capacity for self-regulation need concern us.

There is another form of decay, and it involves the second manner of defining power, as the possession of the capacity to make critical decisions, and of empire, as the relationship between emperors and domains. Lane and Stenlund's definition suggests that the relationship of the emperor to decision-making elites is the key to the definition. A strong form of imperial rule involves the ability to make binding decisions on other members of the polity. This ability must obviously exceed that of run-of-the-mill presidents and prime ministers, and it can do so only if it involves the capacity to override the decisions of other political institutions and to make decisions of a legislative, judicial, and executive variety. In other words, the power of emperors must be relatively absolute for their decision-making capacity to be considered imperial. A weak form of such absolute rule would be the ability of the emperor to set the agenda for other political institutions, including executive, legislative, and judicial ones. From this perspective, imperial decay involves the growing inability of a formerly absolutist leader to override the decisions of other elites or to make willful decisions in the legislative, executive, and judicial fields. It is self-evident that the absolutist ambitions of emperors are justified ideologically, in terms of the emperor's peculiarly personal capacity to make correct decisions and guide the empire.

There is one more dimension along which empires have to be examined— their territorial configuration. Some empires are territorially continuous; others, those with overseas dominions, are not. This seemingly trivial distinction has two important implications. First, territorial continuity facilitates the integration of an empire's diverse regions, societies, and populations. And second, the integration of center and periphery and of periphery and periphery creates interperipheral ties and the potential for solidarity among the empire's manifold regional elites. Such native elites, who are distinct from the emperor's representatives in a region, are always and everywhere present in empires in general and modernizing empires in particular. Indeed, my definition of empire, as a relationship between a hegemonic center and a peripheral civil society, implies their existence. These regional elites, as we shall see, play an important role in accelerating imperial decay and bringing about imperial collapse.

IMPERIAL DECAY

It will be useful at this point to illustrate how these conceptual insights relate to the Habsburg, Russian, and Soviet empires. First and foremost, all three entities can indeed be considered empires, in both senses of the term. The historical Habsburg crown lands, with Vienna as their core, served as the center of the Habsburg Empire, while the other territories represented the periphery. Of course there were variations over time and over space. The degree of control varied, being smaller with regard to Hungary, Croatia-Slavonia, and Lombardy, and larger with respect to Bohemia and Moravia. And, after the *Ausgleich* of 1867, Hungary acquired substantial autonomy within the Empire except in matters of foreign policy, monetary policy, and trade policy.

The Romanov realm was even more obviously imperial. St. Petersburg and Moscow represented the metropolis politically, economically, culturally, and socially, while the vast provinces extending in an arc from Finland through the Ukraine, Transcaucasia, and Turkestan to the Far East formed the periphery. As with the Habsburg realm, imperial control varied—being lesser in Finland, the Baltic region, Bukhara, and Khiva, and greater in Poland, Belorussia, the Ukraine, and Transcaucasia.

European Russia in general, and the area spanning the Moscow-Leningrad axis, has served as the center of the Soviet empire: traditionally, its institutions have made the decisions that materially affected the Soviet periphery. That periphery, however, must be defined as including not only the USSR's "internal empire" (the non-Russian republics) but also its "external empire" (the former people's democracies of Eastern Europe). In the Soviet case, as in that of the Habsburgs and Romanovs, central control of the periphery varied from country to country and from republic to republic, historically being greater in the Ukraine, Belorussia, East Germany, and Czechoslovakia, and lesser in the Baltic republics, Poland, Hungary, and Transcaucasia. The functional equivalent of Habsburg Hungary is best represented by the formerly Communist countries of Eastern Europe.

All three entities were also empires in the second sense of the term. Just as the Habsburg emperors and the Russian tsars wielded pivotal decision-making power, so, too, the leaders of the Communist party of the Soviet Union have traditionally been able to impose their will on, and at a minimum to set the agenda of, their entourage in the Politburo and Central Committee and, to a lesser degree, parallel institutions within the polity. Even with the introduction of collective leadership in the post-Stalin era, there has never been much doubt that supreme authority resided in the Party leader, be he Nikita Khrushchev, Leonid Brezhnev, Yuri Andropov, or Mikhail Gorbachev.

There is a final point of comparison worth pursuing: that all three empires obviously underwent decay. As Robert Kann suggests, it is arguable that the Habsburg Empire was in a process of more or less permanent decay from the time it incorporated Bohemia, Moravia, and Hungary in the early part of the sixteenth century.[12] Central control over the crown lands was always tenuous; local diets tended to persist, as did local laws, customs, elites, and their prerogatives. The centralizing reforms of Maria Theresia and her son Joseph II attempted to remedy some of these faults and transform the system into some approximation of a Western-style state. Nevertheless, although an efficient bureaucracy was eventually put in place and the military transformed into a modern, if woefully inadequate, fighting force, the center's tug-of-war with truculent elites in the crown lands never ceased and perhaps even intensified in reaction to the centralizing measures implemented by Joseph. In any case, although Francis I tolerated little dissent, the provinces in general and Hungary in particular were never fully subordinated and, in 1848, they emerged to assert their rights or to make new demands on the center. Franz Joseph's subsequent experiment with neoabsolutism ended with his defeat by Napoleon III at Solferino, while his unwillingness to countenance a looser arrangement for the crown lands came to an end with the Compromise of 1867. Thereafter, the centrifugal tendencies exerted by Magyars, Czechs, Poles, Italians, Serbs, and others accelerated and remained a permanent, indeed an increasingly dangerous, threat to the integrity of the imperial polity until its collapse in 1918.

Very similar processes were evident in Russian as well as in Soviet history. Although the Muscovite empire was in the process of expansion throughout all the centuries of its existence, its hold over earlier acquisitions became rather more tenuous by the end of the nineteenth and certainly by the beginning of the twentieth century. Decay was manifestly in evidence in Finland, the Baltic region, and Poland in the nineteenth century, and throughout the rest of the empire in the early twentieth, especially after the reforms of 1905-6 permitted peripheries to mobilize in opposition to the center.

The centralizing reforms initiated by Peter the Great and continued assiduously by Catherine, which were so alike in spirit to those implemented by the centralizing reformers of the House of Habsburg, Maria Theresia and

Joseph II, only partly succeeded in integrating the borderlands, especially those acquired from Poland. To be sure, an administrative system was created, governers were placed in power, and laws were rationalized and to some degree made uniform throughout the empire. But although much was achieved in the way of transforming Russia into what Marc Raeff calls a "well-ordered police state," the transformation remained far from complete and, worse still, was severely shaken by the Napoleonic Wars.[13] Most significantly perhaps, the reforms provoked a reaction on the part of regional non-Russian elites—Swedes, Baltic Germans, Poles, and others—who insisted on retaining their traditional rights, customs, and prerogatives.[14] In this sense, the Russian tsars, like the Habsburg emperors, never succeeded in overcoming the regional fragmentation of their domain, and may even have played a critical role in transforming what used to be mere regional self-interest into the quest for autonomy. Over time, especially toward the end of the nineteenth century, modern national elites, representatives of the eponymous nations—Finns, Estonians, Latvians, Lithuanians, Belorussians, Ukrainians—added their voice to the chorus of peripheral opposition to the encroachments of the center.

Like the Russian and Habsburg empires, the Soviet empire experienced a steady if differentiated process of decay. The acquisition of lands, at first of the republics and later of the East European states, took place in the first three decades of the Soviet imperial experiment, between 1917 and 1948. By the early 1950s it appeared as if the Soviet empire, with the exception of Yugoslavia, had achieved near-monolithic unity. The non-Russian republics had been bludgeoned into submission during the 1930s, while the East European states were Stalinized after the war. Soviet imperial history after Stalin's death, however, is largely a record of progressive, and occasionally very convulsive, imperial decay. East European regional elites—and masses, of course—revolted in 1953, 1956, 1968, 1970, 1976, 1980, and, finally, in 1989. Events in the non-Russian republics were far less dramatic—until the massive disturbances of 1989—but no less significant. All the republics acquired a life of their own in the 1960s, 1970s, and 1980s. And although the center retained control over the republics, they developed republican bureaucracies with regional interests, native intelligentsias with republican foci, and dissident elites with nationalist aspirations. The upshot of these developments was that, by the 1980s, there emerged in all the republics the equivalent of local Communist party machines, called "mafias" by self-righteous Soviet sources, that ruthlessly pursued their own interests, very often to the detriment of the interests of the center or the empire as a whole.[15] The names of Volodymyr Shcherbyts'kyi, Dinmukhamed Kunaev, Sharaf

Rashidov, and other satraps exemplify the empire-building tendencies of republican Party bosses.

Decay was also evident in the second form of imperial rule—that by an emperor. In all three instances the decision-making prerogatives of the emperors declined over time. The enlightened absolutism of Maria Theresia and Joseph II was followed by the unenlightened absolutism of Francis I, but they all shared the characteristics of imperial decision makers. Although to some degree bounded by Metternich, Francis was still able to impose his will on the political system—if not, perhaps, always able to bring about the desired effects, as was the case, most poignantly, with Joseph II—to a far greater degree than the mature Franz Joseph. Although Franz Joseph adopted the methods of Francis in the 1850s, he abandoned them soon thereafter, with the result that some approximation of limited imperial rule emerged in the Habsburg realm, with all the autonomy for courts, parties, press, and other institutions that imperial self-limitation entails. Moreover, although the emperor remained supreme for all his life, his supremacy was largely limited to questions of foreign and military policy. Indeed, insofar as the Compromise of 1867 signaled the transformation of the Habsburg domain into a *kaiserliche und königliche* realm, Franz Joseph's imperial jurisdiction was roughly reduced by half.

The process of imperial decay was somewhat less advanced in the Russian case, but no less evident by the time of Nicholas II's rule. The fundamental break with the traditional absolutism of the Russian tsars occurred with the accession to power of Alexander II. His predecessors, like those of Franz Joseph, enjoyed a markedly greater concentration of decision-making authority: Peter the Great and Catherine the Great stand out, of course, as does Nicholas I. Alexander's reforms, although coming from above and therefore testifying to the continued centrality of the imperial office, had the effect of reducing imperial prerogatives by devolving some power to local elites. The relative diminution of the autocracy continued throughout the nineteenth century, and accelerated in the early part of the twentieth, partly as a consequence of Nicholas's being a weak-willed and barely competent ruler, but mostly as a result of the fact that other elites were co-opted into the political process both before and especially after the near revolution of 1905. By the time of Nicholas's abdication in early 1917, it is at least arguable that imperial prerogatives had decayed to such a degree that the real power behind the throne was a half-crazed monk and a variety of court elites scheming behind the emperor's back.

The decay of imperial decision-making powers is perhaps most striking in the Soviet case. Although frequently the target of savage criticism by his comrades, Lenin was unquestionably the central figure within the Bolshevik elite, both in the years of exile and underground existence and until his disability in 1922. Despite being decidedly less charismatic an individual and far less brilliant a thinker and political activist, Stalin managed to acquire even greater powers than Lenin by the end of the 1930s, so much so that he held virtually absolute sway over political institutions as well as possessed the capacity to make as many key decisions as he wished.[16] Decay began to set in with Stalin's death. Khrushchev still possessed much of the centralizing elan of Stalin, but Brezhnev explicitly adopted a policy of collective rule—albeit one that increasingly came to resemble a weak form of Stalin's cult of the personality—whereas Gorbachev for all practical purposes abandoned the arbitrariness of his predecessors. Although he has amassed enormous powers as president, they are unlikely, or so he claims, ever to exceed his mandate as the legal head of a state purportedly ruled by law.

ABSOLUTISM

Why did imperial decay afflict the Habsburg, Soviet, and Russian imperial systems in so similar a manner? Why do we encounter the decay both of empire, as a system of control between center and periphery, and of imperial rule? Perhaps most important, are these two processes related? I suggest that absolutist rule lies at the heart of the answers to both questions and represents the link between both forms of imperial decay. Simply stated, my thesis is that absolutism engenders pathologies that lead to its own degeneration, a fact that, in territorially continuous empires, necessarily leads to the decay of the center's control of the periphery.[17]

For it to function properly, an ideal type of absolutism requires information and resources in large, if not quite absolute, amounts. Information is critical to absolutism, as absolute rulers cannot impose their will on society without maximally accurate knowledge of the environment within which their decisions are made. Resources, in particular material and financial resources, must be present in relative abundance, lest absolutist rulers be incapable of effectively imposing their will and, thus, maintaining their rule. In order to acquire such huge amounts of resources and information, ideal absolutism must empower a network of agents to extract taxes and to acquire detailed data about conditions of life in the absolutist ruler's realm. In the ideal absolutist world, prefects will accumulate resources and information and pass on all that they acquire, minus their wages, to the center. Ideally, resources will be neither squandered nor hoarded in the process, and information will not be distorted.

As long as prefects function only as representatives of their lords, they will perceive their role as exclusively extractive and accumulative and will fulfill their mandate according to the plans of the ruler. The weakness of such an arrangement, however, is obvious, as a prefect without strong ties to and knowledge of some region is less capable of acquiring the requisite information and resources than an agent familiar with the region. Few roots may guarantee the loyalty of prefects, but they undermine their short-term ability to perform their duties. Inevitably, therefore, under this arrangement emperors do not acquire the information and resources they need.

Ironically, the preferred short-term alternative, which permits prefects to establish roots in the regions they oversee and in effect become vassals, has insidious long-term consequences for the absolutist ruler. Once prefects establish themselves as vassals and think of their domains as inheritances, they place their own interests either ahead of or, at least, on a par with the presumed interests of the center. Marc Bloch has described this process with regard to feudal society, which can serve as an analogue of the sort of system we are investigating.[18]

As soon as vassals begin acting as if they were masters of their own domains, the flow of information and resources from periphery to center becomes distorted. Only information that tends to enhance the reputation of vassals will be passed on to the center, and only resources that cannot be siphoned off into the vassal's own coffers will get transferred to the center. The result is that the emperor, who cannot function as an absolutist ruler without massive amounts of correct information and extensive resources, acquires diminishing amounts of both, as an increasing number of prefects become vassals and an increasing number of vassals pursue their interests with the determination that comes with local authority.

How would a degenerating absolutist regime of the sort I have described proceed to resolve its problems? Its first impulse might be to purge local vassals and replace them with more trusted representatives. But this tactic only brings the absolutist regime back to the starting point of the degenerative process. Increasing central supervision of the activities of vassals, say, by dispatching another set of supervisors to supervise the vassals, only enhances the inefficiencies or corruption involved in the original relationship by adding another layer of potentially corruptible and inefficient bureaucrats to an already corrupt and inefficient system. Nor is devolving more authority to the local satraps an acceptable option, as it only reinforces the localist tendencies of the lord's vassals. Instead, the only option that emperors can pursue in order to reestablish equilibrium between their imperial ambitions and the information and resources they possess to fulfill those ambitions is to *deabsolutize*—that is, to embark on willful decay of the second type of imperial relationship, that involving pivotal decision-making authority.

Deabsolutization has several consequences for absolutist rulers, some positive, some negative. First and foremost, by reducing the amount of resources and information emperors require to maintain themselves as emperors, deabsolutization alleviates the problem of inadequate resource and information endowment. But second, reducing imperial ambitions means increasing the powers of advisers, ministers, and other members of the imperial entourage who partake in decision making. In this manner, the imperial relationship between emperor and elites undergoes a significant transformation: whereas formerly the emperor exercised absolute power over both the entourage and vassals, under the new arrangement the entourage joins the emperor in exercising imperial authority over the vassals. In a word, the elite splits into a centrally based imperial faction and a regionally based subordinate one.

In turn, this split has several far-reaching consequences for absolutism. First, it erodes the ideological legitimacy of imperial rule by extending the aura of imperial infallibility to the mere mortals in the entourage. As this erosion continues, an empty ideological space will emerge in the center of the polity. Second, the split in the elite increases the autonomy of the vassals by cutting them off from and, to a significant degree, turning them against the center, especially the entourage. Regional interests are given greater coherence and legitimacy by the center's consolidation against the periphery. Third, the split enhances the emperor's affiliation with the center—specifically, with the distinct society and population comprising it. Even if emperors resist this identification, there is little they can do to prevent it, as the forces set loose by deabsolutization work to contract the transimperial breadth of the emperor's authority and to focus it on his immediate bailiwick, the center. More likely than not, such an affiliation will assume ethnic overtones, and the emperor will increasingly appear as the ruler of the metropolitan population and society. And fourth, the split between entourage and vassals provides regional elites with the opportunity to assert their own interests and to forge coalitions with the vassals against the center. Initially, such cooperation is likely to be based on self-interest only; in time, as the imperial ideology erodes, a normative justification will emerge as well.

Although any number of competing ideologies can in principle step in to challenge the absolutist ideology, the one that is likely to have the greatest resonance in the modern era is nationalism. Nationalism—or the belief that nations should enjoy political sovereignty—is tailor-made for regional elites who wish to legitimize their own aspirations to self-rule.[19] By virtue of its hegemonic hold on the modern mind, nationalism is available for elite use if and when they find it useful for their purposes. Regional elites will either create distinct societies where these did not previously exist or begin to transform the characteristics of their still distinct societies, territories, and populations into attributes qualifying them for political sovereignty.

As regional elites clamor for greater authority to determine their own affairs and as vassals assert their interests with greater vehemence against the center, both will join forces to assert their increasingly common interests against the center. Indeed, at that point, they are likely to form tentative coalitions on the basis of regional nationalism. And as both elites coordinate and intensify the willful siphoning off of information and resources and the periphery increasingly escapes the center's control, imperial decay sets in—by definition, of course.

Imperial decay is facilitated by the fact that absolutism is unable to reproduce itself efficiently. Successions in absolutist states are rarely brief, painless, and stable. On the contrary, the normal procedure for replacing absolutist rulers is for wars of succession or, minimally, for court intrigues to erupt, and for periods of extreme instability, imbecile rule, or ineffective governance, all of which squander state resources, to be the norm. The situation is aggravated by the fact that the absolutist ruler's personality is an important factor in the system of imperial rule: if dynamic, an emperor can work wonders; if lethargic, a ruler can accelerate decay and complicate transitions.[20] Not only does such waste incapacitate the center and prevent it from overseeing its vassals and controlling the periphery, but, worst of all, it weakens the state. Indeed, all the consequences of absolutist rule—the emergence of unruly vassals and regional elites, imperial decay, delegitimation, nationalism, and, of course, succession struggles—significantly weaken the state, the next conceptual link in my theoretical chain.

STATE DECLINE

Ironically, it is the extractive, administrative, and military capacities of the state—as a political organization that extracts resources and administers a territory in order to maintain the military capacity it needs to survive on the international arena[21]—that are the casualties of absolutism. First of all, absolutism results in the less efficient accumulation of information and the less efficient acquisition of resources. And second, absolutism and its necessary consequence, deabsolutization, induce the emperor's vassals to act as their own lords, thus leading to the fragmentation of the administrative apparatus of the state. The upshot is that absolutism, paradoxically, promotes the degeneration of states, as monopolizers of violence and extractors of information and resources, thus undermining their capacity to compete internationally. Other things being equal, we expect the international status of territorially continuous empires and their ability to withstand the military pressures of more or less coherent nation-states or multiethnic states to decline over time. In a word, imperial *states* inevitably decline.

Although modernization is not a necessary or sufficient condition of international decline, it does facilitate it. If economic and technological conditions are more or less stable, we expect state decline to proceed more or less steadily. Once we inject the intervening variable of modernization, however, we expect the decline of imperial states to accelerate for two reasons. First, modernization enhances the appeal of nationalism to regional elites. And second, modernization makes it even more difficult for the imperial state to keep abreast of the technological achievements of other, less fragmented, states.

The literature on the relationship between modernization and nationalism is enormous and needs no repeating here. Scholars such as Karl W. Deutsch argue that modernization enhances interethnic competition, which in turn translates into a greater awareness of ethnic markers and a subsequent willingness to translate these markers into political advantages in the competition for scarce resources.[22] Other scholars, such as Anthony D. Smith, see modernization and the rise of the scientific state as leading to a spiritual crisis of regional intelligentsias who then search for solace and security within their ethnic communities.[23] Still other scholars, for example, Ernest Gellner, see modernization as encouraging states to impose unitary languages as the functional prerequisite of efficient industrialization and urbanization.[24] Finally, some analysts view modernization as raising the educational and cultural level of the populace and thereby converting it into nationally conscious individuals who think and act as members of nations and not of mere ethnic communities.[25]

Whichever one's preferred theory, all of the presumed consequences of modernization enhance the distinctiveness of imperial peripheries and provide excellent arguments for regional elites to pursue their own interests in the language of nationality and nationalism. Competition underscores the importance of ethnicity, scientific states lead to a search for roots in the nation, state imposition of uniform education produces a reactive reassertion of the truly authentic (the ethnic roots), while mass education forges a nation out of a vague community. Modernization, in other words, enhances the strength, appeal, and legitimacy of protonationalist regional elites.

No less worrisome than the emergence of nationalist sentiments is the fact that decaying empires cannot keep pace with the modernizing efforts of more coherent states, inasmuch as technological innovation and dissemination are facilitated by coherent administrative structures that can implement the economic decisions of the center as well as by a surplus of resources permitting states to embark on such ambitious economic projects. Although fragmented or relatively poor states can undertake such campaigns and be successful in achieving some of their goals—Austria's experience in the late nineteenth and early twentieth centuries, like Russia's in the same time period, or the USSR's in the 1930s, clearly supports this proposition[26]—they will always lag behind their more cohesive competitors and be incapable of sustaining such intensive modernization drives over the long run.

So far, my argument resembles that of Paul Kennedy, namely, that great powers decline when their economic and technological capacities lag behind their military needs.[27] But as Charles Kupchan argues, explaining objective decline is relatively unproblematic. Rather more difficult is accounting for the fact that central elites, who by and large are aware of decline, invariably do too little to stop it. According to Kupchan, empires can pursue five possible strategies to stem decline:

1. Form alliances in order to increase military and economic capability and to reduce the number of potential adversaries;
2. Expand the frontiers of the empire to establish secure borders and/or to extract human/material resources from new territories;
3. Mobilize the domestic economy and extract more resources from existing overseas territories in order to increase output of war-making goods;
4. Withdraw or disengage from peripheral theaters in order to free assets for more important missions and to reduce the number of potential adversaries;
5. Enhance reputational and prestige effects through posturing, verbal threats, and preemptive actions in order to enhance the credibility of deterrence and mask the relative loss of material power.[28]

Significantly, the one course decaying empires are unlikely to pursue at all, or only as a last resort, is withdrawal or disengagement. Such a move would not only be a sign of weakness, but it would also convey the wrong signal to all the domains under the center's control and, indeed, encourage their separation. Although it is impossible to say which particular policy response the absolutist rulers of declining states will adopt at which particular time, we must assume that they will first embark on some or all of the alternatives to withdrawal—alliance formation, further expansion, economic mobilization, or reputation enhancement.

Alliance formation is the easiest response, but it does the least to address the source of international decline—imperial decay. Alliances can temporarily rectify the strategic imbalance with other international competitors, but they are unlikely to alter dramatically the decaying empire's overall standing in the international system of states. Quite the contrary, by attaching the decaying empire to some other power, probably an ascendant state capable of protecting the empire, an alliance is likely to institutionalize the decaying empire's decline and actually reduce the empire to permanently second-rate status. Besides being unpalatable for absolutist rulers, permanent decline undermines the legitimacy of both empire and rulers and subordinates emperors to the foreign policy considerations of their allies. Habsburg subservience to Germany, especially after 1879, is typical of the dangers that lie ahead for empires that embark on such a move.

Frontier expansion is another option that is unlikely to help for long, if at all. In addition to the fact that the expenditures in men, money, and matériel that such expansion involves strain the capabilities of declining empires, frontier expansion only aggravates the problem of imperial decay by increasing the number of recalcitrant provinces under the putative control of the center.

Mobilizing the domestic economy for greater resource extraction is an equally problematic response to a declining empire's needs. Due to the weakness of the center and its relative incapacity to modernize, the empire will be hard-pressed to mobilize an economy for its own war-making ends. And even if the center is able to fuel economic growth, it is unlikely to keep pace with its international competitors.

Enhancing imperial prestige is the least costly solution to the empire's problems, but it is also least effective. Conditions may improve temporarily, but, in time, competing powers will realize that there is little substance to the declining empire's bluff. Worse still, such prestige enhancement is likely to be conveyed in language that asserts the reputational primacy of the center, perhaps even of the ethnic groups identified with it, thereby leading to the further alienation of regional elites.

At some point, the absolutist rulers of declining empires logically will consider the only remaining option, that of strategic withdrawal. But we should not expect emperors to accept complete decolonization immediately, as such a move would be irrational in terms of their presumed desire to preserve the integrity of the state, their own absolutist rule, and the maximal longevity of the empire. It is far more likely that emperors will permit either all or some of the periphery to enjoy a moderate degree of autonomy vis-à-vis the center. But for all its possibly positive short-term effects, this half-measure ultimately backfires by increasing the regional identification of vassals, enhancing the stature and demands of protonationalist regional elites, contributing to the deabsolutization of the center, further delegitimizing the imperial ideology, and, thus, only accelerating imperial decay. At best, therefore, the imperial center will be able to stem its international decline, but only at the cost of accelerating its imperial decay. An arrangement such as this is not only inherently unstable, but it is likely to collapse if and when a crisis threatens to demolish this carefully arranged house of cards.

CRISIS

Crises, which I define as genuinely life-threatening conditions on whose resolution the survival of a system depends, are not mere problems, catastrophes, or the like. Systemic crises, like the crises undergone by medical patients, can have only one of two consequences: survival or death.[29] Systemic survival implies the continuation of the precrisis social, political, economic, and other structures that characterized a system. Systemic death is tantamount to revolution, here defined as a fundamental and rapid systemic transformation, or to destruction in war. Systemic crises, then, are the conditions that logically precede revolutions and destruction in war; that is, they are either revolutionary situations or defensive wars, and, as such, they are conditions of dual sovereignty.[30] It is such crises, I suggest, that force hitherto indecisive vassals and protonationalist regional elites to abandon empire.

Crises have this consequence for several reasons. With regard to the center and the empire as a whole, crises represent deadly attacks on the ruling ideology, thus contributing to the further erosion of the center's legitimacy in the eyes of the population in general and of regional elites and vassals in particular. Crises expose absolutism's aspirations and pretensions to infallibility and reveal it to be a highly fallible, perhaps even uniquely fallible, system of rule. Second, crises represent enormous drains on the resources of the center: troops, finances, military matériel, industrial goods and agricultural produce, propaganda, and other resources must be channeled into the anticrisis effort.

Resource mobilization of so massive a kind under the economically inefficient and politically fragmented conditions of a decaying empire will not only divert the energy, time, and attention of the center from its problems on the periphery, but it will also compel the center to engage in a pell-mell economic and military mobilization that is sure to aggravate the center's relations with the periphery, to inflame the nationalist passions of regional elites, and to lead to economic disruptions and perhaps even economic collapse. In turn, peripheries will respond to crises by losing faith in the authority and leadership skills of the center, by intensifying their resistance to the center's encroachments on their resources, and by rejecting the attempts of the center to extend more or less absolute rule over the polity in general and the drifting periphery in particular.

It is difficult to imagine how so internally weakened a center can withstand the assaults of more advanced external adversaries. When defeat in war comes, the protonationalist regional elites who had enjoyed some autonomy before the crisis, and who probably acquired a greater degree of autonomy during the crisis, will step into the emerging power vacuum and take charge of de facto independent states. Once the center disintegrates, they will have no other choice.

In contrast to wars, which a weakened empire is more or less slated to lose, revolutionary assaults will probably be repulsed for two reasons. First, the resources of revolutionaries are likely to be far fewer than those of the imperial state, however weakened its condition. And second, the threat of revolution will spur the regional elites and vassals to join forces with the central elites, with whom they have a stake in the continued maintenance of the existing social order.

Although chances are that revolutions from below will be crushed by a coalition of all elites, revolutions from above—those massive transformations initiated by the state itself—serve as the functional equivalents of outside assaults, such as wars. Should absolutist rulers decide, for whatever reason, to embark on revolutionary transformations of their domains, then protonationalist regional elites and vassals will have every reason to resist such massive encroachments on their territory, authority, and economic well-being by forging still closer alliances against the center, utilizing nationalist and separatist slogans, as well as, sooner or later, embarking on actual political independence as the only remaining means of protecting their bailiwicks against the assaults of the center. Will the periphery succeed in breaking away from the imperial fold? Only if the revolution from above results either in the massive weakening of the central state or in its collapse. Were the center to turn against itself in internecine fighting, then the empire would effectively be dissolved. As there would no longer be a center to maintain a relationship of control over the periphery, the periphery would have no choice but to become de jure what it already is de facto—independent. Imperial collapse, then, can occur only if a crisis so incapacitates the center that protonationalist elites and vassals take charge for the simple reason that there is no longer anyone in the center to prevent them from doing so.

One final question remains to be answered before I proceed to show how this ideal-typical scheme relates to the historical experience of the Habsburg, Russian, and Soviet empires: How and when do such earth-shattering crises arise? There is no way to predict when any of the above three crises—war, revolution from below, or revolution from above—will break out. It seems certain, however, that some such crisis necessarily is the fate of territorially continuous, absolutist-ruled empires. War with a strong adversary is always a likelihood due to the fact that elite attempts to stem international decline will actually increase the declining empire's difficulties with some of its neighbors. Alliance formation will appease some states, infuriate others, and entangle all in a series of possibly dangerous commitments. Frontier expansion and prestige enhancement will aggravate the decaying empire's relations with its neighbors. Economic mobilization is likely to worry stability-minded adversaries who will respond with mobilizations of their own. Finally, the half-measure of granting some segments of the periphery greater autonomy within imperial bounds is virtually an open invitation to attack or interference by outside adversaries. When wars do not occur, then attempts at revolution, both from below and from above, are likely to come. We know from the theories of Ted Robert Gurr, Chalmers Johnson, Samuel P. Huntington, Charles Tilly, and Theda Skocpol that decaying empires, deabsolutizing regimes, growing illegitimacy, absolutist intransigence, political fragmentation, relative economic decline, and growing nationalism are the grounds in which revolutionary parties, groups, and movements flourish.[31] Although we must assume that the state will keep them in check as long as there are no constraints on its actions, that ability will fade if and when international decline reduces domestic resources while attempts to halt it actually deplete them.

Revolution from above will take place if the emperor, who possesses the pivotal decision-making powers to adopt such a radical course, decides that only a thorough regeneration of the state can save both state and empire from decay and decline. As Ellen Trimberger suggests, the conditions that accompany imperial decay and state decline could induce a visionary ruler to embark on a major transformation from above and a war against the existing state, no less than they could impel societal revolutionaries to strike out against the existing system and attempt to rejuvenate it from below.[32] But Trimberger's analysis overlooks a critical factor—the absolute ruler himself. Said Amir Arjomand rightly points out that the personal weakness of the Shah of Iran had a decisive impact on the ability of his "neo-patrimonial state" to withstand the onslaught of the revolution.[33] By the same token, we expect strong, manipulative, and charismatic emperors to be a necessary, perhaps even a sufficient, condition of revolutions from above. The examples of Peter the Great, Stalin, Mao Zedong, Hitler, and, perhaps, Gorbachev appear to substantiate this proposition.

IMPERIAL COLLAPSE

The last time we encountered the Habsburg, Romanov, and Soviet empires was to suggest that all fit our definition of empire and that all had undergone processes of imperial decay. For my argument to be complete it is now necessary to illustrate the following points: that their imperial ideologies clashed with nationalism, that all underwent state decline, that attempts at halting state decline failed, and that crises acted as the catalysts that eventually toppled the decaying empires and declining states.

The imperial ideologies of all three empires were explicitly supranational. The Habsburgs legitimized their rule in terms of their family's historical role as the holders of the crown of the Holy Roman Empire, as the protectors of Christendom, and as the carriers of Central European culture. The Romanovs claimed to be tsars of Rossiia, the descendants of Rus', and the defenders of the Third Rome. In turn, the Soviet Communists referred to their role as vanguard of the proletariat, the bearers of the correct line, and the trustees of historical progress. Despite this universalist appeal, each of the imperial ideologies betrayed a particularist slant: the Habsburgs for the Germans and the Romanovs and the Soviets for the Russians.[34] In this sense, the seeds of delegitimation were embedded in the ideologies themselves.

Delegitimation assumed full force, however, only after each of these empires became increasingly associated with the ethnic group populating the metropolis. Once the Habsburgs appeared German and the Romanovs and Soviet appeared Russian, there was little they could do to justify their ostensibly supranational rule vis-à-vis peripheral elites and masses. Elite insubordination in general and growing elite and popular appropriation of nationalism in particular were the result. Hungarian truculence with respect to Vienna, Italian pursuit of self-determination, Czech insistence on regional autonomy, and the utilization by all regional elites of the language of nationalism marked the final decades of Habsburg rule. The Romanovs had to contend with national and nationalist movements in Finland, the Baltic region, Poland, the Ukraine, Georgia, Armenia, and Turkestan. Finally, the Soviets encountered national communism in the non-Russian republics in the 1920s and 1930s, in Yugoslavia, Poland, Hungary, Czechoslovakia, and Romania in the cold war period, and, once again, in the republics in the 1960s, 1970s, and 1980s.

International state decline is also an obvious point. Although it underwent a process of impressive modernization in the latter half of the nineteenth century, possessed a highly competent and dedicated officer corps, and performed quite creditably in World War I, the Habsburg army was clearly an inferior fighting machine, especially in comparison to the ascendant powers of the nineteenth and early twentieth centuries.[35] The Empire's good fortune consisted in the fact that its enemies on the battlefield, at least in World War I, were decidedly inferior. But when, as in 1866 at Sadowa and in 1859 at Solferino, the Habsburg forces had to compete with more modern armed forces, they generally performed far worse than with antagonists to their east and south.

The Russian army was no less a lumbering giant than the Habsburg army. Its poor performance in the Crimean War, its crushing defeat by Japan in 1905, and its inability to survive intact the rigors of trench warfare with Germany and—even!—Austria-Hungary in World War I are sufficient testimony to tsarist Russia's apparent decline. The quality of the Russian officer corps and general staff left much to be desired; military training was largely perfunctory; and supplies and ammunition were scarce, so that the army, when it marched into battle in 1914, was ill-prepared and unequipped to deal with one of the strongest fighting forces of modern Europe, the German army.

The international decline of the Soviet empire became no less apparent in the 1980s. Although the USSR possessed ample nuclear weapons, it was incapable of using them to pursue its political goals. Instead, it was hampered by a bloated army rent by ethnic conflicts, lacking in sophisticated military equipment, uncertain of the loyalty of its Warsaw Pact allies, and unable to win a war in Afghanistan. The Soviets, like the Russians before them, possessed sheer numbers of men and matériel, but they were falling behind the West in general and the United States in particular, especially after the latter's commitment to the Strategic Defense Initiative exposed the fundamental technological weaknesses of the Soviet system.

In all three empires, attempts were undertaken to prevent international decline, but in none was voluntary strategic withdrawal ever considered until it was too late and the empires were on the verge of collapse. Autonomy alone was granted to Hungary by the Habsburgs, to Finland, Bukhara, Khiva, and the Baltic region by the Russian tsars, and to parts of Eastern Europe and some republics by the Soviets. Instead, the three empires first adopted the other four policy options noted by Kupchan: alliance formation, frontier expansion, economic mobilization, and prestige enhancement. The Habsburg Empire searched for salvation in its alliance with Germany, Russia sought the help of England and France, the USSR embarked on deténte with the West. The Habsburgs seized and annexed Bosnia, Russia expanded into the Balkans and Central Asia, and the Soviets invaded Hungary, Czechoslovakia, and Afghanistan. The Habsburg and Russian states supported industrialization, while the Soviets forced the rate of economic and military growth so as to keep pace with the West. Finally, all three imperial states engaged in posturing, bluffing, and blustering: the Habsburgs most visibly in their continued intransigence with regard to the Balkans in general and Serbia in particular, the Russians with respect to their self-styled messianic role as defenders of all Slavs, and the Soviets as the vanguard of the proletariat, a rising superpower, and the protector of the Third World.

These attempts at enhancing security generally served only to alarm their competitors, who proceeded to embark on arms buildups, economic expansions, alliance formations, and bluffing of their own. Indeed, in the case of the Habsburgs and the Russians, their unconsidered bluffing, military aggressiveness, and alliance formations embroiled them in a war that eventually proved to be fatal to their states. The Soviets managed to avoid such a fate, although the aggressive foreign policies of Brezhnev unintentionally enhanced the coherence of NATO and, worse still, provoked the Americans to rearm. By the mid-1980s, it was clear that the Soviets lacked the economic and technological capacity to keep up with the United States and to maintain the enormous burdens of empire.

The crises that eventually befell the Habsburg, Russian, and Soviet empires weakened all three imperial centers, virtually draining them of political vitality, and pushed the protonationalist regional elites and disloyal vassals to assert their self-identity and to pursue their own interests, even to the point of repudiating the weakened center and embarking on independence. War crushed the central state, impoverished the periphery, and weakened center-periphery ties in the Habsburg and Russian cases, while

Gorbachev's *perestroika* did the same for the Soviet empire. Once the center had imploded and the dominant half of the imperial relationship had in fact ceased to exist, the subordinate part was left on its own and was virtually forced to take the path of national independence. Of course the impulse to pursue centrifugal policies was already there in all three cases; yet it was the crisis that brought "push to shove" and impelled the borderlands to search for independent solutions to their problems.

THE COLLAPSE OF COMMUNISM IN EASTERN EUROPE

Most striking about recent developments in the East European people's democracies and the non-Russian republics is that the impetus for dissolution came from Gorbachev and the policies that go under the name of *perestroika*. It is Gorbachev's war against the Soviet party-state that led to the crisis that not only brought about the collapse of the USSR's external empire but that also threatens to undermine its internal empire. Gorbachev effectively discredited the imperial ideology, thoroughly blackened all of Soviet history and values, reined in the secret police, permitted popular mobilization, attacked the Party apparatus, threw the economy into chaos, failed to replace the central Party authorities with a viable institutional alternative, and clearly signaled that Soviet military intervention in Eastern Europe was a thing of the past.[36] All of these—intended or unintended—consequences of his policies provided the incentive for the Communist and anti-Communist elites in Eastern Europe and the non-Russian republics to strike out on their own, to forge coalitions, and to abandon Moscow.

Most East European Communist regimes had begun embarking on distinctly autonomist roads in the 1960s and 1970s as part and parcel of the process of decay that engulfed the Soviet system after de-Stalinization in the 1950s. Yugoslavia and Romania were, of course, in the forefront of these developments. By the middle to late 1980s, however, all the other East European states joined them in more or less explicitly renouncing Moscow's sovereignty. Poland and Hungary did so by contemplating democratic and market reforms, while Bulgaria, Czechoslovakia, and East Germany asserted the primacy of their state interests by rejecting Gorbachev's new course. The upshot of these developments was that, by 1989, Moscow's imperial relationship with Eastern Europe had for all practical purposes ceased to exist. As *perestroika* devastated the metropolis, the East European vassals were effectively left on their own to determine their fates and were forced, by the crisis unleashed by Gorbachev, to come to terms with their societies and regional elites.

The collapse of the Soviet empire in Eastern Europe was, thus, the factor that triggered the collapse of these regimes. After being cut loose from the USSR's protection, the people's democracies were forced to fend for themselves. As the coercive capacity of their secret police apparatuses to place limits on antistate activity was a function of the threat of Soviet military intervention, the East European states were compelled to rely on normative and instrumental means to elicit popular compliance in their existence.[37] But their normative appeal was minimal—especially after years of brutal dictatorship in Romania, Bulgaria, Czechoslovakia, and East Germany—while their instrumental capacities were virtually nil, due to the profound decline of their economies since the 1960s. Why these states had degenerated to such a point in the first place—a development that cannot be understood without reference to the contradictions of the totalitarian state—is an issue that cannot concern us here.[38] Most important for our present purposes is the fact that, under conditions of such weakness, the Communist regimes were fated to collapse quickly and almost effortlessly. They did so *simultaneously* because their regional elites, the Polish, Czech, Slovak, Hungarian, German, Romanian, and Bulgarian democratic oppositions, had been in contact with one another since the 1970s (thanks to the integration of the Soviet empire's peripheries), were watching developments in the bloc closely, and to some degree were coordinating their oppositional efforts. Once the Polish and Hungarian oppositional elites succeeded in extracting major concessions from Moscow's former vassals in 1989, it was only a matter of time before the other oppositions emulated them and pressed their own demands. The political opening they all awaited came in September 1989, with the physical opening of Hungary's border with Austria. As mass flight manifestly illustrated the impotence and illegitimacy of the East German regime, oppositions throughout the region correctly interpreted this event as a signal to turn against Moscow's remaining erstwhile vassals, abandon whatever coalitions they had enjoyed with them, and seize power. Not surprisingly, as soon as the opposition elites gave these regimes a push, all—with the exception of Romania, whose security forces were independent of their Soviet counterpart—collapsed immediately.[39]

THE FUTURE OF THE SOVIET UNION

Which way will the Soviet Union go? Will it follow in the footsteps of the Russian Empire, which collapsed, only to be reestablished by a ruthless revolutionary state-building group? Or will it disintegrate along the lines of Austria-Hungary? If current trends continue, the second option is far more likely. For one, there exists no countrywide revolutionary organization that could aspire to the sort of state-building role played by the Bolsheviks.[40] No less important, one of the major differences between the subordinate elites of the Habsburg Empire and those of tsarist Russia was that the former were experienced, numerous, and capable of ruling their respective countries: after all, they had been tolerated by the emperor for some fifty years before the Empire finally collapsed. In contrast, the non-Russian elites were inexperienced, few in number, and incapable of building states in opposition to the Bolsheviks. Soviet non-Russian elites, with seventy years' experience in administering symbolically sovereign republics, clearly fit the mold of the regional Habsburg elites.

Finally, regional Habsburg elites all possessed relatively developed economic bases for their state-building activities: the Poles controlled the economic resources of Galicia, the Czechs inhabited the most industrialized region of the Empire, and the Hungarians had run a separate economy for some sixty years. In contrast, very few of the non-Russian state-building elites possessed these advantages, and even when they did, their capacities were far fewer than those of the Bolsheviks, who were in control of the industrial, communications, and urban heartland of the country. In contrast, the East European countries functioned as semi-independent political and economic units for several decades, while the non-Russian republics possess relatively well-developed economies, cities, and infrastructures—all thanks to the quasi-federal structure of the USSR and its pursuit of policies of relative economic equalization.

At present, national Communist tendencies are accelerating in all the non-Russian republics and coalitions between republican Party vassals and regional popular fronts have formed or, alternatively, the popular fronts have come to dominate the political arena completely. If present trends continue, two sides will eventually emerge—a strongly ensconced but increasingly irrelevant emperor, be he Gorbachev or someone else, and a variety of secessionist coalitions in the republics. If, as seems certain, Gorbachev will not succeed in building sufficiently strong central institutions to replace those he has destroyed, if the economy either worsens or continues to stagnate for many years to come, and if the newly independent states of Eastern Europe come to enjoy some material and economic support from the West, then the incentive for non-Russian republics to follow in their foot-steps—to abandon a sinking ship and align themselves with a rejuvenated

Eastern Europe, a dynamic West, or culturally proximate countries in Asia or the Middle East—will prove to be irresistible.

The necessary condition of dissolution, the existence of skilled elites, is present. When one considers that the sufficient condition, the crisis brought about by Gorbachev, and two facilitating conditions, the availability of substantial resources in all the republics and the absence of a Russian revolutionary party likely or even able to exert control over the borderlands, are also at hand, then it appears inevitable that the entire Soviet empire will soon join the Habsburg and Romanov realms in the dustbin of history.

CONCLUSION

What, then, can we say about empires and their decline and collapse? First, imperial decay appears to be inevitable. Although no social or political entity is eternal, the distinctive feature of empires may be that their degeneration is immanent in the very system of imperial rule. Empires, in a word, are inherently contradictory political relationships; they self-destruct, and they do so in a very particular, by no means accidental and distinctly political, manner. Second, imperial collapse appears to be no serendipitous occurrence, stemming as it does from the policies imperial elites adopt in order to halt state decline. And third, imperial collapse is irreversible and imperial revival impossible where center-periphery relations are such that the elites and resources of the periphery outweigh or balance those of the center. That empires do not last is, thus, a trite proposition and one this study has taken no pains to make. But that the end of empires appears to come about in a manner more or less determined by the imperial relationship itself and that the reasons for imperial revival are also to be found in the nature of that relationship—these, surely, are propositions worth noting and debating.

NOTES

I wish to thank Walter Clemens, David Good, Ersin Kalaycioglu, Allen Lynch, Andrew Nathan, Richard Rudolph, and Jack Snyder for their helpful criticism of earlier drafts of this essay.

1. For a recent discussion of this issue, see Grzegorz Ekiert, "Transitions from State-Socialism in East Central Europe," *States and Social Structures Newsletter*, no. 12 (1990):1-7.

2. See Richard Pipes, *Russia under the Old Regime* (New York, 1974).

3. For a discussion of this argument, see Paul A. Roth, *Meaning and Method in the Social Sciences* (Ithaca, N.Y., 1987).

4. On the importance of concepts, see Giovanni Sartori, "Guidelines for Concept Analysis," in *Social Science Concepts*, ed. Sartori (Beverly Hills, Calif., 1984), 15-85. See also Theda Skocpol, *States and Social Revolutions* (Cambridge, 1979), especially the theoretical chapters.

5. Robert Gilpin, *War and Change in World Politics* (Cambridge, 1981); Joseph A. Tainter, *The Collapse of Complex Societies* (Cambridge, 1988); Arnold J. Toynbee, *A Study of History* (Oxford, 1962); S. N. Eisenstadt, *The Political Systems of Empires* (Glencoe, N.Y., 1963); Michael W. Doyle, *Empires* (Ithaca, N.Y., 1986); Johan Galtung, "A Structural Theory of Imperialism," *Journal of Peace Research* 8 (1971): 81-118; Herbert Kaufman, "The Collapse of Ancient States and Civilizations as an Organizational Problem," Shmuel N. Eisenstadt, "Beyond Collapse," and George L. Cowgill, "Onward and Upward with Collapse," in *The Collapse of Ancient States and Civilizations*, ed. Norman Yoffee and George L. Cowgill, (Tucson, Ariz., 1988), 219-76.

6. Doyle, *Empires*, 45.

7. George Lichtheim, *Imperialism* (New York, 1971), 5.

8. Jan-Erik Lane and Hans Stenlund, "Power," in Sartori, *Social Science Concepts*, 395.

9. Anthony Giddens, *The Nation-State and Violence* (Berkeley, Calif., 1987), 20.

10. For the classic discussion of political systems, see David Easton, *A Framework for Political Analysis* (Englewood Cliffs, N.J., 1965).

11. On the concept of civil society, see John Keane, ed., *Civil Society and the State* (London, 1988).

12. Robert A. Kann, *The Habsburg Empire: A Study in Integration and Disintegration* (New York, 1957).

13. Marc Raeff, *Understanding Imperial Russia* (New York, 1984).

14. Edward C. Thaden, *Russia's Western Borderlands, 1710-1870* (Princeton N.J., 1984).

15. See Gregory Gleason, *Federalism and Nationalism: The Struggle for Republican Rights in the USSR* (Boulder, Colo., 1990).

16. Some revisionist historians disagree with this view. In particular, see J. Arch Getty, *The Origins of the Great Purges: The Soviet Communist Party Reconsidered, 1933-38* (Cambridge, 1985).

17. Much of the subsequent analysis draws on the essays of Kaufman and Cowgill in Yoffee and Cowgill, *The Collapse of Ancient States and Civilizations*.

18. Marc Bloch, *Feudal Society* (Chicago, 1970), vol. 1.
19. For a detailed conceptual discussion of nationalism, see Alexander J. Motyl, *Sovietology, Rationality, Nationality: Coming to Grips with Nationalism in the USSR* (New York, 1990), 46-58.
20. See Sidney Hook, *The Hero in History* (Boston, 1955).
21. The view of the state as being embedded in domestic and international relations draws on Skocpol, *States and Social Revolutions.*
22. Karl W. Deutsch, *Nationalism and Social Communication* (Cambridge, Mass., 1966).
23. Anthony D. Smith, *Theories of Nationalism* (New York, 1972).
24. Ernest Gellner, *Thought and Change* (London, 1964).
25. See Otto Bauer's writings on this subject in Tom Bottomore and Patrick Goode, eds., *Austro-Marxism* (Oxford, 1978), 102-17.
26. See David F. Good, *The Economic Rise of the Habsburg Empire, 1750-1914* (Berkeley, Calif., 1984); John Komlos, *The Habsburg Monarchy as a Customs Union: Economic Development in Austria-Hungary in the Nineteenth Century* (Chicago, 1983).
27. Paul Kennedy, *The Rise and Fall of the Great Powers* (New York, 1987).
28. Charles Kupchan, *The Vulnerability of Empire* (Unpublished manuscript), chap. 2, p. 11.
29. See Alexander J. Motyl, "Reassessing the Soviet Crisis," *Political Science Quarterly* 104 (1989): 269-80.
30. On the concept of dual sovereignty, see Charles Tilly, *From Mobilization to Revolution* (New York, 1978).
31. See Ted Robert Gurr, *Why Men Rebel* (Princeton, N.J., 1969); Chalmers Johnson, *Revolutionary Change*, 2nd ed. (Stanford, Calif., 1982); Samuel P. Huntington, *Political Order in Changing Societies* (New Haven, Conn., 1968); Tilly, *From Mobilization to Revolution*; Skocpol, *States and Social Revolutions.*
32. Ellen Trimberger, *Revolution from Above* (New Brunswick, N.J., 1978).
33. For a discussion of the importance of personality in "neo-patrimonial states," see Said Amir Arjomand, "Iran's Islamic Revolution in Comparative Perspective," *World Politics* 38 (1986): 383-414.
34. See Kenneth Minogue and Beryl Williams, "The Revenge of the Particular," in *Thinking Theoretically about Soviet Nationalities*, ed. Alexander J. Motyl (New York, forthcoming 1991).
35. See István Déak, *Beyond Nationalism: A Social and Political History of the Habsburg Officer Corps, 1848-1918* (Oxford, 1990).
36. For a more detailed discussion of this argument, see Alexander J. Motyl, "Totalitarian Collapse, Imperial Disintegration, and the Rise of the Soviet West: Implications for the West," in *The Rise of Nations in the Soviet Union: American Foreign Policy and the Disintegration of the USSR*, ed. Michael Mandelbaum, (New York, 1991), and "Empire or Stability? The Disintegration of the USSR and the West," *World Policy Journal* (forthcoming).

37. I discuss the normative, instrumental, and coercive supports of state stability in *Will the Non-Russians Rebel? State, Ethnicity, and Stability in the USSR* (Ithaca, N.Y., 1980).

38. For a detailed treatment of the degenerative tendencies of the totalitarian state, see Motyl, *Sovietology, Rationality, Nationality*, 59-71.

39. See Bernard Gwertzman and Michael T. Kaufman, eds., *The Collapse of Communism* (New York, 1990).

40. Theda Skocpol develops this point in "Social Revolutions and Mass Military Mobilization," *World Politics* 40 (1988): 147-68.

3

The Soviet Union and the Habsburg Empire: Problems of Comparison

William O. McCagg, Jr.

I

Friedrich Nietzsche proposed a century ago that God was dead. In 1989 an American Foreign Service officer pronounced that history also had reached its end. Neither of these men, of course, was thinking of an actual death. Nietzsche wished merely to suggest that after hundreds of millennia of human civilization, man had suddenly since 1789 lost his confidence in the benevolent guidance of an abstract deity. Francis Fukuyama meant comparably that suddenly since about 1980 man had lost faith in the fundamental twentieth-century Marxist (and positivist) idea that history is leading "upward" toward some postliberal final stage.[1] But these two necrologies highlight the peril facing anyone who dares in 1990 to write about world affairs. The rush of events is accelerating, mortally challenging all prognoses based on accepted knowledge.

Just two years ago, in mid-1988, it would not have seemed realistic at all to suggest comparisons between the Soviet Union and the Habsburg Empire. On the one hand, the Soviet multinational dominion in Eastern Europe was then still an unassailable pillar of the world political order. Even the clear-sighted observer, Zbigniew Brzezinski, still felt constrained in his new book on the "failure" of communism, not to predict a coming general collapse of Soviet power, much less any breach in the Berlin Wall.[2] And on the other hand, 1988 was the seventieth anniversary of the failure and collapse of the Habsburg Empire. To all but specialists in its history, that old *Reich* seemed then wholly dead and certainly irrelevant to present-day political problems. The ice was melting, of course. Two years ago martial law had been lifted in Poland and economic reformers were reintroducing "capitalism" at a fairly rapid pace in Hungary. But even in April, 1989, Charles Gati, a normally venturous Hungarian-American political scientist, pronounced that he had yet to see any "systemic" change in the structure of "totalitarianism" in the Communist countries.[3] And in June, 1989, there were still credible rumors circulating in Budapest that a "hard-liner" intervention was in the offing for Hungary, which would be led by East Germany, Czechoslovakia and Romania (perhaps with, perhaps without, Soviet participation) in the spirit of the Brezhnev Doctrine.[4] Amidst circumstances such as those, it seemed provocative, rather than realistic, to suggest that somehow society might profit from comparing the multinational Soviet Union to the Habsburg Empire, as if the former were on the brink of disintegration and the latter had something practical to tell. Coincidentally, of course, the principal structures of Communist party control did disintegrate in Poland and Hungary, allowing a free election and the emergence of a non-Communist government in the former, and the rehabilitation of the rebels of 1956 in the latter. The revolutionary deluge of the fall of 1989 has made the Stalinist Empire in Eastern Europe as irrevocably a thing of the past as the Habsburg Empire itself. Within the Soviet Union itself, moreover, in republic after republic a new nationalism has found roots, giving rise to vocal strivings for home rule and even independence from Moscow's control. The nationality rebellion has gone so far, that in the Russian Republic there is serious discussion of the possibility of "going it alone," without the imperial borderlands, so as to avoid the pull and tug of all their demands. In this situation, a comparison of the Soviet polity with the Habsburg *Reich* seems logically unexceptionable. Indeed, the crisis with Lithuania seems virtually a replay of the drama that the Habsburgs played out with Serbia eighty-five years ago, and one can spot immediately a dozen other parallels between Moscow's problems and Viennese experience.

But let it be underlined that this is the way the situation seems at the time of this writing, in the summer of 1990. I cannot guarantee that in the near future, or even at the moment of the publication of these remarks, they will have the same feeling of relevance. Their value, and the value of the various essays that follow, lies first of all in their testimony about the peculiar excitement of the moment in which we live, and only secondarily in their seriousness as scholarship and as political advice.

II

Several solid frameworks justify comparison of the two multinational empires with which we are concerned. The first emerges simply from geography. The Soviet Empire in its broader manifestation—the Soviet "bloc" or Warsaw Pact of 1955—included most of the vast Central and East European regions that used to belong to the Habsburgs. Of course, very little of onetime Habsburg Austria's territory fell in 1945 directly under Moscow's rule: only the Carpatho-Ukraine, Eastern Galicia, and northern Bukovina have been parts both of the Habsburg Empire and of the Soviet Union. But for a time at the end of the war, the only parts of old Austria-Hungary not in Stalin's hands were Trieste, Carinthia, part of Styria, the Tyrol, and tiny Vorarlberg. Only in 1948-49, because of the Stalin-Tito break, did the Soviets lose control over Slovenia, Croatia, Dalmatia, Bosnia, and the Vojvodina. Only in 1955, after the Austrian State Treaty, did Moscow's troops withdraw from Vienna, Upper and Lower Austria, and the Burgenland. All the rest of the Habsburg Empire remained under direct Soviet influence until the past few years. And in the Yugoslav lands the Soviet political system has survived. On evacuated Austria, Moscow has effectively imposed military and political neutralism down to the present day.

Because of this territorial overlap, and because certain "landless," or "nonhistoric"[5] former Habsburg peoples—notably the Jews and the Ukrainians—figure significantly in Soviet Russia, it is patently legitimate to compare and contrast the political adventures of this, that, or another onetime Habsburg land, or people, under the rule first of Vienna, then of Moscow.[6] In Hungary, particularly, there is a great plenitude of egregious parallels between the experience under communism and the earlier record under the Habsburgs. In 1945, for example, as in the late seventeenth century, Hungary was suborned to a new authority by a "liberating" military conquest. In 1956, as in 1848, the country made a disastrously violent bid for freedom, which culminated in reimposed military absolutism. In the 1960s, as in the 1860s, a "turncoat" Hungarian national leadership worked out a systematic compromise, which sacrificed the principle of independence in exchange for socioeconomic special treatment. By the 1980s, as in the 1880s, Hungary was the most privileged and prosperous single unit of a dominating empire.

Such precise parallels are anything but universal in the overlap regions under discussion. In Bohemia, for instance, a key Slavic province of both the Habsburg and Soviet European empires, the political records are not at all similar. In the nineteenth century the Czechs pursued almost without interruption a disruptive political line against Habsburg power, and in the end they played the most conspicuous single role in bringing the Habsburg Empire down. In the Soviet era, however, the Czechs (for whatever good reason) were compliant to Soviet intrusions in 1945, compliant in 1948, compliant to a degree in 1952, and passive in 1956. Then in 1966-68 they completely broke with all the previous patterns of their behavior, challenging Soviet rule perhaps more effectively than any other nation did in all of Eastern Europe; and they got squashed for their pains. Whereupon for twenty years after 1969 they were massively compliant once again, and they broke out in 1989 only after the successful rebellion in East Germany had guaranteed them that their revolt would work. Is there any parallel worth dwelling upon here? Even the often-cited prominence in Czech history of years ending in "8" broke down in 1988, when nothing happened.

Likewise, in the South Slav and Polish experiences under first Habsburg, then Soviet rule, many, many details are different. It is frequently said, for example, that the way Serbia defied Austria-Hungary in the years before World War I foreshadowed the way Tito's Yugoslavia defied Stalin after 1948. Once one penetrates below the surface, however, one must admit that before 1900, neither Serbia nor Croatia did much to challenge the Habsburgs. Croatia, notoriously even collaborated with Vienna against "freedom-fighting" Hungary. But Tito's Yugoslavia has remained a constant thorn in the Soviet side virtually from the moment of the consolidation of a Soviet Empire in Europe. Correspondingly in Poland, despite certain real parallels between Soviet and Habsburg rule, the details were all different. No doubt the imposition of Habsburg and Russian control alike over that country was preceded by its devastating destruction in many wars. Within both empires, Poland at an early date received a special position. In both there was a national upheaval that culminated in brutal reimposition of imperial power. Nonetheless, precise study brings to light massive and self-conscious differences in behavior between, for example, the restrained revolutionary Poland of 1956 and 1980-81, and the hot-headed, fiery Poland of 1830, 1846, and 1863. If Wojciech Jaruzelski self-consciously imitates Józef Pilsudski in his efforts to seem the savior of a Poland "reborn," there was simply nobody in nineteenth-century Poland (not to mention Habsburg Galicia) who could be compared to the succession of Communist party First Secretaries, Boleslaw Bierut, Wladislaw Gomulka, and Edward Gierek. Further, there are few significant national minorities in the Soviet-made Poland of today, whereas in Habsburg Galicia (and even in tsarist-ruled Congress Poland) the presence of national minorities was nearly the whole story; yet Soviet Poland contained a vast "stolen territory" in Silesia and Pomerania, which had no parallel whatsoever in the Poland of the nineteenth century.

Even in the contrasts, however, one may frequently find edifying results from systematic study of the overlap territories of the two empires. And the same may be said of the significant "overlap peoples." Look at the Jews, for example, who in both empires have played a disproportionately large role in what might be called "the imperial middle class."[7] There are here many parallels, as with the Hungarians. Both the Habsburg Jewry, which centered in turn-of-the-century Vienna, and the Soviet Jewry of Stalinist Moscow emerged through massive emigration from the lands of prepartition Poland, the classical home of the Ashkenazim. The migration of the first preceded the revolutions of 1917-20 and the Holocaust, and the migration of the latter postdated those cataclysmic events. But in both empires demographic movement brought on massive transformation of Jewry from ghetto "backwardness" into membership in the educated professions—indeed, into wholly disproportional prominence in areas such as medicine, the law, literature, and scientific research. In both empires Jews were prominent in revolutionary movements, yet also conspicuously loyal to the ruling state, and behind the scenes in both empires they sometimes came very close to the real centers of power.

But alongside all these parallels in Jewry's career in the two empires, there is a dramatic contrast that allows one to pinpoint the real difference between the two empires' treatment of nationalities. The Habsburg Empire was essentially Liberal from 1860 until 1918, and despite its random anti-Semitism, at no time did it systematically persecute its Jews, who remained therefore a pillar of the political and social system. The Soviet state, on the other hand, for all its doctrinaire commitment to human emancipation, remained more than absolutist in its politics, and coerced its Jews, along with everyone else, toward the appointed dogmatic goals. Consequently, though Soviet anti-Semitism has over the decades been far less vocal and conspicuous than the anti-Semitism of the Habsburg Empire, the Soviet Jews became in the late 1960s the first Soviet nationality group to go into opposition.

One can point to similar interesting patterns when one studies the Western Ukrainians, who under Habsburg and Soviet rule alike have been the most articulate of all the elements within the Ukrainian nation, striving for independence against all neighbors—and against all odds.[8] But even without them, our point seems established: because of territorial and popular overlaps, it is patently legitimate to compare and contrast the Soviet and Habsburg empires, different as they may have been.

III

We can also see parallels and contrasts between the Soviet Union and the multinational Habsburg Empire in the methods and instruments the two states used to control their territories and populations. The reason is above all that through the history of precisely these two empires, one can trace an experiment in constitution making for multinational polities, which has been continuous since the eighteenth century.

The Habsburgs started the game by attempting after 1740 to build a modern autocratic state centering in Vienna.[9] For over a hundred years, though they tolerated substantial autonomies in various crownlands, they turned ever more rigorously toward centralized royal absolutism. Then after the revolutions of 1848 and the lost wars of the 1860s, they acknowledged the force of modern nationalism. They reversed course and committed themselves to the theory that they might survive as rulers of a multinational world through systematic reduction of their central authority. Thereafter in each of their dominions they encouraged the writing of liberal constitutions, organizing the Austrian half of the Empire according to a federal constitutional pattern, while sticking in Hungary to centralist constitutionalism. Behind the scenes, of course, they tried to bolster their remaining institutional power through policies of manipulation. They proved themselves masters of the game of playing one nationality against another, as well as of "muddling through."

This theory failed them in 1918; and at that very moment the new Soviet state went to work at building up a new type of autocratic control behind remarkably similar constitutional arrangements.[10] In the onetime borderlands of the tsarist empire, Lenin and his colleagues applied a federal principle, just as the Habsburgs had done in post-1867 Austria. In Russia they used centralized arrangements, such as the Habsburgs had employed in Hungary. Their new system learned explicitly from Habsburg experience;[11] and one must admit that their constitutional arrangements, cruel though they may be, have lasted for over seventy years, quite a bit longer than the Habsburg system of 1867. Only today is it proving necessary to engage in radical reworking of the Leninist nationality settlement.

Beyond this basic continuity between the central Habsburg and Soviet constitutional experiments, one may note peripheral parallels between how the two empires approached the government of multinational regions. For example, the Habsburgs treated some areas as "satrapies"—units that were not considered integral parts of the civic state but that were not foreign either; and the Soviet Union has elevated the satrapy model to big business. Under the Habsburgs, the most conspicuous satrapy was Bosnia-Herzegovina, occupied by the army in 1876-78, but not formally annexed until 1908, and even then ruled ambiguously by the Austro-Hungarian joint Finance Ministry, rather than by the Vienna or by the Budapest constitutional governments. In the Soviet Empire satrapy status has been the norm in Mongolia, North Korea, and throughout the vast territories in Eastern Europe that the Red Army conquered in 1944-45. To everybody's knowledge, all these territories have for forty years and more been largely subject to Soviet influence. However, Moscow has actually ruled through behind-the-scenes coordination between the Soviet and regional Communist parties; between the Red Army and the local Communist-dominated armies; and between the KGB and local police agencies. Outwardly Moscow has encouraged all of these lands to retain the symbols of their former independence, and to seem much more independent than the Soviet Union's own republics.

And alongside the satrapies, both empires have relied on another type of indirect dominance—satelliteship—that involves even less overt rule, but a good deal of voluntary self-limitation. In the Habsburg political system, Serbia fell into this category through most of the late nineteenth century, as did for lesser periods of time the Romanian principalities. In the Soviet case one may mention here the special positions of neutral Austria and Finland, and also that of Afghanistan before 1979. The reason both these empires could have satellites was that both relied heavily throughout their existence on systematic diplomacy, ensuring control at home through massive manipulation of the external environment. Need one more than mention, to establish this reality, the pivotal role of Count Metternich in establishing the political system of the Habsburg Empire in the first half of the nineteenth century? Or the dominant role of the Bismarckian alliance system in preserving the Empire, despite all its internal difficulties, through the last four decades of its existence? Or the Habsburg byword, *Divide et impera*, which was also Stalin's? And what has the international political system, which we know as the "cold war," been, if not a massive diplomatic distraction of world attention from demands for a "rollback" of the Stalin-won empire behind the iron curtain? It is in no way an exaggeration to say that both the Habsburg and the Soviet empires became as broad as they both for so long were, because the diplomats of the two states (aided in the Soviet case by the foreign Communists) were adroit at manipulating both the interests of outsider states and the mythologies of the greater world.

Let us turn now from comparing the techniques of ethnic rule employed in the two empires, to a comparison of their specific instruments of control, and first of all to the most prominent of these, their armies.[12] Study immediately shows remarkable parallels. For example, the old Habsburg army and the Soviet army alike were dominated by the central population of the empires in which they existed, the Germans and the Russians, respectively; and in each the language of command has been the language of those people, with minimal concession to minority languages. Yet as is well known, both armies recruited indiscriminately from all territories of the state, regardless of civic constitutional autonomies; and each has been remarkably successful at generating and preserving a supranational patriotism that transcended local nationality. This is not the place for more extensive discussion of such matters, but it can be stated forthright from these two examples that strong supranational military organizations are probably advantageous instruments for ensuring political dominance in multinational regions.

In the bureaucracies and the police organizations also there is clear evidence that both empires have, for long periods of time, had considerable success at surmounting national differences.[13] Because of its modernity and benevolence, Joseph II's bureaucratic Austrian state was as appealing to the peoples over which it ruled after 1780, and in some degree all the way down to 1918, as was the more explicitly revolutionary Leninist state to the benighted populations of tsarist Russia after 1917. Correspondingly, the pre-1860 Habsburg Monarchy was in its day as much a byword for successful police rule as was Stalinist Russia in ours. And both the bureaucracies and the police of these empires have been notably supranational (if not, in point of recruitment, entirely without bias). But here, of course, differences of degree and quality patently separate the two empires. Increasingly over the hundred and fifty years of its existence the Austrian state bureaucracy became a paragon of incorruptibility: the Soviet bureaucracy has become if anything the reverse—increasingly a cesspool of venality. Both these bureaucracies built modern educational and economic systems that indelibly changed the subject populations, hauling them out of an often primeval agrarian parochialism. But whereas the Habsburg system collapsed under the impact of external blows, the Soviet system is collapsing under its own weight. And as for the police, it must be said that neither Metternich's terror organization, nor Alexander Bach's, ever approached in its violence, or in the scope of its operations, the record of the GPU, not to mention Stalin's NKVD and MVD, or the post-Stalinist KGB. The Habsburg Empire simply had no gulag, nor for all its preoccupation with nationality problems, did it ever consider the sort of deportation of whole nationality groups, which Beria's police undertook at the end of World War II.

Any systematic organizational comparison of the Habsburg Empire and the Soviet Union must come to grips not only with the formal organizations of control just mentioned, but also with the complex of ideological-political control instruments that were known in the Habsburg case as "aristocracy and church" and in the Soviet Union as "Communist party." And here the differences seem transcendent. No doubt one can argue for comparability. One can propose, for example, that the revolution abolished aristocracy and church in Russia, and that consequently the new organizational forms of postrevolutionary Russia could not explicitly label themselves "aristocracy" and "church"—that one should look at the organic functions of the Soviet new class and official ideology, and recognize how similar these were (despite the twentieth century) to what had existed before. The fact remains, however, that the Communist party elite in the Soviet Union, even seventy years after the revolution, has not become an aristocracy even in the absolutely essential point of legitimizing family property. Nepotism is by all accounts pervasive in the Soviet system, but it is flatly illegal.[14] And much the same is true of the Communist party's ideology, which is as antireligious today as it was at the moment of its ascendancy in 1917. Marxism-Leninism, for all the power it legitimized for its followers, has simply never been able to become an established religion of the popular masses. It was from the start, and is today at best, an opiate for the educated classes—for the intellectuals.[15]

It would be difficult here to carry on with systematic comparisons between the organizations of the Habsburg and Soviet empires, because the next step is to mention economic organizations, and that would involve recognition of the total divergence of the two economic systems. The one was private capitalist; the other, all-pervasive state socialist. But in a way there is no need to pursue those differences, because we have already produced a relative proof: we have said enough to establish the fundamentally greater comparability between these two states, than between perhaps any other two multinational world powers of modern history.

Look, for example, at the fate of another comparison. In 1988, a well-known Western observer of current developments in Eastern Europe, Timothy Garton Ash, proposed a comparison between the decay of the Soviet Union and that of the Ottoman Empire.[16] Why? First of all, he claimed, because one could anticipate in the Soviet Empire a "long, slow process of imperial decline in the course of which one could see an unplanned, piecemeal, and discontinuous emancipation, both of the constituent states from the imperial center and of societies from states." Ash prophesied that this would occur "mainly by uncoordinated independent action, whether individual, collective, or national, by pressure from below or from outside, in an overall context of growing relative backwardness." And then he proceeded to point to various institutional parallels between Ottoman and Soviet society: the armies were multinational; the supranational Ottoman class allegedly resembled the Communist elite; the institutions of Islam allegedly resembled the Communist party; the tolerance of religious millets resembled the Soviet tolerance of national entities; the corruption and violence were similar; and so on and so forth.

Ash's principal point has already been disproved: in the two short years since he wrote, the Soviet Empire has undergone a rapid process of dissolution that bears no comparison whatsoever to the two centuries of slow rot that finally did away with Ottoman power. Further, from what I have already said, it should be evident how much more striking are the parallels between the Habsburg Empire and the Soviet Union, than between the Ottoman state and the Soviet one.[17] There was virtually no territorial or demographic overlap between these last two, such as binds the former, nor was there any such continuity of political theory as binds Vienna and Moscow. In addition, the Ottoman army was hardly ever, even in its last years during World War I, a popular army, such as the universal service-based Habsburg army clearly was, and such as the Red Army has been from its inception. If the Ottoman army was "multinational," this was because of its origins in the Janissary Corps, which consisted originally of slaves recruited among the subject nationalities. The Red Army has never been in any way a slave corps.

One can carry on by noting that both the Habsburg and Soviet elites have been basically national in character, defending, respectively, German Magyar and Russian rule in the two modern empires. The Ottoman elite contrastingly was genuinely supranational, and in no way aimed to preserve Turkish ethnic rule. Even the governing language of the Ottoman Empire was Turkish only in structure. In vocabulary and script it was overwhelmingly Arabic and Persian, and quite incomprehensible to illiterate Turks. Nor is it fair to say that Islam, the official "ideology" of the Ottomans, was really anything like the official ideology of the Soviet Union, which had its roots in the European philosophical Enlightenment, just as the Habsburg state ideology did, and which aped a Russian Christianity, which was not all that far from the Christianity of the Habsburg state. Islam, almost by definition, is anti-Enlightenment and anti-Christian.

None of this is to suggest that to compare the Soviet Empire's decay with that of the Ottoman state is wholly sterile. It is simply to underline how much more alike were the Habsburg and Soviet empires, and how much more comparable to each other they are, than either is (*tacet* Karl Wittvogel and Alexander Yanov) to the Asiatic despotisms of the East.[18]

IV

I have argued that we can compare these two empires because of their territorial overlap and because of similarities in their methods of political control. In addition, there is a third solid framework. It regards what one may call the "era-specific functions" of the two empires, and in many ways it is the most interesting of all.

To introduce this sort of comparison, let me recall the famous letter that the Czech historian František Palacký wrote to the organizers of the German National Assembly in Frankfurt am Main in the spring of 1848, in which he referred to Austria as a "European necessity" that would have to be invented were it not extant.[19] What did Palacký mean? In part, he was referring to the threat posed by Germany's unification to the pronouncedly mixed ethnic society that existed (and still exists) in East-Central Europe. Palacký recognized that the ruling classes throughout the area then spoke German, and often were German; and he felt that only the preservation of a separate Habsburg Empire would allow all those nationalities to resist German pressure and to articulate themselves.

Palacký was referring, second, to the political-religious mission that the Habsburg Empire had carried out during recent centuries by defending Europe's eastern frontier against Ottoman assaults. In 1848 the Ottomans were no longer a threat to Europe, but Palacký explicitly revised the Habsburg mission to cover the defense of Europe against the expansive tyranny of tsarist Russia. Without such a bulwark, he said, the Russians would be all over Central Europe.

Meanwhile, Palacký made a third point, and this is where he elevated the Habsburg Empire from being an Eastern European necessity to being an All-European necessity. He proposed that the conflicts between the nationalities of Eastern Europe (and notably the Germano-Slavic conflict) constituted a European problem. The victory of any one group (for example, the Germans) over the others could only, he claimed, work to Europe's (and humanity's!) disadvantage. So he argued that it would relieve Europe of political headaches, were a just and powerful Habsburg state to take the responsibility for keeping these conflicts permanently in equilibrium. His argument was highly self-interested, and on its face was a device for giving the Czechs access to political power. But it contained the notion also that Western Europe was "baroque" enough without its eastern rim: Palacký saw the Habsburg Empire as a "European necessity" because it relieved Europe of the burden of its eastern multinationality.

As is well known, during the second half of the nineteenth century the Habsburg Empire ceased to be effective in these functions. The causes of its eclipse were of course manifold. They included a basic conflict between the rigidity of the Habsburg state and the dynamism that modern schooling brought to the subject nationalities. The state insisted on dynastic law, on aristocratic primacy, on Catholic faith, and only after that on modern liberal ideas. The new education began with the modern idea of human and national rights, and gave primacy to abstract reason and modern technology above tradition. Only an explosion could result from such juxtapositions. In addition there were basic conflicts between the instinctive conservatism of the rulers, and the force of modern capitalism in a period when everywhere in Europe vast populations were abandoning the agrarian countryside in favor of huge urban industrial conglomerations. And also the Empire was challenged, indeed thrust aside, on the West by the new German *Reich*, and pulled apart from the East by the spectacle of new tiny national states emerging in the once-Ottoman Balkans.

It is worth emphasizing, however, that the Habsburg Empire ceased to be a "European necessity" above all because Europe itself with extraordinary vigor "took off" in the late nineteenth century, battering with its fantastically rapid modern growth any and every institution left over from the past, taking onto its own shoulders the responsibilities that Palacký had perceived to be the Habsburg Empire's—interfering in and usurping Habsburg affairs, speaking directly to the peoples of the East, turning them against Vienna and all it stood for. In the end, moreover, the Empire did not collapse because of its own problems alone, although it started the war that killed it, and no doubt deserved its fate. The Empire collapsed in 1918 because of its involvement in a European cataclysm—because of a catastrophe that nearly brought the whole vast gorgeous complexity of Western Europe to ruin.

Now let us move on to observe that the same European cataclysm of 1914-18 brought on the destruction of the tsarist empire, which for three centuries had governed another multinational region, the vast Eurasian steppe that stretched from the Ukraine to the Pacific Ocean. The situation in Eastern Europe at the end of the war was thus quite different from what it had been in 1848, when Palacký perceived the need for a European defense bastion in the East: now from Vienna all the way to the edge of China there was disorder, rebellion among the nationalities, civil wars within the larger nations. Not since the Mongol period of the Middle Ages had Europe's eastern frontier been so exposed. It does not matter that no great Turkish invader was poised to come in through the Balkans, or that there was no Mongol threat to Europe's safety in Siberia: the imminence of strife and destruction on a huge scale was unmistakable. And a new kind of character-istically twentieth-century threat had emerged to attract Europe's attention to the disaster: the probability that someone would have to pay for it all was immense.

Western Europe itself was in no position to meet this challenge; witness the weakness of the various interventionist expeditions sent to Russia in 1918-21. England and Italy were exhausted, France was bled white, and an American task force had forced the Central Powers into political collapse. Besides, Western Europe had its hands full after 1918 just intervening in the former Habsburg lands, enlarging the Balkan statelings and creating a new Poland. Northern Eurasia was altogether too much for Europe to put back together again.

Enter the Bolsheviks! Lenin and his colleagues had seized power in the Russian cities almost by default in the fall of 1917, and (*tacet* the Sisson documents) in no way because any European countries encouraged them to do so. They held onto power through 1918 because of the geographical remoteness of their strongholds and the sheer disunity of their opponents. They established their hegemony over the multinational Bridge of Asia in 1919-21 only with the greatest difficulty, and with no help from outside. But when they achieved victory, and in 1920-24 established the constitutional Soviet Union, they did so with Europe's consent. This consent was often reluctantly given and grudgingly received. The Soviet Union remained essentially an isolationist power throughout the interwar period. But pre-cisely that isolationism underlined what had happened: the Bolsheviks had taken the disorder of Eurasia out of Europe's hands, and off Europe's shoulders, because Europe could not and would not do the job itself. And in this sense, may one not suggest that the new Soviet Union responded to Europe's needs, and was thus a "European necessity" just as much as the Habsburg Empire had been in Palacký's day? If it hadn't come into existence, would not something like it have had to be created?

One may reinforce this argument by projecting it further, for the great drama of twentieth-century Europe's history was by no means ended with the settlements of 1919-24. As is well known, the new Europe began stumbling almost from the start. It included, as equal partners to the old Western liberal state system, no less than twelve new or greatly enlarged states in the multinational East (thirteen, if one includes Turkey). From the start these states proved an *embarras de richesses*—too expensive, too complex for the state's good. All of them had major economic, class, and ethnic problems that, together with inexperience, led some of them within the decade onto paths of political illiberalism.[20] After 1921, when Italy, one of the allegedly great powers of the West that were supposed to keep the system "free," stumbled into fascism, the discontented flocked to imitate it, especially in the disunited East. By 1929, when the great economic depression lamed the economies of the Western world, the forces of stability in Europe were therefore parlously weak.

Just as one may blame the rotting of the Habsburg Empire on many factors, so also the collapse of interwar Europe.[21] Some have called the crisis "the inevitable crisis of industrial capitalism," others speak of "imperialist overextension," and still others have been impressed by the cultural and especially by the scientific breakthroughs that destroyed the simple faiths of the nineteenth century, and made the young twentieth century world a "world without Truth" (or of too many "truths"), too complex for the ordinary mind to grasp. But an important cause was clearly also that the new Europe of the interwar period was too "baroque" for its own health, too enormous, too spread out. When the crisis came, it hit the East first and brought on a debacle of liberalism there. Austria and Hungary, principal economic centers, went bankrupt. Authoritarian nationalism spread everywhere. Virtually every disposition of the 1919 peace settlement came into question. And this Eastern European debacle fanned the German anti-Liberal hysteria of the early 1930s. It abetted the rise of Austrian-born Hitler to power in Germany in 1933, and justified his catastrophic launching within six years of a new European war.

Enter Stalin! The Soviet dictator was, of course, reluctant to get involved in Europe, very much so.[22] In the period of Hitler's rise to power, Stalin maintained the Soviet policy of isolationism; then, during the years of Germany's rearmament, he made motions toward participating in a general front against fascism. But for all practical purposes he was wholly preoccupied during the 1930s with the great industrial drive at home, and with the great purges; and in 1939, disillusioned by Munich, he struck a bargain with Hitler that actually permitted the new European war to erupt. For two years between 1939 and 1941, Stalin stood resolutely against Russia's reinvolvement in European affairs.

To no avail. In June 1941 the leading European power of the day, Hitler's Germany, attacked the Soviet Union, forcing Stalin to rejoin the anti-Fascist coalition. During the four-year-long struggle that followed, Stalin's Russia not only survived but played the single greatest role in the absolute defeat of Hitler's Germany, and of all save two (Spain and Portugal) of Hitler's imitators in Europe. This accomplishment alone revalidates the proposition that the Soviet Union must be considered in some fashion as a "European necessity"—a factor without which Europe could not have recovered its equilibrium. Nor does the case end there.[23] By the end of the war Stalin's power had extended over the entirety of the multinational zone whose direct membership in Europe had caused such problems after 1918. The Red Army had even split up Bismarck's Germany, whose unification had played so great a role eighty years earlier in disrupting the Habsburg *Reich*. For two or three years after 1945, there was hope of a Soviet withdrawal, or at least of a political reliberalization of this vast belt of lands—a hope that culminated in the American proposal in 1947 of a self-help economic program, the Marshall Plan, for rebuilding the Europe that had been created in 1919. But in 1948 it became clear that Stalin's forces would not retire, but instead would roll down an "iron curtain" across Europe from Lübeck to Trieste, simply removing from Western Europe's shoulders all responsibility for Europe's "problem zone."

It was because of that Stalinist retreat into isolationism in 1948 that Western Europe has been able to achieve the shape it has today.[24] The Marshall Plan funding was not squandered on the more economically backward East, as it might have been had it not been for Stalin, but was concentrated on rebuilding the already well-modernized West. Indeed, because Stalin's Empire was so threatening to Western Europe, the American Congress probably provided much more funding for the Marshall Plan than it would have had Eastern Europe also had to be rebuilt. Certainly the Americans bound themselves to Europe through NATO, and through every sort of economic involvement, more tightly because of the cold war threat, than they ever would have allowed had Eastern Europe been "free." Further, during the two decades that followed 1948, specifically in the context of defense against Stalin's Empire, Western Europe got rid of its principal old problems: its militarism, its nationalism, its economic parochialism, its colonial involvements, and ultimately its political disunity. The Europe we know today—the Europe that is headed toward political unification in 1992—is the direct result of Stalin's division of Europe in 1948.

May it be argued from these facts that all the horrors of Stalinism were a "European necessity" in a sense analogous to František Palacký's definition of the Habsburg Empire?[25] This seems a huge oversimplification of what happened. In the name of part of Stalin's work—his foreign policy in Europe—such a thesis would cast on all his works a sanction they hardly deserve. He himself was a man of appalling oversimplifications, and there seems no merit in justifying any of them by coining a new one.

We keep the issues separate, denying that, just because Stalin's defeat of Germany contributed to Western Europe's postwar success, therefore the gulag and the whole Empire of Fear inside the Soviet Union from 1928 to

1953 was the precondition of that success. Nonetheless, despite this denial, our fundamental argument seems wholly valid. It is inconceivable that without the cold war, and with Eastern Europe free and Germany united, Western Europe would have achieved the democratic structure, the demilitarization and decolonization, and the economic unity and prosperity that it boasts today. To this extent the Soviet Union, and the Stalinist Empire, have been European necessities, over seventy and forty years, respectively, in exactly the same sense that the Habsburg Empire once was.

V

My purpose in this essay has been to demonstrate that indeed the Habsburg Empire and the Soviet Union are comparable—that because of their territorial overlap, their common methods of rule, and their common functions vis-à-vis the multinationality of Eastern Europe, and vis-à-vis the historical development of Western Europe, it is legitimate to scrutinize them side by side. Let me now conclude by pointing to yet one further functional relationship between the two empires.

The Habsburg Empire was an experimental ground. From the 1840s to the 1870s all Europe recognized that the constitutional arrangements being worked out on the Danube were models that might be tried out elsewhere. Later on, after the turn of the century, it became conventional for Europeans to look down on what was happening there—to consider the multinational society there as something one might see in a zoo, and to mock its cacophony. But still the Habsburg Empire was the experimental ground on which Europe tried out the methods through which it hoped to govern its colonies. After August 1914 a Viennese intellectual, Karl Kraus, even labeled the dying Empire an "experimental institute for the end of the world," and this is the way many historians tend to look at it today.[26]

The Soviet Empire is a wholly parallel experimental ground. During and after the Russian civil war, the Bolsheviks had no concept of where they were headed: they were modernists, intent on doing things differently and better than they had been done before, and however one deplores their methods and their product, one must recognize that it has been *the* greatest and most adventuristic political experiment of the twentieth century. Correspondingly, one may recognize that the nationality crisis of 1989-90 is nothing new and transient. The national complexity of Eurasia was there in suppressed form all through the long quiet years under Stalin and Brezhnev. And its presence may ultimately be the explanation of why Stalin and Brezhnev felt obliged to be so utterly rigid for so long. In the old Habsburg Empire, Franz Joseph chose to accept the noise and turbulence of his nationalities because he was an optimist and hoped he could prevail. Stalin and Brezhnev chose to suppress the turbulence, and to pretend their nationalities loved one another, because they knew very well from personal experience in the Caucasus and in Moldavia, that given free voice, their nationalities would lapse into hate.

And in their disintegration, the two empires are also comparable experimental grounds. One should not be distracted by the fact that Franz Joseph's Empire disintegrated because of a European war, whereas today the Soviet Union is not at war, and does not even seem threatened by an armed conflagration. The Great War was a European catastrophe whose precise analogy is the catastrophe that grips the Soviet Union today. Behind the Soviet crisis is a typically twentieth-century disparity between political aspiration and practical economic capacity: Moscow simply could not meet the cost of keeping up with the Americans in point of weapons and computers, while going to Mars and at the same time feeding the Soviet population. Behind the crisis lies, moreover, a breakdown of Soviet society's infrastructure that foreshadows the breakdown taking place in every modern industrial society; and a destruction of the natural environment that foreshadows what is happening everywhere else. An end of the world is with us all, just as it was in Karl Kraus's day; and we may see our own future in the Soviet Union's present crisis just as clearly as he perceived it in the rot of the Habsburg Empire after 1914. This above all is why the comparison and contrast of the two empires is so apt.

NOTES

1. Fukayama, "The End of History?" *National Interest*, no. 16 (1989): 3-18.
2. Zbigniew Brzezinski, *The Grand Failure* (1988; reprint, New York,1990), 254-55.
3. Lecture at a faculty seminar, East-Central Europe Institute, Columbia University, March 1989.
4. See my report "June Journey," in the American Association for the Study of Hungarian History, *Newsletter*, January 1990.
5. This term was developed by Karl Renner and Otto Bauer at the turn of the century during theoretical debates in the Austrian Social Democratic party. See Robert Kann, *The Multinational Empire*, 2 vols. (New York, 1950), 2: chap. 20.
6. The best general history of the Habsburg Empire is probably still C. A. Macartney, *The Habsburg Empire, 1790-1918* (London, 1968). For the experiences of the various nationalities, see Adam Wandruszka and Peter

Urbanitsch, *Die Habsburgermonarchie, 1848-1918*, vol. 3 (Vienna, 1980). For roughly parallel records of Soviet-dominated Eastern Europe, see Zbigniew Brzezinski, *The Soviet Bloc: Unity and Conflict* (Cambridge, Mass., 1971); J. F. Brown, *Eastern Europe and Communist Rule* (Durham, N.C., 1988); and Joseph Rothschild, *Return to Diversity* (New York, 1989).

7. On the Jews in the Habsburg Empire, see my *History of Habsburg Jews, 1670-1918* (Bloomington, Ind., 1988). On the Soviet Jews, see Benjamin Pinkus, *The Jews of the Soviet Union* (Cambridge, 1988); and Nora Levin, *The Jews of the Soviet Union Since 1917*, 2 vols. (New York, 1988).

8. See Paul Magocsi, *Galicia: A Historical Survey and Bibliographic Guide* (Toronto, 1983).

9. The classic discussion of the Habsburg Empire's constitutional development is Josef Redlich, *Das österreichische Staats-und Reichsproblem*, 2 vols. (Vienna, 1920, 1926). But see also Robert A. Kann, *The Habsburg Empire: A Study in Integration and Disintegration* (New York, 1957), and the same author's contribution in *Die Verwaltung*, vol. 2 of Wandruszka and Urbanitsch, *Die Habsburgermonarchie 1848-1918*, chap. 1.

10. See Richard Pipes, *The Formation of the Soviet Union*, rev. ed. (New York, 1968); and for material about later Soviet nationality policy, the essays in Jeremy Azrael, *Soviet Nationality Policies and Practices* (New York, 1978).

11. The Leninist and Stalinist theories of nationalism were both devised in pre-1914 Austria on the basis of study of the Austro-Marxist nationality theories; see Pipes, *The Formation of the Soviet Union*, 36ff.

12. For the Habsburg army and the ethnic question, see István Déak, *Beyond Nationalism: A Social and Political History of the Habsburg Officer Corps, 1848-1918* (New York, 1990). For comparable data on the Soviet army, see S. Enders Wimbusch and Alex Alexiev, "The Ethnic Factor in the Soviet Armed Forces," *RAND*, R-2787/1 (March 1982).

13. For the Habsburg bureaucracy and police system, see *Die Verwaltung*. For the Soviet administrative system, see Merle Fainsod, *How Russia Is Ruled* (Cambridge, Mass., 1970); and Jerry Hough and Merle Fainsod, *How the Soviet Union Is Governed* (Cambridge, Mass., 1979).

14. See M. S. Vozlensky, *Nomenklatura: The Soviet Ruling Class* (Garden City, N.Y., 1984).

15. But see the interesting essay on Soviet ritualism in Christel Lane, *The Rites of Rulers. Ritual in Industrial Society: The Soviet Case* (Cambridge, 1981); and Vladimir Shlapentokh, *Soviet Public Opinion and Ideology: Mythology and Pragmatism in Interaction* (New York, 1986).

16. Timothy Garton Ash, "The Decay of Empires," originally published in the *New York Review of Books*, September 29, 1988; republished in *The Uses of Adversity* (New York, 1990), 242ff. The Soviet-Ottoman analogy has been spelled out also by John Evans in a lecture at the Kennan Institute in Washington, D.C., on February 5, 1990.

17. For a systematic discussion of Ottoman institutions in the light of modern political science, see Bernard Lewis, *The Emergence of Modern Turkey*

(London, 1968); and Lewis's *The Political Language of Islam* (Chicago, 1988).

18. Karl Wittvogel, *Oriental Despotism* (New Haven, Conn., 1957); and Alexander Yanov, *The Origins of Autocracy: Ivan the Terrible in Russian History* (Berkeley, 1981).

19. Palacký's letter is conveniently available in Charles and Barbara Jelavich, eds., *The Habsburg Monarchy* (New York, 1959), 18-23.

20. Hungary was a revanchist power, and vigorously anti-Socialist from late 1919 on. Poland did not achieve frontiers until 1921-23, and was economically so unstable that Józef Pilsudski felt obliged to seize power against the constitution in 1926. Terrorism dominated Bulgaria from 1923 to 1925. Greece had its first dictatorship in 1925-26. Austria experienced its first civil war in 1927. The King seized power against the constitution in Yugoslavia in 1928: see C. A. Macartney and Alan Palmer, *Independent Eastern Europe* (New York, 1962); and Hugh Seton Watson, *Eastern Europe Between the Wars* (reprint ed., Hamden, Conn., 1962).

21. For the following, see H. Stuart Hughes, *Contemporary Europe: A History*, 3rd ed. (Englewood Cliffs, N.J., 1971).

22. See Adam Ulam, *Expansion and Coexistence*, 2nd ed. (New York, 1974), chaps. 8-9; Trumbull Higgins, *Hitler and Russia* (New York, 1966); James E. McSherry, *Stalin, Hitler, and Europe*, 2 vols. (Cleveland, 1968-70); and D. C. Watt, *How War Came* (London, 1989). For the thesis that Stalin really wanted a pact with Hitler all along, see Stephen Cohen, *Bukharin and the Bolshevik Revolution* (New York, 1973), 360 and 469. Despite a flood of new material published in 1989 in the Soviet Union on the fiftieth anniversary of the Stalin-Hitler rapprochement, and the utter destruction of the orthodox Soviet explanations, there seems to be no new confirmation of Cohen's argument.

23. For the ambiguities of the postwar period, see my *Stalin Embattled, 1943-1948* (Detroit, 1979); and Vojtech Mastny, *Russia's Road to the Cold War* (New York, 1978).

24. On the building of the new, post-World War II Europe, see Robert Wegs, *Europe Since 1945* (New York, 1977).

25. For this sort of argument, see Theodor Von Laue, *Why Lenin? Why Stalin?*, 2nd ed. (Philadelphia, 1971).

26. Kraus referred to the Empire as a *Versuchstation des Weltunterganges* in his editorial in *Die Fackel* about the assassination of Franz Ferdinand in June 1914: see Heinrich Fischer, ed., *Gesammelte Werke von Karl Kraus*, 14 vols. (Munich, 1952-67), 8: 418.

4

Language and National Identity

Miroslav Hroch

Every attempt to describe the historical development of different countries runs the risk of trying to compare the incomparable. This danger can be avoided if the comparison adheres to certain principles—"rules of the game." One such rule is that in comparing historical events, even if they did not occur at the same time, we are able to distinguish fundamental analogous features or relations.

We are looking at comparable units, if we compare identical phases of national movements, even if they did not occur at the same time. In this case, the synchronic comparison follows analogous historical situations. In each of the national movements in the Habsburg Monarchy and in tsarist Russia, we can distinguish three phases. These movements started with a period of scholarly interest in national language, history, or geography (phase A), continued in a period of national patriotic agitation (phase B), and achieved their success definitively as a mass movement (phase C). Comparing each of these three phases we are able to distinguish fundamental differences, but eventually also construct a model of national transformation.[1]

Unlike the comparison of the Habsburg Monarchy and tsarist Russia, the comparison of the Habsburg Monarchy and the modern-day Soviet Union is not without difficulties. In this case, we are not analyzing similar stages of national movements, or comparable social and political systems and structures, but processes that are analogous only in perhaps one marginal sense: the multinational character of the two states.[2] Interethnic relations and conflicts occurred in both situations under very different social, political, and international circumstances. But even this parallelism gives some possibility for comparing ethnic relations in two such different societies. Nevertheless, we must not overestimate our results. They yield some interesting similarities, without being able to offer a basis for generalizations or even a model of national movements or of the disintegration of multinational empires.

That is why my contribution has two levels of unequal scientific perfection: the comparative one, concentrated on the Habsburg Monarchy and tsarist Russia, and an additive one that attempts to find some analogies between the past and the present. I shall devote my attention here to the role of linguistic programs and linguistic demands.

This limitation follows from another rule of successful comparison; namely, the subject of comparative analysis should be only one of the fundamental features of the compared situations or movements. In this essay, it will be the relation between language and national identity in the national movements within the Habsburg Monarchy and the Russian Empire. This comparison perhaps offers some analogies with actual national processes in the modern USSR. That is why we first have to analyze the national movements in both multinational monarchies.

These movements were not simultaneous. When Estonian and Latvian patriots began national agitation in the 1860s and 1870s, the Czech and Croatian national movements had already undergone their phase of national agitation (phase B) and entered their mass phase (phase C). The national movements in the Baltics entered phase C only at the beginning of the twentieth century, and the national movements in White Russia and in the Russian Ukraine did not arrive at phase C at all before 1917.[3] Seeking analogous features between current developments in the USSR and the Habsburg Monarchy is justified only if we consider the present movements in the Baltics and the Ukraine as a kind of repeat performance of the unsuccessful phase C in their national movements. For us the basic problem is whether and why in all these situations, language—or better, the linguistic program—played such an important role.

It is beyond question that one of the analogous features and problems of both empires was their multinational character. Before the national movements started, this multiethnicity posed an administrative problem: how to enable different ethnic groups to communicate among themselves and with the state administration, without causing problems.

The situation changed when signals announced a "national revival," the national movement of small, and until this time nondominant, ethnic groups to obtain all the attributes of existing nations—their own national culture, differentiated social structure, and some degree of political autonomy. In all instances, in the forefront of demands was the call for a national language.[4]

It would be too simple to compare only the formulations of linguistic demands. What we are concerned with here is their interpretation, the purpose of their political and social function. Such an interpretation will have to be carried out in two steps: first, for the two empires until their breakup after World War I, and second, for the two empires and the current Soviet Union.

If we ask ourselves why language was foremost in national movements, we are facing a problem we cannot resolve without differentiating in terms of time, place, and above all content. What we usually call the "linguistic program" of a national movement, in fact, covers several aims that did not come into existence at once but were born gradually, with demands made earlier merging with ones formulated later. In other words, the later-formulated linguistic programs were unthinkable without previous aims having been shaped and realized. From this viewpoint we can distinguish four strata of the national linguistic program which to a large extent are in line with the four steps or stages of creating such a program.

1. An interest in language as a subject of scientific research and of aesthetic value becomes primarily a celebration of the language. Briefly stated, this interest is usually linked to Enlightenment scholarship, on the one hand, and on the other to the influence of Johann Gottfried von Herder. Both can be accepted only partially. The Czech Jesuit Balbin wrote a celebration of the Czech language in the second half of the seventeenth century; other celebrations appeared roughly at the same time as the work of Herder, but independently of him.[5] But it is without doubt that Herder added a principled ethical and philosopical justification to the celebrations of the aesthetic, historical, and emotional values of a language. In his view, language expresses a nation's way of thinking, one so perfect that in itself it is the same as national thinking. And without national thinking the national character cannot emerge, nor can a nation as a social and cultural community.

2. Language as an expression of national character could exist only as a written or literary language. We cannot imagine spoken language as an instrument of national identification. Only the written standard identifies the individual speaker with a larger, national community. This gave rise to a further step in the linguistic program: efforts to create linguistic standards, cultivation of a new language, and its "purity."[6] In brief, this involved three aims: (a) self-identity of literary language, i.e. the question whether such languages that do not have their own literary tradition (e.g., Estonian, Finnish, and Slovene—in contrast to Czech or Polish) have the right to exist;

(b) the standard codification of this language; and (c) the cultural intellectualization of the language. Only then could a language become an equal to the language of the "ruling" nation. Science as well as literature and literary translation served this purpose. Utilizing a new literary language was the moral duty of all intellectuals from the ranks of the nondominant ethnic group. Such was the demand of the Jungmann generation in Bohemia, the Štúr generation in Slovakia, and the later demands of Estonian, Lithuanian, and Ukrainian radical patriots.

3. Normalized and codified written language could fulfill its role only if it was mastered by members of the given ethnic group. Therefore, another goal was included in the national program: to have a new written language taught in schools and to ensure that it became the language of instruction at all grade levels. Different national movements achieved varied results in these efforts. The Czech movement was the most successful, even before 1848, whereas efforts toward Slovak teaching and learning were thwarted by "Magyarization" after 1870 and in the Baltics by Russification: in Lithuania since the 1860s, in Estonia and Livonia since the 1880s.[7]

4. The highest—and, in terms of the time the latest—component of the linguistic program was the demand that the written language of the former nondominant ethnic group be equal to the language of the ruling nation—in our analysis to German or Russian. The idea was that this language would become the language of administration, of the judicial system, and of markets in areas where the given ethnic group was in the majority. The logic of things also gave rise—either implicitly or explicitly—to the demand that in areas occupied only or in the majority by members of the nondominant ethnic group its written language should become the ruling language and that German or Russian should be used only in relations with the central authorities. The Czechs, Croatians, and, of course, the Magyars achieved partial success in this respect within the Habsburg Monarchy, whereas in tsarist Russia only the Finns realized these goals.[8]

The first and second of these four steps were born during phase A of the national movement, or at least they are typical for the mentality of this phase. The third and fourth steps are typical of phase B, but they remained a part of the national program also during phase C. This does not mean that the first two disappeared during phase C. All four components of the linguistic program were born gradually, yet the older component was integrated into the later ones. Thus it happened that admiring and celebrating the language remained contained for the most part in the linguistic program and in the national mentality of a small nation, even when the language was not threatened by assimilation and its administrative use had been secured. In other words, at a time when the written language of a small nation found a firm place in society, the mythological image of the national language was not confined to its actual role—to mediating social communication.

This quest became an ideological mission and acquired a purpose besides that of simple language communication. It became a symbol of national identity and cultural independence and assumed a new, supralanguage and supracommunicative function. This adoring and overestimating of the language can be found in the mentality of small nations in both multinational empires during the period of the national movements and even afterward, when these successful movements were victoriously channeled into establishing a national state. This mentality could not and still cannot be understood by members of ruling nations, who have regarded their language simply as an instrument of communication.

The adoration of the language sometimes became the object of criticism—for being reactionary, old-fashioned, illiberal, and shortsighted.[9] But criticism does not take historical circumstances into account, circumstances that contributed to this linguistic program's becoming decisive among the majority of national movements. That is why we have to explain, not judge, the role of the linguistic program in various phases of the national movement.

The resistance of the Bohemian estates against Habsburg centralism at the end of the eighteenth century used the argument, among others, that the Czech language was a specific second language in Bohemia. That is why the estates supported celebrations of this language as well as scientific activities of the small group of patriots during phase A. When the self-awareness of Czech-speaking artisans grew stronger, their language—even if they still did not learn it in its written form—became a symbol, an articulation of their resistance to the German-speaking patriciate and the state bureaucracy. The same was true at the time of the emancipation of Estonian and Latvian small peasants vis-à-vis the German landlords and the German "Literates," and of the western Ukrainian peasants in relation to the Polish aristocracy.

We know of other instances where conflicting interests were expressed in terms of linguistic demands. The expansion of the opportunities for social advance in Bohemia and other Habsburg lands after serfdom was abolished, in the Baltic lands after the 1820s and especially after the 1860s, gave members of the nondominant ethnic groups greater access to education than before. But the condition for successful studies was mastery of the language of the ruling nation: German in the case of the Habsburg Monarchy, German or Russian in the case of tsarist Russia. This was not only a matter of technical problems in teaching the language, but also a question of linguistic aptitude. A bitter feeling of being disadvantaged could well have been fed after completing higher education; another handicap was born in this instance for newly educated men from the oppressed ethnic group. The choice of the official language and the medium of education determined which groups had access to better jobs.[10]

Why could language articulate to such an important degree the interest and conflicts that, in fact, had very little or nothing in common with language? Why did it take on a political role? The deeper reasons can be sought not in the philosophical influence of Herder or among patriotic agitators, but in the processes of social transformation. Economic growth and the advance of innovations in the economy and administration presupposed social mobility and communication. K. W. Deutsch defines a nation as "a product of a complementary communication."[11] Mobility and communication needs compelled a growing number of individuals to become literate and capable of the standardized presentation of messages. Such growing interdependence raised language use to a new level. For the individual, language and culture became "his real entrance-card to full citizenship and human dignity."[12] Communication is, of course, impossible without a standardized language. Care for the standardized written language is needed for "operational individuals" (to use Gale Stokes's terminology) to feel satisfied. That is one of the reasons why these "operational individuals" advocated "linguistic nationalism."[13]

This does not sufficiently answer the question why "operational individuals" did not turn to standardization and routine use of the ruling state's language, but chose instead a more complicated path for their mother tongue. During a certain time, the educated members of the nondominant ethnic groups did in fact use a different language on the job (*langue du pain*), the written form of the ruling state's language, rather than that used in the family (*langue maternelle*), which was usually a spoken, nonwritten language. At the beginning of the national movement there was only an extremely limited use for the written form of the language of the nondominant ethnic group in the role of the *langue du pain*. One of the aims of the national movement's linguistic program was, as we already know, to abolish this kind of bilingualism and insist that the mother tongue and the written language be the same. Only such a language was suitable as a precise linguistic instrument for all educated persons.[14]

Only in this way was it possible to bring about the cultural entity that covered internal differentiations and conflicts within the national society. The main results of studying the form of the mother tongue, of course, had an additive educational effect as well because it strengthened national consciousness among educated members of the nondominant ethnic group.

Another important factor in the sphere of social relations should be mentioned among the roots of overvaluing the linguistic program of small nations. Their leaders came from the lower strata of the social structure and they had to address their appeals to the same groups. Whether these were primarily artisans, as in Bohemia, or farmers, as in Estonia and Lithuania, they always were social groups who during phase B of the national movement had no political experience or education. These social groups could hardly have become inspired by a politically articulated program of civil rights before the revolutions of 1848-49 and similar movements. The linguistic demands were basically closer and more understandable to them. They adopted them and passed them on to subsequent generations. That is why linguistic demands became for several decades the most suitable vehicle for articulating various interest group conflicts in advanced modern societies—conflicts in which the interest group differences are matched by differences in language.

II

Let us now move on to the second component of our problem, the additive part of comparative observations. What can an analysis of the role of language and the linguistic program in both pre-1914 multinational empires tell us about the nationality problem in the contemporary multinational Soviet state? We know very well the strong role played by linguistic programs and differences in the current political disintegration of the Soviet federation. What explains the role of linguistic demands in these centrifugal efforts? Do they really constitute the main factor, one of the decisive reasons? Or do they only appear to do so? What can we learn from the preceding comparison of nineteenth-century national movements?

Some fundamental lessons can be learned about the important supra-linguistic role of the linguistic program. I stated earlier that an unsynchronized process of modernization gave the language in both empires a supracommunicative role. This had several stages and modifications which can be compared with the actual situation in the USSR. We could express these analogies with the nineteenth century in five points.

1. Language during the nineteenth century began to be used as an instrument of agitation at a time when members of the nondominant ethnic group had no political experience in a civic society and therefore could hardly set out political argumentation and slogans calling for civil rights. After fifty to seventy years under a dictatorship the mentality of the masses is similar:

language, the linguistic program, and culture play a political role also in the outlying republics of the Soviet Union. It is difficult to say to what extent the national identity supplies the need for democracy and civic rights. National freedom is regarded as a guarantee of civic rights: in this regard the situation is different from tsarist times.

2. The linguistic difference under political oppression became an argument used by the national movement against the German bureaucracy in the Habsburg Monarchy and the bureaucracy in tsarist Russia. In the Soviet Union, the character of political oppression changed, compared with that experienced in the nineteenth century, but Russian remained the official language of public life, of the bureaucracy, and as a result of this it has become for the members of a small nation a symbol or even an instrument of political oppression. In contrast, the language of the oppressed nation is automatically identified as the language of liberty.

3. An awareness of linguistic identity became fundamental during the nineteenth century, when the old feudal regime was disintegrating. The idea of linguistic identity brought together, in a national movement, new ties among people belonging to different social groups and political camps. Similarly, at a time when the planned economy and Soviet centralism are disintegrating, when old ties are crumbling, language suddenly and spontaneously assumes an integrating role.

4. The linguistic program, which at the beginning of the national movement had already become a source of symbols and stereotypes, maintained its own position when the national identity was being formed (i.e., during phase C). Even for those who were members of a small nation and who held administrative, economic, or educational positions, the language was usually more than just a means of communication: it remained a symbol of political goals and at the same time a source of prestige. Even though every person of the newly emerging Czech (and later Croatian, or more particularly the Slovenian) elite knew German, and every member of the Ukrainian intelligentsia in Galicia knew Polish, using the mother language became for each one a matter of honor, prestige, and national identity. When the Soviet system pushed out the mother languages of the small Baltic nations from a large part of the administration and schools, this became a source of tension and dissatisfaction, although the Soviet actions fell far short of being a threat of Russification. Defense of the charismatic mother tongue became again a matter of national identity and political prestige.

5. A more realistic comparison of motivations is to be found under the surface of events. Beginning with a certain stage of the national movement (at the end of phase B or, at the latest, at the beginning of phase C), a struggle

for positions in the administration ensued. The local intelligentsia of the Czechs, Slovenes, or the western Ukrainians in the Habsburg Monarchy and of the Estonians, Lithuanians, and others in Russia had difficulty accepting the fact that the higher offices in their regions were filled from the ranks of the ruling German or Russian nation. These officials were placed in positions by the central authorities and did not need to know the literary language of the domestic population. Similar to this is the experience of the small nations in the USSR: the Russian-speaking *nomenklatura* bureaucrats come from the center and tend not to know the local languages. Under such circumstances Russian became not only a means of communication but also a symbol of political (i.e., national) oppression.

What lessons can be drawn from these five analogies? One can argue against their validity by saying that the need for the linguistic program was lost when the principles of equality of nations and languages were realized—when, for example, at the end of the nineteenth century Czech had already penetrated the schools and administration. The same applies, formally, to the Soviet republics, where the local languages were put on the same level as Russian. A state of equality determined by law and the constitution should not give rise, theoretically, to conflicts. But this is true only in theory.

At the same time, another criticism is significant. The linguistic program is less represented in the national movements of the Soviet Union than it was in the movements of the nineteenth century. But who knows what will happen in the rapidly changing current situation? In any case, one difference is certain: of the four stages of the development of the linguistic program in the Habsburg Monarchy and tsarist Russia, only the last two are important today—namely, to win equal rights for the language of nondominant ethnic groups in the schools and to make it dominant in the administration of its territory.

How do we explain the surviving linguistic conflicts between Russian and the languages of nondominant ethnic groups or nations? In the Austrian half of the Habsburg Empire—just as in the Soviet Union today—an asymmetrical equality of nations, and therefore an inequality of two theoretically equal languages, was obtained. While a growing number of members of small nations had to master the language of the ruling nation, whether German or Russian, in the interest of their own work and professional success, members of the ruling nation did not have to learn the language of the subservient nation, although they constituted the minority of the subservient nation's population. And moreover, they refused to learn it because they regarded only their own language (i.e., the language of the ruling nation) as useful, as an important "world" language. The same unequal situation between the languages of ruling and small nations also developed under Soviet rule.

This asymmetry also had its sociolinguistic implications. If we distinguish between the spoken and written (literary) language, then written language is considered to be a second language that must be learned. The same applies to the relation between the language of a small nation and the language of the ruling nation, viewed as a second language. Therefore, children of the educated strata, and often also of the wealthy strata, are at an advantage where the spoken language at home is close to the written language and where the language of the ruling nation is routinely represented. These children quickly learn to write correctly in the ruling language and eventually also in the written language of their mother tongue. In contrast, children from families who have received no, or only an elementary, education are at a double disadvantage; that is, they have difficulties studying in both languages. This socially determined differentiation is perhaps valid for the nineteenth century, just as it is for the Soviet Union. Moreover, then and today bureaucracy was linked to a growing formalization of the language. Therefore demands grew in a multinational state for maximum mastery of the written language of the ruling nation.

Members of a small nation, and especially of the lower, uneducated classes of this nation, were therefore disadvantaged by the unwillingness of the members of the ruling nation to accept a real, and not merely an asymmetrical, equality of both languages. If the German-speaking minority in Bohemia and Moravia, in Slovakia, in Prussian Poland, or in the Slovenian areas refused to learn the language of the majority of these regions, then this had its logic insofar as German was the common medium of communication within the Empire. But after the emergence of independent states after 1918, this unwillingness to share true equality with the language of the small nation, being now a state language, became totally illogical and led to an explosive situation.

This, probably, is the key parallel and the most important historical lesson for the present outlying Soviet republics especially the Baltic states. Just as the German minority refused to accept Czech as an alternative language of communication in Czechoslovakia, today the Russian minorities (for instance, in the Baltic States) refuse to learn the language of the local inhabitants. If the unwillingness of the German minority led to the acceleration of national tension and prepared the ground for the fall of the Habsburg Monarchy and later for Czechoslovakia's instability, then the same dynamic threatens the development of free republics in the Baltics and elsewhere. At the same time, the experience of the Habsburg Monarchy and of its sucessor states demonstrates that the acceptance of a two-language mutuality could be the only alternative, the only way to avoid—without using force—a new accumulation of explosive ethnic conflicts.

This hypothetical prognosis is based on a concrete historical experience: the dissolution of the multinational Habsburg Empire signified the end of its great power ethnic politics, but the possibility of national conflicts remains alive.

All these parallels and analogies between the developments of the nine-teenth century and the Soviet Union are not based on new research by a Soviet specialist. They are only the hypothetical result of comparative observations made from a perspective that incorporates the experiences of the nineteenth century. My aim is not to bring to light new facts about the current developments in Eastern Europe but rather to inspire Soviet specialists with some new viewpoints.

NOTES

1. For more about the comparative method and the periodization of national movements see M. Hroch, *Social Preconditions of National Revival in Europe* (Cambridge, 1985), 18ff.
2. Here I am comparing not synchronically but diachronically, i.e., along the historical vertical axis; in this kind of analysis we cannot examine two territories, but only two periods of development in the same territory. That is why it is useful to put the multinational Russian state into the comparison as a way of joining the nineteenth-century Habsburg Monarchy and the modern-day Soviet Union.
3. On Croats see M. Gross, "On the Integration of the Croatian Nation: A Case Study in Nation Building," *East European Quarterly* 15, (1981); on Estonians and the periodization see E. A. Jansen, "Eesti talurahva teadvuse rahvusliku kujunemisest XIX sajandil," in *Eesti talurahva sotsiaalseid vaateid XIX sejandil* (Tallinn, 1977), 109ff.; on Lithuanians, M. Hellmann, *Grundzüge der Geschichte Litauens und des litauischen Volkes* (Darmstadt, 1966); on Ukrainians, P. R. Magocsi, "The Ukrainian National Revival: A New Analytical Framework," *Canadian Review of Studies in Nationalism* 16, (1989): 45ff.
4. E. Lehmberg, "Zur Betonung der Sprache," in *Der Nationalismus* (Hamburg, 1964), 1: 171ff., 2: 34ff.; J. A. Fishman, *Language and Nationalism: Two Integrative Essays* (Rowley, Mass., 1972), 40ff.: P. R. Magocsi, "The Language Question as a Factor in the National Movement," in *Nationbuilding and the Politics of Nationalism*, A. S. Markovits and F. E. Sysyn eds. (Cambridge, Mass., 1982), 220ff.

5. On Czech glorifications of the language see A. Pražák, *A národ se bránil* (Prague, 1946).

6. On the importance of language codification see R. L. Lencek, "The Role of Sociolinguistics in the Evolution of Slavic Linguistic Nationalism," *Canadian Review of Studies in Nationalism* 16, (1989): 99ff.; E. Niederhauser, "Language and History: National Traditions in Eastern Europe," in *Small Countries and International Structural Adjustment: A Collection of Hungarian and Swiss Views, Proceedings of the Second Hungarian-Swiss Roundtable 7-11 April 1981* (Budapest, 1982); B. Anderson, *Imagined Communities* (London, 1983), 71ff.; B. Bernstein, *Class, Codes and Control, 1. Theoretical Studies Toward a Sociology of Language* (London, 1971), 15ff.

7. K. J. Čeginskas, "Die Russifizierung und ihre Folgen in Litauen unter zaristischer Herrschaft," in *Commentationes Balticae* 6-7 (1959): 1ff. and 85ff.; E. Uustalu, *The History of Estonian People* (London, 1952), 136ff.; H. Kruus, *Grundriss der Geschichte des estnischen Volkes* (Tartu, 1932), 156ff.

8. J. H. Wuorinen, *Nationalism in Modern Finland* (New York, 1931); Th. Rein, *Juhana Vilhelm Snellman II* (Helsinki, 1928), 533ff.

9. Against H. Kohn's criticism see V. A. Kemiläinen, *Nationalism: Problems Concerning the Word, the Concept, and Classification* (Jyväskylä, 1964), 122ff.

10. G. H. Mead, *Mind, Self, and Society* (Chicago, 1934), 135ff; J. Hermann, "Bilingualism versus identity," in *Multilingual Matters* (Philadelphia, 1988), 227ff.

11. K. W. Deutsch, *Nationalism and Social Communication* (Cambridge, Mass., 1953).

12. E. A. Gellner, "Nationalism and the Two Forms of Cohesion in Complex Societies," Radcliffe-Brown lecture in *Social Anthropology* (1982): 158.

13. Gale Stokes, "Cognition and the Function of Nationalism," *Journal of Interdisciplinary History* 4 (1974): 537ff.; see also J. A. Fishman, "Social Theory and Ethnography: Neglected Perspectives on Language and Ethnicity in Eastern Europe," *Ethnic Diversity and Conflict in Eastern Europe* (Santa Barbara, Oxford, 1980), 87ff.

14. Gale Stokes, "Cognitive Style and Nationalism," *Canadian Review of Studies in Nationalism* 9 (1982): 10ff.; J. Chlebowczyk, *Procesy narodotwórcze we wschodniej Europie środkowej w dobie kapitalizmu* (Katowice, Cracow, 1975), 41ff., 122ff.

THE NATIONALITIES

5

Nationality Problems in the Habsburg Monarchy and the Soviet Union: The Perspective of History

John-Paul Himka

I

My essay sketches the history of the nationality question in both the Habsburg Monarchy and the Soviet Union. It is not, however, intended solely as background for more specifically focused studies because I hope here to bring insights to the comparative problem explored in this volume from the perspective of the discipline of history. I will be paying close attention to problems of historical time and historical timing, and I will be using a methodology frequently employed by historians. Historians often set aside the models and rigorous definitions of other social scientists in favor of abstractions concerning concrete historical developments. In this essay, I will attempt to generalize the process of development of each of the two nationality problems at issue in order to allow for their comparison as historical processes. I hope, in other words, to distill the salient features of each of the nationality problems as seen over the course of their histories; these distillations, in turn, will lead to contrasts and parallels. This method, I readily admit, demands *bricolage* and cannot avoid disputable generalizations, but every method must put up with its own limitations in order to arrive at its own insights.

For a historian, the principle and striking difference between the nationality problems of our two great powers is that they played themselves out in two radically different historical epochs. The Habsburg Empire faced the nationality problem from 1526 to 1918, the Soviet Union, from 1922 on. At least for historians, these dates are highly suggestive. The modern era began in the early sixteenth century, notable not only for the formation of the Habsburg Empire but also for the Renaissance, the Reformation, explorations, and the rise of capitalism. The era of European dominance commenced in the several decades around 1500, and came to an end, as did the Habsburg Empire, only as a result of and during the world war of 1914-18. The period of the Great War and after, the period of the Soviet Union and its nationality problem, is an entirely different era, for which the death camp at Auschwitz—once sleepy Oświęcim in old Galicia—strikes me as the most pertinent symbol.

II

The history of the nationality problem in the Habsburg empire can easily be divided into three periods: (1) from 1526 to around 1772, before the principle of nationality (or, to use the more familiar, later terminology, nationalism) became a serious factor in politics; (2) from 1772 to 1848, when the nationality problem per se was incubating in Austria; and (3) from 1848 to 1918, when the nationality problem dominated, transformed, and contributed to the destruction of the Empire.

The first of these periods began when, after the battle of Mohács in 1526, the lands of the Bohemian kingdom as well as Hungary became united with Austria under the Habsburg scepter. Although Austria had long ruled over non-German, Slavic-speaking areas—indeed, this was, so to speak, the original entelechy of the *Ostmark*—it was only in 1526 that some of the principal sources of future national conflict were acquired. The actual absorption of Hungary was a drawn-out process, lasting into the late seventeenth and early eighteenth centuries, when the land was finally completely wrested from the Turks and the last of the major anti-Habsburg rebellions was put down. The annexation of Galicia from Poland in 1772 was another major acquisition of the prenationalist era that would become an important component of the Habsburg Monarchy's nationality problem in the future.

Even in this early period, before the national question as such had appeared in European politics, there were elements of national conflict in the realm of the Habsburgs. Political and confessional conflict in Bohemia, culminating in the battle of White Mountain in 1620, often had strong overtones of Czech-German antagonism. The resistance of the Magyar gentry to the Habsburg dynasty was also a mixture of national as well as political and religious opposition. By acquiring Galicia in 1772, the Habsburgs became involved in the Polish question, which developed rapidly into a full-blown nationality question of the modern type. In the period from 1526 to 1772 the Empire acquired the three "historic" national problems that would loom so large in its subsequent evolution.

During the same early modern era, not only were the elements of the Czech, Hungarian, and Polish problems put in place, but also those of the Austrian German problem. For it was in this period that the Habsburg emperor lost factual hegemony over Germany while absorbing large non-German populations to the south and east.

The second period in the development of the Habsburg nationality problem lasted from roughly 1772 to 1848. The *terminus ad quem* is well defined by the revolutionary events of 1848-49, by which time the national question in the Monarchy had clearly acquired political valence. The *terminus a quo*, however, that is, 1772, the year of the first partition of Poland, is largely a marker of convenience, since the whole period from the middle of the eighteenth century to the Congress of Vienna was transitional. Two great processes differentiated the second period from the first. One of these processes was the emergence of nationalism as a political force and doctrine almost throughout Europe.[1] The period between 1772 and 1815 saw the disappearance of the Polish state and attempts by Poles to restore it, the American and French revolutions, the Napoleonic Wars, and the German nationalist reaction to the French Enlightenment, best represented by the writings of Johann Gottfried von Herder. From here on in, nationality problems were to be a prominent aspect of European—and then later, world—history. The other great process differentiating the period 1772-1848 from the preceding period was the movement of reform initiated by the Austrian enlightened absolutists Maria Theresia and Joseph II (1740-90). They added a new and crucial dimension to the Austrian nationality problem by awakening the hitherto dormant "nonhistoric" peoples of the Empire.

Austria's great enlightened monarchs were the victims of reason's cunning; striving to forge a unified and in many respects administratively uniform state, they unwittingly initiated a great diversity and constructed the time bomb that, prematurely detonated by world war, blew their monarchy into fragments a century and a half later. For it was they who took the trouble to educate the clergy in even the Monarchy's most godforsaken regions, creating almost overnight intelligentsias of the most varied native tongues.

It was also they who established Vienna as a great center of learning for the whole monarchy and gathered here the most promising representatives of the new intelligentsias they had brought into being. The latter compared notes and experiences and made of the imperial city a major seat of Slavic and East European studies;[2] or put another way, Vienna became a clearing-house for the "heritage-gathering" work of the first phase of national movements.[3] With the reform of the postal system, roads, and communications in general, the enlightened absolutists connected the remotest corners of the Monarchy with the rest of European civilization. It was now possible for a pastor somewhere in the Carpathians to read periodicals and books that linked him with greater European civilization and developments.[4] World-historic events began to impinge on peoples that had hitherto been regarded, without excessive exaggeration, as "nonhistoric," that is, standing outside the general historic process.

Furthermore, the enlightened absolutists made serfs the subjects of law and in manifold other ways elevated both their status and sense of dignity. In a situation where almost entire nationalities were subject to serfdom (e.g., the Romanians of Transylvania, the Ukrainians of Galicia and Bukovina, the Slovaks of Hungary), the elevation of the serf inevitably had national consequences. The abolition of serfdom in 1848, which can rightly be regarded as the culmination of reforms originating in the mid- to late eighteenth century, made the national consequences much more visible, and entire peasant nations strode upon the stage of history during the revolution of 1848.[5]

In the third period, the seven decades from the revolution of 1848 to the collapse of the Empire in 1918, the nationality question dominated the politics of the Habsburg Monarchy. The restoration of the Empire in 1849 was in significant measure due to the Monarchy's success in playing the "nonhistoric" nationalities off against the "historic" nationalities: Czechs, Slovenes, Croats, Romanians, and Ukrainians (Ruthenians) against Germans, Magyars, and Poles. (The Czechs were a borderline nationality, with features of both historicity and nonhistoricity; in 1848-49 they were clearly ranged with the nonhistoric peoples.) The dynasty tried to transcend the nationality problem in the 1850s, the era of neoabsolutism, but defeat in war in 1859 and 1866 and the establishment of a *Kleindeutschland* in 1871 forced Vienna to seek a solution to it instead. There was a great deal of wavering in the years from 1860 to 1871, but when the dust had settled, the dynasty had come to the solution of sharing power among the three indisputably historic nations: the Germans, the Poles, and the Magyars.

The most far-reaching concessions, of course, were made to the Magyars in the Compromise of 1867, which gave the historic Hungarian *natio* (i.e., the Magyar gentry) a free hand in historical Hungary. In this large piece of East-Central Europe, the national issue and closely related social issues were the determinants of political life, which was entirely geared to the suppression of any national consciousness other than Magyar consciousness. The cost of maintaining Magyar hegemony was high—namely, the retardation of Hungary's political, social, and cultural evolution; in some respects Hungary resembled tsarist Russia more than it did its Austrian state partner.

In the Austrian part of the Monarchy after 1867, considerable concessions were made to the Poles in Galicia; in return, they gave stability to Cisleithanian politics and indirectly and directly helped to preserve the dominance of the Germans over the Czechs in Bohemia.[6] Nonetheless, the expansion of education and political enfranchisement in Austria made the various nationalities ever more insistent on what they considered to be their due, and Austria's nationality problem grew increasingly intractable. Although the solution of 1867-71 had been to put power in the hands of the historic nations (and, in the case of the Poles—as for the Hungarians—in the hands of the most historic part of the nation, the gentry), the next several decades saw the rapid maturity of the so-called nonhistoric peoples.[7] The years from 1867 to 1914 saw the acceleration of the work begun by the enlightened absolutists. The deliberate fostering of capitalist development and the introduction of compulsory education radically improved the position of formerly plebeian peoples. The swift advancement of the Czechs vis-à-vis the Germans in Bohemia and the slower, but steady advancement of the Ukrainians vis-à-vis the Poles in Galicia are cases in point. These same decades also saw a profound change that went well beyond anything the enlightened absolutists had imagined, namely, the democratization of political life. Key moments were the introduction of civil liberties in 1867-68, the restitution (after the revolutionary prelude of 1848-49) of a parliament in 1867-73, and the widening of the franchise in 1897-1907. This democratization of political life could not help but undermine the hegemony of the historic nations, which were under heavy siege by the eve of World War I. Moreover, the same processes that mobilized the nonhistoric nations also had a politicizing effect on the masses of the historic nations. Socialist and peasant parties emerged and grew among the Germans and Poles of Austria, but so did nationalist parties of a new kind, infused with anti-Semitism and an unabashed national egoism that championed the domination and assimilation of subject peoples. Nationalism penetrated to the masses, even making profound inroads into the Austrian social democratic movement, and the more nationalism seeped into the fibers of Austrian society, the more national tension mounted. The world war of 1914-18 placed great strain on the internal cohesion of all participants, including the Habsburg Monarchy. The latter's defeat at the hands of powers intent on carving it up was also a major factor in its dissolution in the autumn of 1918. There can be no question that the Empire was on the road to dissolution prior to 1914, but there can also be no question that the world war greatly accelerated the process.[8] That the Habsburgs' multinational empire did not die an entirely natural death is suggested by a great many facts: for example, that Magyar hegemony was still intact at the eve of the war and that after the war many Hungarians still wanted a Habsburg monarch; that the Czechs true to Palacký's dictum of 1848, reinvented the old empire, albeit in truncated form, as Czechoslovakia; that the Ukrainians of Galicia required another decade or so under Habsburg rule to attain the national maturity that would have ensured their independent existence vis-à-vis the Poles; that the Empire still functioned as a viable economic unit,[9] and so on. Although in the last two decades of the Monarchy's existence, there were some violent clashes between nationalities (assassinations, gunfights at universities, even some mass murder of civilians during the world war), I think it is safe to say that the nationality problem in the Habsburg Empire was over before it became really nasty. I believe that this largely accounts for the present nostalgia for the days of the Habsburg Monarchy: relatively speaking, but *only* relatively speaking, the nationalities muddled through and worked out their differences in a peaceful and orderly fashion. It is really a shameful and painful commentary on the twentieth century and its political culture that one can look back at the dying years of the Habsburg Monarchy and in hindsight regret its passing.

III

When we cross the divide of 1914-18, we enter into a new era, with new ideologies and, related to these, new, qualitatively more destructive methods of solving political conflicts. The war and its immediate aftermath saw the emergence of two dynamic and clearly related political movements: communism and fascism. World War I was also notable for the new kind of destruction that humankind unleashed on itself—the destruction produced by technologically advanced societies. The Napoleonic Wars had also constituted a world war, fought in Haiti and Egypt as well as Russia and Spain, but it was a world war between technologically rather primitive forces. World

War I was of a completely different order of destructiveness. It was fought among industrial powers, and machine guns and poison gases, barbed wire, and trains—not sabers and muskets, horses and wagons—determined the outcome. During World War I, fifty thousand men could perish in an afternoon. The new kind of violence carried over into the politics of the immediately postwar period as East-Central Europe, and particularly the former Russian Empire, was racked by civil war and national conflict. World War II, of course, went much further. And in our own day, we have developed the capacity essentially to annihilate ourselves entirely. This is a different era from that which the Habsburgs confronted. It is also an era the Soviet Union did much to shape.

If the nationality problem in the Habsburg Monarchy came into being over time and then evolved, but never quite reached a natural culmination, the same cannot be said about the nationality problem in the Soviet Union. This state was born amidst and from revolutionary upheaval that was both social and national in character. While Lenin was consolidating the power of the Soviets, the Habsburg Empire cracked apart along national lines and the Russian Empire lost many of its western territories to new national states: Poland, Lithuania, Latvia, Estonia, and Finland (and to a national state already in existence: Romania). The nationality problem was a determining factor in the final form that the Soviet state took, the union created in December 1922. From the beginning, and in intensified form, the Soviet state faced the problem that Austria confronted only in its twilight: the management of politically conscious, ambitious nationalities. The great difference between the Habsburg and Soviet situation is accurately reflected by the difference in the constituent parts of these two multinational powers. Whereas the Habsburg Monarchy was a congeries of kingdoms, duchies, and other crownlands with great historical significance, but scant national content, the Soviet Union was formed of republics, autonomous republics, and autonomous regions, all designed on the national principle, with little or no regard for historical precedents.

The nationalities that formed the Soviet Union had originally been under tsarist rule, of course, and this to some extent mitigated the nationality problem that the Soviet Union inherited. In contrast to Austria, whose fostering of education helped create and develop its nationality problem, the old tsarist regime deliberately cultivated ignorance, which impeded the development of any mass political consciousness, including national consciousness, and restricted the formation of national intelligentsias. Moreover, tsarism's consistent discrimination against the languages, cultures, and autonomous aspirations of the non-Russian nationalities had also helped keep nationality problems in check, especially since this policy was pursued with much more brutality than the related policy in Habsburg Hungary. But by the time the Union of Soviet Socialist Republics was formed, the nationalities of the former tsarist empire were no longer so passive. Many had, in fact, detached themselves from Russia entirely (Poles, Finns, Latvians, Estonians, Lithuanians, Romanians), and others had at least tried hard to do so (Ukrainians, Georgians). The revolutionary years 1917-21, as well as the rehearsal for these in 1905-7, saw the intense politicization of the masses and consequently the rapid development of national consciousness throughout the territory of the future Soviet Union. The slogan of national self-determination had been popularized by the most skillful of Russian propagandists, the Bolsheviks, who ended up masters of the land.

Soviet policy of the 1920s intensified national consciousness. The Soviet state's radical program of universal literacy and compulsory education, both in the national languages, created much more mobilized nationalities. The division of the landlords' estates and, more important, the disappearance of the landlord class helped bring the submerged nationalities into greater prominence. This was the result of the destruction of the old regime's administration. Peasants migrated to the cities, changing their national character. Moreover, the policy of indigenization (*korenizatsiia*) adopted by the party in April 1923 called for local personnel to assume the administration of the national republics, thus directly nationalizing politics and politicizing the nationalities. By the late 1920s, the Soviet Union was a union of strong, and waxing, nationalities. In a section of the globe where national oppression and dissatisfaction remained rife in the 1920s, the Soviet Union stood out as an exception. It exercised considerable attraction on members of national minorities in the new East European states, as evidenced by the national composition of their Communist parties. Its attraction for the Belorussians and Ukrainians of Poland in the 1920s was particularly noticeable.[10]

It is interesting to speculate how the Soviet Union would have ended up, had it continued on the same trajectory as it was following in the 1920s. Even though various nationalities of the USSR were growing ever more conscious in the 1920s, and some had surpassed Habsburg levels of national consciousness, there was not much evidence of conflict among them. One of the reasons for this, of course, was the thoroughgoing social revolution that lay at the foundation of the Soviet state. In the old Habsburg monarchy, a factor contributing to the intensity of national antagonisms was precisely that the national differences so often coincided with social differences. The struggle between historic and nonhistoric nationalities had often been a new form of the struggle between nobles and peasants; the resentment of the Jewish population by peasant peoples, which was often an important building block in the formation of their national consciousness, corresponded to a pre-existing economic antagonism.[11] All this was essentially missing in the wake of the Bolshevik victory. It is conceivable, although there is no way to know for sure, that the Soviet Union could have continued to evolve as a viable multinational state in which friction among the various nationalities would have been minimal.

Of course, already in the 1920s there was strong evidence of countervailing tendencies, tendencies that became absolutely dominant in the political life of the Soviet Union in the 1930s. Right from the beginning, when the structure of the USSR was under debate in 1922, Stalin put forward a much more centralist vision of the union than leaders of the national republics or even Lenin found palatable. In the following spring Stalin purged his first prominent party member: the Volga Tatar Sultan-Galiev, arrested and tried for nationalist deviations.[12] In 1926 Stalin launched an attack on Ukrainian national communism in the persons of Shumsky and Khvylovy.[13] Backing Stalin were all those Russian chauvinists who had been drawn into the administration and military in the early years of the Soviet regime, particularly in republics such as Ukraine where Bolshevik rule had been established as the result of the suppression of a national independence movement.[14]

Why Stalinism emerged victorious in the 1930s is, of course, the subject of a wide-ranging and long-standing debate among historians and other interpreters of the Soviet Union. Here I will limit myself to two observations relating to this problem of causality. First, I believe that one can show that most aspects of what is considered characteristic of Stalinism have some link with the nationality problem. For example, the mass incarceration and liquidation of writers and other cultural figures in the USSR in the 1930s affected the intelligentsias of the nationalities in a particularly acute manner. Not only was the incidence extremely high, but affected were young and fragile cultural infrastructures. Or take what so many perceptive observers consider to be the real turning point into full-blown Stalinist terror, collectivization.[15] It is not at all hard to prove that in terms of demographic losses, it affected Ukrainians and Kazakhs disproportionately.[16]

Second, although the Stalinists themselves liked to depict what they did in the 1930s as the exacerbation of class war, I am unprepared to accept this claim. To be sure, the state and party killed certain strata of the population en masse, but a contest among classes in any Marxian sense was certainly absent during this process. I do think, however, that it is not hard to see that Stalin and his cohorts touched off *national* warfare in the 1930s and created the nationality problem as a *problem* for the USSR. It was they who began a fierce persecution of the non-Russian nationalities, they who reversed the previous party policy of indigenization in favor of Russification, they who decided to resurrect many of the Russian national myths of the old tsarist regime, and they who made a pact with the fascist devil in order to expand Soviet imperial rule over the Baltic peoples, Western Ukrainians, and Western Belorussians. In short, it was they who ended the relative multinational peace in the USSR and established the conflict between a Russian ruling nation and non-Russian subject nations that has characterized the Soviet Union for over half a century.

The year 1941 revealed the depth of disenchantment with the Stalinist regime on the part of the non-Russian nations. Many Ukrainians, Belorussians, Lithuanians, Latvians, Estonians, Karelians, Moldavian Romanians, Tatars, and others looked to the German invaders as potential liberators. Only the racial madness of the Nazis and a savagery surpassing even that of the Stalinists prevented the Germans from capitalizing on the initial, naive goodwill of the non-Russian nationalities. Even when cured of their illusions about the German invaders, many non-Russians did not want the Russians back. A case in point is the Ukrainian Insurgent Army (UPA), which waged a suicidal guerrilla war against both the Nazis and the Soviets (the latter were unable to extirpate the insurgents until about 1950). And of course, hundreds of thousands of non-Russians preferred emigration to the West over return to their occupied homelands.

The last years of Stalin's rule saw mass arrests and deportations of Lithuanians, Latvians, Estonians, and Ukrainians; the deportation from their homelands of entire small nationalities (such as the Crimean Tatars or Soviet Germans); the suppression of Yiddish culture, complete with the murder of major Yiddish writers; and the emergence of an ever more vociferous Russian chauvinism, complete with a vile anti-Semitism. It is hard to say how all this would have turned out had Stalin lived much beyond 1953.

De-Stalinization in the mid-1950s and early 1960s brought some relief to the Soviet nationalities, but it did not change the nature of the Soviet nationality problem in any fundamental way. The men who were carrying out de-Stalinization had themselves been implementers and products of the Stalinist system they were trying to modify. They inevitably set limits to de-Stalinization that were very confining: an end to mass terror, especially against Communists, but no institution of civil liberties or representative government and the retention of the Communist power monopoly and repression as an implement of policy; retention as the basis of the economy of centralized, primarily heavy industry and collectivized agriculture; liberalization of the censorship in the non-Russian republics (and the restoration of Yiddish literature), but retention of Russian political control and cultural hegemony. It is a great pity that these hesitant first reforms were followed not by a second wave of more far-reaching reforms but by a reaction that underscored the limits of de-Stalinization. In this reactionary period, the non-Russian dissidents emerged. Over the two decades from the mid-1960s to the mid-1980s these dissidents were treated in an increasingly brutal manner, more and more reminiscent of the classical period of Stalinism.[17] The dissidents were the product of the meager liberalization in the cultural sphere that de-Stalinization entailed. Even a paltry democratization generated proponents of the rights of nationalities. The national question became inextricably linked with the question of the democratization of the USSR: the preservation of Russian hegemony demanded the retention of censors and the secret police.

IV

The late 1980s witnessed the second wave of de-Stalinization, the Gorbachev reforms. A significant part of the party leadership had come to a decision that a democratic restructuring of Soviet society was so necessary that the consequences had to be risked. Political prisoners were released and a limited freedom of speech and assembly was tolerated. Partially free elections were also held. Of all the problems that have emerged in the Soviet Union in the course of Gorbachev's restructuring, none has become so critically acute as the nationality problem. As this essay was being written, Lithuania declared its independence from the USSR and Gorbachev bullied it into at least partial submission; the central authorities felt constrained to invade Azerbaijan; anti-Soviet guerrilla warfare broke out in Armenia; and secessionist sentiments became dominant in Estonia and Latvia and strong in Moldavia, Ukraine, and Georgia. This has all been the result of essentially only a few years of democratic reform. The Soviet Union's nationality problem, compared to that of the Habsburg Monarchy, has been undergoing compressed development. This compressed development in the USSR has made the national question a much more explosive issue than it ever was in the Habsburg Monarchy. The old joke about the Monarchy's situation being hopeless but not serious has more than a kernel of truth to it. The centripetal direction of the Monarchy's evolution was clear and the insoluble nationality problem formed the very matrix of politics, but the actual unfolding of the problem proceeded at a tolerable rate. Such is clearly not the case in the Soviet Union.

Several reasons seem to account for the sudden exacerbation of the nationality problem in the USSR, which caught many Western analysts of the Soviet Union by surprise. In both Austria and the USSR, democratization inevitably produced national consequences. In Austria's case, however, these consequences were produced and confronted gradually, while the USSR must, having postponed their resolution for so long, face them in a much more powerful concentration. But the concentration is also more powerful as a result of the much greater mobilization of the population in the USSR than in the Habsburg Empire. Not only is the Soviet population much more literate than that of old Austria-Hungary, but communications technology has been revolutionized since the days of *Národní Noviny*. It is much easier and cheaper to print than it used to be, and unofficial, uncensored periodicals have proliferated in all the non-Russian republics. Even in Belorussia, for example, there were a dozen such periodicals by early 1989 with a circulation of between five and ten thousand.[18] Moreover, national movements have been able to take over the official press as well as television and radio, entirely in the Baltic republics and partially in others. The very instruments of totalitarianism have thus been turned against their former master and placed in the hands of movements for democracy and national sovereignty. The new movements draft their manifestos and register delegates to their congresses on computers; they make professional-quality videos of their demonstrations and concerts; they fax their latest communiqués to co-nationals and press agencies abroad. Yet another reason for the intensity and rapidity of the development of national tension in the USSR is that the underlying problems are so acute. The national grievances aired in the newspapers and parliament of the Habsburg Empire never included anything so dreadful as the mass graves of Kurapaty forest. The Habsburg Empire was not (until the war) in as deep an economic crisis as the Soviet Union now is; and it never knew the sort of ecological damage wrought by the phosphate mines in Estonia or the Chernobyl nuclear disaster in Ukraine and Belorussia. There is almost no moral cement holding the USSR together. It is no accident that Gorbachev, master of the media though he may be, cannot command the popularity either in Russia or in the non-Russian republics that Franz Joseph enjoyed throughout his realm.

It is too early to tell how the national question in the USSR will ultimately be resolved. Perhaps the question will be resolved by the breakup of the multinational empire into independent national states. This was, after all, how the issue was concluded in Austria-Hungary; the sheer compressed force of the nationality problem, combined with the economic collapse of the old regime, could well have the same effect on the USSR as defeat in war had on the Monarchy. Or perhaps the events of 1988-90 in the Soviet Union will turn out to be the compressed equivalent of the 1848-71 period in the Habsburg Monarchy. Sir Lewis Namier once said of the Compromise of 1867 in Austria-Hungary that "it had been imposed on the contracting parties by the inherent necessities of their political situation and by the logic of events. Its intricacies no human mind could have thought out."[19] Perhaps the new Soviet Union that will emerge from the current crisis will be just such a ramshackle realm with a variety of "deals" for various nations: an *Ausgleich* for the Balts or the Ukrainians, Croatian status for this republic, Polish status for that nationality—in any case, a departure from the centrally imposed relative uniformity that had characterized the USSR in the past. Or perhaps the intensity of national discontent will lead to a decision on the part of the authorities to stop the experiment with democracy and reimpose dictatorial rule from the Russian center. There are certainly historical precedents for this. In 1867 Hungary passed up democratization of political life in favor of the preservation of Magyar hegemony. It is important to reemphasize, however, that Hungary belonged to another era and that the suppression of the non-Magyar nationalities never included mass arrests, let alone mass deportations or mass murder. The historical precedent of the USSR itself in the 1930s is much more sinister. At the present moment, moreover, with the release of long-pent-up and unprecedented national grievances, with the compressed and powerful development of national movements, it would take a great deal of twentieth-century-style violence to return to anything like the status quo ante. The Soviet Union stands at a critical crossroads.

NOTES

1. See the excellent account in Roman Szporluk, *Communism and Nationalism: Karl Marx versus Friedrich List* (New York and Oxford, 1988), 79-85.
2. Eduard Winter, "Wien als Mittelpunkt der Slawistik und der Einbruch des romantischen nationalen Denken in Vormärz," *Wissenschaftliche Zeitschrift der Humboldt-Universität zu Berlin*, Gesellschafts- und Sprachwissenschaftliche Reihe, 17, no. 2 (1968): 209-12.
3. The term "heritage gathering" was coined by Paul R. Magocsi. The heritage-gathering stage of national movements corresponds to Miroslav Hroch's "Phase A": "The beginning of every national revival is marked by a passionate concern on the part of a group of individuals, usually intellectuals, for the study of the language, the culture, the history of the oppressed

nationality. These individuals remained without any widespread social influence, and they usually did not even attempt to mount a patriotic agitation, in part because they were isolated, and in part because they did not believe it would serve any purpose. Their interest was motivated by a patriotism of the Enlightenment type, namely an active affection for the region in which they lived, associated with a thirst for knowledge of every new and insufficiently investigated phenomenon." Miroslav Hroch, *Social Preconditions of National Revival in Europe: A Comparative Analysis of the Social Composition of Patriotic Groups among the Smaller European Nations* (Cambridge, 1985), 22-23.

4. An excellent example is the Ukrainian awakener Iosyf Levytsky, who translated Schiller and Goethe while ministering to the parish of Shklo, a village about halfway between L'viv and Jaroslaw.

5. See especially, Roman Rosdolsky, *Engels and the "Nonhistoric" Peoples: The National Question in the Revolution of 1848* (Glasgow, 1986).

6. There is an outstanding study of Austropolonism in the form of a biography: Joanna Radzyner, *Stanislaw Madeyski 1841-1910: Ein austro-polnischer Staatsman im Spannungsfeld der Nationalitätenfrage in der Habsburgermonarchie* (Vienna, 1983).

7. See Otto Bauer, "Erwachende Völker," *Der Kampf* 7 (January 1, 1914): 145-51.

8. Of course, it should be kept in mind that the outbreak of war was in part the result of Habsburg nationality politics.

9. "Perhaps the forces emanating from the nationalities conflict were rendering the economic union obsolete from a political standpoint. On the eve of World War I, however, the economic union still stood intact." David F. Good, *The Economic Rise of the Habsburg Empire, 1750-1914* (Berkeley, Los Angeles, and London, 1984), 123.

10. See especially Janusz Radziejowski, *The Communist Party of Western Ukraine, 1919-1929* (Edmonton, 1983).

11. John-Paul Himka, "Ukrainian-Jewish Antagonism in the Galician Countryside during the Late Nineteenth Century," in *Ukrainian-Jewish Relations in Historical Perspective*, ed. Peter J. Potichnyj and Howard Aster (Edmonton, 1987), 111-58.

12. Richard Pipes, *The Formation of the Soviet Union: Communism and Nationalism 1917-1923*, rev. ed. (Cambridge, Mass., 1964), 260-62.

13. James E. Mace, *Communism and the Dilemmas of National Liberation: National Communism in Soviet Ukraine 1918-1933* (Cambridge, Mass., 1983).

14. The case is made well and briefly in Szporluk, *Communism and Nationalism*, 218-19. "From the start it was Trotsky's policy to utilize the ex-officers of the imperial army to help to build the Red Army. . . . In 1918 ex-officers and ex-non-commissioned officers numbered 7/8ths of all commanders." Leonard Schapiro, *The Origin of the Communist Autocracy: Political Opposition in the Soviet State, First Phase 1917-1922*, 2nd ed. (Cambridge, Mass., 1977), 238.

15. For example, Z, "To the Stalin Mausoleum," *Daedalus* 119 (1990): 314.

16. Janusz Radziejowski, "Collectivization in Ukraine in Light of Soviet Historiography," *Journal of Ukrainian Studies* 5, (1980): 3-17; Robert Conquest, *The Harvest of Sorrow: Soviet Collectivization and the Terror-Famine* (New York; 1986); Maksudov, *Poteri naseleniia SSSR* (Benson, Vt., 1989). Some Western Sovietologists had been at great pains to minimize the number of deaths by famine in Ukraine and Kazakhstan at the end of the collectivization drive. The great mass of material on the famine published in the Soviet press itself in 1988-90 has made these efforts at denial seem unsound.

17. For example, in the Ukrainian republic the first major arrest and trial of dissidents took place in 1965-66. About two dozen, mainly young intellectuals were rounded up and sentenced. Most were again at liberty in the early 1970s. In 1972 these dissidents and dozens more were again arrested. Most of these were rearrested while still in the camps or in exile (generally on fabricated criminal, not political, charges) and were not freed until granted amnesty by Gorbachev in 1988. The 1970s and early 1980s saw several suspicious murders of cultural figures in Ukraine, the death of several dissidents in the camps, and the use of psychiatric hospitals as places of incarceration.

18. Jan Zaprudnik, "Belorussian Reawakening," *Problems of Communism* 38 (1989): 45. *Národní Noviny* had a circulation of 2,400 in 1848. Stanley Z. Pech, "The Press of the Habsburg Slavs in 1848: Contribution to a Political Profile," *Canadian Journal of History* 10 (1975): 40.

19. "The Downfall of the Habsburg Monarchy," in *Vanished Supremacies: Essays on European History, 1812-1918* (London, 1958), 114.

6

A Subordinate or Submerged People: The Ukrainians of Galicia under Habsburg and Soviet Rule

Paul Robert Magocsi

In the context of the theme of this conference, "Great Power Ethnic Politics: The Habsburg Empire and the Soviet Union," the Ukrainians are unique. They are the only indigenous people in the former Habsburg Empire to experience the direct rule of the Soviet Union in the years since 1945. Specifically, the Soviet-ruled territories that before 1918 had been part of the Habsburg Empire comprised the western Ukraine—areas known as East Galicia, northern Bukovina, and Transcarpathia. The largest of these western Ukrainian lands was East Galicia, which will be my focus here.[1]

In comparing Habsburg and Soviet methods of rule in East Galicia, it is possible to address factors such as the administrative, economic, military, and nationality policies of the two regimes. The concern here will be primarily with the nationality question. Also, in keeping with the comparative nature of this exercise, it might be instructive to speculate whether the Habsburg approach to the Ukrainian nationality question has any relevance as a model for consideration by present and future Soviet policymakers.

HISTORICAL BACKGROUND OF GALICIA

The territory of East Galicia did not enter the Habsburg polity until 1772, when Austria participated in the first partition of Poland. At that time, the Habsburgs acquired the former Polish palatinate of Rus' (which in medieval times coincided more or less with the principality of Galicia) as well as parts of two other former Polish palatinates (Sandomierz and Cracow) that were west of the San River and south of the Vistula River. Together this new territorial acquisition on both sides of the San River became known as the kingdom of Galicia and Volhynia, or, for short, simply Galicia. It was the part of Austrian Galicia east of the San River where Ukrainians were in the majority (71 percent in 1849; 62 percent in 1910) that will be referred to here as East Galicia. It became part of the Soviet Union briefly in 1941-42 and then definitively after 1945.

It is useful to remember that East Galicia occupied only a quantitatively small part of the Ukrainian problem as a whole. Even when East Galicia was combined with northern Bukovina and Transcarpathia, together these Habsburg Ukrainian lands accounted for at most 12 to 15 percent of the total Ukrainian land mass and population. Yet despite their relatively small size in the total Ukrainian context, the western Ukrainian lands, in particular East Galicia, were to play an enormously positive role in preserving the Ukrainian national idea during the nineteenth century. In fact, at the very same time when tsarist oppression had stopped the Ukrainian movement dead in its tracks in the Russian Empire, the Ukrainians living under the relatively more benign rule of the Habsburgs were able to develop Ukrainian nationalism into a viable movement for themselves and for their descendants.

THE PHENOMENON OF NATIONALISM

When examining the Ukrainian nationality question, whether in East Galicia or the Ukraine as a whole, it is useful to keep in mind certain conceptual issues. Nationalist movements can be divided into two basic categories, which might be called intelligentsia-inspired national movements or nationalism, and state-imposed nationalism.[2] Intelligentsia-inspired national movements emanate from below or, if you will, from the bottom up. They occur among groups who live in multinational states where a language, culture, and identity other than their own are dominant. The group's often self-proclaimed leaders—the nationalist intelligentsia—seek to convince the group's members that they form a distinct nationality and as such deserve at the very least cultural autonomy, if not political autonomy, or even independence. The second category, state-imposed nationalism, emanates from above, and occurs within already existing independent states. The governments of these states hope to gain the allegiance of their subjects by convincing them that they are united because they belong to a given nationality, whose primary function is loyalty to the existing government and social structure.

The Ukrainians were a stateless people, so their national revival obviously belonged to the intelligentsia-inspired variety of nationalism. However, living in the Habsburg and neighboring Russian empires, Ukrainians were also exposed to the state-imposed nationalisms of those states. Thus, at the very same time when the Ukrainian national revival was unfolding, the Habsburg and tsarist authorities were also trying to implement their respective state-imposed nationalisms. The manner in which those two imperial authorities tried to transform Ukrainians into loyal Habsburg or tsarist subjects was to have an indelible imprint on the Ukrainian self-image and on the manner in which Ukrainians identified themselves in national terms. In short, the Ukrainian national revival of the late nineteenth century—as well as the Ukrainian national psyche ever since then—was marked by two seemingly contradictory phenomena: a hierarchy of multiple loyalties versus the principle of mutually exclusive identities.

In multinational states, it was and still is natural to find individuals who feel perfectly comfortable with one or more "national" loyalties or identities. In the case of Ukrainian lands in the nineteenth century, it seemed normal for a resident to be simultaneously a Little Russian (Ukrainian) and a Russian. The best-known example of such types comprised the Cossack officer stratum, whose members, because they strove to become recognized as members of the Russian noble estate, seemed to become assimilated and therefore Russified. Besides these Cossacks-turned-nobles, several intellectuals followed a similar path. The most famous was the writer Nikolai Gogol, a Ukrainian who published only in Russian. These and other "Little Russians" consciously felt that a harmonious union existed between their attachment to the "province" of Little Russia and to Russia as a whole.

On the other hand, as the Ukrainian national revival evolved, some of its leaders became convinced that in order for the movement to survive, the otherwise natural hierarchy of multiple loyalties or national identities had to be replaced by a framework of mutually exclusive identities. Thus, one could not be a Russian from Little Russia, or a Pole from the Ukraine; one had to be either a Russian or a Ukrainian (the latter term was favored over Little

Russian precisely to accentuate the degree of perceptual difference), or a Pole or a Ukrainian. One could not be both.

But how did these conflicting principles of multiple loyalties versus mutually exclusive identities affect the manner in which Ukrainians could function in the specific territory of East Galicia, which was ruled by both the Habsburg Empire and later the Soviet Union? In effect, both the Habsburg Empire and the Soviet Union tried to force their respective versions of a state-imposed nationalism upon Galicia's Ukrainians. For the Habsburgs, this took the form of promoting loyalty to an imperial dynasty; for the Soviets, on the other hand, the goal was loyalty to a classless and eventually nationless Communist state. What were the results of the Habsburg and Soviet approaches to the phenomenon of Ukrainian nationalism in Galicia?

GALICIA UNDER THE HABSBURGS

In the case of Habsburg rule, which lasted from 1772 until 1918, it must be said that the final balance sheet was, from the standpoint of Ukrainian nationalism, quite positive. Already in the 1770s, when Galicia first became a Habsburg land, Empress Maria Theresia together with her co-regent and successor, Joseph II, initiated a series of reforms that were to have a positive impact on what was still the embryonic stage of Ukrainian nationalism. From the outset, the Habsburg authorities clearly distinguished Galicia's Ukrainians, whom they called Ruthenians (*Ruthenen*), from Russians, the nationality with whom they frequently had been and were still to be confused.[3] Other Habsburg contributions included: (1) an improvement in the status of the Greek Catholic church, which was almost exclusively the religion of Galicia's Ukrainians, and which was made equal to the Roman Catholic church (1774); (2) the introduction of universal elementary education in the vernacular language (1777); and (3) the establishment of the first modern schools of higher learning specifically for Ukrainians—the Studium Ruthenum at the University of L'viv (1787) and the Greek Catholic seminary called the Barbareum in Vienna (1775).

These positive precedents were to be repeated, in particular at certain critical periods in Habsburg history. Thus, in 1848 it was really at the instigation of the Habsburg authorities that the Ukrainians as a group began to participate in the political world and, thereby, to enhance the status of their national movement. In that year alone, Ukrainians established their first political organization (the Supreme Ruthenian Council), their first newspaper (*Zoria halytska*), their first cultural societies (Galician Rus' Matytsia and

National Home), and their first modern military formations (the Ruthenian National Guard and the Sharpshooters Battalion). Furthermore, they participated actively as members of the newly established Austrian parliament (Reichstag), and they received their first permanent center of higher learning, a Chair of Ruthenian Language and Literature at the University of L'viv. All of these achievements led some contemporary Polish nationalists to quip that it was the Habsburgs (especially the Galician governor Franz Stadion) who "invented" the Ukrainians.[4]

This midcentury boost to the Galician Ukrainian national movement was subsequently tempered by the ups and downs of Austrian political life during the last seventy years of Habsburg imperial history. Yet despite the increasing dependence by the Habsburg authorities on Galicia's Poles as the group of choice to rule the province (in particular after 1868), the Ukrainian national movement continued to make remarkable advances through the creation of numerous cultural organizations, publishing houses, newspapers, and political parties. In the most critical realm of education, the number of Ukrainian-language elementary schools during the last four decades of Habsburg rule rose from 1,293 to 2,510 and secondary schools from 1 to 5.[5] Moreover, nine new Ukrainian university chairs (small departments in North American university terms) were created at the University of L'viv.

Finally, the Habsburg authorities even stepped in on the side of Ukrainians with regard to the internal nationality conflicts that raged between those rival members of the intelligentsia who argued that the local East Slavic population was Russian and those who said that they were part of a distinct Ukrainian nationality.[6] Habsburg authorities clearly favored the pro-Ukrainian orientation. The most significant contribution in this regard was the 1893 decision of Galicia's provincial school board, which declared in favor of vernacular Ukrainian as the only acceptable language to be taught in schools and to serve as the linguistic medium to represent the Ukrainian nationality.

This is not to say that Galicia's Ukrainians got everything they wanted. The province was never divided into separate Polish and Ukrainian entities, nor was a Ukrainian university ever established, two of the group's long-standing demands. Nor did Polish domination of the upper and middle levels of the Galician administration ever change. Yet, while Galicia's Ukrainians did not fare terribly well in comparison with Galicia's Poles, in comparison with their national brethren across the border in the Russian Empire the contrast could not have been greater.

In tsarist Russia, there were until 1905 no legal Ukrainian political parties, no cultural organizations, no newspapers. There were never any Ukrainian-

language schools at any level, and the Ukrainian language itself was officially banned from 1863/1876 to 1905. It was in the context of these realities
that, despite criticism leveled by political and civic activists against certain
aspects of Habsburg rule, Galicia's Ukrainians were until the very end of the
empire's existence in late 1918 to remain its loyal "Tyrolians of the East."[7]

GALICIA UNDER SOVIET RULE

Even before the Soviet Union came to rule East Galicia definitively after
1945, the achievements in Ukrainian national life stemming from the Habsburg era had already been largely undermined. With the collapse of the
Habsburg Empire in 1918 and the end of the Polish-Ukrainian war of
1918-19, Galicia came under Polish rule. Under Poland, the number of
cultural institutions decreased, most Ukrainian-language elementary schools
became bilingual Polish-Ukrainian schools, and all but one of the Ukrainian
university chairs was abolished.[8] Then, when the Soviet Union first annexed
the region in the aftermath of the German-Soviet destruction of Poland in
September 1939, many of the remaining institutions from the "feudalistic"
Habsburg days were closed. Soviet rule was interrupted by the German
invasion of June 1941, but it was renewed with the arrival of the Red Army
in the fall of 1944.

With the end of World War II, the Soviet Union became the dominant
force throughout all of East-Central Europe, and the inhabitants of East
Galicia were subjected to a new version of state-imposed nationalism. In
effect, the new rulers were to foster the Ukrainian aspects of East Galicia,
but only to the degree that they fit into the Soviet predilection for an
acceptable hierarchy of multiple loyalties.

On the one hand, the Ukrainianization of East Galicia as carried out by
the Soviets took the form of the expulsion through population exchange of
most of the remaining Poles living in the towns and countryside.[9] Polish was
also replaced in the educational system as elementary and secondary schools
were either made purely Ukrainian or bilingual Ukrainian and Russian.
Analogously, the former dominant Polish institutional presence in cities like
L'viv as well as in numerous towns throughout East Galicia came to an end
as Polish cultural organizations and Roman Catholic churches were replaced
by Ukrainian institutions.

On the other hand, all the former Ukrainian political, cultural, and
religious institutions that had existed before 1945 were abolished. And if
their association with the Habsburg "feudal" and Polish "bourgeois" past

was not enough to make them unacceptable, the fact that some may have existed (or were restored) during the three years of German occupation (1941-44) provided the Soviets with the ultimate justification for their abolition—their very existence during the war years made them "collaborationist" and "fascist." The most important of such organizations was the Greek Catholic church, which under the nearly half-century leadership of its patriarchal-like leader, Metropolitan Andrei Sheptyts'kyi (1865-1944), had in itself become an integral part, if not the very essence, of Galician Ukrainian national identity. Following the precedent of nineteenth-century tsarist Russia, Soviet authorities arranged for a church council (Sobor) at L'viv, which in 1946 abrogated the union with Rome. This meant that Greek Catholicism was made illegal and all its former adherents, should they wish to remain Eastern-rite Christians, had to become adherents of the Russian Orthodox church.[10]

Thus, under Soviet rule, all the former institutions, national symbols, and historical events that until then had been associated with a Ukrainian self-identity in Galicia were outlawed and removed from public life. For instance, the pre-Soviet Ukrainian national flag and national anthem, or the heroes of Galician Ukrainian history, especially during the recent twentieth-century struggle against Polish and German rule, were now branded as aspects of Ukrainian "bourgeois nationalism," a phenomenon that could and frequently was considered a crime against the Soviet state. Galician Ukrainians could remain Ukrainian, but only if they were specifically Soviet Ukrainian.

And what did Soviet Ukrainian mean? In essence, being Soviet Ukrainian meant forgetting everything that previously had been considered positive in the Galician past, in particular since the onset of Habsburg rule in 1772, as well as events, regardless of when they happened, that were associated with the Polish presence in the area. There were a few exceptions to this general condemnation of the last two centuries. The most outstanding of these exceptions was the late nineteenth-century belletrist and publicist, Ivan Franko (1856-1916), who because of his socialist inclinations could be claimed as a precursor to Communist activists in the twentieth century. Aside from his own talent, Franko was raised by the Soviets to the level of a national hero, with the University of L'viv and several streets and squares being named after him, not to mention the frequent republication of his writings and numerous conferences about his career. In addition to Franko, Soviet Ukrainian ideology included the glorification of a group of otherwise little-known and relatively unimportant leftist and Communist leaders and events in interwar East Galicia and, in particular, the World War II struggle against local "collaborationist" Ukrainian bourgeois nationalist leaders.

However, more problematic for Ukrainians living under Soviet rule was the unresolved issue of multiple loyalties versus mutually exclusive identities. Under Habsburg rule, these seemingly contradictory principles could coexist, because in Austrian Galicia Ukrainians could function within the socially and politically acceptable imperial Habsburg framework of a hierarchy of multiple loyalties without having to give up their own national identity. In short, an East Slav from Galicia could be simultaneously a Ukrainian national patriot and a loyal Habsburg subject. Both identities were compatible.

This was in decided contrast to the Russian Empire—and for that matter to the Soviet state that succeeded it. In tsarist Russia, accepting the idea of a hierarchy of loyalties effectively meant that a resident of the Ukraine or, as it was known then, Little Russia, was at best a Little Russian. In the absence of any Little Russian or Ukrainian language schools, all means of written and oral communication outside one's native village would be Russian. In such a situation, being a Little Russian became, *nomens omens*, simply a lower or less advanced form of Russian identity. Moreover, the entire ideological complex of tsarist society did not recognize the Ukrainian or Little Russian past as anything more than an appanage of Russian civilization. Hence, the residents of medieval Ukrainian territory and the language they spoke were considered "Old Russian," the states they inhabited were referred to as Kievan "Russia" or the Galician "Russian" kingdom, and a leader like the seventeenth-century hetman, Bohdan Khmelnytskyi, was just another Russian Cossack.

Whereas the Soviets recognized Ukrainian as a distinct literary language and Ukrainians as a distinct people, their interpretation of the historical past as presented to several generations through a centralized school system proved to be not much different from what was taught in tsarist days. Even the view that Ukrainian was a distinct language was at times undermined by Soviet policy, which already in the late 1930s argued that all Ukrainian students must be fluent in the Russian language and that Ukrainian must be brought steadily closer to the Russian language in alphabet, vocabulary, and grammar.

Finally, the Soviet understanding of the hierarchy of multiple identities was best represented by a three-stage evolution that Marxist-Leninist ideologists expected to take place among all nationalities living in the Soviet Union, but most especially among the three closely related East Slavic peoples—Russians, Belorussians, and Ukrainians. Those three stages—*rastsvet* (flowering), *sblizhenie* (drawing together), and *slianie* (fusion)—were expected to culminate in a situation that would replace distinct nationalities with a new Soviet nation (*sovetskaia natsiia*) or "historical community of people—the Soviet people (*sovetskii narod*)."[11] Thus, while the hierarchy of multiple loyalties in the Germanic Habsburg world allowed for the survival and even flourishing of a Ukrainian nationality, in the Soviet Union multiple loyalties provided for a gradual process of Russian assimilation or at the very least the persistence of a "lower" form of Russian identity, whether it was called by its old name, Little Russian, or its new one, Ukrainian.

THE PERSISTENCE OF HISTORICAL TRADITION

In a real sense, the traditional conflict within the Ukrainian national psyche between acceptance of multiple national identities versus mutually exclusive identities persists to this day. While it is true that the Habsburg heritage has contributed to making Galicians the most nationally conscious segment of the Ukrainian population, they represent the exception in the Soviet Ukraine. In fact, it is the persistence of a hierarchy of multiple loyalties among perhaps three-quarters of the Ukrainian population that has led to only a passive commitment on the part of Ukrainian society as a whole to the kinds of demands for national autonomy or even independence that since the beginning of the Gorbachev era have been made with increasing frequency in the Baltic and Caucasian republics.

The differing aspects of Ukrainian self-identity are related in part to geography. The Ukrainian SSR, with its 50 million inhabitants and 604,000 square kilometers, is an enormous country, second only to the Russian SFSR in the Soviet Union. In a real sense, one can speak not of one but of four "Ukraines": (1) western Ukraine; (2) the central or Kiev-Poltava region; (3) the far eastern Donbas and lower Dnieper industrial region; and (4) the southern Black Sea Littoral and the Crimea. Of these four regions, only one, the western Ukraine, in particular former Habsburg-ruled Galicia, has demonstrated the strongest manifestations of Ukrainian patriotism and nationalist activity during the Gorbachev era.

As for the other regions, much of the eastern Ukraine and the Dnieper industrial areas are inhabited by ethnic Russians who are oblivious, if not openly opposed, to Ukrainian national concerns. This is also the case along the southern Black Sea Littoral and the Crimea, where a Ukrainian presence has never had any long-term historical roots. As for the ethnic Ukrainians in the eastern and southern regions, they may have the name "Ukrainian" inscribed on their identification papers under the rubric of nationality, and they probably use Ukrainian as their operative language (or more likely a Russian-Ukrainian jargon known as *surzhyk*), but most still lack any commitment to the current political movement that wants to enhance the status of Ukrainian culture.

Certainly, the central region of Kiev (including the city of Kiev) and Poltava, which gave the Ukrainian language the basis for its modern literary standard, have more nationalist potential. But even there centuries-old administrative and religious traditions work against the kind of Ukrainian distinctiveness that would allow for a clearly defined demarcation from the Russian world. After all, this part of the Ukraine has been under Muscovite/Russian rule since the mid-seventeenth century. Moreover, it shares the common tradition of Orthodoxy with Russians, which in many ways is as strong a bond, if not stronger, than the national one that would link Orthodox Ukrainians with their Greek Catholic brethren in Galicia. Thus, even in the heart of the Ukraine—the Kiev and Poltava regions—not to mention the eastern and southern Ukraine, the idea of a hierarchy of multiple loyalties, which perceives Ukrainianism as only one aspect or lower stage of a larger Russian, or perhaps Soviet identity, is a tradition that is still alive and well.

The geographical disparity and limited concentration of Ukrainian nationalist activity were revealed most graphically in March 1990, when the first relatively free elections were held in Soviet Ukrainian territory, specifically for deputies to the Ukrainian Supreme Soviet. The Communist party was opposed by the so-called Democratic Bloc, a heterogeneous coalition of individuals and organizations dedicated to transforming the Ukrainian SSR into a truly Ukrainian state. The Democratic Bloc, therefore, could be said to represent the Ukrainian national movement in its present form.

Of the 450 seats that were contested, the Bloc won less than one-quarter, or just over 100 deputies. The Bloc, moreover, won significant victories only in two areas: Galicia (43 of 47 seats) and the city of Kiev (15 of 21 seats). As for the rest of the country, the Bloc garnered a mere 15 percent of the vote in the central and eastern Ukraine, while in the peripheral areas of the Crimea, Transcarpathia, and Bukovina it won no seats at all.[12]

This internal divisiveness is precisely what is of most concern to organizations like the Popular Movement for Reconstruction in Ukraine, better known by its acronym RUKH, which since its establishment in September 1989 has been in the forefront in trying to renew Ukrainian cultural and spiritual life and to transform the Ukrainian SSR into a truly Ukrainian state. While RUKH is not calling for independent statehood, it does wish to see the Soviet Union became a federation of equal republics in which the Ukraine would have complete control over its own cultural and economic affairs. The culmination of these efforts was the declaration of Ukrainian sovereignty made by the Ukrainian Supreme Soviet on July 16, 1990.[13]

But goals and declarations aside, RUKH's greatest difficulty remains to convince the vast majority of Ukrainians throughout the country—and not simply those who live in Galicia or the city of Kiev—that they should give up their multiple loyalties for a mutually exclusive national identity. In short, the battle against Little Russianism is far from won in the Soviet Ukraine, and until it is, nationalist organizations like RUKH will be limited in their efforts to mobilize society as a whole to carry out the kind of changes it would like to see.[14] The Ukrainian situation reminds one of what Václav Havel has recently repeated so eloquently about his own Czechoslovak society, namely, that the greatest danger to the well-being of the nation comes not from the external forces of a repressive state but from the moral failings within individuals, whose very personas are crossed by walls that divide their own souls.[15]

But what about Soviet policymakers at the center in Moscow? Most are committed to the idea that the Soviet Union should survive, even if the relationship of the center to the constituent republics will probably have to change in the direction of a real federation of national states. If that is the goal, then the Habsburg experience in Galicia might be worthy of consideration and even emulation.

Like the Habsburgs before them, the Soviets could, in theory, satisfy the instinctive need for national self-pride if it encouraged an end to the tsarist and now Soviet version of multiple loyalties, one in which the Russians play the role of the supposedly older and wiser brother vis-à-vis the Little Russians or Ukrainians. This approach has always contributed to a blurring of distinctions between Russian and Ukrainian cultures and to suspicions on the part of Ukrainians that they are constantly under the threat of national assimilation. Like the Habsburgs, the Soviets need to view Ukrainian national self-pride not as a threat but as a healthy phenomenon that needs to be encouraged in a Ukrainian polity that must be treated as an equal partner in the inevitable political transformation of Soviet society.

It is interesting to note that even the more sanguine of Ukrainian nationalist leaders realize that accommodation with the component parts of a restructured Soviet Union is a prerequisite for the Ukraine's survival. Dmytro Pavlychko, head of the Taras Shevchenko Ukrainian Language Society and recently elected deputy to the Ukrainian Supreme Soviet, who was in the forefront in calling for Ukrainian sovereignty and who remains committed to "total independence," nonetheless admits that "an immediate secession from the Soviet Union is, first of all, impossible."[16] Notwithstanding the reaction of the present Soviet government to such a move, Pavlychko concedes that "we [Ukrainians] are not yet mature enough as a people for complete independence. There are many Russified Ukrainians; there are many who will view such a step negatively."[17]

Thus, both sides are aware that the achievement of their respective political goals requires mutual accommodation. The Habsburg efforts at accommodation with the empire's nationalities—as belated as they always came—were in the case of groups like the Ukrainians of Galicia (the loyal "Tyrolians of the East") quite successful. However, the Habsburg experiment ultimately failed because of the catastrophe of World War I. In the present geopolitical configuration, an external threat to the Soviet Union does not seem likely. There is, however, a greater possibility for internal upheaval prompted by nationality conflicts or the enormous economic difficulties. But in the absence of either an external or an internal threat, the Soviet authorities have an opportunity to improve on the Habsburg experience not only by accommodating the Ukrainian national movement but also by working with it to restructure the political relationship between the countries that at present comprise the Soviet Union.

NOTES

1. For an introduction to the historical background and a survey of the extensive literature on Ukrainian-inhabited Galicia during both Habsburg and Soviet rule, see Paul Robert Magocsi, *Galicia: A Historical Survey and Bibliographic Guide* (Toronto, Buffalo, and London, 1983), esp. chaps. 5, 6, 8, and 9.

2. The following discussion is taken from Paul Robert Magocsi, "The Ukrainian National Revival: A New Analytical Framework," *Canadian Review of Studies in Nationalism* 16 (1989): esp. 49-52.

3. The confusion, not only among the Habsburg authorities but among the Galician Ukrainian populace as well, derived in part from the fact that the people called themselves *rus'kyi*, which sounded to the untutored ear like *russkyi* (Russian).

4. For details on the early stages of the Ukrainian national revival in Galicia before 1849, see Jan Kozik, *The Ukrainian National Movement in Galicia, 1815-1849* (Edmonton, 1986).

5. Ann Sirka, *The Nationality Question in Austrian Education: The Case of Ukrainians in Galicia, 1867-1914* (Frankfurt-am-Main, 1980), 75-95 passim.

6. The Galician Ukrainian national movement actually experienced an internal struggle between an intelligentsia that accepted the principle of a hierarchy of multiple loyalties (the Old Ruthenians and Russophiles) and an intelli-

gentsia that favored the idea of mutually exclusive identities (the Ukrainophiles). See Paul Robert Magocsi, "Old Ruthenianism and Russophilism: A New Conceptual Framework for Analyzing National Ideologies in Late 19th Century Eastern Galicia," in Paul Debreczeny, ed., *American Contributions to the Ninth International Congress of Slavists* (Columbus, Ohio, 1983), 2:305-24.

7. On the question of Ukrainian loyalty to the Habsburgs, see Paul Robert Magocsi, "Ukrainians and the Habsburgs" (unpublished manuscript).

8. The decline in Ukrainian national life for Galicia's Ukrainians during the interwar years is outlined in Bohdan Budurowycz, "Poland and the Ukrainian Problem, 1921-1939," *Canadian Slavonic Papers* 25 (1983): 473-500.

9. During the interwar years when Poland ruled "Ukrainian" East Galicia, the number of Polish settlers increased by 300,000, so that by the 1930s ethnic Poles comprised 39.5 percent of the urban population and 21.1 percent of the rural population. With the onset of Soviet rule in 1945, nearly 750,000 of the Poles still remaining moved westward to the restored state of Poland. For details on the fate of Poles, see Joseph B. Schectman, *Postwar Population Transfers in Europe, 1945-1955* (Philadelphia, Pa., 1962), 151-79.

10. On the importance of Sheptyts'kyi in Galician Ukrainian life and the subsequent demise of the Greek Catholic church, see Paul Robert Magocsi, ed., *Morality and Reality: The Life and Times of Metropolitan Andrei Sheptyts'kyi* (Edmonton, 1989).

11. Cited in Kenneth C. Farmer, *Ukrainian Nationalism in the Post-Stalin Era* (The Hague, 1980), 63.

12. "Elections to Ukraine's Supreme Soviet: A Report by the Helsinki Commission," *Ukrainian Weekly*, April 8, 1990, 8-9.

13. The text of the Declaration on State Sovereignty of Ukraine is given in English translation in the *Ukrainian Weekly*, July 22, 1990, 1 and 7.

14. On the persistence of Little Russianism in the Ukrainian mentality at present, see Mikola Riabchuk, "Ukrainskaia literatura i malorossiiskii 'imidzh,'" *Druzhba narodov* 50 (1988): 250-54, and in particular the interview conducted by Roman Solchanyk: "Mykola Ryabchuk Speaks on 'Little Russianism,'" *Ukrainian Weekly*, September 3 and 10, 1989, 2 and 12 and 2 and 12.

15. Havel expressed these views in his 1990 New Year's speech to the Czechoslovak nation and again in an address to the Polish parliament, the latter reprinted in English translation as Václav Havel, "The Future of Central Europe," *New York Review of Books*, 37 (1990):18-19.

16. "Inside Ukrainian SSR Politics: Interview with Dmytro Pavlychko," *Ukrainian Weekly*, August 5, 1990, 12.

17. Ibid.

7

National Autonomy in Russia and Austro-Hungary: A Comparative Analysis of Finland and Croatia-Slavonia

Sergei A. Romanenko

At the beginning I would like to answer one of the questions raised by the organizers of our conference: Is it possible in principle to conduct a comparative analysis of Austria-Hungary and the Soviet Union? It is possible, but only from the point of view of a discussion of politics or of the state and law. It is possible if we consider the interrelationship of ethnic community and the state in a purely abstract, theoretical manner. It is possible if we strive to answer the following questions: First, does every nation always aspire to gain state independence to the fullest degree? And second, does the essence of self-determination consist of just the gaining of this independence in and of itself? It is possible if we define clearly the subject of comparison: tendencies or coincident stages in ethnic and social development; forms of the nation-state structure; mechanisms of political power; and similarity of courses pursued in specific political situations or cases of direct adoption, whether by central authorities or national and public movements, of neighboring countries' experience.

It is wrong, however, to build a policy toward the USSR on the basis of an analysis of Austria-Hungary's development and disintegration. First of all, these countries represent entirely different historical periods and have a different social basis. Second, a unique national-state structure has been formed and a different political culture has been developed in the USSR for over seventy years. Finally, it is wrong to ignore the peculiarities of the psychological situation in the USSR, especially its ethnic and religious aspects. Therefore it seems more correct, from the point of view of a historical science, to make a comparative analysis of the Habsburg and the Romanov dynasties.

I do not intend to answer at once all the questions that are raised with the comparison of the two countries. Rather, I have limited myself primarily to the comparison of two autonomous national-political territories, Croatia and Slavonia within Austria-Hungary and the Grand Duchy of Finland within the Russian Empire. This will enable us to understand the essence of autonomy as a historic phenomenon, to examine the change of ideas about it in the course of historical development in different countries and nations.

It would be good to emphasize one more detail. Within the Soviet Union there is almost a total lack of studies of the history of national movements in Russia. This is not accidental, since Soviet scholars were given the task of proving the absolute historical validity of natural laws that led nations to preserve the almost comprehensive national-territorial community of our multinational state. At the same time, as T. M. Islamov points out in this volume, the historians who studied Central and Southeastern Europe were given an entirely opposite task: to understand the basis for the inevitable disintegration of Austria-Hungary and the creation of several independent countries.

Even so, our point of view is that it is possible to apply the methodology for studying national movements in Central Europe to the history of national movements in Russia.

Russia and Austria-Hungary, the two states covering almost entirely two historic-geographical regions (that is, Central and Eastern Europe), had much in common in the late nineteenth and early twentieth centuries. Those common features were the poor development of capitalism as compared to Western European countries; the uneven economic development of various regions of the state; the structural differences within the economy; the multinational populations; the formation of nations for the majority of peoples within their domains; sudden fluctuations of the level of these peoples' development; and monarchy as the form of government. The Habsburg and the Romanov monarchies were evolving in the same direction—from medieval to modern statehood. In the sphere of political relations this was manifested in a step-by-step transition (though not always a final one) from authoritarian to constitutional-liberal government, and in the sphere of national-state structure from centralism to decentralization, possibly to federal structure.

Both monarchies had to keep a balance between the two opposing tendencies existing in any multinational state: centrifugal and centripetal. The focus of political struggle and, accordingly, of programs of national movements was on the question of national self-determination, and of a possible way of reaching it within the framework of existing multinational states. This notion may seem controversial, but one of the most important instances of coincidence in the history of the two monarchies was that neither the Austrian Germans nor the Russians had completed the process of forming nations, and their imperial ideas, which were manifested in centralist policy and the concept of an indivisible state, performed a sort of compensatory function in the ethnic self-consciousness of both state-forming peoples.

Together with this there existed profound differences in inner political development and national-state structure. The ways in which the two monarchies were created and their operating principles were far from similar. Practically all the peoples inhabiting the territory of the Habsburgs had their special political and juridical status, which contained elements of national statehood. In Russia, with the exception of Poland and Finland, there was a centralist pattern of national-state structure. At the same time, there existed in Austria-Hungary a system of rather developed national representative bodies both on the state and local levels. Such bodies were practically nonexistent in the Russian Empire (except for the Polish Sejm, the Parliament in Finland, and to a certain extent the state Duma). Also, as opposed to the Russian case, in Austria-Hungary nations neither enjoying full rights nor forming states contained the majority of the population. With all its weak points and contradictions the monarchy in Austria-Hungary was of an authoritarian-constitutional character; in Russia, power had a more authoritarian-totalitarian character and this remained true up to February 1917.

The totality of these circumstances called forth common features and specific developments of national movements of the peoples in these two states, and shaped their ideologies, political programs, and methods of struggle and forms of organization. The growth of national political party structures that was an integral component of the national self-determination process was under way in both states. Political parties were becoming the principal form of the national movements.

The panorama of national-political concepts—centralist, conservative, liberal, radical, and revolutionary—was practically similar, though each of these trends had its national and "state" peculiarities. On the whole, one can say that almost all the parties, except for revolutionary groups, spoke in favor of preserving the integrity of a state. They saw the possibility of national self-determination within the framework of existing borders along with conducting liberal and democratic reforms to a greater or lesser degree. The right of nations to self-determination right up to their separation, which was recognized by Social Democracy, did not mean the demand of state disintegration.

The vital importance of the national question increased in both states in the course of their development from medieval to industrial societies. The problem of autonomy was a separate one, however, since it dealt with the basic question of the existence of a state and its integrity, namely, the idea of the territory of "their own" states; this is one of the most sensitive points in the national consciousness of the peoples in the process of state formation—the Russians, the Austrian Germans, and the Hungarians. In the late nineteenth and early twentieth centuries, the two states faced the necessity of broad political and national-state reforms. Heated polemics were launched on the question of the future of national autonomy, which hid a more general question of the choice between centralist and decentralist policy in the sphere of national relations. Generals and Social Democrats, literary workers and top-ranking officials were taking part in sharp debates in the press and in literary and scholarly publications. In fact, this was a reflection of the gradual and general sharpening of international relations in Europe at the end of the nineteenth and the beginning of the twentieth century, leading eventually to the great international armed conflict, World War I, which had incalculable consequences.

The statesmen and public at large of the two states had been watching their neighbors' activities attentively. As Vladimir I. Friedson has shown, Russia utilized the experience of the Habsburgs in developing their military border by building up its own military settlements.[1] The idea of autonomy for Croatia perhaps went back somehow to that of Finland. In 1905-07 the leaders of national movements and the public in general were actively interested in developments in Russia. Russia, in its turn, tried to learn a lesson from the results of the 1848-49 revolution and to transfer to Russian soil the mechanism for settling disputes among the nationalities.

In Austria-Hungary the problem of autonomy was most closely interwoven with the general principles of national-state structure, with the problem of the very existence of the Monarchy as a united multinational state. Any change in the status, rights, or competence of Croatia's and Slavonia's autonomy would inevitably break the delicate balance of forces and interests established in the dualistic system of 1867-68. The position of Finland was different. It was situated on the outskirts of Russia and initially, since 1809, had possessed broad autonomy. The change of its status, even its separation, would not have affected the principles of the Russian centralist state. But the question of Finland's autonomy had great military-strategic and political-psychological importance for the Empire as a whole.

If we consider the problem of autonomy as an internal problem of a multinational state, then it is necessary to analyze it as a form of political self-determination of an ethnic community in the transition period from a medieval society to an industrial one. It is important to estimate which of the tendencies inherent in this process prevails at a given historic moment; to observe whether there is a tendency toward the preservation or disintegration of a state; to discover the balance of political centrifugal and centripetal tendencies, as well as of intra- and interethnic integration processes; and finally, to consider possibilities of alternative development. The transformation of autonomy based on a feudal political-territorial principle into national-political territorial autonomy in the course of developing ethnic communities leads to the change of the very principle of autonomy, which is then interpreted as specific national statehood within the framework of a united multinational state. It inevitably leads to a clash with the concepts of all-Empire state ideas and laws, and raises the question of political self-determination for the ethnic community that was playing a part in state formation.

If autonomy was considered earlier as a guarantee of an intact multinational state, whether because of military-strategic considerations as in Finland, or as a method of maintaining balance in the complex multinational political structure, or as a concession to a national movement as in Croatia and Slavonia, then along with strengthening the process of political self-determination of peoples not enjoying full rights, autonomy becomes a disintegrating factor in the view of the central authorities. The authorities face a dilemma—to preserve or not to preserve the safety of a state. And if to preserve it, then in what way: by centralist measures or decentralization of a national-state structure, by federalization, confederalization, or raising the status of autonomy? Peoples not enjoying full rights have another option: to remain or not to remain within a multinational state, to agree or to refuse to have sovereignty and statehood curtailed in any case. They must decide how to build relations with national minorities within the framework of autonomy including the minorities of a state-forming nation throughout the Empire. It is here that questions are asked and replies to them are still being sought: Can an ethnic community be the subject of state law? How can one combine general democratic principles and the rights of national minorities?

If we are asked to consider the problems of autonomy from the point of view of the appearance and development of historical-geographic regions, then we can avoid making national and state peculiarities absolute. We regard this as being even more justifiable in the given case, since multinational states, at the frontiers of which autonomies emerged, covered almost entire historic-geographic regions. Each of them was a specific world within its own state traditions and international relations, religious and political psychology. Finland was born at the frontiers of Russia, which possessed Eastern Europe, and of Sweden, which embraced Northern Europe. Croatia, Slavonia, and also a territory that was under the national-church autonomy of the Serbs, were situated at the frontier of Austria-Hungary, a powerful Central European state that was gradually losing its might and influence in Southeastern Europe, and of the Ottoman Empire. The frontiers of these countries and regions coincided to a great extent with the borders of spreading Christian religions (Orthodox, Lutheran, and Catholic) as well as Islam.

The autonomous status of Croatia and Slavonia fixed in the 1868 Hungarian-Croatian agreement was based on the historic law of a Croatian medieval state that existed in the tenth and eleventh centuries. Later on, Croatia voluntarily, though under the threat of external danger, recognized by the decision of the Sobor the power of Hungarian kings in 1102, and in 1526 recognized the power of Ferdinand Habsburg. It was confirmed by the Croatian Pragmatic Sanction of 1712.[2]

In 1868 a state community composed of Hungary and the kingdoms of Dalmatia, Croatia, and Slavonia was proclaimed. Emperor Franz Joseph was at the same time crowned as Hungarian and Croatian King, and he held the title of King of Croatia. But Croatia and Slavonia were granted autonomy within the framework of the Kingdom of Hungary while Dalmatia found itself in the Austrian part of the Monarchy and was granted the status of a common province. Thus, the ethnic territories of the Croatians and the Serbs within the Monarchy and the territory of the Tribune Kingdom recognized intact by law turned out to be split between two parts of the dualist state, each of them being a parliamentary monarchy with its sovereignty and statehood. They were united in the person of the monarch. There was nothing like all-Empire law in Austria-Hungary. The Hungarian-Croatian Agreement, a kind of basic law of Croatia, was at the same time Article XXX of the Code of Hungarian Law.[3]

According to the Hungarian-Croatian Agreement, Croatia and Slavonia were granted "political autonomy" within the composition of the Kingdom of Hungary, and its population (regardless of ethnic origin) was granted the status of "a political nation." Croatia and Slavonia were granted legislative authority and power in all the affairs of home policy, religion, and justice. According to the Agreement, its territory, bodies of executive power, its representative organ, the Sobor, and also the flag, the coat of arms, and the anthem were considered its attributes. There existed three departments in the autonomous government: home affairs, education and religion, and justice. The establishment of the department of religion and church in the government gave the Catholic religion, which was practiced by the overwhelming majority of Croatians, the significance of being a state religion. The establishment of this department also turned religion into an ethnodifferentiating feature in the public mind, since the name of the autonomy coincided with the ethnonym of the Croatians and with the name of their medieval state. In 1913 the department of "national economy" was added.[4]

The head of the executive power was the ban, who was neither formally nor juridically subjected to the Sobor but was appointed by the Emperor on the recommendation of the chairman of the "common" Council of Ministers in Budapest. In fact, the ban was not accountable to the Sobor, and his appointment was not in any way connected with the results of elections. The office holder was deprived of any military powers, a point that was stipulated specially. Thus Croatian national units were not part of the Reichswehr and Honvéd.

Clerks and officials for both the bodies of the "common" departments on the territory of Croatia and for autonomous ones proper were recruited in accordance with the Agreement of 1868, that is, "from the citizens of the Kingdom of Dalmatia, Croatia, and Slavonia."

The Sobor was gradually losing its estate nature, but the Croatian aristocracy preserved in it its right to personal representation alongside the elected deputies. Property, educational, and age qualifications were characteristic features of the electoral system. Before the 1910 reform, only 2 percent of the population enjoyed the right to vote, and after it was put into effect this rose to 6 percent. The increase in the number of people enjoying the right to vote did not result in a diminution of the political role of Serbian parties that represented the minority of the population. After 1887 there were eighty-eight constituencies and, accordingly, elected deputies. The number of deputies from each nationality living on the territory of Croatia and Slavonia was neither legislatively nor administratively fixed. The established ratio of Croatian and Serbian deputies in the Sobor of three to one roughly corresponded to the ratio of the Croatian to the Serbian population in the autonomous territory.[5]

The Croatian language was considered an official language in the legislative as well as judicial spheres. According to law, Croatian representatives could use their language both in the "common" Parliament of Hungary in Budapest and in their activities as members of the Hungarian delegation at the talks with the Austrian delegation. Forty-four representatives of Croatia, elected by the Sobor from its members, sat in the "common" Parliament of Hungary. Direct elections to the all-state Parliament were not conducted on the territory of Croatia. By the Agreement of 1868, Croatia was provided with the presence of four elected deputies of the Sobor and one representative of the aristocracy in the Hungarian delegation. But neither the Sobor, nor its delegation in the common Parliament, nor its five representatives in the delegation were regarded as a national-political representation having the right to its own opinion. The decisions of the autonomous Sobor had to be confirmed by the Emperor, the King of Croatia. The members of the Croatian delegation in Parliament were obliged by law to "discuss and settle all the matters considered as common absolutely independently and without any instruction like all other members of Parliament."[6] The right to speak their native language was of no real, practical advantage because this language was unknown to and hated by the overwhelming majority of the other deputies. The fact that the Hungarian language was not known (and the Croatians refused on principle to learn it) led to dramatic and comical cases when after speaking unanimously against a bill they suddenly voted for it.

As for executive bodies, the interests of Croatia were supposed to be represented by the minister without portfolio in the common Parliament; this person had no responsibility before the autonomous bodies but was responsible to the "common" Parliament as were all the members of the Cabinet. In addition, there existed "Croatian sections" in the four ministries of the common Hungarian government: finance, trade and industry, agriculture, and public works.

Unlike the Croatian situation, Russia got Finland as a result of its victory in the 1808-9 war with Sweden. According to the Peace of Fredrickshamm, it was established that "these areas ... from now on will be the property and possession of the Russian Empire," and the Russian Emperor would have the title of "Grand Duke of Finland." The Manifesto of Alexander I determined the status and laws of the newly born Grand Duchy. It "confirmed and certified the religion, basic laws, and rights and privileges which every estate of this duchy in particular and all the subjects inhabiting it so far enjoyed and promised to keep them in unbreakable and obligatory effect and strength." By the "basic laws" the Emperor is thought to have meant Swedish legal acts, such as the 1772 form of government resolution and the 1789 act of union and security, though they were not mentioned specifically anywhere.[7] [Thus Finland, which had never had its own state law, and the Finns, who did not have their own state, received special status within the Russian Empire thanks to the preservation of the existing laws of the Swedish centralized state, which had never granted Finland special status.] Laws functioning in the former state formations retained their legal force in both states. And, de facto, they also remained in historic consciousness one of the most important elements of national self-consciousness.

In 1809 Finnish "nobility and knights" swore an oath of loyalty during the Lantdag (the four-estate representational body) in Borgå Porvoo.[8] Since there was no nobility of Finnish origin (as opposed to Croatian), the upper classes of Finnish society were Swedes by nationality. And their dominant position was preserved in many cases in the life of the Grand Duchy many years later. (According to the 1890 census, the Finns accounted for 85 percent of the population while the Swedes comprised 13.5 percent of the population of the autonomous region.)[9]

In 1809 a government senate was established to rule the Grand Duchy, and in 1816 it was renamed the Imperial Finnish Senate. In 1826 the post of State Secretary of Finnish Affairs was created. In 1809 it was determined that no change in Finland's basic laws could be made without the consent of the Lantdag. The leading role in the Lantdag was played by the representatives of Swedish nationality, since they made up the majority of the nobility and the urban population. Up to 1863 the Imperial government ruled Finland without convening the Lantdag, though it took care not to violate formally existing laws by its decrees and resolutions. In 1869 the Lantdag Charter was adopted, according to which the Lantdag was to be convened once every five years. In 1882 this term was shortened to three years. In 1886 the Lantdag was given the right of legislative initiative. According to the estimates of General M. M. Borodkin, in the 1890s, 30 percent of the population in Finland enjoyed the right to vote. Of this, approximately two-sevenths were rural (mainly Finnish) and one-third were urban (basically Swedish).[10] The Grand Duchy was directly ruled by a Governor-General appointed by the Emperor.

The meaning and status of Finland's autonomy changed in the course of the little more than one hundred years during which this territory was part of Russia. This differentiates the experience of Finland from that of Croatia, whose juridical position changed little from 1868 to 1918. In 1808, according to the adopted "Provision of Establishing Government," all matters were to be discussed in "the language currently used," which was Swedish. From the very beginning, the Russian language was excluded from state and public life of the Grand Duchy. In 1863 the Finnish Lantdag made a decision that Russian was not a compulsory subject in the schools.

Petersburg decided in 1900 to introduce the Russian language every-where, including the Senate, as one of its main steps toward Russification. In 1903, in order "to mobilize greater preparedness," the Russian language was introduced in the Finnish railway system.[11] It is worth noting here that in 1907 the Hungarian Parliament under the Vekerle government adopted the so-called railways pragmatics, which, among other things, required that railway workers and officials in the territory of Croatia know the Hungarian language; this was in direct violation of the Agreement of 1868.[12] These two laws were later annulled, both in Russia and in Hungary.

One language problem is closely connected with the question of the right of natives of Russia to serve in Finland. Since 1903 Russians were allowed to work as state civil servants, and they were given the right to buy immovable property.

Acts similar to those that limited rights adopted earlier by Finland were passed by central authorities in other regions too. In 1809, the Manifesto on Finnish Troops was adopted, and it preserved the situation existing in Finland under Swedish rule. The Manifesto was later continued and in 1878 the rules of military service were issued in accordance with which Finnish troops were organized to "defend the throne and the Motherland." Only citizens of Finland could serve in Finnish regiments, and they took a special oath of loyalty to their Motherland. In 1883 the first Finnish battalions were organized. Later a cavalry unit was also formed. From 1901 to 1904, measures were taken to eliminate Finnish units, which were now regarded as a threat to the existence of a united army. Single, empirewide military rules were introduced in the Empire though they were later canceled by the Manifesto of October 22 (November 4), 1905.

In 1880 Finland began to produce its own coin, a mark, which since 1877 had been "tied" to the French franc. Measures were taken to unite the money systems of the Empire and the Grand Duchy in 1904. In keeping with these measures, the gold ruble was to be circulated in the territory of Finland as a unit of payment equal to the gold mark, its rate of currency compared to the ruble being 2.66:1.[13] Early in the nineteenth century, sections of the Russian State Bank were being set up in Helsinki and other cities of Finland. Finland had its own customs system in trading with Russia and Western Europe.

As opposed to the Croatian lands, which were economically the most backward regions of the Empire, Finland gradually became a more advanced region compared to other parts of the Russian state. This, however, did not save it from the misfortune at the turn of the century that affected Croatia as well—mass economic emigration to the United States.

The sharp change of policy toward the autonomy of Finland could be seen earlier in the reign of Alexander III, and the Manifesto of 1891 solidified the change. Tendencies toward centralization in the policy of the Romanovs and the government in St. Petersburg were increasing. They reached their apex in 1899, when, for the first time, the Manifesto of Nicholas II contained the notion of all-state (all-Empire) legislation. Although the Manifesto confirmed that "the Grand Duchy of Finland, becoming part of the Russian Empire, enjoys . . . special institutions as regards its internal government and legislation which fit the living conditions of the country," the rights and powers of these institutions were drastically cut.[14] By issuing this Manifesto the Emperor gave himself the right to promulgate acts concerning Finland without the consent of the Lantdag. The Manifesto of 1899 was received with universal indignation in Finland, and the Lantdag declared this Manifesto void in the Grand Duchy.

Soon afterward, however, the Russian emperor released the 1905 Manifesto (October 17) in which he was forced to yield to the growing resistance of the population of Finland. Although the Manifesto referred to Finland only as "the Finland area," it canceled most of the centralist and Russifying measures adopted earlier.[15] The main result of the Manifesto was the creation of an electoral system for this autonomous region which was the most progressive of the contemporary electoral systems in Europe; it provided for direct election, general and equal suffrage, and the secret ballot. Women could also take part in elections. The new election law had not only an all-democratic character. Granting general suffrage drastically diminished the political influence of the Swedish minority.[16] There was a similar situation in Hungary, where the Hungarian national movement was fighting the introduction of general suffrage because of the fear of being in the minority during the elections. The Vienna government of General Fejérváry used the threat of introducing this suffrage in 1905 to blackmail the opposition.[17] The Croatian national movement also fought against general suffrage in Hungary because of the fear that it would undermine the special status of autonomous Croatia.

Despite gains, the government in St. Petersburg gradually returned to a centralist policy. Like their neighbors, the Habsburgs, the Romanovs saw centralist policy as the opportunity to retain the unity of the state as an empire. But in reality this kind of policy only strengthened centrifugal disintegration tendencies. A manifesto regarding all-state legislation was issued in 1910, and a program to liquidate autonomy was worked out. In 1912 the first all-Empire act of equal rights for Russia and Finland was promulgated. These measures were characterized in newspapers published by the Serbs of Austria-Hungary as the end of Finland's autonomy.

The periods of encouragement for broader autonomy followed by attempts to strangle and to eliminate it are surprisingly similar and almost contemporaneous in the policies of both countries. From 1881 to 1903, the regime of personal power of Ban Count Khuen-Hédérváry was established. After the Count retired, the ban was T. Pejačević, who was forced to lead a government formed largely under the influence of the opposition, which won the 1906 elections.

After a compromise was made between Austria and Hungary, the necessity of such compromises disappeared, and the "soft ban" was first replaced by A. Rákóczy and then by P. Rauch. They ruled Croatia with the dissolved Sobor. In 1910 N. Tomasic became ban, and during this period the election law underwent a limited reform. But a "hard-line" time came again when S. Žuvai and then D. Onkelkhauser became ban and later "the King's Commissar." Žuvai, as well as I. Škerlec, the last ban before the beginning of the war, were the targets of an abortive assault by the nationalists, who were supporters of terrorist methods of struggle.

Tsar Nicholas II needed as governor-general N. P. Bobrikov who, since 1897, had been zealously conducting a policy of doing away with autonomy. After he was killed by a terrorist in 1904, several other persons such as I. Obolensky, N. N. Gerard, and General Beckman and General Geizen were appointed Governors-General. They all had to take into consideration the growing national movement and to make compromises, since they realized that the central government had neither the strength nor the possibility to pursue a hard-line policy in Finland.

The position of the national minorities, the Serbs in Croatia-Slavonia, and the Swedes in Finland, is of special interest. The national-ecclesiastical autonomy of the Serbian population was something like a remainder of once broad privileges received by it in the seventeenth and eighteenth centuries. The basis of "Serbian historical rights" as interpreted by those involved in the national movement was that "top privileges" were granted by several legal acts. The laws of 1790-91, which were promulgated by the State Assembly of Hungary, granted Serbs civil rights and limited their advantages in the spheres of school education and funds. The 1848 law guaranteed equal rights in religion, and the law of 1868 dealt with nationalities and autonomy. The last legal act that determined the rights, functions, and powers of national ecclesiastical autonomy put an end to its political importance from the juridical point of view. This autonomy embracing both the territory of South Hungary proper (Bachki and Banat) and Croatia and Slavonia had some important elements of national statehood—the patriarchal council and a national-ecclesiastical Sobor elected in seven dioceses and having seventy-five deputies.

The jurisdiction of the autonomous bodies officially and juridically was limited to the problems of education and religion. They could not deal with the spheres of economy and finance. All the decisions of the Sobor as well as the results of the elections of patriarch and bishops were supposed to be confirmed by the Emperor, who was officially considered to be the head of the national-ecclesiastical autonomy. The law on autonomy, though formally granting the Serbs special status, in fact limited their civil rights and made their interests clash with the interests of other non-Hungarian peoples, first and foremost the Romanians and the Slovaks. National-ecclesiastical autonomy denied the political sovereignty of the Serbs and underlined their ethnic-cultural individuality.[18]

The law on nationalities (which was passed after the law on autonomy) stated that "since all the citizens of Hungary in a political way make up one, indivisible, united Magyar nation, then its citizens enjoying equal rights are all the citizens of the Motherland no matter what nationality they are."[19] The law formally guaranteed freedom to use national languages in the low and middle administrative levels, and in village and district courts, and it also obliged educational bodies to see to it that citizens of any nationality living as a compact group received education in state institutions in their native language. However, since the second half of the 1870s a policy of expanding Magyarization had been launched. In 1887, the Sobor, under pressure from Budapest, passed a resolution to hand all matters dealing with national-ecclesiastical autonomy in Croatia and Slavonia to the "common" government. This not only limited the rights of the Serbian population but was a direct violation of the Agreement of 1868.[20] In 1912, national-ecclesiastical autonomy was virtually abolished by order of the Emperor.

The remaining Swedish population in Finland had occupied part of the coastline of Finland since the time of Swedish kings. This concentration of the Swedish population differed from that of the Serbian population in Croatia, which was living practically throughout the entire territory. Also different from the Serbs, the Swedes did not have any special status, though in many cases they had a dominant position. The Swedish nobility and citizens played a leading role in the political and spiritual life of the country, while the Finns were represented mainly in the village population. There was no such confrontation between the Serbs and the Croatians, though there was no Serbian nobility in Croatia. In addition, conflict between the urban population and village dwellers did not occur.

The Croatians and Serbs were ethnically related peoples, the Finns and Swedes were not. The Croatians and Serbs had many elements of language, culture, and territory in common. By law, however, the Croatian language was the official language in Croatia. Besides, the Croatians were Catholics whereas the Serbs were Orthodox Christians. The Swedes and Finns had little in common as ethnic or linguistic communities. The Finnish language belongs to the Finno-Ugric language group, but the Swedish language belongs to the German group of languages. The Swedes and Finns, however, were united by one political tradition, by the same rights, and by the same religion, Lutheranism.[21]

It is interesting to analyze the evolution of policies toward minorities that were carried out by the authorities in autonomous areas. During his rule Ban Count Khuen-Hédérváry fought against the national Croatian movement and often turned to the Serbian population for support. This, together with the growth of movements for self-determination, exacerbated the conflicts between the national groups. His adherents followed a more even-handed political course, which, however, on the eve of the annexation of Bosnia and Herzegovina and during the crisis of the Balkan Wars, gradually acquired an openly anti-Serbian slant. It became typical of the ruling circles to accuse the Serbs of treason. A similar, though also different, evolution could be observed in Finland. In the middle and the second quarter of the nineteenth century, the Russian government supported the national and cultural demands of the Finnish population, which was seeking equal rights with the Swedes, who traditionally dominated political and spiritual life.

In 1863 the Finnish and Swedish languages were declared to be equal, and in 1886 the Finnish language was introduced in primary schools. But later, within the framework of increased common centralist and Russifying tendencies in the policies of St. Petersburg, and in connection with the growth of the Finnish national movement, central authorities gave up the support of cultural and political demands of that movement, blaming it for its cooperation with the Swedes who were striving to harm the security of Russia and to return Finland to Sweden.

The principles of historic state law, natural law, and the idea of a nation as an ethnic and social community were interconnected with the programs of the national movements. Gradually the medieval concept of a nation as a political community was replaced by the idea of a nation as the totality of a people having a common origin, language, culture, self-consciousness, character, way of life and thinking, and historical destinies.

Political parties were forming simultaneously in Croatia and Finland. Practically all parties in Finland emerged in 1906 except for the Social

Democrats and Old Finns. In Croatia this process lasted a bit longer, from 1905 to 1910, and the balance of ideological-political forces, which often did not coincide with the social and national structure of society, became clear. Similar types of parties existed in both autonomies. The national conservative movement was represented by the National party and the Old Finns.[22] The national-liberal party wing was made up of the main parties of the Croatian-Serbian coalition, the Croatian Rights party, the Croatian People's Party of Progress (united in 1910), and the Serbian National Party of Independence. This party, like the Swedish People's party, was the main political representative of the national minorities.[23] There appeared also parties of Christian-Social orientation, such as the Catholic parties in Croatia (Croatian Workers party, Croatian Christian-Social Rights party) and Lutheran parties in Finland (Christian Workers Union of Finland).[24] The Croatian Christian-Social parties were based on the national-radical positions of pan-Croationism. The Serbian National party could be considered to a certain degree to be their analogue and antipode.[25]

Social Democrats became constitutional much earlier than the rest of the parties in both autonomous regions, in 1894 in Croatia and in 1899 in Finland. These parties were independent of the larger Social Democratic parties in Russia, Hungary, and Austria.[26] The peasant parties were the Party of the Brothers, (of A. and St. Radić), the Croatian People's Peasant party, and the Finland Agrarian Union.[27]

The parties of all orientations in both autonomous regions put forward similar demands for general and equal suffrage with the secret ballot, as well as for freedom of the press, speech, association, and assembly. National-political demands differed not only because of the peculiarities of the positions of each region, but also because of the status and interests of each of the four nationalities and the layers making up the social foundation of every party.[28]

The national-liberal forces of both regions created Croatian-Serbian and Finnish-Swedish political blocs respectively. This was demonstrated by the formation of a united body, the Croatian-Serbian coalition, the only such example in all of Austria-Hungary.[29] The parties in Finland—Young Finnish and Swedish Peoples—retained complete political independence from each other, but they set up "the bloc of constitutionalists." Both blocs at practically the same time in 1905 entered the political arena, and their first steps were successful enough. But if the coalition had a common program and preserved the programs of separate parties, the constitutional bloc did not have such a program. Initially the coalition united many parties, but gradually it became the union of only two parties—the Croatian and Serbian parties, just like the bloc.

Almost none of the parties had a program for seceding from the multinational state and creating an independent national country. The parties in Finland mainly dealt with improving the constitution. The liberals were for an entirely new constitution, and the conservatives were for keeping old laws and also for the abolition of all laws and resolutions made after 1895. Their program lacked the term "national self-determination." The parties in Croatia had similar demands. They fought for the abolition of laws and resolutions that weakened Croatia's autonomy.

Croatian and Serbian liberals underlined the right of nations to self-determination and considered that it could be realized within the framework of the existing state by conducting political and social reforms. Since the South Slav question was closely connected with the problem of reforming the whole country, they put forward their own draft reform. In 1905-7, the Coalition supported the Hungarian national movement, and it hoped to gain broader autonomy for Croatia if the movement won in its fight with the dynasty for broader common rights for Hungary. Later, after the annexation of Bosnia and Herzegovina, hopes for the support of the Hungarians were lost because they became less tolerant of non-Magyar nationalities.

The political parties of Finland did not present nationwide plans for transformation. They were only striving to widen the spheres of authority and the rights of the autonomous region. At the same time the conservatives, the Old Finns, understood that only the liberation movement in Russia had brought freedom to the people of Finland.[30] Even the most radical draft plans, such as the Tammerfors Manifesto, which reflected the point of view of the left Social Democrats and which contained the demand to create a provisional government and convene the National Assembly instead of the Lantdag, did not exclude the possibility of maintaining unity with Russia if reforms were enacted.

The main points of polemics that took place in national movements concerning the character of documents determining the status of autonomous regions were similar. The Finnish national movement supported by the Swedish movement took the position that the Borgå Lantdag represented the agreement of the two states, that Finland was not a province of the Russian Empire; it had its own statehood. This position was met with indignation in St. Petersburg.[31]

The Croatian national movement also described the 1868 Agreement as the union of two equal political entities. But if the liberals thought that Croatian statehood was not lost, the radical movement confirmed the opposite and demanded the creation of a Greater Croatia. Naturally, the very question of a union with equal rights was not acceptable to Hungary in 1868.

The orientation of other demands of the national movements in Finland and Croatia was almost the same. They called for wider rights for autonomous representative institutions in running the economy, first of all, and a solution to the problem of taxes and finance. Since Croatia had no customs system of its own, the creation of one was actively discussed. One of the leading parties of the Coalition, the Croatian Rights party, spoke against establishing a customs union between Austria and Hungary, but declared that it could agree to the creation of one in Croatia if Dalmatia were added to it and if Croatia, Slavonia, and Dalmatia were legally committed to common economic aims.

Since there had been no national military units in Croatia, the Croatian opposition, like the Hungarian one, demanded their creation and deployment on their own territory (as part of the Reichswehr naturally).

But Croatian-Serbian and Finnish-Swedish relations differed greatly. The Serbs in Croatia fought for their recognition as practically a second "political nation" and sought the preservation of those privileges that had been granted to them within the framework of national-ecclesiastical autonomy. The temporary way out of the situation, which constantly posed threats of intranational conflicts, was found in the concept of a "united nation" that was used by the Croatian-Serbian coalition. According to this concept the Croatians and Serbs formed one nation, and therefore the Serbs could enjoy the same rights as the Croatians did. In fact, however, it was different because this theory virtually denied the existence of the Serbian nation in Croatia. The fact that there was a difference in the national-political status of the two nationalities, that in keeping with the traditions of the Habsburg Monarchy they were subject differently to state law, constantly confronted them. Croatian politicians wanted to attach to "political autonomy" an ethnic character and to turn it in the full sense of the word into national-political autonomy for their nation. Serbian politicians wanted to turn this ethnic-confessional autonomy into a political one.

The nature of relations between the Swedes and Finns was different. The Swedish People's party did not intend to grant the Swedish population its own political-legal status. The basic problem in their relations was language, since Swedish had for a long time been dominant in culture and education. The programs of the Finnish and Swedish People's parties in many cases coincided. Their main idea was to ensure full equal rights to the two languages and to ensure the language rights of the minority. On the whole, each of the parties tried to solve these problems by proceeding from universal democratic principles and not from the rights of its own nation. The relations between the Finns and Swedes did not have the character of a struggle between two peoples, as was the situation in Croatia. However, both the Serbian and Swedish liberals entered the coalition with the Croatian and Finnish liberals and declared their recognition of the aims of the Croatian and Finnish national movements, respectively.

An essential element of ethnic self-consciousness is the awareness of belonging to a family of other peoples related to one's own nation. These sentiments and theories are manifested with greater force by peoples in multinational states when they do not enjoy full rights and when the processes of political self-consciousness and self-determination came late. The dreams of having its own "great" state which would embrace the maximum possible territory and hopes of obtaining the dominant position for its own national culture in this state were psychological reactions to many centuries of being forced into an inferior position. Respective concepts were based on the well-known adage of that period that the communities of society, state, and nation were based on the idea of coincidence of state frontiers and ethnic territories.

"Pan" ideology has its roots in the imperfect development of a given ethnic community and its incompatibility with its legal status both within the autonomous regions and the entire multinational state. With regard to other nations, pan ideology inevitably reproduces the pattern of the existing multinational state. Pan ideology in Croatia proceeded in all its versions from the principles of historic state law, the political traditions of the Habsburg Monarchy, and the concept of a "united Croatian nation" which was similar to the idea of the "united Hungarian political nation." Pan-Finnish ideology, which began to spread at the beginning of the twentieth century especially in Karelia, replicated the Swedish and Russian traditions of ethnocentrism and political centralism. If the South Slavs regarded a nation as "the source of all rights in a state,"[32] Russia had a different tradition: the position of the state stipulated the status of a nation. Thus peoples not having full equal rights inevitably developed a hostile attitude toward the state-forming nation.

The pan ideology of the Croatians and Serbs existed in several versions. At first it was Pan-Croatianism and Pan-Serbism. The former denied not only the rights of the Serbs but also the very fact of their existence in the territory of Croatia; the latter aimed at uniting the South Slavic peoples under the crown of Serbian kings. The second version of the pan ideology was South Slavism, the concept of national and political unity of the Croatians and Serbs (as it was interpreted by the Croatians) and the establishment of equal rights of two ethnic communities in the territory of Croatia and Slavonia (as it was interpreted by the Serbs). Both these concepts considered it desirable to join the South Slavs and Slovenians in a possible political formation. The third version was Austro-Slavism—an idea embracing all Slavic peoples of the Monarchy. It stipulated keeping intact its character during the process of transforming the national-state structure. The majority of members of national movements among the South Slavs favored the combination of the second and third versions, namely, the creation of a political formation of the South Slavs within the boundaries of the Monarchy. The ideas of common Slavic community and solidarity also played an important role. Their latest rise was connected not only with the internal situation in Austria-Hungary but also with sharper Slavic-German relations, with the formation of two opposing military blocs.

The Finns, like the Croatians and Serbs in Austria-Hungary, were not ethnically isolated in the Russian Empire. Their relatives included the Ests, Livs, Votyaks, and Mordovians.[33] The Karels represented some specific subethnos of the Finnish nation. The idea of collecting all these peoples under the leadership of the Finns in a united state with an ethnically related population arose in some political circles in Finland. But early in the twentieth century it did not have a substantial social base. In contrast, the idea of creating Great Croatia within Austria was quite widely supported.[34] Besides, the idea was spearheaded against Russia and the Russian people and was not at all aimed against the Swedish minority, the bearers of Finnish statehood.

Finnish politicians claimed Karelia (the Olonez gubernia in the Russian Empire) while Russian generals, in their turn, could not forgive Alexander I for giving the Vyborg gubernia as a concession to Finland. The Croatians and Serbs mainly claimed the uniting of their territories in accordance with the 1868 Agreement. The problems of Bosnia and Herzegovina, which Croatian chauvinists considered to be ethnically pure Croatian territory, stood separately. Chauvinist sentiments in Croatia were directed first of all against the Serbs and not against the ruling peoples. One of the main obstacles in Croatian-Serbian relations was the recognition by the Croatian side of political community with the Serbs while also recognizing their own ethnic individuality. At the same time those representing the South Slav orientation often used in reference to the Serbs and other Slavic peoples the descriptive word "brother," which was not used among the Finns with reference to related nations.

The different versions of pan ideology among the Finns and South Slavs were united by the desire to build a new multinational political formation, whether it was within the frontiers of existing states or beyond them. Being taken as the basis of state construction, all these concepts inevitably led to the denial of the rights of other nations, even those that were ethnically related, to sovereignty and national individuality; states built on this basis developed according to the same laws as other multinational states. Ethnocentric relations that could not lead to a weakening of contradictions were typical of all of them. They inevitably sharpened again and this time among ethnically related peoples. The pan-national ideological structures of the Croatians, the Serbs, and the Finns reflected the peculiarities of two worlds, Western European and Slavic Eastern European.

Although the South Slav question touched upon the very basis of the Habsburg Monarchy, Croatian and Serbian politicians did not plan to establish contacts with national movements of other countries. The only exception to this was during the short period of the "new political course" in its relations with Budapest, and at the time (1908) there was a widespread passion for neo-Slavist ideas. They aimed at preserving the status of Croatia legally with no revolutionary upheavals. At the same time the opinion in Finland was that it must become, if not the center of revolutionary movement in Russia, at least a force rendering considerable help to Russian revolutionaries.

The year 1906 proved to be one in which political parties in Russia were being formed, and these parties treated the question of integrity and transformation of the Empire in different ways.[35] Analyzing the political situation in Russia, they considered the experience of Austria-Hungary and clearly understood that in the regions with mixed populations existing types of autonomy did not solve the national problem but, on the contrary, might even sharpen it. They took as a particular example, Croatian-Serbian relations in Croatia. In addition, the constitutionalists presumed that if policies granting greater autonomy and federalization were to be carried out in Russia before a democratic constitution was granted and before guarantees of personal and public freedom were issued, then the population of the Empire would become split and the liberation movement in Russia would suffer the fate of a similar movement in Austria in 1848. Then national contradictions and ambitions of every nation to bring to the foreground their own demands led to the final victory of absolutism over the disintegrated public forces.[36]

The experience of Austria-Hungary was used by the central authorities in St. Petersburg as well as by Finland's representatives. They obviously took into account the status and experience of the related Hungarian nation to solve international political conflicts. In 1909 a Russian-Finnish commission was set up "to work out the draft rules of the order of promulgating all-state laws concerning Finland." The members of the commission representing Finland put forward a draft plan for setting up delegations that were to pattern the relations of Russia and Finland according to Austro-Hungarian norms. After the commission session naturally rejected these proposals, the situation in the common Parliament repeated itself, since the commission members from Finland, in keeping with the resolution of its creation, were allowed not to know the Russian language.[37] The possibility of historic alternatives in the development of Russia and Austria-Hungary was conditioned by four elements. First, there existed a social alternative in bourgeois-socialist development; second, there was a political or state alternative—to be a monarchy or a republic; third, there were ethnic-political alternatives—the preservation or disintegration of a united multinational state; and fourth, there was a national-state-centralist structure alternative—to be federative or confederative.

The disintegration of Austria-Hungary and the formation of several independent states did not bring a solution to the national question in Central Europe nearer, nor did it ensure the rights of nations to self-determination. This can also be said about the preservation of the biggest part of the national-territorial complex of the former Russian Empire.

As the analysis of the programs of various peoples' national movements in Russia and Austria-Hungary shows, the decentralist transformation of the multinational state, attaching to its separate parts any sort of autonomous status and thereby transforming the status into a federation, does not necessarily reflect a tendency to split the multinational state. But the question of whether ethnic community can be subject to state law remains unanswered even today.

One should seek to find the causes of stronger tendencies to disintegration of both empires in the marked changes in their situations immediately preceding and during World War I. Militarization inevitably led to the breach of normal economic, social, and political links, and centralization tendencies in the policies of the central authorities inevitably increased the resistance of the various peoples and old, dormant decentralist tendencies.

NOTES

1. Vladimir I. Friedson, "Vojna Kraina i voina naselia u Rusii," in *Voina Kraina. Poviesni pregled.— Historiografiia—Rasprave* (Zagreb, 1984).
2. *Vengersko-horvatskoe soglasheniie 1868 g.* (St. Petersburg, 1910); *Formirovaniie natsionalnikh nezavisimykh gosudarstv na Balkanakh (konec XVIII—70-e gody XIX v.)* (Moscow, 1985), 248-51; *Beuc I. Poviest instituciia drzvane Vlasti kralevine Hrvatske, Slavonije i Dalmacije* (Zagreb, 1985), 275-90.
3. *Istoriia Vengrii* (Moscow, 1972), 2:260.
4. M. Vladislavljevic, *Polož hrvata u Austro-Ugarskoj* (Belgrade, 1937), 39.

5. F. Supilo, *Politika u Hrvatskoj* (Zagreb, 1953), 113-14.
6. *Vengersko-horvatskoe soglasheniie*, 34.
7. M. M. Borodkin, *Finlaiandskaia okraina v sostave Rosiiskogo gosudarstva* (St. Petersburg, 1910), 7, 14-15; M. M. Borodkyn, *Finliandsky vopros v Rossii* (St. Petersburg, 1905), 18. *Akty dlia vyasnenyia politicheskogo polosheniia Velikogo knyashestva Finliandskogo* (St. Petersburg, 1908), 13.
8. Ibid., 21-22.
9. *Enciklopedicheskii slovar "Brokagauz i Efron,"* T. 70-71.
10. M. M. Borodkin, *Iz noveyschenii istorijii Finlajandii* (St. Petersburg, 1905), 183.
11. Ibid., 162.
12. M. Gross, *Vladavina hrvatsko-srpske koalcije, 1906-1907* (Belgrade, 1960), 178-202; *Istoria Vengriji* 2:415, 417.
13. M. M. Borodkin, *Iz noveyschenii istorjii Finliandii*, 165.
14. M. M. Borodkin, *Finliandskii vopros* (St. Petersburg, 1905), 28.
15. *Akty*, 181-82; M. M. Borodkin, *Finlaiandskaia okraina*, 90-95.
16. *Enciklopedicheskii slovar "Granat,"* 43:701-2.
17. *Istoriia Vengrii*, 2: 393-94.
18. *Srpska pravoslavna mitropolia karlovahk po podacima od g. 1905* (Sremsky Karlovci, 1910); *Tumach povlastica, zakona, uredava i drugih naredenja srpske narodne crkvene autonomije u Ugarskoj, Hrvatskoj i Slavoniji* (Novi Sad, 1897).
19. *Istoriia Vengrii*, 2: 262-63.
20. S. Sidak, M. Gross, I. Karaman, and D. Sepich, *Povijest hrvatskog naroda, 1860-1914* (Zagreb, 1968), 133.
21. *Enciklopedicheskii slovar "Brokgauz i Efron,"* 70:953-58.
22. I. Ibler, *Hrvatska politika. III. 1904-1906* (Zagreb, 1914/1917), 355-57, 481-92, 519-20; *Politicheskii partii v Finliandii* (St. Petersburg, 1909), 21-38.
23. *Program i organizacija hrvatske puchke napredne stranke* (Zagreb, 1906); *Program i pravilnik hrvatske stranke prava (chlanice koalicije)* (Zagreb, 1907); *Hrvatska ujedinjena samostalna stranka* (Zagreb, 1911); *Program srpske narodne samostalne stranke* (Zagreb, 1903); *Polititcheskie partii v Finliandii*, 41-43, 45-49.
24. *Politicheskii partii v Finliandii*, 85-87; *Program hrvatske krshc.- soc.stranke prava. U Zagrebu, 1906*; *Program Hrvatske radnichke stranke u Zagrebu* (Zagreb, 1906).
25. *Starchevicheva hrvatska stranka prava* (Zagreb, 1907); *Khjizica za chlanove srpske narodne radikalne stranke* (U Novome Sadu, 1907).
26. *Istoriski archiv Komunistichke partiie Iugoslavie* (Belgrade, 1950), 4:56-58; *Politicheskii partii v Finliandii*, 62-83.
27. A. Radich, *Sabrana djela*, T. VII (Zagreb, 1936); *Politicheskii partii v Finliandii*, 98-102.

28. The author intends to give a detailed comparative analysis of the programs of different types of political parties in Finland and Croatia in a forthcoming article.
29. I. Ibler, *Hrvaska Politika*, pp. 372-73, 389-90, 465-69.
30. *Politicheskii partii v Finliandii*, 18.
31. G. Abov [M.M. Borodkin], *Iz istorii uchenii finliandskogo gosudarstvennogo prava* (St. Petersburg, 1895).
32. *Program i organizacija hrvatske puche napredne stranke*, 3.
33. *Panfinskaia propaganda* (St. Petersburg, 1906).
34. *Starchevichesa stranka prava* (Zagreb, 1907).
35. *Sbornyk program v politicheskyh parti v Rossii* (St. Petersburg, 1906), 1:18-19, 27-28; 3:21 -22.
36. *Sbornik programm*, 3:75, 64, 65.
37. M. M. Borodkin, *Finliandskaia okraina v sostave Rosiiskogo gosudarstva*, 110-11.

8

From Empire to Empire: Russian versus Asian Revolutionaries, 1917 - 1920

Henryk Szlajfer

It is my intention in this chapter to point out certain aspects of relations between Russian and Asian revolutionaries at the time of the revolution and the civil war of the years 1917-20. I want to concentrate on the conflicts that took place in connection with the reincorporation of Central Asia into the Russian state. These were diffused conflicts that concerned the main political and social goals of the revolutionary changes, and the role of the Asians in the revolutionary process as such; these were national conflicts that were disintegrating the old tsarist empire, and social conflicts that favored the policy of reintegration of the old empire around the new center of power. Last but not least, these were conflicts about the limits of national autonomy within the framework of the new empire. Each of these conflicts separately, and all of them together, had an impact on the ultimate form of this empire. My hypothesis is that although the establishment of the Soviet Union put a damper on the Asians' aspirations for independence, and especially on the concept of a multiethnic Asian community based on Islam and Revolution, nonetheless, the strong Asian resistance forced the Russian Bolsheviks to revise fundamentally their original concept of the "nationalities policy" (first of all, the concept of the legal and administrative structure of the revolutionary empire).

Disregarding its largely fictitious character, federalism was the Asians' bitter victory of a kind. From the present-day point of view, the federal structure of the Soviet Union and the related policy of the territorial concentration of nationalities constitute a peculiar Achilles' heel in the Soviet state system. It is worth remembering here that more than thirty-five years ago, the young historian Richard Pipes gave particular emphasis to precisely this aspect of Russo-Asian relations when he wrote: "From the point of view of self-rule the Communist government was even less generous to the minorities than its tsarist predecessor has been. . . . On the other hand, by granting the minorities extensive linguistic autonomy and by placing the national-territorial principle at the base of the state's political administration, the Communists gave constitutional recognition to the multinational structure of the Soviet population. . . . this purely formal feature of the Soviet Constitution may well prove to have been historically one of the most consequential aspects of the formation of the Soviet Union."[1]

THREE REVOLUTIONS AND THE QUESTION OF INCORPORATION

Analyzed in terms of the seizure of power in October 1917, the Russian revolution appears primarily as a great *journée revolutionnaire*—an urban and European one. Yet that same revolution, seen as a process encompassing not only October, but also the civil war, appears as a complex combination of three types of revolutionary change: urban-cum-proletarian, peasant, and national-cum-anticolonial. Superimposed on this combination to an increasing degree is the process whereby the new state was created and institutionalized.

During the destruction of the old order, this state-building aspect of the revolution is not yet so explicit, especially in the sphere of foreign relations. The transition to the phase of constructing the new state order takes place gradually; this is by no means a single act involving an immediate break with internationalism, seen as the firm desire for a revolution that goes beyond the bounds of nation and state. This would in any case be impossible, given the dominant ideology, the prevalent demagogy, and—most important—the pragmatic requirement that political action be undertaken to protect the new order, including action based on the propagation of revolutionary fervor.[2]

The process of "étatizing" the *journée revolutionnaire* produced parallel contradictions within the former Russian Empire. The strength these contradictions acquired and the form they assumed varied, however, in different areas of public life and in particular regions. This uneven development was rooted in the uneven pace of the three types of revolutionary change mentioned earlier. While the central Russian part of the old empire was beginning to institutionalize the new order, the old order was still being demolished in the Euro-Asian part and the Asiatic hinterland; moreover, in the latter regions, this process was taking place alongside foreign intervention and attempts to reinstitute the old power apparatus, or in some cases even attempts to establish independent non-Communist states.

This had a direct effect on the process of incorporating the hinterland within the new state. The uneven development of the "regional" revolutions was expressed in a phenomenon that at first glance appears truly astonishing: the political (and even ideological) coexistence of Marxism, in its Communist version, with revolutionary anticolonial nationalism of frequently explicit religious form. Particularly before the introduction of War Communism and the policy of *Kombieds*,[3] and subsequently also during the New Economic Policy (NEP), this phenomenon expressed itself in the coexistence of Russian communism and traditional forms of agriculture in large parts of the hinterland; in a limited instrumentalization of conflicts in the countryside and the associated expropriations; and in the relative tolerance shown toward Islam.

Consequently, in certain sections of the hinterland the Russian urban-cum-proletarian revolution was seen as a promise of national and social rebirth, as a positive factor in the struggle against the traditional representatives of "the one and indivisible Russia." Recollecting the situation in the Caucasus, the Bolshevik leader Anastas Mikoyan notes that "in the years of the Civil War, the Daghestani Bolsheviks frequently made use of active militants from the Pan-Islamic movement to support them in their struggle."[4] In a similar vein, the Tatar revolutionary Mir Said Sultan Galiyev wrote in 1921: "In the ranks of the Red Army of the Caucasus are found shariy'at squadrons and units."[5] Describing the situation among the Volga (Kazan) Tatars, Sultan Galiyev stresses that a group of "Red *mullahs*," linked to the movement for Islamic religious reform (*jadids*), had appeared on the side of the Bolsheviks.[6] Finally, let us note the example of the fanatically puritan group of Kazan Tatars that called themselves "God's Regiment of Vaisov" and that supported the Bolsheviks.[7] An Islamic historian slightly exaggerates in thus generalizing these tendencies: "The majority of the Muslims in Russia, especially the intellectuals, believed in the religious and national freedom promised by the Bolsheviks, and started to support the Soviet regime."[8]

This coexistence and collaboration was of course limited in nature. What was still implied was the principle of incorporation within a Russian state, albeit accompanied by a restriction of certain symbolic features of the domination of European Russia. When this basic principle was challenged, force sooner or later became necessary and the previous peaceful coexistence came to an end. The right to secede from the former empire, proclaimed in the Declaration of Rights of the Nations of Russia on November 15, 1917, and reaffirmed on December 3 that year in the appeal "To All Toiling Muslims of Russia and the East," was treated in "dialectical" fashion, in accordance with Lenin's interpretation that this right was comparable to the right to civil divorce. In extreme circumstances a "divorce" may perhaps be granted, but this does not mean it should be encouraged.[9]

In the Asiatic hinterland factual incorporation as a basic tenet of state building was applied with rigorous consistency; this is attested to by the brief histories of the independent states of the Caucasus and Central Asia, and also by the fierce struggle for the Ukraine at Russia's European borderlands. Where diplomatic and military constraints led to the acceptance of the creation of formally sovereign states, this was regarded as an interim concession, as can be seen in the examples of the Republic of the Far East, a buffer state set up in 1920 and reincorporated into Russia in November 1922, or the republics of Khiva and Bukhara.[10] This does not of course mean that excessive emphasis was placed on the principle of integration during the phase when the old order was being destroyed; on the contrary, fierce battles were fought to moderate this principle and highlight the right to national autonomy. The national renaissance of the Asiatic peoples was at this time of prime importance in waging a succesful struggle against the Whites. Any opportunities to gain these peoples' support on the main fronts of the war were utilized to the maximum.

This explains why in the first period of the civil war (up to the Eighth Congress of the Russian Communist party [RCP]), the Russian center of the revolution did not object to the creation of relatively autonomous national Communist parties (e.g., a Muslim one). The establishment of the Bashkir Autonomous Soviet Socialist Republic was one of the concessions that persuaded Ahmed Zeki Validov-Togan's Bashkir regiments to break with Kolchak.[11] The mobilizing value and propaganda attraction of the slogan of "self-determination" were enhanced by the fact that in the years 1918-20 the Asiatic hinterland was in practice either cut off from the Russian center of the revolution or occupied by the Whites and armies of the Entente. In April 1923, Stalin forcefully reminded his Russian colleagues that "if in the rear of Kolchak, Denikin, Wrangel and Yudenich we had not had the so-called 'aliens,' the oppressed peoples, who disorganized the rear of these generals . . . we would not have nailed a single one of these generals."[12]

KAZAKHSTAN AND TURKESTAN: DIFFERENT FORMS OF
THE RUSSIAN EXPANSION

The uneven development of the revolutionary process took on extremely complex and dramatic form in Central Asia (mainly Kazakhstan, previously Steppe General Gubernatorstvo, and Turkestan, previously Turkestan General Gubernatorstvo).

On the one hand, in Turkestan the national renaissance of the Asiatic peoples not only failed to provide support—even tactical support—for the Russian center, but also practically from the outset took on the character of an anti-Russian and anti-Bolshevik movement, largely controlled by the traditional political and religious elites. The few exceptions to this included the grouping of "Young Bukharans," influenced by reform Islam and Pan-Turkism, who sought Bolshevik support.

On the other hand, it should be stressed that in those areas of Central Asia where White forces were operating, particularly in Kazakhstan, it proved possible to repeat the project of tactical cooperation between Muslims and Bolsheviks. The most obvious example here is the Kazakh national party Alash Orda, which until 1919 had attempted to function on its own, with assistance from the Whites. Disillusioned with the positions of Kolchak and the ataman Dutov, this party entered into negotiations with the Bolsheviks and subsequently began collaboration with them (ignoring warnings of the Bashkir leader Zeki Validov-Togan)[13]—which ended, as in the case of Bashkirs, in the reestablishment of Russian domination and the destruction of Alash Orda.

These differing reactions in different parts of Central Asia were partly the result of their history prior to 1917; in the main, however, they stemmed from the different forms assumed by Russian expansionism.

As regards the steppe territories inhabited by the Kirgiz and Kazakhs, some authors estimate that 32-56 million hectares of the best land were transferred to Russian and Ukrainian colonists and the Public Land Fund between 1880 and 1916.[14] Cossack settlers received some 43-45 hectares on average, while Russian and Ukrainian peasants received an average of 11 hectares.[15] The effect of these land annexations and the arrival of appproximately 1.5 million Russians and Ukrainians—other estimates put the figure at 3 million—were dramatic changes, usually for the worse, in the life-style and husbandry of the Kazakhs, who were hitherto nomadic.[16] Attempts to rectify matters by a policy of encouraging the Kazakhs to settle on the land yielded no results for the same reasons: "Although the Kazakhs formed at least 50 percent, and in some areas 75 percent, of the farming population, they owned only 20 percent of the sown fields."[17]

In contrast, Russian expansion in Turkestan took on different, indirect forms: "Migration to Turkestan proper, where pressure of existing population was unfavourable to settlement by Russian peasants, was negligible."[18] In this region the Russians' expansion and domination were primarily based on the state bureaucracy, army, and Orthodox church, and also on the penetration of the merchant class. The latter, drawn by the region's "white gold" (cotton), managed to give the local economy a strong commodity character within a relatively short time (particularly in the Fergana Valley), with the pauperization of part of the peasantry and the generalization of a system of sharecropping. As a result, Turkestan lost its self-sufficiency in food and the economy became dominated by cotton.[19]

This type of expansion on the one hand accelerated social differentiation in the countryside (with an increase in the numbers of sharecroppers), while on the other hand it helped to reinforce the dominance of traditional political and religious/cultural structures. The latter effect was rooted in the role played by the elite controlling the basic socioeconomic structures, in maintaining—in the face of growing social polarization—what might be termed a system of collective social security. This system, thanks partly to Islam, operated relatively effectively, not only as an "ideological superstructure," but also as an important element in reproducing the "economic base" (as was the case with communal and clan control over the irrigation systems).

As can be seen from the brief outline presented above, differing reactions to the Russian revolution in these areas of Central Asia were rather to be expected. Yet, given that the people of Turkestan had less dramatic experience of Russian expansionism than their counterparts in Kazakhstan, it might have been assumed that resistance in the latter region should hypothetically be stronger. Let us recall that less than two years had elapsed since the bloody, anti-Russian uprising of the Kirgiz, Kazakhs, and sections of the Uzbeks in 1916. This uprising took a toll of seven thousand Russians dead or missing and nine thousand colonists' farmsteads burned.[20]

However, the Kazakhs were hard hit by government repression. Some estimates put the number killed at over two hundred thousand, with a further three hundred thousand fleeing to China.[21] Even if the first figure is inflated, the losses were undoubtedly substantial. I believe this must have been a significant factor in the history of the Kazakhs after 1917. On the other hand, we shall note that in its evolution toward collaboration with the Bolsheviks after 1919, the Alash Orda encountered no opposition from Islam, which had yet to sink firm roots in the region, having become the majority religion there fairly recently. It has been emphasized in this connection that the Alash Orda was largely the product of reform-oriented Muslim intellectuals and traditionalist clan leaders appealing to native, non-Islamic Kazakh tradition.[22] In this sense the party was to some extent open to the slogans of change and reform raised by the Bolsheviks and to their promises of national and economic equality. In sum, the nationalism of the Alash Orda was not of the fanatically religious and traditionalist type, geared exclusively toward the past. Hatred of the Russians and a feeling of being culturally alien were secondary factors compared to the dramatic impact of the land (and pasture) question, a question of survival in general. In this context, the evolution of Bolshevik policy in the final stages of the civil war was of key importance. In addition to an awareness of the increasing military superiority of the Red Army, the most important consideration was that the policies of the Whites were even worse and held out little chance of either national autonomy, even limited autonomy, or a redistribution of the land grabbed by the Russians.[23]

In Turkestan, Bukhara, and Khiva, the deep interpenetration between Islam and the basic living and working conditions and the continued existence, almost totally intact, of the traditional social and cultural/political structures (despite the rapid commercialization of agriculture mentioned earlier) made the local population rather unsusceptible to slogans of revolutionary change. Thus, writing in 1921, Sultan Galiyev stressed the exceptional power of traditional Islam in Bukhara and its influence on the whole of Turkestan, and also the fanaticism shown in struggling against religious reformers. In analyzing the possibilities for antireligious propaganda in this region, he pointed out that conditions here were "completely different from those we encounter among the Tatars, the Bashkirs, or the Kirghiz."[24] Underlining the role played by Tatar reform-oriented Muslims before 1917 in encouraging religious modernization in Turkestan, Bukhara, and Khiva, Sultan Galiyev noted that the reincorporation of this region after 1917 was in fact carried out jointly by Tatars and Russians.[25] In general, the demand for national autonomy in Turkestan, Bukhara, and Khiva, along with the opposition to Russian penetration, took on the form of an irredentist force controlled to a large extent by traditionalist elites. The crisis in agriculture, particularly in cotton, and the presence of some three hundred thousand unemployed, starving day laborers and sharecroppers encouraged the spread of anti-Russian attitudes, demands for independence, and religious fanaticism. The short-lived Kokanda government, dominated by the Ulema Association and subsequently smashed by Russians in February 1918, set out a socioeconomic program calling for "the maintenance of private property, of the *shariat*, and the seclusion of women."[26] In the modified, more orthodox version, this program—with its emphasis on Pan-Islamism and its theocratic-cum-religious view of society—was later to become the program of the Basmachis.

THE PAST AS PRESENT

In 1917 and in the first years of the civil war, it was not, however, the aforementioned differences that immediately determined the attitude of the population of Central Asia to the Russian revolution. The primary factor was above all the manner in which the revolution made its appearance in this region.

The European peasant/Cossack population of Central Asia, which was politically—and to a certain extent economically—dominant, along with the Russian inhabitants of the towns, the bureaucracy, and the army, were almost entirely in favor of, first, the February and, then, the October revolution (until the appearance of strong White forces). This support was founded on the straightforward premise that any Russian government that guaranteed law and order was a good one.[27] As a result, the delegates to the Tenth Congress of the RCP in 1921 learned from an authoritative source that in Kazakhstan, for example, "our party includes in its ranks a Communist Orthodox priest, a Russian policeman, and a kulak from Semirechiye who . . . hunts down Kirgiz as if they were wild game."[28] Regarding Turkestan, it has been pointed out that "the Russian soldiers who were sent to Turkestan to suppress the rising [in 1916] played an important part in the Bolsheviks' victory and in their control of Turkestan in 1918."[29] In this connection, let us note the declaration made on November 28, 1917, by the chairman of the Third Regional Congress of Soviets of Turkestan: "One cannot let the Mohammedans into the highest organs of revolutionary authority on account of the uncertain attitude of the local population toward the power of the Soviets, and because the native population lacks a proletarian organization."[30] The fifteen-person revolutionary government of Turkestan contained not one single Asian member.[31] It seems justified to suggest that in reaching Central Asia the Russian revolution acquired a very specific character, initially being seen primarily as a preemptive self-defense by the European minority, threatened by an explosion of dissatisfaction on the part of the Asian millions. The few Bolsheviks of the time who were sensitive to the problem of the East were warning their comrades that the Europeans' revolution had in its first few years basically changed nothing in the traditional pattern of relationships between the nationalities. Safarov, for example, declared at the Tenth Congress of the RCP that Central Asia was witnessing "an automatic continuation of the former colonial relations under the guise and form of the Soviet power."[32]

The fact that a substantial part of this area was cut off from the Russian center in the years 1918-20 and that the Russian revolutionaries were under dual siege (the Whites and the Basmachis) could only aggravate these relations, which came to be symbolized by Red "cavalry raids" on *kishlaks* and *auls*, two types of Asian settlements. The policies of War Communism, the attempts to nationalize both private and *waqf* land and also irrigation systems (in conditions of famine and with no means of ensuring the latter's efficient utilization or even maintenance), the contemptuous attitude to religion and attempts at forced laicization—all these things contributed to a picture of the revolutionary authorities as a new version of the traditional colonial rulers. Even worse, in attacking traditional social relations, the Russian Bolsheviks displayed serious ignorance: by undermining the mechanisms of communal social security, they deepened the desperation of the poverty-stricken *dekhans*. On top of this came a peculiar mixture of revolutionary rhetoric and preservation of the prerevolutionary model of colonial relations in agriculture.[33] I will return to the repercussions of all this later on.

FROM "SELF-DETERMINATION" TO THE NATIONALITIES POLICY

The national-cum-anticolonial revolution in the Asiatic territories of the former Russian Empire was a product of the February and October revolutions in the sense that those made it possible to pose and define the problem of national autonomy. Before 1917, programs of national independence did not reflect the views of most politically active Muslims either in the Kazakh steppes or among the Bashkirs, or even in Ufa and Kazan, the religious and intellectual centers of the Tatar and Islamic renaissance. On the other hand, in Bukhara and Khiva, which had a special status, a tendency toward regional separatism was strongly accentuated, although even here this tendency was already undergoing visible erosion. Other regions, however, were only witnessing the early stage of a reemergence of national thought, expressed in terms of either religious/ethnic unity (Pan-Islamism and Pan-Turkism) or territorial autonomy (the "Tatarism" of the budding middle class among the Volga Tatars). The transition from a religious and cultural renaissance (begun among the Muslims toward the end of the nineteenth century) to political programs of a national and social character had only just started after the revolution of 1905. Nor was the scope of the political demands in question readily apparent. In the case of the Volga Tatars, a group in a very specific situation, being scattered over the area between Baku, Kazan, Orenburg, and Tashkent, these demands sometimes involved cultural autonomy, sometimes territorial autonomy (the concept of Idel-Ural, i.e., a Tatar state including Bashkirs as well, situated between the Volga and the Urals). Prior to 1917, demands for territorial autonomy among the nationalities and ethnic groups concentrated geographically, such as the Armenians, Kazakhs, or Turkmenis, were primarily expressed in concepts of autonomy within a federal structure.[34] Similar demands were aired immediately after the February revolution.[35]

Equally ill defined was the social content of the respective national programs. Or more precisely: this content was extremely heterogeneous. In social terms, the national revolution was perceived both as a process of profound change in socioeconomic structures and as one of restoring or preserving historical forms. This heterogeneity indicates the existence of a differentiation in the levels of internal development attained by particular nationalities and also in the social character of the elites. Simplifying matters somewhat, one could say that the division between reform and traditionalist Islam (between *jadids* and *qadymists*) was particularly sharp in those ethnic groups that had already seen a differentiation in the communities producing their elites. In any case, there was a distinct interdependence between the level of development of particular nationalities and the degree to which national demands were linked to programs of socioeconomic reform.

In this situation, the presented concepts of state independence or of the desirable socioeconomic structure constituted a veritable "Periodic Table" of the historical forms. There was no one single model here, nor could there be. The social base for the programs of national independence (or autonomy) was composed of peasants, workers, and intellectuals, the déclassé noblemen (the "ragged *murzas*" of the Tatars), *mullahs* and *beys*, and nomadic clan chieftains. Nationalism (whether "private" and local or "ideological") found leaders and attracted support in every social group, albeit in different ways, to different degrees and with different social goals envisaged.[36] As a political phenomenon, nationalism arrived in the towns and villages of Central Asia ahead of modern social structures. As a result of the brutal economic, cultural, and political intervention of the Russian Empire, the development of national consciousness among the Asiatic peoples leapt over certain stages of "natural" socioeconomic and political evolution.

From the point of view of the Russian center of the revolution, the national aspirations and projects of the Asiatic peoples were highly suspect; the substantial part of the Bolshevik party apparatus either considered them incomprehensible or viewed them with outright hostility. It was not the done thing to mention this fact afterward, in the late 1920s or 1930s. S. M. Dimanshtein, who was in the East during the revolution and in the 1920s edited the journal *Revolutsiia i Natsionalnosti*, found this out for himself in 1930 when he asserted that ignoring the national question had been a "fairly universal" practice of the Bolsheviks in the hinterland. He came under fire immediately.[37]

The attitude Dimanshtein refers to was not just a question of the pressure of the political conjuncture. In the contemporary Marxist tradition, the gaining of independence by Russia's peripheral regions had never been considered desirable, even less so following the October revolution. The dominant views were expressed either in the naive conviction that the revolution would resolve the "national question" automatically, or in the position that any disintegration or territorial weakening of Russia would constitute a historical setback—from the point of view of the further development of "civilization" in the backward areas. In both those cases, Russian Bolsheviks were direct heirs to the Russian (and European for that matter) imperial tradition; revolution allowed them to legitimize and consolidate this tradition.

In this situation there was little likelihood Asian aspirations toward independence would be given an understanding reception. Of course, the specific conjuncture—the civil war—made it possible to conclude various forms of compromise, to give concessions in order to gain tactical advantage in the struggle against the Whites. In the end, however, the "nationalities policy" was counterposed to the national and anticolonial revolution. This policy's points of reference were: first, the principle of territorial unity of the former empire, and second, the principle of incorporating demands for national autonomy within the framework of a formally federal state structure. Everything within the bounds of this policy was acceptable (for a time, of course), while anything outside these bounds was not. At the same time, mechanisms were established to ensure that the federal territory would not be reduced. The most important of these were the creation of a single, centralized All-Soviet Communist party and the construction of a unified multinational army and security police.

Taken as a whole, this nationalities policy, which involved multiplying the nations and nationalities existing in the hinterland (particularly in the Caucasus)—described afterward by Soviet researchers as the stage of *raztsviet* of nations and nationalities[38]—was conceived as a specific form of mediation between the principle of self-determination in the literal sense and the tradition of Russian centralism. And it made it possible to resolve the dilemma formulated at the Eighth Congress of the RCP in 1918 by Piatakov: "Since we unite economically . . . this whole celebrated 'self-determination' is not worth a fig. This is either simply a diplomatic game, which has to be played in some cases, or it is worse than a game if we take it seriously."[39]

FURTHER REMARKS ON THE EVOLUTION OF THE SITUATION IN CENTRAL ASIA

The development of the Asian national movement in the former tsarist empire was largely determined by its two principal components. The first, which we may define as "Marxist nationalists," as Rodinson does,[40] was in favor of cooperating with the Russian revolution for both tactical and ideological reasons; the second, which Soviet historiography calls the "nationalist counterrevolution," believed the revolution to be in conflict with the Asiatic peoples' aspirations toward independence and also with the traditional social and religious order.[41] Nevertheless, the factor that was to decide the fate of the national revolution and of both these groups and to determine how the national problem was resolved was undoubtedly the policies of the Russian leaders. Safarov, who played a large part in elaborating the Center's policies in the Asian hinterland, stated at the Tenth Congress of the RCP in 1921 that the Bolshevik party "has taken extremely little interest in the national question. The result of this has been a series of unpardonable errors."[42]

In my opinion, only the second part of this statement can be accepted without reservation; as to the first, a series of doubts arises. What Safarov terms a lack of interest was, in fact, the collapse of a particular concept (and practice) of the policy toward the nationalities. The aforementioned mixture of naive internationalism and of a theory of the historical superiority of large state organisms gave rise to specific policy. This policy was well known to the Asian population: Russian centralism, or more precisely, Russia's historic mission in the East. In Turkestan, that mission was carried on in the years 1918-19 by a firmly anti-Asian group of the so-called Old Bolsheviks, led by I. O. Tobolin.[43] What was important in Safarov's speech, however, was that he was warning the center that the revolution in the hinterland was entering a new stage. What was occurring there—largely as a reaction to the measures taken by the Russians in 1918-20—was the gradual fusion of the two above-mentioned currents in the Asian national movement, thereby creating a qualitatively new situation that was threatening the Russian revolution.

In September 1920, less than a year before the Tenth Congress of the RCP, in an address to the Baku Congress of the Peoples of the East, the Turkmen Narbutabekov demanded a change in the policy toward Turkestan; he also appealed to Zinoviev and Radek, who were present at the Congress: "Remove your counterrevolutionaries . . . , remove your colonizers who are now working behind the mask of Communism!"[44] This picture was reaffirmed several months later by Safarov, who asserted that "the Russian kulaks . . . who by a twist of fate become the 'agents' of the dictatorship of the proletariat in the borderlands, have driven the local masses into the camp of counterrevolution."[45]

It was obviously not only—or even primarily—the kulaks who were involved here; the problem was above all that of Russians acting as colonists. Placing the emphasis on the kulaks, however, made it possible to prepare moves that, on the one hand, involved the return to Kazakhs and Uzbeks of the part of the land they had lost, at the expense of Cossacks and wealthier Russian peasants, while, on the other, ensured the maintenance of the support of the majority of Russian colonists.

Thus, in June 1920, even before the Baku Congress, the leaders of the RCP advised the authorities of Turkestan to expel the Russian kulaks from Central Asia and to grant equal land rights to the Asian population and also to Russian smallholders and landless peasants. Advice of this kind, included in the "Circular Letter to All Organizations of the Communist Party of Turkestan," followed the report of the special Russian Turk Komisiia.[46] It is symptomatic, however, that this move was accompanied by a devastating attack against all "national deviationists" among the Muslim Communists in Turkestan.

And once again, the problem of Central Asia did not emerge by a "twist of fate." Safarov realized this full well. The problem lay both in the position occupied by Russians within the colonial structure and also in the policies of the Russian revolutionaries themselves. This produced arrogance and the national and economic discrimination against the Asian population.[47]

All this criticism was taken into account in the RCP Congress decisions, although in a fashion that could not have satisfied the Asian advocates of autonomy or independence inside and outside the Bolshevik party. In fact, the Congress resolution "On the Party's Current Tasks on the National Question" formally and irrevocably dispelled all hope of establishing independent Asian socialist republics. Next, generalizing from the case of Turkestan, the resolution spoke of two deviations: "great-power aspirations, colonization, and Great-Russian chauvinism" and "bourgeois-democratic nationalism, at times assuming the forms of Pan-Islamism and Pan-Turkism (in the East)." Nonetheless, being unable to ignore the threat posed by the rapid increase in the Asian resistance, the resolution went on to say that "Congress considers it necessary to stress the particularly dangerous and damaging character of the former."[48]

Following a meeting of the RCP leadership with twenty-seven delegates from the Baku Congress, personnel purges in Turkestan began at the end of 1920, under the supervision of the central authorities; the purges reached their peak after 1921. It should be stressed, however, that the main targets were the MusBuro (Muslim Bureau) and the local Muslim cadres who were suspected of being under the strong influence of Pan-Islamism and Pan-Turkism. These local cadres, who come from the politically and socially radical faction of Asian nationalism, gained a strong influence at the beginning of 1920, after the Red Army had raised the blockade of Tashkent and after the center had displaced those Russians who had been the most compromised in the eyes of the Asians.[49] In January 1920, formally in connection with the discussion on the administrative division of Central Asia, the Kazakh leader Turar Ryskulov, backed by his followers on the Muslim Bureau, announced a program that aimed at: "1. Formation of a Muslim Turkestani Army; 2. Formation of a Turkic CP; 3. Expulsion of Russian and other 'European' colonizers from Turkestan or at least limitation of their rights in using the land; 4. Creation of a federal union of all Turkic-Muslim territories of the Soviet Union, free of both West European capitalism and Soviet Russian imperialism."[50] Already in December 1919, the Muslim Bureau announced that it was becoming "the highest Muslim party organ in Turkestan."[51] The intervention by Moscow, caused, among other things, by reports by Mikhail Frunze, the Commander-in-Chief of the Red Army in Turkestan, led to the removal of Ryskulov's followers.

However, outside the ranks of the Communist party, in the years 1921-22 a radical turnabout was effected in relation to Islam and Muslim tradition. For example:

1. Religious land (*waqf*) was restored to the *mullahs* and mosques.
2. Obstacles to the development of schools run by *mullahs* were removed.
3. Muslim holidays were recognized, as was the legitimacy of traditional courts and law (*shariat*).

4. A fairly liberal attitude was adopted toward the religious beliefs of Asian rank-and-file members of the Bolshevik party (in Bukhara, 90 percent of the Asian members were practicing Muslims).

5. Antireligious propaganda was restricted to the Russian urban population.

6. The attacks on traditional agrarian relations were curbed—acknowledging, for instance, the importance of clan control over irrigation systems.[52]

7. Furthermore, in 1921, according to official figures, some 246,000 hectares of land taken from Russian colonists and millions of hectares confiscated from the Orenburg Cossacks were redistributed, principally to Kazakhs and Uzbeks, in the most conflict-ridden regions; in Turkestan (around Samarkand), the Asian population received some 66,000 hectares of land.[53]

These conciliatory measures taken by the Russian center did not, however, have an immediate effect and failed to diffuse the crisis. The threat of the two Asian nationalisms' irredenta could, in the short term, be averted only by force. An effect was nevertheless achieved in the long term.[54]

The most spectacular confirmation of Safarov's fears of a gradual unification of the Asian national movement was the defection to the Basmachis in 1920 of Ahmed Zeki Validov-Togan, Commissar for War of the Autonomous Socialist Bashkir Republic in the years 1919-20, and of the majority of the Bashkir government. Almost at the same time, a powerful uprising broke out in Daghestan, while fighting intensified in Bukhara and the rest of Turkestan. Then, in January of 1921, an illegal Socialist party of Turkestan was set up in Bukhara by a group of Asian revolutionaries. In general, it seemed that after a period of disillusionment with the Whites and then of collaboration with the Reds, the region was now entering one of mass Asian resistance to the Russian revolution. In this context it is quite understandable that the Turkestan delegation to the RCP's Tenth Congress—composed of Bolsheviks loyal to Moscow—attacked the ideas of Pan-Islamism and Pan-Turkism with incredible fury.[55] After all, it was Muslim unity that constituted the link between the two currents of the Asiatic national movement described earlier. It is true that this unity was defined in different ways (in conservative-cum-theocratic terms or in revolutionary and socially radically ones), yet it called into question both the revolutionary paternalism of Russia and Europe and the concept of the "Balkanization" of Russian Asia.

ISLAM AND NATION

The case of Turkestan was undoubtedly an extreme one. Yet for this very reason it shows us the most dramatic consequences of the meeting of European communism and the concrete social, religious, and cultural reality of Asia. Some of these consequences resulted from the difficulties involved in translating the concepts of European social and political sciences into the language of Asiatic conditions as well as from ignorance. At the Second All-Russian Congress of Communist Organizations of Peoples of the East, held in the autumn of 1919, the Tatar Sahibgiray made the following realistic observation: "Lack of knowledge [of the East]—this is why we are circling round helplessly and no one is capable of saying anything concrete."[56]

On the other hand, however, the main source of those negative consequences was the specific concept of the nation and the nation-building processes, which was accepted by the Russian leaders and was selectively copying the relevant European experience and which, at the same time, was closely linked with the ideology of the Russian revolution's "civilizational mission" (which, in turn, implied a transformation of the idea and practice of the tsarist empire into those of the Socialist empire). In this situation the conflict with Islamic tradition was hard to avoid.

The power of Islam in Russia cannot be seen as merely the reflex reaction of centuries of tradition; its power was continuously reproduced by colonialism although in different forms (e.g., the transition toward an "open Islam" started by religious modernizers). Writing in 1921, Sultan Galiyev asserted that "Islam was and still is, at least in the eyes of the Muslims, an oppressed religion"; he also stressed that many injunctions of *shariat* "have a . . . positive character."[57] At the same time, the integrative functions of Islam were extended. This produced a situation of "overdetermination" that involved a strict binding of the "national question" (generally understood in religious-cultural categories) to the "social question," with the former distinctly prevailing in the planes of social integration.

The Asian revolutionaries—who usually took part in the Islamic reform movement at the turn of the century, subsequently (until 1917) having involved themselves in socially radical, national organizations—were well aware that pursuing the policy of "class struggle" could not be their topmost priority in Russian Asia. Their primary concern had to be the resolving of the fundamental national problem, namely, the ensuring of political and economic relations of equality with the Europeans. This concern is clearly present in Sultan Galiyev's pronouncements regarding methods of antireligious propaganda in the Muslim community; echoing Narbutabekov's position, he declared: "No antireligious propaganda will give the expected results as long as Muslims have not been liberated and made free and equal Soviet citizens, not only on paper, but in fact."[58] Zeki Validov-Togan, when breaking with the Bolsheviks in 1920, wrote in a letter addressed to Lenin, Stalin, and Trotsky: "We have already explained . . . that the land question in the east has in principle produced no class distinction [between us]. For in the east it is the European Russians, whether capitalists or workers, who are the top class, while the people of the soil (yerli), rich or poor, are their slaves."[59]

Needless to say, those revolutionaries did not reject agrarian revolution; however, they saw it in a more complex context than the one laid down by the established pattern of "pure" class struggle. It is especially true that even in those areas where social conflicts already acquired the form of a struggle between landlords and peasants, as was the case with the Volga Tatars and the Bashkirs,[60] the problem of national demands was by no means extinct. This is why although Sultan Galiyev pointed out factors favorable to the antireligious propaganda concentrated on social questions among the Tatars and the Bashkirs, he did not lose sight either of the fact "of national renaissance of the Volga Tatars" or of the complicated network of national domination, which made Islam more attractive as a form of supraethnic consciousness.[61]

It is obvious that the problem of Islam (and Pan-Turkism) as one of determining the direction of nation-building processes in Russian Asia presented the Russians with an extremely difficult choice. Nearly all major Asiatic revolutionaries opted for the concept of great Asian nations. That, however, involved the establishment of a relatively homogeneous pole opposite to the non-Asiatic population of Russia and, implicitly, the acceptance by the Russian center of a certain version of Pan-Islamism and/or Pan-Turkism. A counterproposal was to take advantage of Pan-Islam's weaknesses and to adopt a policy aimed at strengthening differences among the Asian population and forming nations according to the European model. This was not an artificially created problem in the sense that the "natural laws of development" would imply the first option as the only one to be taken up (as claimed by the Asian revolutionaries).[62] The dramatic aspect of the choice lay in the fact that the second option was realistic as well as historically justified; its existence as an option did not result from Russian pressure alone. If today we correctly recognize as an oversimplification the view that Islam was merely an obstacle to arousing national consciousness,[63] an assessment that overlooked the nation-building aspects of that religion, then it is also an oversimplification to advocate a view that ignores ethnic, cultural, linguistic, and, not least, economic differences that occurred in Russian Asia.[64] After all is said and done, those differences sometimes took dramatic forms such as sharp conflicts between Tatars and Bashkirs, Tatars and Uzbeks, and so on. The opposition between the Pan-Islamic concepts of the nation and the "territorial and cultural" concepts reflected both the conflict between the Asians and Russian centralism (in this case, Pan-Islamism was an instrument for the defense of the religious and cultural identity of the Asians) as well as the conflict stirred up by political ambitions of the Kazan Tatars to whom Pan-Islamism was a convenient instrument for strengthening their role among the Russian Asians.[65] It should be remembered that in May 1917, during the First All-Russian Muslim Congress, the adversaries of Pan-Islamism (and, implicitly, anti-Tatar-minded Asians) claimed that "we must realize that there is not a Moslem nation in Russia" (Zeki Validov-Togan, later a supporter of supraethnic unity among the Russian Asians). When criticizing a defender of the idea of a "Moslem nation," the Kazakh leader emphasized: "Do you have any idea what nationality is? It is the unity of blood, spirit, culture, traditions, language, customs and territory. You cannot create a 'Moslem' nation on the basis of a non-territorial, centralized autonomy. Are you not, incidentally, a Pan-Islamist? We know that behind Pan-Islamism there are concealed the machinations of one nationality [Tatars] to dominate the other!"[66]

In sum, in 1917, the Asian communities in Russia were perplexed. If, on the one hand, the continuity of their religious community told Asians to choose a solution toward ideological unity that would go beyond local patriotism, on the other hand, growing ethnic differences and antagonisms implied "Balkanization." In a word, nothing could be taken for granted and, theoretically, one could choose any of the paths. As usually happens in situations of this kind, force settled the matter—the force of the Russian center at that. In the eyes of Asian revolutionaries that was tantamount to mere interference of the colonial type. The Asian revolutionaries, however, were tardy in realizing that fact and the long-term consequences of the policy of the Russian Bolsheviks. Meanwhile, the latter did not find it necessary to shatter the illusions about their policy at an early stage of the revolution.

From all the evidence available it appears that at the initial stage of the Bolshevik revolution, the first option prevailed. The appeal from December 1917 was addressed, as we remember, to the "Laboring Muslims," not to the Kirgiz or the Uzbeks. Saidbayev is correct in observing that "by turning to the Muslims, the [appeal] was assuming that religious attachment meant here more than the ethnic status."[67] Also later, more or less until 1920, the term "laboring Muslims" did not disappear from the political language of the

Bolsheviks. Such terms as "Muslim languages," "Muslim proletariat" or "Muslim Communists," and "Muslim Army" were in common use.[68] And what is more important, in June 1918, on the initiative, among others, of Tatar leaders Vakhitov and Sultan Galiyev, the Russian Party of Muslim Communist-Bolsheviks was formed. At the end of that year, however, it lost its autonomy and was transformed into a section (Buro) of the RCP. After the Eighth RCP Congress, a statutory ban was enforced on the creation of national (Communist) parties independent of the Russian center. And it is worth mentioning here that the said party of Muslim Communists was showing strong "independent tendencies," claiming, for example, the right to join the Comintern outside the RCP structure. The Turkic Communist party (and the Turkic Republic), in attempting to unite Asiatics (led by Turar Ryskulov in Kazakhstan and Turkestan) shared a similar fate. At the final stages of the civil war, experiments with revolutionary Pan-Islamism and/or Pan-Turkism lost their attraction for the Russian leadership, in particular because the ambitions of Asian revolutionaries were difficult to stifle, whereas their aspirations to autonomy and resistance to the policy of "accelerated" political differentiation of the Asian countryside, as well as their demands for national justice, were increasingly suspect. More and more the center identified Islam with "reaction" and the idea of Muslim (or Turkic) unity with subversion of the revolution. Although Lenin saw the need at the Comintern Second Congress in 1920 to support revolutionary nationalism outside Russia, he nevertheless thought it was necessary to "fight Pan-Islamism" as a counterrevolutionary force that was a "strengthening of the power of Turkish and Japanese imperialism, the nobility, the big landowners, the clergy, etc."[69] The attempts of Tan Malaka, an Indonesian Communist and an activist of Saraket Islam, to make Lenin change his opinion of Pan-Islamism and see the difference between "imperialist Pan-Islamism" and "national-liberation Pan-Islamism" failed.[70]

In such a situation, the plans of Sultan Galiyev, Ryskulov, and other Marxist nationalists to create an autonomous Asiatic pole of Russia and the "world revolution" could not find a following among the Russian leadership. A telegraph conversation held in January 1920 between Frunze, commander of the Turkestan front, and Shalva Eliave, a member of the Turkestan Buro of the RCP Central Committee sheds some light on the Russian leadership's attitude toward Asian revolutionaries' projects. When Eliave asked Frunze about his opinion on projects to create a Muslim army out of, among others, those captive Turkish officers who declared their readiness to fight for the revolution, Frunze, having already had some ideas about the influence of Pan-Islamism and firsthand experience of Ryskulov's activities, answered:

"There should be no separate staff and no Muslim army. Regarding this matter, I and Ilyich [Lenin] exchanged views once again . . . and any talks are out of the question. We will, of course, permit the creation of local [detachments], however, not on the religious but on the national basis."[71]

IN PLACE OF CONCLUSIONS

It would be challenging to show the destruction of the old tsarist empire and the emergence of the new "socialist empire" in a comparative perspective, in the reference to the historical experience of former colonial empires and/or the Habsburg Empire. Such a comparison with regard to the years 1917-20 would probably provide a fascinating experience in the use of John Stuart Mill's "Method of Difference." The fundamental question one wants to ask here is, Why did the Habsburg Empire fall while the Romanov Empire, despite a temporary disintegration, come back to existence as the Soviet Union? Also intriguing is the question of the different historical time in which those two empires lasted at the threshold of their respective disintegration. Why was in the European part of the former tsarist empire the result of disintegration processes similar to the one in the former Habsburg Empire (the establishment of independent Poland, Finland, Latvia, Estonia, and Lithuania, but not Belorussia and the Ukraine), whereas reintegration was the result in the Asian territories?

I hope that this discussion will hasten such a comparative analysis, even by pointing out that although the Russian military power was indeed the last resort, that power was increased by the factors that caused the Central Asian nationalities to disintegrate,—that is, the (delayed) national revival as well as social conflicts.

Despite all the examples I have quoted to the contrary, the Russians were not "lone riders" when reintegrating Central Asia and the Caucasus; tens of thousands of Asians expected the fulfillment of the revolution's promises and thus sided with them. In the years 1917-20, the population of Central Asia saw the "White" and the "Red" Russians. The Whites were thinking about the past and promising nothing, whereas the Reds were exploiting the prospect of national freedom and were promising everything. Also, for the Asian revolutionaries, who were full of energy and hatred for the old social order and traditional Islam, the Russian revolution created the illusion of a march eastward, of the "Russian Muslim proletarian's lance" aimed against "world imperialism and [the] clerical-feudal bourgeoisie." Trostsky was not the only who believed in "world revolution"; so did Vakhitov, Ryskulov,

Sultan Galiyev, and the others. It was for them also a vision of the revolution of the "colored" people against the world of the "whites." Although it is not clear why the Russians were to support such a revolution, what matters is that until a certain time the Asian revolutionaries believed the Russian revolution would open the road to the East for them.

All in all, Asia got divided and this facilitated the reintegration of the empire. From the formal, administrative point of view, that integration was close to the provisions of the Austro-Marxists' programs (the theories of Otto Bauer and Karl Renner), and also to the famous program of Aurel C. Popovici presented in his *Die Vereinigten Staaten von Gross-Oesterreich.* Although it may sound paradoxical, it was no one else but Lenin and Stalin who turned out to be those programs' successors and consistent realizers. In this sense, one can speak of the "spirit" of the Habsburg Empire's nationality policy having left Vienna over seventy years ago—for Bolshevik Moscow.

NOTES

1. R. Pipes, *The Formation of the Soviet Union: Communism and Nationalism, 1917-1923* (Cambridge, Mass., 1954), 285-86.
2. See E. H. Carr, *The Bolshevik Revolution 1917-1923* (Harmondsworth, 1966), 1:79.
3. *Kombieds* were the Committees of the Poor, which united poor and landless peasants and were the mainstay of the policy of War Communism in the villages.
4. A. I. Mikoyan, *Droga walki* (Warsaw, 1985), 1:370.
5. M. S. Sultan Galiyev, "The Tatars and the October Revolution," in *Muslim National Communism in the Soviet Union: A Revolutionary Strategy for the Colonial World*, ed. A. Bennigsen and S. E. Wimbush, (Chicago, 1980), 156-57.
6. Ibid., 153.
7. See Bennigsen and Wimbush, *Muslim National Communism*, 223, and A. Bennigsen and Ch. Quelquejay, *Les mouvements nationaux chez les musulmans de Russie: Le "sultangalievisme" au Tatarstan* (Paris-The Hague, 1960), 83-84.
8. A. Nimet Kurat, "Tsarist Russia and the Muslims of Central Asia," in *The Cambridge History of Islam* Vol.I; *The Central Islamic Lands* (London 1970), 629. Cf. M. Rodinson, *Marxism and the Muslim World* (London, 1979).
9. See I. Deutscher, *Stalin: A Political Biography* (Harmondsworth, 1966), 188. The dispute between Lenin and Stalin in 1922 over the constitutional framework of Soviet Russia not only failed to undermine the principle of factual incorporation but actually transformed this into the sole valid

interpretation of the principle of "self-determination." Cf. M. Levin, *Lenin's Last Struggle* (London, 1975).

10. See Z. Lukawski, *Historia Syberii* (Wrocław, 1981); H. Carrere d'Encausse, *Reforme et revolution chez les musulmans de l'Empire russe: Bukhara, 1867-1927* (Paris, 1966).

11. See S. A. Zenkovsky, *Pan-Turkism and Islam in Russia* (Cambridge, Mass., 1960); B. Kh. Yuldashbayev, "Natsionalnyi vopros v Bashkirii na pervom etapie sovietskogo natsionalno-gosudarstviennogo stroitelstva," *Istoricheskiie Zapiski*, vol. 115 (Moscow, 1987).

12. J. W. Stalin, *Marxism and the National and Colonial Question: A Collection of Articles and Speeches* (London, n.d.).

13. Yuldashbayev, *Natsionalnyi vopros.*

14. Nimet Kurat, "Tsarist Russia and the Muslims of Central Asia," 517; R. Wojna, *Walka o ziemie w Rosji w 1917 roku* (Wrocław, 1977), 35; A. Bennigsen and Ch. Lemercier-Quelquejay, *Le presse et le mouvement national chez les musulmans de Russie avant 1920* (Paris The Hague, 1964), 146.

15. E. Szczepanik, *Radzieckie republiki Azji Srodkowej 1917-1941: Dzieje, gospodarka, spoleczenstwo* (Wrocław, 1987), 9.

16. Nimet Kurat, "Tsarist Russia and the Muslims of Central Asia," 517; M. B. Olcott, *The Kazakhs* (Stanford, Calif., 1987), 90.

17. Olcott, *The Kazakhs*, 98.

18. E. H. Carr, *Socialism in One Country, 1924-1926* (Harmondsworth, 1970), 1:553.

19. See Szczepanik, *Radzieckie*, 11.

20. Nimet Kurat, "Tsarist Russia and the Muslims of Central Asia," 519. E. Yu. Yusupov, in his *Perekhod k sotsializmu minuya kapitalizm* (Moscow, 1987), tries to minimize the anti-Russian aspect of the uprising.

21. Nimet Kurat, "Tsarist Russia and the Muslims of Central Asia," 519.

22. Olcott, *The Kazakhs.*

23. See Carr, *The Bolshevik Revolution*, 1:330-31.

24. M. S. Sultan Galiyev, "The Methods of Antireligious Propaganda among the Muslims," in *Muslim National Communism*, ed. Bennigsen and Wimbush, 155.

25. Sultan Galiyev, "The Tatars." Contemporary Soviet historiography indirectly admits that the reintegration of Turkestan was impossible without external intervention; moreover, the role played by the First Volga Brigade of Tatars in the Fergana Valley is also stressed. See *Istoriia sovietskogo krestiian'stva T.I: Krestiian'stvo v pervoe desatiletiie sovietskoi vlasti 1917-1927*, (Moscow, 1986), 151. Nevertheless, to maintain a sense of balance, a rosy picture is painted of the rapid creation of peasant soviets after 1917, both in Kazakhstan and Turkestan, without stating precisely whether Russian or Asiatic peasants were involved (ibid., 44-45). On the other hand, however, A. Bennigsen, "La révolution importée: Le précédent de l'Asie centrale (1917-1928)," in P. Kende et al., *Le systeme communiste:*

Un monde en expansion (Paris, 1982), is right to point out that such a considerable participation of the Tatars in the struggle for Turkestan made "the war in Central Asia ultimately not acquire the nature of a national-liberation struggle of the local population against Russian colonialists."

26. Carr, *The Bolshevik Revolution*, 1: 336.
27. See O. Caroe, *Soviet Empire: The Turks of Central Asia and Stalinism* (London-New York, 1967), 98f.
28. RKP, *X Zjazd Komunistycznej Partii (bolszewikow) Rosji. Marzec 1921. Stenogram* (Warsaw, 1970), 261 (speech by G. Safarov).
29. Nimet Kurat, "Tsarist Russia and the Muslims of Central Asia," 519.
30. G. Safarov, *Kolonialnaia revolutsiia (opyt Turkiestana)* (Moscow, 1921), 70; A. Bennigsen, "Sultan Galiev: The U.S.S.R. and the Colonial Revolution," in *The Middle East in Transition: Studies in Contemporary History*, ed. W. Laquer (New York, 1958), 402.
31. It was not until May 1918 that the Fifth Congress of Soviets of Turkestan "formally removed the ban on the admission of Muslims to governmental posts." Carr, *The Bolshevik Revolution*, 1:338. The Asian membership of the Communist party of Turkestan was estimated in mid-1918 at a mere 100 (against the total CPT membership of 2,000). Yusupov, *Perekhod*, 74.
32. *X Zjazd*, 263. For more on this subject, see Safarov, *Kolonialnaia revolutsiia*, 86.
33. See *X Zjazd*, 263, and Szczepanik, *Radzieckie*, 104.
34. See Zenkovsky, *Pan-Turkism*; Pipes, *Formation of the Soviet Union*.
35. At the All-Russian Muslim Congress in Moscow in May 1917, where representatives of the Tatars suggested adopting a project of national and cultural autonomy, the majority of the delegates pushed through a program of territorial autonomy on a federal basis. A similar program had been adopted in April 1917 at the All-Muslim Congress in Tashkent. See Zenkovsky, *Pan-Turkism*, and Nimet Kurat, "Tsarist Russia and the Muslims of Central Asia," 522-23.
36. Pipes, *Formation of the Soviet Union*, observes that "in most of the borderlands, there was an alliance between nationalism and socialism" (20). This description is not convincing. It could be extended to cover Armenia, Azerbaijan, Georgia, or, to a lesser degree, the Volga Tatars; it could be difficult, however, to apply it to the Basmachi movement or the Daghestani hill tribesmen. According to Caroe, *Soviet Empire*, among "the local nationals [in Bukhara] there were really three parties, the Conservatives, the Innovators (who were not Socialist) and the Socialists. The Conservatives . . . had most influence with the tribes and their strength was underrated"; in consequence, as far as the Modernizers and Socialists were concerned, the "scales were weighted against them and in the end they failed" (101, 118).
37. S. W. Kuleshov, "Velikii Oktiabr i natsionalnyi vopros (problemy istoriografii)," *Istoriia i Istoriki* (Moscow, 1981), 20.

38. See T. Rakowska-Harmstone, "Die aktuelle Problematik sowjetischer Nationalitätenpolitik Osteuropas," *Zeitschrift für Gegenwartsfragen des Ostens*, no. 7-8 (1985).
39. Quoted in J. Borys, *The Sovietization of Ukraine, 1917-1923. The Communist Doctrine and Practice of National Self-Determination* (Edmonton, 1980), 348.
40. Rodinson, *Marxism and the Muslim World.*
41. The first group was undoubtedly exemplified in this period by Mir Said Sultan Galiyev, chairman of the Central Muslim Military Council of the Commissariat for Defense, a member of the so-called Small Council of Stalin's Commissariat for the Nationalities, and chairman of the Central Bureau of Communist Oganizations of Peoples of the East from mid-1919. In 1923, we are told by Soviet historiography, Sultan Galiyev "was expelled from the RCP for nationalist, anti-Soviet, and anti-party activieties." See M. A. Persits, "Vostochnyie internatsionalisty v Rossii i nekatoryie voprosy natsionalno-osvoboditielnogo dvizheniia (1918-iiul 1920)," in *Komintern i Vostok* (Moscow, 1969), 64. The second group had a number of important leaders, especially among the Turkistani Basmachis (including Toghay Sari, Madamin-bek, Ibrakhim-bek, Kurshirmat, and—from the end of 1921 to August 1922— Enver Pasha). On the chieftain Toghay Sari, see Caroe, *Soviet Empire*, 120-21; on the Chechen sheikh Hadji Uzun, see Bennigsen and Wimbush, *Muslim National Communism*, 209.
42. *X Zjazd*, 260.
43. Yusupov, *Perekhod*, 123.
44. Congress of the Peoples of the East, Baku, September 1920. *Stenographic Report* (London, 1977), 60, 63.
45. *X Zjazd*, 262.
46. *Istoriia i Istoriki*, 257.
47. *X Zjazd*, 265, 267; Carr, *The Bolshevik Revolution*, 1:341.
48. *X Zjazd*, 812, 818-19.
49. Yusupov, *Perekhod*, 82-83.
50. This is the reconstruction made in the official history of the Communist party of Kazakhstan, published in 1963. See Bennigsen and Wimbush, *Muslim National Communism*, 233. For a contemporary opinion on the short-lived activities of the Turkic Communist party, see Mikhail Frunze's notes, quoted in Zenkovsky, *Pan-Turkism*, 247.
51. See Yusupov, *Perekhod*, 82.
52. T. S. Saidbayev, *Islam i obshchestvo. Opyt istoriko-sotsiologitsheskogo issledovaniia* (Moscow, 1978); Szczepanik, *Radzieckie*.
53. Istoriia, 262. Cf. Zenkovsky, *Pan-Turkism*, 223, who presents an even rosier picture regarding Kazakhstan.
54. M. Heller and A. Niekricz, *Utopia u wladzy. Historia Zwiazku Sowieckiego od roku 1917 do naszych czasow. Czesc I: do roku 1938* (Warsaw, 1986), 125 (*samizdat*), stress that the conciliatory policy of the Bolsheviks after

1920 "greatly contributed to the destruction of the Basmachi movement." See also Pipes, *Formation of the Soviet Union*, 260.

55. Cf. *X Zjazd*, 973.
56. Quoted in Persits, "Vostochnyie internatsionalisty," 99.
57. Sultan Galiyev, "The Methods," 146, 147.
58. Ibid., 150.
59. Quoted in Caroe, *Soviet Empire*, 113.
60. Wojna, *Walka o ziemie*, 39.
61. Sultan Galiyev, "The Methods."
62. Cf. Zenkovsky, *Pan-Turkism*, 244.
63. As propagated by, e.g., T. A. Zhdanko, *Specifika etnitcheskikh obshtshnostieii v Sredniey Azii i Kazakhstan' e (XIX-nachalo XX vieka), Rasy i Narody* (Moscow, 1974), 24.
64. Commenting upon possible dangers of Pan-Islamism, Sir Harcourt Butler wrote in 1916 letter to Lord Chelmsford, Viceroy of India: "I have always maintained that pan-Islamism is a feeling and not a force." Quoted in M. Kramer, "Political Islam," *The Washington Papers*, no. 73 (1980): 81.
65. Of the 435 Muslim periodicals published in Russia in the years 1870-1920, 202 were Tatar. Cf. Bennigsen and Lemercier-Quelquejay, 283. *Le presse et le mouvement national chez les musulmans de Russie avant 1920.*
66. Quoted in Zenkovsky, *Pan-Turkism*, 148, 149.
67. Saidbayev, *Islam i obshchestvo*, 64.
68. Ibid. During the fights with Basmachis there also appeared Muslim detachments of "Red Basmachi." See Pipes, *Formation of the Soviet Union*, 183.
69. Second Congress of the Communist International. *Minutes of the Proceedings* (London, 1977), 1:181.
70. See R. T. McVey, *The Rise of Indonesian Communism* (Ithaca, N.Y., 1965), 160-62.
71. Quoted in Persits, "Vostochnyie internatsionalisty," 94.

9

From *Natio Hungarica* to Hungarian Nation

Tofik M. Islamov

An ethnosocial community of different levels of evolution began to be known by the term "nation" long before the proper nations of the bourgeois epoch, nations in the Marxist-Leninist sense of that historic category, became a reality. The word "nation" itself appeared in the majority of European languages between the twelfth and fourteenth centuries. Thus, in Hungary, "nation" was the old French *nasion* in the twelfth century, the traditional English *nation* at the end of the fourteenth century, and a new Magyarian *nemzet* at the beginning of the fourteenth century.[1]

Humankind has long since been striving to come to an understanding of the enigma of people grouping into certain communities, to an understanding of the sense and significance of the material as well as the nonmaterial or spiritual values that tend to cement such communities. One of the earliest known attempts to grasp the meaning of "nation" was undertaken at the beginning of the fifteenth century, and it already contains the wording of some specific and important components of the concept of nationhood. According to a decision of the Great Constantinople Assembly of 1417, "A nation can be understood as a community of people of common origin who have disassociated themselves from another race of people (*gens*), or as a community differentiated from another group of people by language, which shall be regarded as the most important criterion of a nation and constitute the framework of a nation, by God's and human law equally . . . or else a nation can be understood in terms of territorial integrity."[2]

It is quite obvious that the term "nation," as well as its synonym "people," as understood by the Czechs, Slovaks, and some other Slavic groups, was used to describe a community typically existing in a feudal social system that was composed of a population ruled by a feudal seigneur. This was not a nation proper as is characteristic of those in capitalist social systems—or socialist social systems for that matter. A clear-cut differentiation exists between these two perceptions, nation and nationality. The different semantic weight and the obviously different historic and social understanding cannot, however, be interpreted as extremes separated by an insuperable Chinese Wall, in spite of the fact that those two historic categories express different forms of existence of an ethnosocial community in different socioeconomic systems. Hence, while stressing their principal differences, it is necessary to bear in mind that the contemporary nations did not arise in a vacuum. In a sense they were all "products" not only of capitalism but also of all the preceding social formations.

The foundations of any bourgeois nation have been laid over a span of hundreds of years, but the final consolidation of a nation in the transition epoch is greatly accelerated by the decay of feudalism and the advent of capitalism. The dynamism of the outgrowth of a feudal nationality into a capitalist nation has been predetermined by a complex combination of relatively quiet, gradual evolution and extremely rapid and explosive revolution in the periods of great social activity. That is why the formation of a nation—the outgrowth of a nationality into a nation or rather its rise to the level of a nation—might be delayed for centuries and then abruptly accelerate during periods when there is a revolutionary replacement of the old social formation with a new one. The history of modern Europe is full of examples of this type of development. Revolution is known as the locomotive of history, and in that sense it can greatly hasten all social developments, including the process of nation formation. It is therefore absolutely natural that the bourgeois revolutions in Great Britain and France did speed up the consolidation of the bourgeois nations in those countries. Similarly, it was during the Hungarian revolution of 1848-49 that the first stage of the formation of the contemporary Hungarian, or Magyar, nation was completed.

On March 15, 1848, the day the bourgeois revolution in Hungary began, the Magyars emerged as a united nation and challenged the most powerful European monarchies of that time. Against all common sense and sober calculations, they began not only to repel the superior forces of the Habsburg troops and the Russian tsar's army but also to inflict heavy blows upon them.

However, this is only one of the peculiarities of the process of the formation of the Magyar nation that is related to a later period, and here I am interested mainly in the earlier stages of that process as well as in the preconditions and circumstances of the development of the basic characteristic features of that outgrowth of the aristocracy-led *natio Hungarica* into a bourgeoisie-led Magyar nation.[3]

The Hungarian revolution of 1848, as I have stated, sharply accelerated the formation of the Magyar nation though the roots of the nation go deep into the medieval period. Some specific features characteristic only of that nation cannot be explained without reference to their historic background.

As scholars have studied the various economic and political models that can be considered in the formation of nations, they have identified, out of the great variety of forms and types, two main types that can rather conventionally be called French and German. The first, or French, model can be defined as an étatist-institutional model if we have in mind the character of the process of national integration, since it was the French state that came forward as the main integrating factor of that nation. The latter, or German, model can be defined as a cultural and historical model, since it was German ethnic factors, the German culture, and, before that, the German language, that were the main elements integrating that nation.[4] In the German model, as is described in the works of Herder and Fichte, the *Volksgeist* or an allegedly permanent, invariable spirit of the people or nationality always comes to the fore.[5]

The Hungarian model of the nation-building process has some features that have an affinity with both basic types of nation-building models just described, but it does not have complete confluence with either of them. The state and its most important attributes, such as an estate-based constitution, a state-called national assembly, and a state-controlled *comitatus* system, relied on an economic system based on land ownership and on political power that involved a comparatively well-organized social structure and the landlords' high public prestige. This social structure did not stop functioning even during the gloomiest and most difficult period of Turkish conquest and oppression in Hungary from the sixteenth to the seventeenth century. As soon as the chance arose, those feudal establishments were placed at the disposal of the bourgeois reformers and played a major role in national integration in the course of the consolidation of the Hungarian nationality and later of the Hungarian nation.[6] But the language factor and, in the broad sense of the term, the ethnocultural factor were also of great importance. I discuss this in detail below.

In other words, the Hungarian model represented a symbiosis of a "state"-built nation and a "culture"-built nation; it was a combination of those two basic types of nation-building models, *Staatsnation* and *Kulturnation*. Herein lies one of the most important differences between the Hungarian model and other nation-building types in Central Europe, though a certain affinity to the Polish nation-building pattern still can be traced [7]

The specific conditions of the Hungarian national consolidation were described in Kossuth's newspaper *Pesti Hirlap* as far back as 1842 during the heat of the national liberation movement in Hungary, when the newspaper made an attempt to give its own interpretation of the perception of "nation" in general. In its words, "A nationality is a historical fact, and the national language cannot be the only factor of a nationality. For in order to become a nationality, a people should have a common constitution, common perceptions, common interests, and a common need to make progress and develop the country; as for us, we are also united into a nation by our common memory of that great epoch that we survived together."[8] With all the best intentions of giving a generalized definition, the newspaper's reference to the constitution and "that great epoch that we survived together"—in other words, the period of the great rise and fall of the medieval Hungarian Kingdom—shows that the nationality referred to was Hungarian. This gives a Hungarian interpretation to the formula and shows that it was the intention of the leading force of the Hungarian national liberation movement, the middle-level gentry, to trace an organic relationship between the contemporary understanding of a nation to that which their forebears inherited from the medieval estate-based principle.

At the birth of the Hungarian nation proper, that is, the nation of the capitalist epoch, there stood a Hungarian folk midwife. She represented a group composed of Hungarian nationals, a group whose formation should be traced deep into the past centuries when the Hungarian feudal state was beginning to be formed and when the Hungarians began to adopt Christianity, which later became a unique ideological and, in a way, cultural foundation of that nation.

The state has always been a promoter of the process that encourages the development of both the base and the superstructure of any social system and especially encourages the process of economic consolidation of different parts of the historically occupied territory of an ethnosocial community. Most often, the newly born feudal, noble-led European states included some territories populated by various nationalities. This is true even in the "pure" nation-states of Western Europe such as France and Great Britain. They are always referred to as classic models of single-nationality states although they came into being—and this is an established historical fact—as a result of the unification of different ethnic groups driven together by force. Suffice it to say that even in 1789, when the French nation as such was really formed, one-fourth of the French population could not speak French.

It is not within the ethnic structure that the main difference between the way nations formed in Western Europe and in East-Central Europe should be sought. The main difference between the two regions should be sought in the different rates and methods of their socioeconomic developments, which had conditioned the rebuilding of nations in those regions. The initial starting positions were similar, however and the feudal states rose both in Western Europe and in East-Central Europe more or less simultaneously. The feudal kingdoms in Central Europe, such as the Polish, Czech, and Hungarian realms, were at one time only slightly or not at all inferior, either in population or in power, to the British and French kingdoms. A considerable lag in the historical development of the eastern part of the European continent occurred starting from the sixteenth century. Whereas in the Western European countries there was a gradual ripening of the capitalist economic system with a dominating role played by the cities, and the feudal economic system had already embarked on the road of decay, in the countries of Central Europe there was a marked process of feudal consolidation started by the advent of the so-called second serfdom, which hindered social development in that region.

Here one finds the main snag that brought about the sluggish development of nation building in Central and South-Eastern Europe as compared with that of Western Europe. It was really a delay and not a slowdown, for these two concepts have different meanings. Because of the later transition from feudalism to capitalism, and hence from the feudal nationality to a bourgeois nation, the process went on much faster in Central and Eastern Europe than in Western Europe. It took Eastern Europe a few decades or at most a century, whereas in Western Europe it took several centuries. And this is the second cardinal difference. It can be explained by the fact that in spite of the negative consequences of the division of labor in Europe, which had begun before the period of actual nation building, in spite of the ever-deepening economic and social lag of the countries and peoples of the eastern part of Central Europe, these countries still had a chance to enjoy the results of economic, social, industrial, and technological development, scientific ideas, cultural advances, organization of production processes and social relations that had occurred elsewhere. The adaptation of those basic material and spiritual values gained by humankind in its steady movement toward further progress tended to require the construction of appropriate objective conditions.

Thus it was the decay of feudal relations in Western Europe and the gradual development there of capitalist relations, along with appropriate transformations of social relations and of the entire social superstructure (including the sphere of culture and ideology) that had great significance for the creation of the forms and theoretical foundations that could stimulate such adaptations to progress even in those Central European countries that were still lagging behind in socioeconomic development.

In East-Central Europe however, where all the features of the historical process common for the region as a whole were present, the conditions for the forming of a new kind of ethnosocial community—for the transformation from feudalism to capitalism—were far from similar for all the peoples of that region. Because of these inequalities, the process of nation building varied during the bourgeois epoch, not only in the Habsburg Empire, but also in Hungary, which preserved its relative independence even within the Habsburg system. It is self-evident that in general in multinational Hungary the opportunities for members of the dominating community, the Magyars, were much greater than those of Slovaks, Ruthenians, Wallachians, or even the Croatians and Serbians who enjoyed certain feudal privileges. Of particular significance was the preservation of the important attributes of the feudal state such as the landowners' tightly knit groups with their organizational and political experience and their representative organs—the *comitati* councils and the State Assembly, both of which were convened regularly—and also the Hungarian feudal estate-based constitution. The official recognition of the Hungarian constitution by the Royal Court in Vienna handicapped, despite all of the efforts of the Crown, the transformation of the Habsburg Empire into a centralized absolute monarchy by Western European standards. It was for that reason, as well as a number of historical peculiarities surrounding the relations between Hungary and the Habsburgs, that the latter failed to reduce Hungary to the rank of ordinary province, as was the case with Bohemia and Moravia after the Battle of White Mountain.

An important factor that affected the transformation from feudal nationality to bourgeois nation was the peculiar class structure in Hungarian feudal society and the relations between the elements of that structure that were expressed in the activity of the legislative bodies and in the ideology of the ruling classes of that society. I mean here in the first instance the unequally great political prestige and social weight of the landlord class (i.e., the privileged estates) compared to the relative weakness of the state. The Crown's power was weak even during the great flourishing of the medieval Hungarian Kingdom in the second half of the fifteenth century in the reign of Mátyás Hunyadi (Matthias Corvinus). In Hungary as well as in neighboring Poland,[9] the royal power failed ultimately to overcome the particularism of the nobility and put an end to feudal anarchy. This was one of the most important reasons for the disintegration of those two Central European states. To it I should also add the backwardness of urban development, typical for the region, and the concomitant economic and political weakness of the trading and manufacturing classes, the forerunners of the bourgeois class. That is why, unlike in the West, there was no absolutist state typical for the period of mature, late feudalism characterized by the superiority of the Crown over the estates and a certain equalization of the social structure that could create more favorable conditions for the rise of a capitalist economy. The great contrast between Eastern and Western Europe is illustrated by the fact that in Hungary, all the secular and clerical aristocracy as well as the nobility were not subjects of the Crown but rather "co-owners" of the state. They were collective guardians of the mythical Sacred Crown, which was vested with attributes of judicial power as the main sovereign of the Hungarian state and as an image of that state. In accordance with the Hungarian constitution, the estates equally and jointly with the royal authority were the sole legislators of the state and the executive power at the level of the *comitati* administration; power, in other words, was completely exercised by the nobility. Nor were the peasants and all the other representatives of the underprivileged estates royal subjects: they were subordinate to the privileged estates.

Hungarian feudal ideology and political thinking admitted only one major social division: the privileged estates that constituted the *natio Hungarica*, that is, the aristocrats, and the underprivileged subjects of those members of privileged estates who made up the *misera plebs contribuens*, or poor tribute-paying commoners.

The Hungarian estates managed to preserve a considerable part of their medieval political prerogatives and social privileges even under Habsburg domination, and the dynasty, though it certainly attempted to do so, was unable to do anything against it. Here is an interesting example that could throw light on the character of the relations between the privileged estates and state power. In 1764, in the heat of most vigorous efforts of the royal court in Vienna to extend the policy and institutions of absolutist centralism to Hungary as well, the State Assembly of Hungary forbade the circulation of a book published in Vienna. This book included instructions from the royal court stating that sovereign power theoretically was subject to no restriction and hence mandatory taxation of the nobility was justified. The Hungarians sentenced the book to a public *auto-da-fé*. The author of the book was Adam Kollár, a man of Slovak origin who was Maria Theresia's royal librarian. The Habsburg Empress had to approve the verdict of the estates, but she paid them back in the same coin the next year when she ordered an anonymous Magyar booklet opposing Kollár's thesis to be publicly burned in the main square of Pozsony (Pressburg; Bratislava).

The perception of the nobility's nation, *natio Hungarica*, the nation of Hungary—but not a Hungarian (Magyar) nation—was deprived of any ethnic meaning; it was first of all a class conception and secondly a territorial and political perception. It covered a community of people who belonged to the dominant class and lived within the limits of one and the same political entity. In the foreground there was in that case an estate that possessed classlike solidarity, but in fact it was indifferent to which nationalities and ethnic groups composed the said "nation" of the privileged. It was just as indifferent to the recognition of those by whose labor the "nation" was fed, indifferent to the enserfed Magyars, Wallachs, or Slavs. But the landlords of all nationalities—Magyars, Germans, Slovaks, Wallachians, Serbians, Croatians, both assimilated and nonassimilated, Hungarian-speaking and ignorant of that language—were all regarded as members of *natio Hungarica* with equal rights.[10] In that respect, the Serbian Church Council was typical in asking that special Serbian privileges be recognized in Hungary. The State Assembly turned down the petition and said, "We believe they are all *Hungarians*. . . . We declare them as well as all the *nationalities* populating the Kingdom of Hungary and other territories related to it *Hungarians*, i.e., our fellow countrymen."[11]

In this text I have stressed two terms, "Hungarians" and "nationalities." The first showed the State Assembly's chauvinistic scorn for the non-Magyars, and they expressed a wish to have them assimilated by force and violence as soon as possible. The latter term admitted the presence of the non-Magyar peoples and to a degree recognized their rights since they were declared "Hungarians" and "fellow countrymen." So the word "Hungarian" was used in a double sense. First, it was used to cover all the inhabitants of that country regardless of their language, religion, or nationality. In that sense, like an old and now-forgotten Russian term, *Vengerets* (which was in use in the 1920s and 1930s and even until the end of World War II), it denoted citizenship, that one belonged to a country or a state but not to a nationality. And in that sense, by the way, it was also applied to the Magyars by the representatives of the non-Magyar ethnic groups who could clearly differentiate a Magyar from a Hungarian (*Vengerets*, *Ungarnländer*, or *Hungari*). With the application of that term, those peoples connected the presence of a "Hungarian" consciousness, a consciousness of belonging to Hungary as a common homeland for all those nationalities and ethnic groups, a sense of belonging to Hungary, which was considered to be a special political and territorial community apart from any ethnic or folk-bound, national self-consciousness whatsoever.

But in the course of nation building and with the rise of national self-consciousness, the intensification of the nationalist movements and international contradictions in Hungary, the "Hungarian" consciousness was forced out by more specific ethnic terms or ethnonyms—Slovak, Serbian, German, Wallachian, Romanian, and so on. A similar process was going on with the ethnic Magyars, but to trace it, "to capture it," was much more difficult, since for the definition of both perceptions, the broader state and political perception and the narrower ethnic perception, the Hungarian language knew only one word, "Magyar," an ethnonym that was applied to the whole multinational kingdom "Magyarsag," which means in translation the country of Magyar, "Magyaria." Nevertheless, in the sense that we are interested in the history of the evolution of the autonomous *natio Hungarica* and "Hungarian nation," or the "Magyar nation," to be more exact, we must look at the complete process during which the feudal conception of nation was gradually replaced with a new bourgeois or ethnic conception.

This conception expressed itself as a planned effort to attach a Magyar national character to that polyethnic state in spite of the fact that the ethnic Magyars constituted only half of the population of the state (though they of course represented the largest ethnic group in that kingdom). At the time of the rise of bourgeois nationalism, not only the objective interests but also the subjective designs and aspirations of all the nationalities populating Hungary were seized with a drive to national consciousness and were pointed against their common enemy, Habsburg feudal absolutism.

The pan-Hungarian national rush was led by the bourgeois-minded Magyar nobility whose leaders sincerely believed in the possibility of the gradual, peaceful, and nonviolent creation of a united Hungarian nation. One of the most prominent of those leaders, Miklos Wesselenyi, a Transylvanian magnate and liberal, sincerely hoped that all the nationalities populating that country would very soon turn into Magyars—first in mind and feeling and then in language—due to a sense of gratitude to the ethnic Magyars for the abolition of serfdom and other progressive reforms. But later, in his *Word of Deeds of Magyar and Slavonic Races*, Wesselenyi wrote, "As long as those nationalities tend to stick to their languages and their national peculiarities they—the latter—must be placed under the protection of the constitution and government."[12]

Though a considerable part of the Hungarian territory that had fallen to Ottoman domination since 1541 was liberated with the decisive participation of the Habsburg Empire, the Habsburgs nevertheless failed to conquer Hungary by force of arms and declare it a conquered territory, which, according to feudal law, would be a sufficient reason for abolishing the Hungarian constitution and pursuing unification. The attempts to ignore the estate-bound privileges of the Hungarian landlords and their constitution at once caused a powerful outbreak of armed resistance supported by massive riots by the peasants. The first of these riots occurred in the course of the Austro-Turkish Wars in 1683. The second one, under the leadership of Prince Rákóczi Ferenc II in 1703 to 1711, nearly brought about a complete liberation of that country from Habsburg domination but failed as a result of a sudden improvement in the international situation in favor of the Habsburgs. The attempt ended with the conclusion of the peace treaty signed at Szatmár in 1711 favoring the Empire. This was an official international document that determined the rights and obligations of each of the parties in the conflict. In the document's most important clause the Habsburg Crown officially recognized the Hungarian constitution and pledged to rule that country only in agreement with the Hungarian estates, to respect the privileges of the Hungarian landlords and nobility, and to convene the Hungarian National Assembly regularly. Any further observation of the conditions of the peace treaty of 1711 was naturally related to the balance of forces of the two parties in conflicts at any moment. In any case, at the coronation of the Hungarian sovereign, those conditions were always confirmed by both parties. The only exception occurred at the crowning of Joseph II, but his refusal to wear the Hungarian crown ended, as is known, in a most miserable fiasco.

Thus the Habsburg domination that had been unfolding in Hungary starting from the second decade of the eighteenth century proved to be forever weak and limited, both in form and in fact. This limited domination is clearly seen in the independent administration that was carried out through the Hungarian Royal Chancery and the Office of the High Commissioner as well as by the independent economic territory that was separated from all the other Habsburg domains by the Hungarian customs system.

Another factor of great importance for the character and rates of the transformation of the Magyar nationality into a Magyar nation was the force and tenacity of freedom-fighting traditions that had been consolidating for centuries, first in anti-Ottoman and then anti-Habsburg campaigns. The historical self-consciousness of the Magyars was deeply affected by the events in the war of 1703 to 1711, during which its participants, who fought heroically, proclaimed the slogan "For Fatherland and Freedom!" That slogan was brought forward with the purpose of overcoming the antagonistic class contradictions that divided the main mass of the people, the serfdom-bound peasants, from the landlord-led nobility. It carried a certain ideological weight, indicating that the nation-focused consciousness was evolving toward the nation-worshiping, jingoistic ideology of the new epoch. However, the state-control factor was simultaneously a "drag" with regard to the movement from feudalism toward capitalism and with regard to the formation of the nation, since state control was closely connected with the feudal administration. In practice it tended to fight for the preservation of all the privileged estates' rights and liberties while at the same time it drastically distorted nation building as well as the bourgeois transformation of a feudal society.

The Hungarian nobility as a class always fought in the first instance for its own self-seeking interests and estate-bound privileges, and thus it could notably reduce the sphere of influence of foreign authority in that country. But at the same time, the nobility most willingly accepted the assistance of the foreign administration in subordinating the millions of serfs and in oppressing the continual drive of the bourgeois elements toward the economic and social rise of bourgeois society. In that respect, the role of the nobility was a reactionary one, and it remained such until the nobility became involved in the process of bourgeois capitalist development in that country. Until that time, the Hungarian nobility stubbornly rejected all attempts by "enlightened absolutism" to regulate the numerous feudal duties and obligations the nobility placed on their subjects, to have the subjects released from personal bonds, to reduce the landlords' arbitrary whims, and to introduce a more progressive system of general taxation. But the struggle of the nobility against the supercentralization and Pan-Germanizing efforts of Habsburg absolutism that took the shape of a broad anti-Habsburg campaign in Hungary in 1790-91 already carried, in a sense, some features and peculiarities of the national-liberation movement of the bourgeois epoch. That is why the anti-Habsburg movement of 1790-91, which threatened to become a national uprising, should be regarded not only as the last estate-protecting campaign of the Hungarian nobility (which put an end to the nobility-dominated stage of the national-liberation movement in Hungary) but also as the beginning of a new stage. This campaign was a milestone in building the Magyar nation as well as a step forward in the development of its self-consciousness that was caused by the retreat of the mighty empire. It was at that time that the Court in Vienna retreated from its attempts to centralize and Germanize the Hungarian state, which one might now call a state within a state.

That stage—that is, the events in Hungary at the end of the reign of Joseph II—was preceded by a stage of cultural and linguistic progress that is usually called the Age of Enlightenment in the history of Hungary. Concerted efforts were made by the Hungarian, or rather the Magyar, nationality to overcome the old feudal backwardness and to boost both material and spiritual progress by promoting education and in particular, science as a means of eradicating obscurantism, superstition, and apathy.

The eighteenth century is of course known as the "Age of Enlightenment." This powerful philosophical movement began in Great Britain, reached France, and then spread all over Europe. Eventually, all the European nationalities and countries, including the least advanced and prepared in all respects—economic, social, and cultural—accepted the ideas of this bourgeois renaissance. The scale and scope of the acceptance of those ideas, principles, and slogans propagated by the great enlighteners had a direct relationship to many factors that helped to determine the general socioeconomic, cultural, and ideological development of Hungary, a region located between Germany and Russia, with Italy and Austria on one side and the Ottoman Empire on the other. This renaissance did not pass unnoticed by the Great Sultans, who were cocksure of their cultural superiority over Europe.[13]

The rate at which Enlightenment ideology spread varied considerably within Central and Southeastern Europe and followed along the same lines as those movements that laid the groundwork for the transition from feudalism to capitalism. Thus, the nationalities and countries of the Central European region found themselves in a more favorable position than the Balkan nationalities whom they had overtaken by at least one phase of historical development. This happened despite the fact that some of the Balkan countries—Greece, Serbia, and the Danubian Principalities—had come to their national state systems much earlier than the nationalities in Central Europe who had long been subordinate to Habsburg absolutism or the Russian tsar's despotism.

The spread of Enlightenment ideals in the countries of Central Europe coincided with the initial phases of a new stage of socioeconomic development, which occurred first in the cultural sphere and were characteristic of the period during which there was an outgrowth of the nationalities of the feudal epoch into the qualitatively new ethnosocial communities of the bourgeois epoch. Figuratively speaking, the Enlightenment has been interpreted as the initial stage of the National Renaissance.

Questions concerning the role of the state and the importance of a native feudal class of landlords and nobility during nation building have been discussed with great interest by scholars. According to Emil Niederhauser, an outstanding expert on the problems of nation formation within the areas of Central and Southeastern Europe, these factors could bring in "a number of advantages in the fight for the so-called national goals," but he also warns that "it would be wrong to overestimate the role of those factors in accelerating or facilitating [the process of formation,] for the nationalities who had their own feudal class were far from being in any more advanced, more advantageous position than the others." [14] It is absolutely true that we should not overestimate the role of state control in the process during which a nation is formed out of a nationality. The experience of the first semi-independent states that later became fully independent states in the Balkan Peninsula, such as Serbia, Montenegro, and the Danube Principalities, shows the presence of state control in that process. This state control, however could in no way accelerate the transition to capitalism or the formation of actual nations in those Balkan states. Further, the rate of development of the Czechs in Austria and the Serbs and Romanians in Hungary into nations was much greater than that of their fellow nationals on the Balkan Peninsula. Nevertheless, we can infer from Niederhauser that he would rather underrate the role and importance of state control in the nation-building process than overestimate it. Hence the problem remains open for further discussion and closer analysis. According to L. A. Obushenkova, "For the formation of a nation, the presence and activity of a class of national landlords and nobility in Poland and Hungary had both positive and negative aspects." [15]

Thus, regardless of the presence or absence of state control in the nation-building process (at least in its most rudimentary form), regardless of whether the ethnosocial structure of the society was complete or incomplete, and regardless of which ethnic group or religious community a nationality might belong to (as was the case with the Serbian and Wallachian ethnic groups), the process of the outgrowth of nationalities into nations in those two regions reveals the emergence of different "types" as early as the epoch of the Enlightenment.

It was the German Enlightenment that was the most important for the dissemination and assimilation of the ideological heritage of the European Enlightenment among the nationalities of the Central European region. [16] The reason for this lay not only in external pressure that may have been applied or in the mechanical consumption of values bred and promoted by the Enlightenment. It lay rather in a complicated ideological and cultural process that could be described as a cultural confluence and even cooperation, if we take it for granted that the theoretical concepts of Herder and Schlözer that had such a great effect on the hearts and minds of the romantic pioneers and "awakeners"—from Dobrovský and Kopitar to Kollár and Brodziński—had their sources deep in the culture and history of the Slavonic nationalities, including the Russians.

The German Enlightenment was effective under the specific conditions in Central Europe for many reasons. Not only had conditions there been prepared for certain historical transformations by the end of the eighteenth century, but, in addition, the Enlightenment had to do the same kind of work in Germany as in Central Europe. One might say that the Enlightenment laid ideological and theoretical foundations for the national liberation movement.

That the Enlightenment was an occurrence of social activity whose worldview was rooted in John Locke's philosophical concepts, as well as a movement that preceded the bourgeois transformation of society, has never been unanimously agreed. The majority of scholars engaged in the study of late eighteenth- and early nineteenth-century culture and social thought are more or less agreed only in recognizing that the Enlightenment as a whole, or at least some of its individual elements, was of great importance for the ideological and theoretical preparation of the national liberation movements, in particular, in Central and Southeastern Europe. Where the opinions and analysis tend to diverge is with regard to the structure and main components of the Enlightenment.

In one of his early works (1897), written only as an analysis of the views of one of the Russian "bourgeois enlighteners" of the 1860s, but not as a theoretical observation or thorough appraisal of the Enlightenment, V. I. Lenin identified three basic features: a denouncement of "serfdom and all its manifestations in economic, social, and legal spheres, . . . an enthusiastic encouragement of public education, municipal administration, social liberties, European standards of life, . . . and an assertion of the interests of the working people, mainly of the peasants who were not yet fully freed from serfdom or who were only in the initial stages of emancipation from serfdom in the epoch of the enlighteners, a sincere belief in the fact that the abolition of serfdom and its remnants will bring about common prosperity and a sincere desire to work for it."[17] This characterization contains some important methodological guidelines for describing the Enlightenment also in the countries of East-Central Europe, where the peasants "were not yet fully freed from serfdom," which could be proved by the fact that the peasant emancipation reforms carried on by "enlightened absolutism" were just under way in the Habsburg Empire. And we become even more convinced of this fact when we read the lines where Lenin stressed the antifeudal essence of Enlightenment in the broad sense of the word as a social movement opposing all the products of the feudal social system in the economic, social, and legal spheres. The universality of the conditions in all the countries and regions that have not yet survived a bourgeois revolution is indicated by Lenin's phrase "European standards of life." He later added a phrase regarding the necessity of "a generally comprehensive Europeanization of Russia." This indicates the necessity of a radical and complete reconstruction of that country based on the bourgeois-capitalist socioeconomic system and the introduction of bourgeois forms of organization and functions throughout the social structure.

Lenin could also clearly fix the chronological limits of the Enlightenment, which he tied to those times when "new socio-economic relations, with all their contradictions . . . were still at the embryonic stage."[18] So, in a broad sense, the term "Enlightenment," or to be more exact, "the epoch of Enlightenment," could be used to describe all the social developments characteristic of the transition from feudalism to capitalism. That was true for the nationalities possessing national sovereignty or state independence, or at least some rudimentary forms of these things. Many analysts, however, are apt to label the various stages in the history of the nationalities of Central and Southeastern Europe suffering under foreign domination as "Renaissance" or "National Renaissance."

An important precondition for disseminating the ideals of the Renaissance in the broader layers of society in the Habsburg Empire was the reform of the educational system—the universities, high schools, and elementary schools—during the period from the 1750s to the 1780s. As we know, such reforms were carried out under the banner of Pan-Germanization. But since education at the elementary schools was conducted in the native language of the nationalities concerned, those imperial reforms could objectively encourage not only the elimination of illiteracy and an expansion of the stratum of educated people, but also the development of the national languages and cultures. The importance of those reforms was so great with regard to the latter that E. B. Winter, a scholar in the former German Democratic Republic, has concluded that the cultivation of the national languages in the public schools could be "the first phase of the National Renaissance" for the nationalities in the Habsburg Empire.[19]

Winter, like some other analysts, does not point out any principal difference between the concepts "Renaissance" and "National Renaissance," and he uses them interchangeably. He stresses, however, that the efforts made toward the development of "literature in the native language," or the development of a national literature, shall constitute "the first enlightening phase of a National Renaissance."[20]

It was not only the fiction of the subordinate nationalities, but even that of the dominant nationality, such as the Austrian Germans, that took up the cause of the national interests; in fact, the men of letters were the first to realize how their dear backward Fatherland compared with Prussia and Saxony. It was that painful sensation of backwardness and the overwhelming desire to overcome it that was artistically interpreted in "The Adventures of the Pious Hero Aeneus," a story written by the Austrian Alois Blumauer. Another outstanding figure of the epoch of "enlightened absolutism," Josef Sonnenfels, attempted in his *Man without Prejudice*, an influential weekly magazine he founded in 1765, to draw public attention to the Empire's backwardness and to reveal its roots, which, according to him, were in the Roman Catholicism of the Counter-Reformation. He therefore advocated an enlightened Catholicism. So it was really the public understanding of that backwardness and the resulting attempts to find ways and methods to overcome it and foster socioeconomic progress by the abolition of some of the more deplorable manifestations of the baroque Counter-Reformation— for example, the heavy corporal punishment of a high school student—that became a starting point for the development of "Austrian patriotism" or "Catholic Austrian enlightened patriotism."[21]

The generation of Hungarian Enlightenment thinkers who emerged in the last decades of the eighteenth century were heirs to an oppressive legacy. The disintegration of the kingdom into three parts, the never-ending large and small wars with foreign invaders along with the ensuing chaos and destruction, the fall of once-prosperous cities, the displacement of the civilian population, the razing of whole districts, and finally the religious clashes after the beginning of the Counter-Reformation—all these had a ruinous effect on Hungarian culture. The Renaissance culture that had been so important throughout Europe, and that had blossomed in Hungary during the reign of King Mátyás Hunyadi (Corvinus) at the end of the fifteenth century, died. Hungarian, whose unique linguistic norms were created in the sixteenth century and were based on the northeastern dialects, yielded to the West-Hungarian, East-Hungarian, and Transylvanian dialects as the basis of the written language, and ceased to make progress as a literary language. The Bible was translated into Hungarian by Roman Catholic linguists on one side and by Protestant philologists on the other. This brought about two different Hungarian orthographic norms, although the differences, like those between many regional literatures, were not so great. The stunting of the natural evolution of linguistic development brought about an impoverishment of the main word stock, its monoseme. Latin gained ground because Hungarian was scarcely sufficient to satisfy the combined needs of people in daily life, warfare, and religious service. Hungarian texts of the seventeenth and eighteenth centuries therefore contain a number of Latin words and phrases.

Latin became predominant in the arts and sciences, in particular in historical science and law as well as in politics, and Hungarian literature remained bilingual for a long time.

The epoch of Enlightenment, as a broad concept and not as the traditionally narrow conceptualization of "Enlightenment," tends to coincide with the initial period during which the foundations were laid and the components were formed that would become part of building the Hungarian nation in the spiritual sense. This happened in Poland and the Czech lands as well.[22] This great epoch was opened by György Bessenyei (1747-1811) or rather by his play, *Tragedy of Agis* which was based on an ancient theme. The question may arise as to whether such an accurate fixing of the limits of that period is justified. "The publication of that drama in 1772 ushered in the commencement of the Hungarian Enlightenment,"[23] wrote the authors of the second volume of *History of Hungary* in 1972, evidently paying tribute to this specific periodization of Hungarian history. In so doing, these authors were guided by the idea that it was Bessenyei who pioneered the modernization of the Hungarian language and the development of national literature, art, and science. It was also Bessenyei who proposed that a Hungarian Academy of Sciences be established for that purpose.

There is no doubt that Bessenyei is extremely important, not just for Hungary and not simply because it was his *Agis* that, with two other books published in 1772, ushered in an entirely new epoch in Hungarian culture, as the authors of *History of Hungary* claim. The question remains as to whether the aforesaid periodization is indeed so well grounded and flawless.

Factual material collected by Hungarian scholarship during the last decade, the scientific research done by a whole constellation of brilliant scholars of Hungarian history and the history of its culture (one need only mention such names known both in the USSR and in Hungary as Emil Niederhauser, Kaman Benda, Domokos Kosary, Istvan Störer, Bela Köneczi) could make one somewhat skeptical about the periodization.[24] Kosary addresses the question of periodization in his fundamental work, *Culture in Hungary from the Eighteenth Century* (1980). There he presents a colossal amount of factual material and draws some conclusions that could shatter the traditional chronology of Hungarian cultural history. Kosary analyzes the material he collected on religion and the Church, education and schools, the press and the arts by juxtaposing and opposing the culture of the late baroque to the culture of the Enlightenment at three cultural levels: that of the aristocracy, that of the nobility, and that of the masses. At the same time he delineates the interaction of these levels, while taking into account the influence of world culture in that epoch. Kosary is inclined to assign the beginning of the Enlightenment epoch in Hungary to the 1750s or the first half of the 1760s. Apart from its broad systematization of the unusually rich and varied factual material on culture, one of the main advantages of Kosary's giant work, which is innovative in design, coverage, and a complexity of method, is that it has convincingly proved that the eighteenth century, until its last third or quarter, cannot be scientifically regarded—from the point of view of progress in the arts and literature—as a definite period of darkness, failure, and confusion, or as an "a-national century" in the history of Hungarian culture. It was during the first decades of the eighteenth century that Hungarian language and culture found themselves in an even more difficult position than in the seventeenth century.

The polyethnic nature of the Hungarian state, the continuous coexistence of several "national" cultures within the framework of a single state, brought about some interesting forms and patterns of cultural interference and cooperation of all the components of that historical process. A similar process can be observed in Austria, in particular in Vienna. The cooperation between different cultures in Hungary produced such a rare phenomenon in which one can find the representation of several national cultures in one personality. Such was Miklós Zrínyi, a Hungarian magnate of Italian-Dalmatian-Croatian origin who made a tremendous contribution to the development of Hungarian literature as he persistently fought for the restoration of the former grandeur of the Hungarian Kingdom through the reunification of its three parts into a new united kingdom. At the same time, Zrínyi was a champion of Croatian cultural traditions. His masterpiece of Hungarian poetry called *Szigeti Veszedelem* incorporated the stories of the Croatian epic. That masterpiece was then translated into the Croatian language, published by Peter Zrinsky in Venice, and became a literary classic in Croatian literature as well. Similarly, Mátyás Bél contained the attributes of German, Hungarian and Slovakian cultures in one person. Mihai Vitkovich was a Serbian poet who could compose his poems in his native Serbian and in the Magyar and Slovak languages with equal grace. Among others who were similarly gifted were the Slovak Hviezdoslav (Pavol Országh).

Even more striking was the fact that Hungarian culture was geographically decentralized. There was no single center of culture, but rather many such centers were scattered around the periphery in the territories with mixed population, in the Transylvanian Mountains, in the cities the Ottoman invaders failed to reach or take over, and in the northwestern and northeastern sections of the country. In the city of Pozsony, which became the seat of the Hungarian State Assembly after that country was taken over by the Habsburgs, the first Hungarian-language newspaper and magazine were published. An earlier newspaper, the *Pressburger Zeitung*, was printed in German from 1764 to 1929. That newspaper, as well as the more recent paper, *Magyar Hirmondo* (published in Hungarian), was edited, published, and printed by D. Tal'yari, a Magyar who was brought up in a German environment. It was also he who in 1783 founded the first Slovak newspaper, *Presspurske Novini* which was printed in old "biblical" Czech, a language spoken at the time by the Lutheran Slovaks in that country. Just a few decades later Pest and Buda became the greatest centers of cultural life, not only for the Magyars, but also for the Serbs (whose periodical was *Matice Srpska*), the Slovaks, and the Transylvanian Romanians.

The most prominent event of epic importance in eighteenth century Hungarian cultural life was the Racio Educacionis of 1777, a nationwide, state-controlled school reform. The significance of this reform was that for the first time in the country's history, education was declared to be a state rather than a Church concern. It was quite remarkable that simultaneously with the passing of the school bill, the state university was also secularized and transferred from Trnava (Nagyszombat in Hungarian), first to Buda and two years later to Pest.[25]

Thus the first step was made to pass control of the educational establishments to the state, although the schools and universities remained under the auspices of the Church for a long time. In addition, the system of education was unified, starting from the elementary school, which consisted of a three-year course in which students were taught in the native language, to the Latin-speaking gymnasiums, the Royal Academy, and the university.

In the spirit of "enlightened absolutism," the bill that reformed the educational system set forth a goal to schools: "To educate useful citizens." The "useful" spheres of knowledge were Latin, arithmetic, the natural sciences, geography, national history (which consisted of worshiping the dynasty), and the German language, which would become official in Hungary. In the 1780s during the reign of Joseph II, an attempt was made to have mandatory general elementary education for children, between the ages of six and twelve. The law threatened recalcitrant parents with severe punishment. Although well-to-do families paid for high school and university education, it was free for needy gifted children, who were also entitled to scholarships and fellowships. The universities opened new faculties with chairs of veterinary medicine, agriculture, physics, and engineering.

A special education fund, created with the property of the Jesuits that had been confiscated by the Crown in 1773, provided the financial foundation of the reform. This included 3 academies, 41 gymnasiums, and some other educational establishments. The total number of middle educational establishments in Hungary, including Croatia and Transylvania, was 126: 79 Roman Catholic schools and 47 Protestant schools.

The progressive national intelligentsia in Hungary continued to make persistent and varied efforts, sometimes with striking resourcefulness, to introduce the Magyar language in Hungary. In 1777 the Piarean Gymnasium in Pest began to arrange public discussions in philosophy in the Hungarian language just to prove that the language was adequate for that purpose.

In the epoch of Enlightenment, an important landmark in the consolidation of national culture was the development of the national mass media and periodical press in Hungary. *Magyar Hirmondo* (1780-88) published in Pozsony, was the first newspaper in the Hungarian language. *Magyar Museum* (1788-92), published in Košice, was the first Hungarian-language magazine. The popular scientific magazine, *Mindenes Djutemen* (1789-92), published in Komárom, was the first magazine of that kind in the Hungarian language.

The development of the Enlightenment in Hungary was cut short by the Habsburg Crown, which cruelly repressed progressive forces in Hungary after the disclosure of the so-called Jacobin Conspiracy in 1795. The new censorship restrictions sharply reduced the activities of publishers and printers and curtailed the circulation of printed materials as well. Triumphant reactionary forces took control and mercilessly attacked even the slightest manifestation of free thinking and dissent; by the beginning of the nineteenth century all political activity in Hungary had been completely suppressed. As a result, literature came to the forefront in the country's social life and assumed some political functions as well. It was then that the national and political involvement of Hungarian literature increased dramatically. This is why we can better understand the tendency to exaggerate, to a degree, the social and political function of literature as a nearly unique "guarantee of the existence of a nation and later a mouthpiece of the ideals of bourgeois development."[26]

It is self-evident that a national literature worthy of its highest designation has never been just a form of social consciousness but has always been the voice of the nation, a loudspeaker for proclaiming the progressive ideas of the time, to give voice to the social aspirations of the masses, to shape and propagate the political goals of the national liberation movement long before the appearance of any official political program of that movement. But as soon as the Hungarian State Assembly was reconvened, the activity of the *comitati* was restored, political periodicals and trends were revived, and embryonic political parties came into being, literature naturally ceased to be either the unique or the principal champion of the national liberation movement. The go-between function of literature also ceased to operate. Although literature remained the mouthpiece of national liberation ideology, the latter was already officially represented in the political arena. Moreover, the first program for the creation of an independent Hungarian state, national in form and bourgeois in essence, had been worked out by clandestine, republican organizations and prepared by the theoretical tracts of a Jacobin leader, József Hajnóczy, in the mid-1790s, that is, at a time when Hungarian literature was not able to carry on such work.

Today it is quite clear that there can be no modern nation, neither bourgeois nor socialist, without a proper economic foundation and a system of socioeconomic links that can help to consolidate a young and growing organism into an integrated national body. Neither can there be a nation without a national culture that includes the spirit of self-consciousness, a spirit that inspires the young organism to grow further, making it unmatched, simultaneously different from and similar to, other nations. The cultural conditions necessary for the formation of a bourgeois nation often used to appear much earlier and to develop much faster than those conditions necessary to provide a proper economic foundation for a nation. From this one can see clearly how great were the roles of language, literature, the elements of national self-consciousness, and other spheres of culture at the initial stages of national consolidation. But doubly great should be those roles for the nationalities who are deprived of their own state system, who have been subordinated to another nation for ages, who do not have their own national ruling classes, who represent some communities of the feudal epoch with an incomplete and imperfect class structure. On such occasions, all those political instruments and levers of their own "national" ruling classes and their own state control system could not be used to accelerate the process of nation forming. The Magyar nationality in Hungary partially possessed such instruments and levers. In that sense, the Hungarian model of national formation is not analogous to any other model in European history.

Taking another position, Polish scholar J. Chlebowczyk attempts to conclude that the politically organized opposition movement of the 1830s and 1840s emanated from a struggle to obtain recognition of the rights of the Hungarian language. In his words, "There arose an opposition camp. The fight for the introduction of the Magyar language rose to the rank of the struggle for national independence."[27]

By then, according to Chlebowczyk, "the struggle for national independence" in Hungary already had an age-old history, whereas "the fight for the introduction of the Magyar language" as the official language of the state was an important, but not the most important, part of the process of consolidating the Magyar nation.

The skillful utilization of medieval institutions and forms of the estate-based state system by the Hungarian nobility in the interests of the bourgeois transformation and for the creation of a national state drew the attention of Friedrich Engels. He observed that "within the period from 1830 to 1848 there was a much more active political life in Hungary alone than in the whole of Germany, and the feudal forms of the old Hungarian Constitution were much more skillfully utilized in the interests of democracy."[28]

The estate- and hierarchy-based constitution, the State Assembly, and the *comitatus* system were the three Leviathans that helped the independent position of Hungary within the Habsburg realm. They were the strongholds the foreign occupation administration could never bring down. Even during the period when feudalism transformed into capitalism, it was these features that remained intact and served the main organizational centers of the Magyar national life. They transmitted the national drive toward independence and, at the same time, were the most important and permanent forums for the expression of public opinion and for the mobilization of the community around the slogans and goals of the Hungarian national liberation movement.

In the light of all that has been discussed here, we cannot accept as fully grounded Fenyö's point of view about the Magyars: "We in this country never had a state-made nation, nor did we ever have the state playing a nation-building role here. Therefore the national liberation movement in Hungary as well as all over Central Europe in general, could recognize the essence of the nation already in the eighteenth century in her language in the first instance and also in those historical and cultural traditions that were manifested in the language."[29]

This modern Hungarian philologist's perception echoes the opinion of M. A. Hevesy, a Soviet philosopher who also discusses the problems of a national revival in Hungary and "the great ideological activity" that accompanied it. Hevesy states: "We could add to that the fact that literature was the only source for the expression of the national self-consciousness of the Hungarians."[30]

Yes, there was a period in Hungarian history that fortunately was not long (it lasted roughly a decade), when Hungarian society was actually deprived of all legal forms or forums for self-expression as a result of the revenge of Austrian absolutism on the Hungarian Jacobins. During that time, literature and language and some other forms of intellectual activity remained the only forms of expression of the public political mind. But the situation began to change for the better after the termination of the war against France, and a further change for the better began in 1825 when, after a long break that had lasted since 1807, the State Assembly was reconvened. From the 1830s to the 1840s, Hungary enjoyed a political boom of an unprecedented scale and strength when the first word belonged to politics directly, but not to literature. The year 1848 was approaching.

NOTES

1. *A Magyar nyelv törteneti-etimologiai Szotara* (Budapest, 1972), II. k., 1012.
2. H. Finke, "Die Nation den spätmittelalterlichen allgemeinen Kozilien," in *Historisches Jahrbuch* 57 (1937); Szucz Jeno, *Nemzet es törtenelem* (Budapest, 1976), 206.
3. On the socioeconomic aspect of the outgrowth of the Hungarian feudal race into a bourgeois nation, see T. M. Islamov, "Nekotorye voprosy ütorii Vengrii Konsta XVII-pervoi polovmyi XIX v," in *Tsentralnaia i IUgo-Vostochnaia Evropa v novoe vremia* (Moscow), 7-31.
4. Of course the Marxist-Leninist philosophy holds that it is the development of the bourgeois way of production that should be regarded as the main nation-building factor.
5. Szucs Jeno, *Nemzet es törtenelem*, 196.
6. K. Marx and F. Engels, *Sochinenie*, 2nd ed., 6:181.
7. J. Chlebowczyk, *Processy narodotworcze we wschodniej Europie Srodj kowej w dobie kapitalizmu* (Warsaw, Crakow, 1975), 12-18; B. Lesnodorski, *Les facteurs intellectuels de la formation de la societé polonaise moderne an siècle des Lumières*. La Pologne au Xe Congres international des Sciences Historiques à Rome (Warsaw, 1955), 167-216.
8. Endre Arato, *A Magyar nacionalizmus kettös arculata a feudalizmusbol a kapitalizmusba valo almenet es a polgari forradalom idöszkaban (1790-1848)*. *A Magyar nacionalizmus kialakulasa es törtenete* (Budapest, 1964), 163.
9. *Pol' sh na putiakh utverzhdeniia i razvitiia Kapitalizma* (Moscow, 1984), 278; see also L. A. Obushenkova's article in that volume.
10. The official language of that "nation" was Latin.
11. L. Szalay, *Das Rechtsverhältniss der serbischen Niederlassungen zum Staate in den Ländern der ungarischen Krone* (Leipzig, Pest, 1862), 94; S. Gavrilovi, ed. *Temišvarski Sabor 1790* (Novi Sad: 1972). Emphasis added.
12. Zsolt Trocsanyi, *Wesselenyi Miklos* (Budapest, 1965), p. 458.
13. S. Akgün, "European Influence on the Development of the Social and Cultural Life of the Ottoman Empire in the Eighteenth Century," in *Revue des Études Sud-Est Européenes* (Bucharest, 1983), vol. 21, 2, 89-94.

14. E. Niederhauser, *Nemzetek születese Kelet-Europaban* (Budapest, 1976), 85.

15. L. A. Obushenkova, "Comparison of the Processes of the Formation of the Polish, Hungarian and Slovak Nations," in *The Formation of the Nations in Central and South-Eastern Europe* (Moscow, 1981), 55.

16. E. B. Winter, *W. von Tschirnhaus und die Frühaufklärung in Mittel und Osteuropa* (1960); Winter E. Barock, *Absolutismus und Aufklärung in der Donaumonarchie* (Vienna, Frankfurt, Zürich, 1971); M. Csáky, *Von der Aufklärung zum Liberalismus* (Vienna, 1981). The authors—under the influence of antiscientific dogmas and concepts of the notorious Ostforschung—try to distortedly interpret the nature and character of the process of mutual enrichment of the national cultures, a process that had a favorable effect on the development of each of those cultures, including the German and the Austro-German cultures, advocating a variety of German "cultural imperialism." A typical representative of that tendentious direction is Fritz Valjavec; see his *Geschichte der deutschen Kulturbeziehungen zu Südosteuropa. III. Aufklärung und Absolutismus* (Munich, 1958). The mutual influence of the culture of the Austrian Germans and that of the neighboring peoples is brightly described in articles by the Soviet scholar D. Zatonsky and Austrian writer D. Sebestien, published in the magazine *Inostrannaia Literatura* (Foreign Literature), no. 10: 176-84.

17. V. I. Lenin, *Polnaia sobranie sochinenie* 2: 519.

18. Ibid., 520.

19. E. B. Winter, *W. von Tschirnhaus*, 176.

20. Ibid., 186.

21. Ibid., 187.

22. The problem of the Czech Enlightenment was comprehensively considered in the works of A. S. Milnikov, who described the process happening in the countries of Central Europe and having a common base and similar external manifestations with the term "Renaissance" or "National Renaissance," which is also often applied to the Slovaks, Slovenes, and various other nationalities of that region. In my opinion, the application of that term to the Czech lands can be justified only by the fact that the Enlightenment epoch in the history of the Czech lands was preceded by an "Epoch of Darkness," and it was in the last third of the eighteenth century that the Czech people really began "to arise from Darkness" to a new life.

23. *History of Hungary* (Moscow, 1972), 2: 95.

24. E. Niederhauser, *Nemzeti megujulasi mozgalmak Kelet-Europaban* (Budapest, 1977); K. Benda, *Emberbarat vagy hazafi?* (Budapest, 1978); Domokos Kosary, *Muvelöses a XVIII, szazadi Magkyarorkszagon* (Budapest, 1980).

25. Before Mohács (1526), and starting from the thirteenth century, a rather large number of Hungarian students used to go to study at the universities of Bologna, Padua, Prague, Paris and particularly Vienna; the university

there was founded in 1363, almost simultaneously with Krakow University, and almost 4700 students from Hungary studied there.

26. I. Fenyö, *Nemzet, Nep-Irodalom* (Budapest, 1973), 6.
27. J. Chlebowczyk, *Processy*, 115.
28. Marx and Engels, *Sochinenie*, 6:181.
29. I. Fenyö, *Nemzet, Nep-Irodalom* 8-9.
30. M. A. Hevesy, *Views of the Hungarian Revolutionary Democrats* (Moscow, 1962), 20.

10

Concepts of Cooperation in Central Europe

Erhard Busek

In mid-1989, a few months before the so-called Velvet Revolution in Eastern Europe, the Washington-based East-West Forum published a book with the (at that time daring) title *Central and Eastern Europe: The Opening Curtain?*.[1] By concentrating on the main questions of the form and tempo of reforms in that region, whether and how the Soviet leadership would adjust to the changes taking place, and whether the iron curtain that Winston Churchill had once described as descending upon the postwar continent would be lifted again, the book attempted an analysis of the developments in the immediate future of Europe.[2] Little could the editors of and contributors to that book know what would be happening during the last two months of 1989, that *annus mirabilis*.

Events in Berlin, Warsaw, Prague, and Budapest in the autumn of 1989 proved how quickly fiction can become reality. At the same time, nothing could have inspired the minds of editors and writers more than the events that overwhelmed Europe after the mass exodus of East German refugees across the "Green Border" between Hungary and Austria had begun in the summer of 1989—with all its consequences and revolutionary changes.[3] Still, it had to happen right there at the Austro-Hungarian border.[4] It had to happen at those borders between two countries governed by contrasting regimes, in a region of the European continent described as *Mitteleuropa* or "Central Europe."

As imprecise as the term itself may be, it is and has been an ideal concept for academic dissection and intellectual controversy. There are several ways of trying to describe it: as a subject apparently buried either in the rubble of the Third Reich or by decisions made in Yalta;[5] at best as an anachronistic utopia, at worst as a stalking-horse for the military and economic hegemony of a strong Germany;[6] and—rather derogatorily—as "a land where the Orient Express stops in the middle of the night at frontier stations with unpronounceable names."[7] Jürg Laederach, a neutral spectator from Switzerland, as neutral as one can be, has defined Central Europe as "a paradise, but with melancholics as its only inhabitants."[8]

Central Europe thus obviously has to do with emotions, not only with geographical areas that are not clearly definable anyway. In the late 1970s and early 1980s it has become the subject of a growing intellectual debate, be it in Claudio Magris's erudite and lively guidebook *Danube*; compact surveys such as Oscar Halecki's *Borderlands of Western Civilization: A History of East Central Europe*, or Alan Palmer's *The Lands Between*.[9]

If concepts for cooperation in Central Europe are to be analyzed, the first point of dispute is in fact geography. Where does *Mitteleuropa* begin and where does it end? Should all of Germany, for example, be included—that dominating mass of land in the middle of the continent having given *Mitteleuropa* a bad connotation by trying twice during this century to control the area permanently? If we followed Rudolf Jaworski's definition of *Mitteleuropa* as "a cultural landscape of great diversity, consisting above all of urban cultural centers (like Vienna, Prague, Budapest) and regions, and much less of complete states and nations,"[10] then probably Hungary, Czechoslovakia, and Austria as they exist today would form such a cultural landscape; but also Cracow and Galicia with Lwów, Croatia, Slovenia, and northeastern Italy (Trieste and the Friuli region), as well as Bavaria and Saxony, would belong to it—all in all, only a rather vague description.

History is a second point of dispute, in the true sense of the word. The idea of Central Europe, of a region somehow belonging together in some sort of union, took on a momentum of its own in the first half of the nineteenth century. After the Congress of Vienna in 1815 the notion that economic success depended on the existence of larger economic areas without trade barriers became quite popular.[11] It was the German economist Friedrich List who proposed a unified Central European trading area after the Deutscher Zollverein had been established.[12] The mid-nineteenth century Austrian Minister of Commerce Karl von Bruck also favored such a "common market," although with little success.[13]

Economic arguments for the unification of Central Europe played a central role from then on. Inside the Habsburg Monarchy, such a unity actually did exist—if only with huge social differences between the *Kernländer* such as Lower or Upper Austria and those on the periphery, such as Bosnia or Bukovina.[14] It was this difference combined with another fact that hindered the successful cooperation between the regions in Central Europe at the time: the national awakening of the numerous ethnic groups living in the lands between the consolidating German Empire under Bismarck and tsarist Russia—the two powerful blocks between which Central Europe was pressed.

For the peoples in Central Europe the nineteenth century was indeed a time of national awakening. It was only after the Revolution of 1848 that the first plans for federalist solutions within the political framework emerged. The most notable example was the plan for a federation of the Habsburg Empire by the Czech nationalist František Palacký.[15] His ideas remained only a plan, whereas the "Compromise" (*Ausgleich*) of 1867 between the Austrian and the Hungarian parts of the Habsburg Empire became a reality. This was an act of political rationality and did not really solve the problems it was supposed to solve. But the *Ausgleich* definitely was the crucial point in the development of relations between Germans and Hungarians, the Empire's two main nationalities during the second half of the nineteenth century. The others were left behind: the different peoples drifted apart, and the positive approach to the manifold plurality of the nationalities inside the Habsburg Monarchy began to disappear. In addition, the power and dynamics of Wilhelminian Germany made the German-speaking part of the Austro-Hungarian Empire more and more unwilling to compromise, especially with the Czechs but also with the other nationalities.[16]

How tragic such politics were for individual cases can be understood by examining the personal fate of the Prague historian and archivist Anton Gindely. As the son of a Czech-speaking mother and a Hungarian father, but with German education, he suffered from the rapid alienation of the nationalities. He finally resigned when the Charles University was separated into Czech and German branches in 1882.[17]

The developments in the second half of the nineteenth century made it easy for German politics to approach Central Europe mainly as a concept that implied economic expansion and political domination of everything east of Germany. The Mitteleuropäischer Wirtschaftsverein, founded in Berlin in 1904, was a concrete step in this direction.[18] It continued in Friedrich Naumann's book *Mitteleuropa*, where Naumann promoted a radical and nationalistic concept of combining Germany and Austria-Hungary.[19] This plan was only thwarted by the political and military events that led to the dramatic end of the Austro-Hungarian Empire as well as of Wilhelminian Germany.

The new order after World War I, imposed upon Europe under the Paris Peace Treaties, created more problems than those treaties were meant to solve. Some of the ethnic groups were worse off in the new Eastern European nation-states than they had been under the Habsburgs. Instead of cooperation, vicious ethnic strife and mischief divided the new nations in the East. Some of these countries were artificial constructions from the very beginning.[20]

In international relations security policy was divisive. Different kinds of alliances were formed such as the "Little Entente" against the "revisionist" states of Hungary and Austria. There was not much confidence in developing partnerships in those days. On the contrary, the new borders, the new restrictions on trade and tariffs, the new prejudices did not foster new ways of cooperation. Instead they caused a sealing off of the new countries from each other. As a result of the worldwide economic depression after World War I, domestic and local social strains prevailed, as well as ominous changes in the balance of powers in Europe. Right-wing strongman regimes seized power in almost all states in Central Europe, those in Italy and Germany being the most dangerous and threatening. The most radical ideas of nationalism, those of National Socialism, finally eliminated the idea of an independent Central Europe almost as radically as Hitler exterminated the Jews, who for centuries had been a foremost element in this continent's intellectual development.[21]

The catastrophe of the war was to be followed by the decisions at Yalta and Potsdam on the division of Central Europe. These two conferences determined the structural changes of Europe for quite a while, especially in breaking up Germany. The epoch of "Stalin's Peace" (to use Oscar Halecki's term) began. Besides the dreadful consequences of the separation of the continent, various occupation armies imposed their governments' social systems and ideological preferences on their respective area of hegemony. The new centers of world power, Washington and Moscow, established their predominant influences throughout Central Europe and by doing so almost succeeded in erasing its identity. At the same time hundreds of thousands of people were expelled from their home countries, resulting in the world's largest migration movement in current history.[22] Almost the whole continent was turned upside down. In 1945 "Central Europe" became invisible to the West. In the domestic politics of the Western allies the notion of an entity called Central Europe disappeared from consideration. It was the age of the monolithic power blocs.

Now there was even less common meeting ground in Central Europe than there had been between the wars. How could there have been any, since the continent was divided by barbed wire fences? In the Western intellectual world, reconstructing Europe after 1945 became synonymous with creating economic and diplomatic cohesion among the Western allies. Western Europe became a sort of supranational economic union confined to the beneficiaries of the Marshall Plan, politically squeezed into the NATO alliance, economically sealed together in the European Community.[23] Eastern Europe, also tied together in the COMECON (Council for Mutual Economic Assistance) and the Warsaw Pact, became a sort of intellectual graveyard. It was a house in which all doors and windows looking westward were sealed and any attempt to break out was halted by military force, either homemade or from "friendly neighbors"—1953 in East Berlin, 1956 in Budapest, 1968 in Prague, and 1981 in Warsaw.

The breaking up of these blocs was impossible for quite a long time. On the contrary, they were developed into fortresses of military power. For example, as a result of the Austrian State Treaty signed in Vienna on May 15, 1955 (a victory of shrewd Austrian diplomacy),[24] the Hungarians attempted to take their own road. They were encouraged by statements like those of U.S. Secretary of State John Foster Dulles, who had hoped that Austrian neutrality could become the model for the Soviet satellite states in Eastern Europe to follow. But when the government of Imre Nagy demanded free multiparty elections and even Hungary's withdrawal from the Warsaw Pact, the Soviets used direct military intervention to crush the Hungarian revolt for independence and later try and execute Nagy for his part in the revolt.[25]

The concept of neutralization for a united Germany, in 1952—from other motives—very much fostered by Stalin himself, and the principle of denuclearization for all of Central Europe, first introduced by the Polish Foreign Minister Adam Rapacki in 1957, later on even for complete demilitarization of the whole continent, remained theory.[26]

The transformation had to come from inside these countries, from people living, fighting and suffering there. Or as Joseph Rothschild put it, "the revenge of the repressed" had to come.[27] The "Prague Spring," the Charter 77 Movement, and the Solidarity movement were such "revenges." The ignorance of the West had to be fought against to bring Central Europe back to the map of Europe.

Help came quite unexpectedly from places such as Friuli in northeastern Italy. Located at another border between the two systems, this region nourished a more localized anticentrist movement. It supported the cooperation of regions, because the governments or whole nations could not get along well with each other: cooperation through neighborhood.[28] For political rapproachment on a European scale more time was needed. In 1975, the Helsinki Final Act of the Conference for Security and Cooperation in Europe was agreed upon and signed by all European nations (except for Albania), as well as by the United States and Canada. This represented the first such agreement since the end of World War II.

The Helsinki Accords proclaimed the full range of democratic and human rights for all of Europe (freedom of assembly, thought, expression, religion, and travel), even if they were not too successfully realized. But it helped the two blocs to merge again.

In addition to the slowly improving political contacts, the dream of unification of the continent was kept alive by intellectuals and dissidents, constantly harassed, jailed, deprived of their positions, and forced to work at menial jobs in their own countries. It was Milan Kundera, one of the most prominent Czech writers in exile, who first decried the impending nonexistence of Central Europe as a region, the disastrous effect of Russian domination in Europe, and Western ignorance of the vital significance of the free and unseparated central lands for the survival of Europe as a whole.[29] In Kundera's wake came other Central European writers, many symposia, and numerous books, all trying to rebuild *Mitteleuropa*, even if only as an imaginary land.[30]

With Gorbachev as the new Soviet leader the pace of change of the geopolitical conditions in Europe began to accelerate, more and more new (and old) visions were also being promoted from semiofficial Western sides. Among others, Washington-based disarmament expert Kenneth Adelman and Boston professor Walter Clemens came out in the summer of 1989 with plans for what they called the "Austrianization" of East-Central Europe. It would have meant some kind of neutralization of Austria's eastern neighbors, which would have remained Moscow's satellites. The grip of dictatorial regimes would have been somewhat loosened.[31]

Reality had already begun to surpass theory. With the flight of tens of thousands of East German citizens through Hungary to Austria, concepts for cooperation in Central Europe became another dimension almost overnight. The German Democratic Republic was still celebrating its fortieth anniversary in October 1989, only to be reduced to a "footnote of world history" after the fall of the Berlin Wall in mid-November. The next to fall was the

Communist regime in Prague, to be followed by Ceauşescu's overthrow through the bloody events in Bucharest at Christmas 1989.[32] This *was* the "revenge of the repressed."

Not since 1848, the "Springtime of Nations," had Europe lived through a year that was remotely comparable to the last few months of 1989.[33] The self-dissolution of world communism was delivered home every evening via television, and at the same time the fear of communism in the West in general instantly dissolved.

After the "Velvet Revolution" we are all faced with a completely different situation from that of the last four decades. After a Central Europe of nostalgia, associated with the search for a historical-cultural identity, after the demilitarized Central Europe of neutralism, now comes a time for a political concept of Central Europe that does work and that provides an answer to the rapid "de-Sovietization" of the former satellites in the area.[34] This means a reorientation of any individual country's geopolitical position, especially that of Austria, which is located right at the Iron Curtain.[35] The problems to be faced are as manifold as the ways and means to solve them. They bring out the best and the worst in the history of the continent.

Central Europe's history is indeed a peculiar one. Its countries are relatively small and it is geographically diverse. The people of this region have fought about everything—the rites and dogmas of religion, political convictions, and ideologies—and these were often the justification for wars of conquest. Europe throughout the centuries was determined by the ebb and flow of many different ethnic groups, which constituted the rhythm of European civilization. Central Europe suffered most and it was here that the tides left their traces.[36] The resulting borderlines were often contested. Most of the new states had always noisily discontented minorities; the demand to redraw maps to meet their aspirations was a permanent political issue.

At the end of the era of the "Pax Sovietica" it turns out that the stability inside the countries of Eastern Europe was sustained only by the presence of the Soviet army. Despite their common communist systems, they never achieved mutual consent, either inside or outside their countries. The "old demon nationalism" has begun to rear its ugly head again. More and more reports from the countries of Central Europe depict the breakdown of ethnic minorities and the possible threats to the prospect of liberal democracy and a sound market economy.[37] The main question is whether those countries will overcome the obstacles of internal and intraregional ethnic, political, and economic divisions. We who have lived in freedom and prosperity in the post-World War II world owe something to those who drew the short straw over forty-five years ago.

It is risky to analyze the most recent history of the East uncritically;[38] but it is just as risky to approach the changing situation from a purely economic viewpoint.[39] While financial aid might improve the employment situation in the "donor country," it need not bring about a structural change in the receiving country's economy—apart from creating conditions of dependence, unwelcome in a unified Europe. Be that as it may, certain basic truths about Europe are irrefutable—whether we consider our old continent a "Common House" (Mikhail Gorbachev) or a system of "concentric circles" (Jacques Delors).[40] Our identity and our common future rest on four assumptions:

1. History: Our history must be fully accepted as a living part of our heritage, which enables us to learn our lessons from it; our history must be accepted in its wholeness, without avoiding the dark sides.
2. Pluralism: Pluralism, in politics as well as in cultural matters, is the essence of Europe, the element that shaped the continent. Only a sound regionalism will help us to tackle, across national borders, the problems of the various ethnic groups and their nationalistic feelings.
3. Being different: Why is this continent so fascinating? We take pride in our different languages, different customs, different peoples. We take pride in it because European unity is based on diversity.
4. A multilingual continent: This fact calls for special consideration and acceptance. We ought to realize that, over and above a mere literal translocation, we must look for the meanings behind the words and acknowledge the particular qualities of the individuals as well as of the nations.

Notwithstanding the need for visions (which are the bases of all efforts in political and cultural affairs as well as in the world of science and economics), there are a number of practical problems that must be solved in the very near future. Introducing democracy and a free market society at the same time seems to create one of the greatest difficulties. Democracy in our neighboring countries will succeed only with our active support, including financial assistance—but money is not enough. Western democracy as such is neither to be exported nor should it be used as an instrument to patronize other nations.

It is necessary to continue an inter-European discussion about Europe's contribution to the world. European tradition has a great deal to offer. This applies to the field of political systems as well as to cultural matters and to coexistence between nations.

In the near future there is little hope for solutions on a grand scale. In order to solve the pending problems and to keep our chances alive, however, we shall have to take many little steps—but take them quickly.

NOTES

1. William E. Griffith, ed. *Central and Eastern Europe: The Opening Curtain?* (San Francisco and London, 1989).
2. On Churchill and the Iron Curtain see Fraser J. Harbutt, *The Iron Curtain: Churchill, America, and the Origins of the Cold War* (New York and Oxford, 1986).
3. One of the first publications to cover the new development was Patrick Brogan, *The Captive Nations. Eastern Europe, 1945-1990: From the Defeat of Hitler to the Fall of Communism* (New York, 1990).
4. Andreas Oplatka, *Der Eiserne Vorhang reisst. Ungarn als Wegbereiter* (Zürich, 1990).
5. Andrew Nargorski, "Are There 3 Europes? The Concept of Mitteleuropa Is Staging a Dramatic Comeback," *Newsweek*, March 23, 1987, 12.
6. Tony Judt, "The Rediscovery of Central Europe," *Daedalus* (Winter 1990), Vol. 1: 25.
7. Edward Mortimer, "The Rebirth of Central Europe," *The Times* (London), June 30, 1989.
8. Ilse Leitenberger, "Lehrstunde 'Mitteleuropa'," *Die Presse*, July 8-9, 1989.
9. Magris, *Danube* (London and New York, 1989); Halecki, *Borderlands of Western Civilization: A History of East Central Europe* (New York, 1952); Palmer, *The Lands Between: A History of East-Central Europe since the Congress of Vienna* (London, 1970).
10. Rudolf Jaworski, "Die aktuelle Mitteleuropadiskussion in historischer Perspektive," *Historische Zeitschrift*, 247 (December 1988): 544-45.
11. Günter Bischof and Emil Brix, "The Central European Perspective," in: *Europe and the Superpowers: Essays on European International Politics*, ed. Robert S. Jordan (London, 1991), 218.
12. Arnold Suppan, "Der Begriff Mitteleuropa im Kontext der geopolitischen Veränderungen seit Beginn des 19. Jahrhunderts," *Mitteilungen der Österreichischen Geographischen Gesellschaft*, 132 (1990): 197.
13. Klaus Koch, *Österreich und der Deutsche Zollverein (1848-1871)*, in: *Die Habsburgermonarchie 1848-1918*, vol. 6 (Vienna, 1989).
14. Paul Kennedy, *The Rise and Fall of the Great Powers: Economic Change and Military Conflict from 1500 to 2000* (New York, 1989), 216.
15. Erhard Busek and Emil Brix, *Projekt Mitteleuropa* (Vienna, 1986), 62, Oscar Halecki, *Borderlands of Western Civilization*, 328ff.
16. J. Kren, "Nationale Selbstbehauptung im Vielvölkerstaat: Politische Konzeptionen des tschechischen Nationalismus 1890-1938." in: *Integra-*

tion oder Ausgrenzung: Deutsche und Tschechen 1890-1945, eds. J. Kren, V. Kural, and D. Brandes (Bremen, 1986).

17. For the life of Gindely see Brigitte Hamann, *Anton Gindely. Ein altösterreichisches Schicksal*, in *Nationale Vielfalt und gemeinsames Erbe in Mitteleuropa*, ed. Erhard Busek and Gerald Stourzh (Vienna, 1990).

18. Suppan, "Begriff 'Mitteleuropa'," 199. The "Mitteleuropäischer Wirtschaftsverein" soon after its founding also set up a Hungarian branch (in late 1904), and that even before an Austrian branch in 1905! *Meyers Großes Konversations-Lexikon* (Leipzig and Vienna, 1906), 13:917.

19. Friedrich Naumann, *Mitteleuropa* (Berlin, 1915).

20. For Yugoslavia and Austria, for example, see Stefan Karner and Gerald Schöpfer, eds., *Als Mitteleuropa zerbrach. Zu den Folgen des Umbruchs in Österreich und Jugoslawien nach dem Ersten Weltkrieg* (Graz, 1990).

21. Bischof and Brix, *The Central European Perspective*, 221.

22. Alfred M. de Zayas, *Nemesis at Potsdam. The Anglo-Americans and the Expulsion of the Germans: Background, Execution, Consequences* (London, 1977).

23. Judt, *The Rediscovery of Central Europe*, 26.

24. Gerald Stourzh, *Geschichte des Staatsvertrages 1945-1955. Österreichs Weg zur Neutralität* (Graz, Vienna, and Cologne, 1985).

25. George Mikes, *The Hungarian Revolution* (London, 1957); Ferenc Feher and Agnes Heller, *Hungary 1956 Revisited: The Message of a Revolution— a Quarter of a Century After* (London, 1983).

26. For Stalin's initiative to neutralize Germany see Rolf Steininger, *Eine vertane Chance. Die Stalin-Note vom 10. März 1952 und die Wiedervereinigung* (Berlin and Bonn, 1985); for the Rapacki Plan see Palmer, *The Lands Between*, 339f.; for the concept of neutrality in Central Europe see Jochen Löser and Ulrike Schilling, *Neutralität für Mitteleuropa. Das Ende der Blöcke* (Munich, 1984); and for a view of the concept of neutrality in general see Alan T. Leonhard, *Neutrality: Changing Concepts and Practices* (New York and London, 1988).

27. Joseph Rothschild, *Return to Diversity: A Political History of East Central Europe Since World War II* (New York and Oxford, 1989), 147f.

28. One of the first institutions to promote cooperation across borders was the Istituto per gli Incontri Culturali Mitteleuropei, founded in Gorizia in 1966. See *Kadmos—L'Informatore Mitteleuropeo* Marzo 1990, 1.

29. Judt, *The Rediscovery of Central Europe*, 31.

30. Some of those distinguished writers were György Konrad, Václav Havel, Czeslaw Milosz, Danilo Kis, Mihály Vajda, and Milan Simecka. Three of the more recent books on the topic are Sven Papcke and Werner Weidenfeld eds., *Traumland Mitteleuropa? Beiträge zu einer aktuellen Kontroverse* (Darmstadt, 1988); Hans-Peter Burmeister, Frank Boldt, and György Mészáros, *Mitteleuropa. Traum oder Trauma? Überlegungen zum Selbstbild einer Region* (Bremen, 1988); and Arno Truger and Thomas H. Macho, eds., *Mitteleuropäische Perspektiven* (Vienna, 1990). Three of such symposia held during the last five years were "Heimat Mitteleuropa"

(Vienna, 1986), "Mitteleuropa: Dream, Nightmare, Reality" (organized by the Friedrich Ebert Foundation in 1987) and "Central Europe: Illusion or Chance?" (Cracow, 1989).

31. Kenneth Adelman, "New Ways in East Central Europe," *Washington Post*, July 16, 1989; and Walter C. Clemens, "Models of Neutrality," *International Herald Tribune*, August 10, 1989. Later on, Henry Kissinger joined in with "Superpowers and the New Europe," *Washington Post*, October 10, 1989.

32. The events in Hungary, Czechoslovakia, Poland, and the GDR in mid- and late 1989 are perfectly described by Timothy Garton Ash, *The Magic Lantern: The Revolution of '89, Witnessed in Warsaw, Budapest, Berlin, and Prague* (New York, 1990). For Romania see Brogan, *The Captive Nations*, 209ff.

33. Elie Abel, *The Shattered Bloc: Behind the Upheaval in Eastern Europe* (Boston, 1990), 243.

34. Jacques Rupnik, "Central Europe or Mitteleuropa?" *Daedalus*, Vol. 1 (Winter, 1990): 273.

35. Erhard Busek, "Ein neues Österreich für ein neues Europa," *Wiener Journal*, Vol. 112 (January 1990): 9f.; Erhard Busek, "Die Entwicklung in Mitteleuropa: Eine gesamteuropäische Aufgabe," *Europäische Rundschau* vol. 18, no. 2 (1990): 3-7; Alois Mock, "Austria's Role in a New Europe," *Austrian Information*, 43 (1990): 5; and Otto Schulmeister, "Ein Schlüssel zur Lage: Österreich muß sich wählen," *Europäische Rundschau* 2(1990): 23-30.

36. Jean-Baptiste Duroselle, *Europe: A History of Its People* (New York, 1990).

37. Time, August 6, 1990. A recent journalistic presentation of rising nationalism in Europe is Günter Nenning, *Die Nation kommt wieder. Würde, Schrecken und Geltung eines europäischen Begriffs* (Zürich and Osnabrück, 1990).

38. A fairly mild analysis of the Hungarian case is Elemér Hankiss, *East European Alternatives* (Oxford, 1990).

39. The phenomenon of change only seen economically has already found its analysts; for example, János Kornai, *The Road to a Free Economy: Shifting from a Socialist System, the Example of Hungary* (New York and London, 1990).

40. For an analysis of Gorbachev's term, see Vitaly Shurkin, *Großbaustelle Europa. Mit Riesenschritten ins gesamteuropäische Haus* (Bad König, 1990); a critical assessment of Delors's concept of "concentric circles" is to be found in *The Economist*, August 4, 1990, 17.

METHODS OF RULE

11

The Soviet Empire Before and After *Perestroika*

Valery A. Tishkov

It is already evident that the Soviet federation cannot be salvaged by "pouring new wine into old bottles," that is, within the framework of the existing constitutional system and the dominant political and conceptual postulates on which it is based. At the same time, however, only the rudiments of "new thinking" have begun to be set forward in the plethora of party platforms, current reforms, new legislation (at both the all-union and republic levels), and the programs of the nationalist and other newly emergent sociopolitical movements that are concerned with this sphere. The activities of our politicians and legislators, as a rule, have been reactive, and they have failed to keep up with the tumultuous pace of events. Perhaps most disturbingly, the profound polarization and obsessive intransigence that characterize our thinking, our manner of speaking, and our argumentation in the field of nationalities issues frequently preclude any kind of consent and communication, not only between ordinary citizens, but among scholar-specialists as well.

I

This was the source of lively debate at the Congress of People's Deputies in determining to whom the man elected to be the country's president must swear his oath—to the citizens, the people, or the peoples of the Soviet Union. Lawmakers, on the suggestion of poet-deputy Yevgeny Yevtushenko, settled on the final alternative of the three, a choice symbolic of the fatal weakness that underlies the Soviet state: the absence of the requisite sense among the citizenry that they belong to a unitary civil society. In all but prehistoric chiefdoms or tribal alliances based on blood kinship, it is precisely such a civil society that creates the foundation for the formation of a state, legitimizes it, delegates its own inherent sovereignty to the power structure, and is the subject of this formation. Historically, communities of people were formed on the basis of a common religion, race, or cultural-linguistic traits, and these factors continue today to facilitate the formation of communities and states. Once states appeared on the historical scene they utilized these common symbols and bonds in order to facilitate the functioning of the mechanisms of public governance and economic relationships. In order to achieve these goals states attempted to foster or even to construct a more or less unified culture among their citizenry, or at least to guarantee a peaceful coexistence between diverse cultural components.[1]

The fundamental core of the political culture of multiethnic states is typically that of the dominant (in terms of numbers, power, and access to resources) ethnic group. Ethnic domination engenders social stratification and competition between individuals and groups within these societies, and produces tendencies both toward assimilation and toward the marginalization of subordinate groups. This holds true even in states where ethnic equality is legally guaranteed and discrimination is prohibited. When the dominant ethnic group in a multiethnic society identifies itself with the nation-state as a whole, and presents itself as a model or referent for other groups to emulate, it presents the subordinate groups with a limited array of choices. They can voluntarily choose the path of assimilation, they can remain within the society and attempt to compete for resources and power, or they can choose the road of separation and form their own autonomous state as a "defensive bulwark" ensuring their own interests.

The era of the collapse of absolute monarchies and colonial empires gave humankind (particularly the peoples of Europe) an idea of enormous myth making and political potential—the idea of the nation as a kind of mediating substance through which a civil society acquires the right sovereignty and power, as opposed to the notion of a divine source of power and its exercise by God's "anointed" in the person of the monarch. This idea encouraged peoples who aspired to build democratic civil societies and to create sovereign states to create national movements. The idea of a national state in its purest form (one people—one state), however, was not realized either in the age of bourgeois revolutions and the collapse of absolute monarchies in the eighteenth and nineteenth centuries, or during the collapse of colonial empire in the nineteenth and twentieth centuries.

The boundaries between states, which have always been determined to some degree fortuitously, have never coincided with the boundaries of ethnocultural entities (people and nations), which because of natural contacts, intermarriage, and general mobility are impossible to delineate by lines on a map. Many people have lived together for ages and, owing to their particular economic and cultural characteristics, have been able to make use of the resources of one and the same territory in different ways, while other peoples have found themselves dispersed throughout the territory of a single state or have been divided by state boundaries.

Over time throughout the world the concept of the nation has become more and more connected with the concept of the state and of a civil community (cf. the United Nations). For the many peoples, however, who are dissatisfied with their status within multiethnic states (and there are at least 3,000 ethnic groups that fall into this category), the idea of the nation continues to be a powerful mobilizing force and has become the basis for claims for the establishment of sovereign civil communities in the form of separate states or autonomous formations, or for the securing of social and cultural interests and rights within such states. Not only in governmental and legal scholarship and practice, but also in virtually all of the programs of the popular fronts and the statements of activists in the various Soviet national movements, one finds that ethnic communities are identified as nations and on this basis are considered to be endowed with the right to self-determination. Even those smaller ethnic groups, traditionally known in the Soviet Union as *narodnosti* or "national groups," are beginning to use this identification and are laying claim to the status of "nation."

The phenomenon can be observed throughout the world: dozens of peoples within various multiethnic states have declared their right to autonomous existence and have laid claim to the designation of "nation" in recent decades. This has been particularly characteristic of peoples who have maintained their traditional way of life and suffered from inferior status, for example, the Naga in India, the Hawaiians and Navaho in the United States, various Indian tribes in Latin America, and the Basques in Spain. At the same time, however, in all of the countries of the world, including India, a country that is even more ethnically diverse than the Soviet Union, the concept of the nation has become identified at the level of legal and sociopolitical practice with the statewide community; for example, in India, the existence of an "Indian nation" is recognized.

In the vast, multiethnic entity that was known as the All-Russian [Rossiiskii rather than Russkii—Eds.] state, in place of the unifying idea of the nation there operated right up to the beginning of the twentieth century the feudal, eclectic formula of "orthodoxy, autocracy, and national character." Yet, even there the development of the quasi-legal notion of an "All-Russian" exhibited a similar logic [the term All-Russian/Rossian derives from the title of the state and denotes a citizen, whereas the term Russkii refers to a member of the Russian ethnic group—Eds.].[2] Both of these concepts later gave way to a denationalized and politicized idea of citizenship that was based on "proletarian and class solidarity," a concept that along with revolutionary and subsequently totalitarian violence, helped the Bolsheviks preserve the state within almost the same boundaries as those of the late empire. It should also be noted that "the right of a nation to self-determination," which was originally inscribed in the programs of the European Social Democratic parties at the end of the nineteenth century, was used by Lenin as a tremendously effective political weapon in winning the non-Russian regions to the side of the "revolutionary center" in the Russian civil war. In the early, liberal years of Soviet power, the peoples of Poland, Finland, and the Baltic region successfully established separate states, whereas in the Caucasus the Red Army restored the territorial status quo ante.

Over time, this slogan met with a complex and contradictory fate. It remained the foundation on which the unconvincing and difficult to implement theory and practice of socialist federalism was constructed. The principle of national statehood was enshrined as the basis of Soviet federalism: a socialist federated state was considered to be composed of ethnopolitical administrative units, in which each "indigenous socialist nation" had "its own" statehood, as opposed to "bourgeois" federations, where the constituent parts were held to be primarily economic-regional formations.[3] In practice, however, economic ties and economic and political interest were taken into account when the borders of the Soviet republics were fixed. This was the case even in instances that negatively impacted the interests of the center and the dominant Russian ethnic group. Thus, for example, when the Kazakh Soviet Socialist Republic was formed in 1936, industrially developed regions with long-standing, predominantly Russian populations were included within the republic's boundaries in order to increase its economic potential.

The Soviet Constitution has always enshrined the Leninist principle of a right to self-determination, up to and including the right to secession. Under conditions of totalitarianism and strict centralization, however, this was transformed into a purely formalistic guarantee as is evidenced by the fact that there were never any procedures devised for its realization. But even at the formal level the law applied only to certain categories of ethnic groups: those with union republic status. The others were arranged along a hierarchical ladder of relative autonomy, down to a level that made no provision for any administrative structure whatsoever. Additionally, among the peoples of the Soviet Union there are those who have been deprived of their statehood and/or of territories they had occupied since time immemorial, as well as those who have suffered border "adjustments" or incursions on their traditional modes of existence.

These issues have immediate contemporary social and political consequences. The question of the "punished peoples" (i.e., the ethnic groups subjected to forced deportation during Stalin's rule) has an especially strong impact on the current situation. This was a classic case of ethnocide. As of January 1, 1953, the total number of special deportees stood at 2,753,356. This figure included 1.2 million Germans; 316,000 Chechens; 84,000 Ingush; 165,000 Crimean Tatars; 100,000 Lithuanians; 20,000 Estonians; 40,000 Latvians; 50,000 Meskhetian Turks; 81,000 Kalmyks; 52,000 Greeks; 45,000 Moldavians; 63,000 Karachai and members of nearly a dozen other peoples.[4]

II

The speech of democratization initiated in April 1985 has placed the Soviet multiethnic state in a complex historical situation. *In the sphere of ecology* (i.e., the condition of the very environment in which various peoples live), we can enumerate an entire series of critical problems. Ambitious economic projects such as the exploitation of the virgin territories, as well as oil and gas resources, and the construction of gigantic industrial and energy complexes and military sites were completed using extensive and often brutal methods. This resulted in the transfer of vast amounts of labor resources, for the most part from the larger ethnic groups (Russians and Ukrainians), from central regions to regions that were the primary residence of other peoples, many of whom had maintained their traditional methods of subsistence (such as herding reindeer, hunting, and fishing among the peoples of the North, and cattle breeding and small-scale irrigated agriculture among the peoples of Central Asia and Kazakhstan). These policies inflicted incalculable losses on the environment. The grazing range for reindeer in the North has decreased by twenty-two million hectares in recent decades while the amount of harmful substances in the rivers and coastal waters of the Arctic Ocean is five or six times higher than maximum permissible levels.[5]

Ecocide was accompanied by elements of ethnocide, that is, the inflicting of direct physical damage on entire peoples—the Karakalpaks around the Aral Sea, Belorussians and Ukrainians in areas contaminated by radiation, the Kazakhs in atomic testing zones. For example, in the span of a single generation the Aral Sea had lost two-thirds of its original volume of water, and each year winds carry away hundreds of millions of metric tons of sand and salt from the three million hectares of sea bottom that have been exposed. Over the last twenty years infant mortality in the Karakalpaki Autonomous SSR has doubled and in 1989 stood at fifty-one percent—twice the national average. Two-thirds of the adult and juvenile populations have serious health problems, and more than 80 percent of women of childbearing age in the region currently suffer from anemia. The very existence of nearly four million people is in jeopardy, and the maintenance of political stability in the region will be directly linked to an improvement in the ecological conditions in the Aral Sea region. The Karakalpaki writer T. Kaipbergenov explains the absence of open conflict in the republic only by the fact that "all the efforts of the people are directed toward one thing—survival. We are not capable of anything: not anger, not searching out the guilty parties; we can only concentrate on one thing: surviving, saving ourselves. . . . Nowadays not only every republic but every autonomous area is like a powder keg."[6]

As a result of the Chernobyl accident and the ineffective response to its consequences, 20 percent of the territory of the Belorussian republic—home to 2.2 million people—is currently contaminated. In five hundred population centers (with a total population of 200,000) the radiation level is more than fifteen curies; in fifty villages it is forty curies per square kilometer. There is an urgent need to resettle 120,000 children, among whom the rate of illness has increased two to three times. In the last two years the problem of the aftereffects of Chernobyl has engendered a sociopolitical movement in Belorussia and has taken precedence over problems of preserving the language and culture. An analogous situation obtains in the Ukraine, where approximately one million people, about a quarter of them children, are living with high levels of radiation.

The *ethnodemographic situation* is the most important factor to consider when analyzing the current state of the Soviet Union. As a result of the aftermath of the war, the low rate of population increase and the collapse of the agrarian economy (especially in the central, non-black earth region), depopulation and social degradation occurred in the regions where the most populous ethnic groups (Russians, Ukrainians, and Belorussians) reside. In the last ten years the rural population has decreased by 3.2 million in Russia and 776,000 in Belorussia.

In the 1990s the Russian people will face a historic moment -the loss of their status as the majority of the country's population (51 percent of the population in 1989). The increase in population among the non-slavic peoples of the Russian federation (with the exception of the peoples of the North) and among the peoples of Central Asia and the Caucasus was and remains significantly greater. Between 1979 and 1989 the population increase among Russians was 5.6 percent; among Ukrainians, 4.2 percent; and for the Belorussians 6 percent; whereas it was 34 percent for Uzbeks, 32 percent for Krighizians, 45 percent for Tadzhiks, 34 percent for Turkmenis, and 24 percent for Azerbaidzhanis.

There has also been an increase in the ethnic homogeneity of a number of republics over the last two decades, as a result of a number of factors: the departure of many Russians (except for the Ukraine, Belorussia, Kazakhstan, Latvia, and Estonia, where the reverse process was taking place) open interethnic conflicts following forcible expulsions (in Armenia, Azerbaijan, and Uzbekistan) and emigration abroad (primarily by Germans, Jews and Greeks). In 1989, 235,600 people left the Soviet Union; in 1990 the figure will be somewhat higher. As a result of this increased ethnic homogeneity one can anticipate the development of even stronger ethnic solidarity and increased efforts aimed at "nation building."

The demographic situation, which cannot be changed quickly either by legislation or government policies, will in the future play an even greater role as one of the objective conditions promoting change in the balance of forces between the center and the periphery in the multiethnic Soviet state. It also underlies the entirely legitimate aspirations of the periphery to a higher status in the central power structures and to a greater role in determining all-union state policy, as well as in the tendencies toward separatism in the event these aspirations are not realized. Demography has direct political ramifications. Whereas Russians, with 51 percent of the population, comprised only 45.6 percent of the People's Deputies of the Soviet Union and 38 percent of the members of the Soviet Union Supreme Soviet in 1989, they can expect to have even fewer seats in the future parliaments. The number of deputies from the peoples of Central Asia will increase significantly as their more numerous younger generation reaches voting age.[7] These trends promise new clashes in the country's highest structures of power.

At the present time every ethnic group in the Soviet Union is attempting to strengthen its representation in governmental bodies at the expense of the rest of the population, and without regard to the fact that this will inevitably produce a countervailing response from groups that will perceive themselves as underrepresented. Such overrepresentation may result from the wording of electoral laws, the shape of electoral districts, or a disproportionate mobilization of the effected populations.

An analysis of the ethnic composition of recently elected parliaments and governments in the union republics confirms the existence of tendencies toward ethnic exclusivity and the disproportionate representation of groups with union republic status. In almost every case these titular groups dramatically increased their representation both in comparison to their share in the population and in comparison with the composition of previous parliaments. The following are representative examples form the latest elections: in Latvia, 139 of 199 deputies to the republican Supreme Soviet were ethnically Latvian; in Estonia, Estonian took 80 of 104 seats; in Kazakhstan, Kazakhs took 194 of 358; and in Kirghizia, 225 of 350 were Krighiz. In an extreme example the twenty-one member government of Moldova is composed of twenty Moldavians despite the fact the Moldavians make up only 62 percent of the republic's population.

Another key demographic factor that influences ethnic tensions and separatist tendencies is the ethnic composition and status of the nontitular population within the republic. In Lithuania the demographic situation is undoubtedly the most favorable for enacting a plan for secession—not only do Lithuanians comprise 80 percent of the population of the republic, but none of the other important minority groups (Russians 9 percent, Poles 7 percent, Belorussians 2 percent) have any kind of autonomous status. Inasmuch as the new law on secession requires a two-thirds majority for a mandate to separate from the Soviet Union, the demographic conditions for secession are much less favorable in Latvia and Estonia. The population of Latvia is 52 percent Latvian, 34 percent Russian, 4.5 percent Belorussian, 3.4 percent Ukrainian, and 3 percent Polish, while the Estonian population is 61.5 percent Estonian, 30 percent Russian, 3 percent Ukrainian, and 2 percent Belorussian. It is certainly possible for a massive reorientation in the attitudes of the ethnic minorities of these republics to take place, but it is highly unlikely, although it should be noted that in a public opinion poll conducted on April 6, 1990, fully 50 percent of the Russian resident in Vilnius supported the declaration of the Supreme Soviet of Lithuania in favor of secession.

The low rate of population increase among the Latvian and Estonians compared to the rest of the population of their republics (1.4 percent and 0.7 percent, respectively, for the years 1979-89) may be partially responsible for bolstering separatist attitudes there. If one extrapolates the rate of population growth that was characteristic of the last decade into the future, the Russian population will equal the Estonian population in fifty-three years, and in

Latvia, Russians and Latvians will be equally represented in sixty-five years.[8] It is precisely this demographic factor that underlies the "migrant" problem in a number of other republics as well. In all the other republics, except Kazakhstan and Kirghizia where the titular nationality makes up a minority or approximately half of the population (40 percent and 52 percent, respectively), the demographic base for the formation of separatist tendencies is quite striking, with titular ethnic groups making up anywhere from 62 percent of the population in Tadzhikistan to 93 percent in Armenia. In Georgia, although the titular nationality represents 70 percent of the total population, minorities like the Ossetians (3 percent of the population) and the Abkhazians (2 percent) inhabit compact territories that have autonomous status, a fact that precludes secession by a simple referendum among the population of the republic. Autonomous Abkhazia and South Ossetia have the right to demand a separate polling of opinion on the question, and barring a forced exodus of these and other minority groups, the Georgians are unlikely to be able to muster the necessary two-thirds vote. On August 25 and September 18, 1990, Abkhazia and South Ossetia respectively declared their complete autonomy. Remarkably, both these declarations were pronounced invalid by the Supreme Soviet of Georgia within a matter of days.

However important demography may be, it should be noted that in many cases it is far from the determining factor, either in the development of the situation or in the choice of a path for national development. In some instances the status of natural resources, the economy, political conditions, and the character of the external surroundings, especially the nature of historical ties and degree of cultural affinity with the peoples of bordering states, exert a more powerful influence on the situation within individual republics and the character of their national movements.

In the *socioeconomic realm*, the economic structure and system of management that developed over decades of centralized arbitrariness has produced a number of disintegratory factors, the most serious of which may be the profound popular dissatisfaction that permeates regions of economic stagnation. In these areas, "the center" and the local party and government bosses are held to bear unconditional responsibility for the contemporary situation. The regional specialization and division of labor that would have been natural in such a large and diverse country were deformed by an economic system that functioned on the basis of senseless and chaotic connections and interdependence, monstrous disproportions, inequitable exchange, and the secondary redistribution of goods by means of individual "bagmen" on passenger trains.

While modern business can be said to operate autonomously from political and ethnic structures in the developed countries, in the Soviet Union these three spheres are inextricably knotted together. One would think that in the RSFSR, where more than half of the country's population is located (147 million people, of whom 81.5 percent are Russians, 4 percent are Tatars, and 3 percent Ukrainians, with the remaining 12.5 percent divided among dozens of other peoples), there would be a sufficient basis for the preservation of the union in the republics' economic foundations. The Russian Soviet Federated Socialist Republic produces 63 percent of the union's electricity, 91 percent of its oil, 75 percent of its natural gas, 55 percent of its coal, 58 percent of its steel, 50 percent of its meat, 48 percent of its wheat, 85 percent of its paper, and 60 percent of its cement. Siberia alone supplies 3.5 times more raw materials than the rest of the country put together. One would expect that the fact that a significant proportion of these resources goes to the other republics at discount prices (e.g., internal Soviet oil prices are only a third of those on the world market) would incline them toward the preservation of unity. No matter how dire the possible economic costs and consequences of secession, however, popular discontent with the standard of living and the prospects for political and national-cultural development has become so great that those costs do not deter the most nationalistic leaders and their many supporters.

The general deterioration in the conditions of social existence that has resulted from the prolonged economic crisis of recent years has weakened the centripetal forces that hold the union together as well as the peoples' hope of changing the situation for the better within the confines of "the harmonious family of peoples." Righting the Soviet economy and setting it on a reliable course will obviously take years, and some economists predict that it may take decades. This has prompted some of the republics, those of the Baltic in particular, which have been keeping an eye on the flourishing economies of the small states of Northern Europe, to seek their own paths in attempting to improve their well-being. These paths are supported not by precise economic calculations but rather by the collective will to achieve the goal of economic prosperity on the basis of their populations' traditional diligence and zeal. These factors can by no means be dismissed as ephemeral, however, particularly in view of the experience of the Japanese, who possess neither extensive territories nor abundant natural resources.

At the same time that the centralized system of management brought about cultural dependence and a low level of social development in a number of regions (particularly in the Central Asian republics), it remains for the time being the only hope for correcting the problems of these regions—on the basis of unionwide economic relationships and budgetary allocations. Moreover, it is precisely within the framework of a strongly centralized union that many local leaders see their opportunity to obtain compensation "on demand" from other regions and republics for what they see as the unjust depredations of the preceding decades.

This issue underscores the primary difficulty confronting the political leadership in the Soviet Union today—the incompatibility between efforts to introduce a market economy as a foundation for further democratization and the improvement of living standards and the measures being taken by union and/or autonomous republics to gain control over "their" natural resources and economic potential as a base for and a guarantee of political sovereignty. It is interesting to note, however, that both the central and the republican leadership share the view that economic decentralization is a matter of the devolution of state control and regulation of the economy from one level of government to another (i.e., from Moscow to the capitals of the individual republics) rather than a question of denationalization or privatization. It is indicative of this situation that the only organized opposition to Boris Yeltsin's "500-day plan" in the Supreme Soviet of the Russian republic came from the representatives of the RSFRS's autonomous republics. These Deputies based their claim to plenipotentiary authority in economic affairs on the status of their regions as "sovereign states" and "members of the federation" that was granted in recent legislation approved at the all-union level. The deputies also maintained that the devolution of economic sovereignty should stop at the level of their economic ministries and not be passed on to the level of collective or individual enterprises.

In the *political arena*, the most dramatic changes in the character of the Soviet federation have taken place during the five years of *perestroika*. Previously in this enormous country, there was in actuality neither civil society nor its necessary attribute—a state based on law. State power became a monopoly of the Party nomenklatura, while the relations between the center and the periphery were based on the mechanisms of "indirect rule" and "clientelism," well known from colonial history and characteristic of certain African countries today.[9]

In the weakly modernized republics of the Soviet Union this system frequently degenerated into feudal clan relationships or produced organized crime structures, neither of which tolerated any kind of opposition. Glimmers of civic responsibility and independent (even nonpolitical) activity appeared only within a few local intelligentsias, but even there the exponents of reform were often compelled to seek refuge at the center. Nationalism as an ideology, and even more as a political activity directed against the center, could not be said to have existed, unless we grant this label to certain isolated expressions in the world of art or the works of scholars in the humanities, especially historians. Their zeal, however, was generally directed toward establishing the priority of the claims of their national group against those of neighboring peoples for territory, cultural heroes, and cultural legacies. Today, however, the "indigenous nationalities" themselves have definitely begun to display signs of local chauvinism, namely, pretensions to inflated status and the aspirations to assimilate small, ethnically related peoples or the sparsely populated enclaves of ethnically different peoples (e.g., the Poles in Lithuania, Gaguzi in Moldavia, Germans and Koreans in Kazakhstan, Tadzhiks and Meskhetian Turks in Uzbekistan, the Pamir peoples in Tadzhikistan, the Kurds, Lezghians, Talyshi, and Armenians in Azerbaijan). Fundamental religious differences have more often been manifested at the level of traditional institutions and village life in the Soviet Union, without penetrating into the relationship between a particular people and the center. Similarly, they have only partially manifested themselves in relationships with peoples of different faiths with whom these groups come into contact. Meanwhile the bloodiest conflicts to date have occurred in Central Asia between groups that share the same religion.

In the more modernized republics, the growth of civic and political consciousness in the post-Stalin era did not generally advance beyond individual manifestations of the dissident movement. This was particularly the case in the Ukraine and Georgia, where local dissidents maintained a primarily political orientation and received support from fellow thinkers at the center. Nationalism among the basic titular ethnic groups was harshly suppressed by the central and local ruling elites, whereas the hesitant attempts by the nontitular nationalities to assert their rights and interests met with rebuffs primarily from the local authorities and with indifference and a reluctance to interfere from the center.

The Baltic may have been the only region in the Soviet Union in which a volcano of mass dissatisfaction on the part of the principal nationality built up during this period. This dissatisfaction, which was based both on their lack of political status within the system as a whole as well as the nature of the existing political order, developed virtually unnoticed by the central and local leadership and even by specialists in the field. This may be explained by the fact that nationalism in these republics did not generally take the form of open protest by individuals or the intellectual products of poets and historians, but of a mass inner opposition and nonviolent civil disobedience. This popular withdrawal from public activity was generally misinterpreted and dismissed as simply an expression of the more reticent temperament of the Baltic peoples. Baltic nationalism was also strongly nourished by recent memories of their brief independent nationhood, by the sympathies of émigré circles, and in part by the support of the international community. The more militant stand of the local churches (Roman Catholic in Lithuania and Protestant in Latvia and Estonia) also played an important role in this region.

In attempting to trace the outlines of both past and current issues that relate to the status of the "national question" in the Soviet Union, it would be counterfactual to deny the high level of interethnic tolerance, interdependence, mutual influence, and personal contacts that were characteristic of most regions of the union throughout the Soviet period. This is attested to by the fact that the Soviet Union up until quite recently had one of the highest levels of interethnic marriages in the world. It is also true that whereas the Soviet Union was practically free of overt interethnic violence during the last sixty to seventy years, in other regions of the world, including some of the most developed democratic countries of the West, ethnic conflicts have been transformed into a peculiar kind of "Third World war" when measured in terms of the material and human losses they have produced.[10]

III

The unexpected and tumultuous growth in interethnic tensions and national movements in the Soviet Union over the last three years cannot be explained as merely a reflection of the worldwide trend toward ethnic revival and the growth of modern, postindustrial nationalism, although these factors have undoubtedly had some influence.[11] Also insufficient in and of itself is the factor of cumulative, long-suppressed discontent with historical injustices or the low level of contemporary social and cultural conditions. In the final analysis, the strongest and most organized national movements are not taking place in the most backward regions of the country nor among the most socially downtrodden ethnic groups. The Russian/Soviet case seems to differ dramatically from the classic (i.e., British) type of empire in which the mother country, located far from its possessions, was able to extract resources and become rich by exploiting other peoples. In the Russian/Soviet type of empire, which is characterized by the unity of the center and the periphery within the same state boundaries, such a system was never able to take hold. The unitary Soviet state, with its ideologized line promoting "the flourishing and growing together of nations," has in general had to "pay" for the union in terms of a diminished investment in the social benefits and culture of the dominant ethnic group.

The most prevalent explanations among Soviet social scientists for the recent manifestations of nationalism in the Soviet Union, in all their varied forms—from political movements for sovereignty and independence to pogroms and the clashes of armed combatants—have been the supposed drawbacks of Soviet nationalities' policy and deviations from Leninist principles. I suggest that it would be far more useful to focus on the inability of the political order to create even rudimentary civil institutions in the form of effective local self-government, or to build functioning political and social structures through which citizens and groups, including ethnic groups, could defend and realize their diverse and particular interests and rights.

As soon as the once omnipotent and all-encompassing power of the party apparatus weakened, the fatal inability of the hierarchy of state structures (the soviets) to regulate and govern social processes and affairs was immediately evident. For millions of Soviet citizens, aroused in the conditions of *glasnost* to social activism, but faced with a dearth of truly effective forms for realizing their demands, appeals to the nation became the sole and the most readily comprehensible basis for collective action and the expression of protest in conditions of social despair and profound political disillusionment.

Nor should one discount the circumstances noted by Zbigniew Brzezinski: "Although communism declared itself to be an internationalist doctrine, in fact it fostered nationalist sentiments among the people."[12] In the realm of ideas, the prevailing communist dogma did indeed engender intolerant nationalism. As far as social practice was concerned, many internationalist forces and relationships were destroyed or failed to be created in the course of the experiment in building socialism. The prerevolutionary cosmopolitan Russian aristocracy, French-speaking and frequently of foreign extraction, readily admitted distinguished émigrés from the borderlands into their ranks. Ironically, in the postrevolutionary period neither three guaranteed seats on the Politburo (for the foremost party figures from the Ukraine, Azerbaijan, and Kazakhstan), nor the often purely formal relations between the creative intelligentsia of the center and the republics, could compensate for this social loss. The Soviet state with its isolated and sluggish economy has proved, unlike its modern capitalist competitors, to be incapable of creating an influential and essentially internationalist social force like the Western business elite. As a result the largely immobile, disconnected multiethnic population of the country received its lessons in internationalism not from everyday life but from the propaganda apparatus and the experience of life in the military barracks that has been required of all young men.

The arrival of television in Soviet homes in the 1970s and 1980s only increased the flow of the official, Russian-language culture, without providing much in the way of enrichment of "horizontal" interethnic contacts. More frequently, though, especially in times of tension and crisis, the blue screen of the "central means of mass information" became an ordinary, domestic lightning rod in the frenzied search for hostile forces and the causes of disorder.

It appears that the nationalism that was spawned by the developments of capitalism and the desire of the bourgeoisie to form "national markets" during the eighteenth, nineteenth, and twentieth centuries is taking its final bow in the postindustrial societies of the West. Interethnic relations in the Soviet Union over the last two to three years, however, suggest that nationalism is well preserved and being reinvigorated in the social conditions we call socialism. This suggests that the phenomenon of nationalism is more a characteristic of a certain stage in the evolution of human communities than it is connected with any particular social order.

Attempts have been made in Western anthropological literature to interpret contemporary nationalism in a new way—as both a system and a mechanism that certain individuals and groups utilize to achieve desired levels of status and well-being, and to become more successfully integrated into modern technological societies. Insofar as all these processes take place within well-defined cultural systems, here too, such factors as ethnic solidarity and a common language play a rather significant role as well.[13] But there is another way to look at the phenomenon of nationalism. In developed, democratic societies where the individual citizen is presented with opportunities to achieve social status and a satisfactory standard of living, ethnicity, economics, and politics represent three weakly interrelated and largely independent systems. In such societies the members of cultural, linguistic, and religious groups typically protect their interests and ensure their groups' autonomy on the basis of individual rights and general democratic principles. Nationalism and exclusive ethnic loyalty arise in the absence of these safeguards, in societies that lack effective political mechanisms for the articulation and achievement of collective aspirations and interests, and where ethnicity, economics, and politics interpenetrate in one poorly functioning system. Clearly the Soviet Union still belongs in this second category.

IV

What, then, awaits the Soviet Union after five years of *perestroika*? What will be the fate of its population of 289 million, composed of more than 130 different peoples? Bloody interethnic clashes and the army's suppression of popular disturbances in a series of republics have already resulted in 1,049 deaths, 8,951 casualties, and 583,200 refugees, according to Soviet Union Ministry of Internal Affairs data for 1988, 1989, and the first nine months of 1990. More that 330,000 people fled Azerbaijan, 173,000 left Armenia, and 64,000 left Uzbekistan during the same period. The main groups of refugees are currently concentrated in Azerbaijan (204,000), Armenia (236,000), and the RSFSR (150,000). Moscow and the surrounding Moscow oblast' have already had to find space for 40,000 refugees, and further migrations of peoples from the Baltic region, Moldova, and Central Asia are expected in the near future.

To all intents and purposes, the legally constituted authorities are powerless to halt either the violence or the large-scale dislocation of populations. Most often the only factor acting to restrain the violence is the fear of reprisals by the opposing side. The authorities themselves, including the forces of law and order—the MVD and even in some instances the KGB—are also ethnically engaged, and frequently sympathize with the national movements. In 1989 criminal charges were brought against 350 people for participation in interethnic conflicts and in the early part of 1990 there were an additional 100 cases, but it is impossible for those charged with law enforcement fully to investigate and prosecute each one.

This has caused gloomy prognoses concerning the inevitable and rapid collapse of the "Soviet empire." Zbigniew Brzezinski predicts the "Balkanization" of Eastern Europe, the "Lebanonization" of the Soviet Union and the transformation of "the existing Soviet bloc into an arena of the most sever national conflicts on earth."[14] Yuri Afanasiev, in an issue of *Time* magazine devoted to the topic of "Soviet deunionization," expressed the view that "the Soviet Union is neither a country nor a state. The Eurasian territory so designated on maps is a whole world of worlds, made up of different cultures and civilizations . . . and the Soviet Union as a country has no future."[15]

Other scenarios are equally possible. The *first variant* envisions the future Soviet Union as a union of autonomous states. Within a number of these states, particularly the Russian republic, provisions would be made for regional self-government. This scheme probably has more proponents than any other, although its proponents differ widely as to specifics. For the ruling center, for many party and government leaders at the republican and autonomous area levels, and for Mikhail Gorbachev most of all, a renewed union is envisaged within the framework of the long-prevailing concept of a federal state structure. This is designed, however, to be a federation "filled with new contents," and created on the basis of a new treaty. A new union treaty is one of the center's most recent concessions: as recently as 1989 the Communist party Central Committee's platform on "The Party's National Policy in Light of the Current Situation" maintained that the choice made in 1922 was immutable and limited itself to a cliché about the "openness of the treaty." But this concession comes far too late, the consultations that took place between an all-union delegation and representatives from the republics at the Kremlin in July and August of this year proved to be fruitless, and a number of republics had recourse to parallel republic to republic negotiations. The formula "fifteen plus one" (the republics plus the center) frightened many of the participants in this historical drama, and it seems likely that the center may find itself transformed into a kind of switchboard for horizontal inter-republican ties, as a part of the infrastructure ensuring their effective mutual cooperation.

The most succinct account of the position of the political center on this question was set forth in the draft platform for the Twenty-Eighth Party Congress that approved at the Central Committee plenum in February, 1990, entitled "Toward a Humane, Democratic Socialism." In the section entitled "Toward a New Federation," both the fate of *perestroika* and the future of the country were directly linked to the sphere of interethnic relations. The causes of the conflicts, however, were identified in the "distortion of the Leninist nationalities policy," while "the main way out of the difficulties [!] that have arisen in this area" was conceived in terms of the realization of the economic and political reforms and the principle of federalism.

The ideological basis of the platform remains "the principle of self-determination of nations in a revitalized Soviet federation," which presupposes the "freedom of nation-state formations to choose their own ways of life, institutions, and symbols of statehood." But at the same time the document states that "we are resolutely opposed to separatist slogans and movements that lead to the destruction of the large-scale, multinational democratic state," and to the loss of all that was "great and worthy that was introduced into the life of our country by the October Revolution," including the "sense of being an equal participant in a great world power."[16]

In his arguments in favor of the establishment of a revitalized federation, Gorbachev emotionally conceded, "We do not yet live under the conditions of a real federation." The critical point in his position is his insistence on preserving the union as fifteen "national states" with the existing hierarchy of national-state formations and guarantees of the rights and opportunities for development of the so-called nonnative populations and national groups within the republics. This formula does not propose any radical change for the Russian republic, first because it does not acknowledge the concept of self determination for civil-territorial communities (regional self-determination), and second, because the self-determination of the Russians on an ethnic basis would be impossible to bring about, as, indeed, it is for the majority of other peoples.

Although the center still has great political and economic power, it cannot in fact realize its program. The central bureaucratic apparatus and other powerful institutions that are fearful of losing unionwide power, in conjunction with the resistance of conservative forces and the inertia of imperial thinking, have blocked the redistribution and decentralization of power in even the most innocuous spheres of life despite the fact that they are confronted with the specter of imminent disintegration. Science, education, and culture, which are the prerogative of state and provincial institutions in every federal system in the world, remain subordinated to the central authorities in the Soviet Union. Even in the new law on the delineation of prerogatives between the center and the union republics and the draft constitution currently being prepared, these powers remain vested in all-union institutions.

The confrontation in the spring of 1990 between the president of the Soviet Union and the Lithuanian leadership seems to have reinforced the old great-power syndrome and has provoked a resurrection of what were only recently considered to be outdated ideological clichés. In one of Gorbachev's speeches to the Twenty-First All-Union Congress of the Komsomol, he referred to the territory of Lithuania as "this coastal frontier which Russia gained over the ages." In another speech he termed "the demon of nationalism" to be "terrible in all its manifestations," and he suggested that "the common goal of the younger generation" should be "the total renewal and development of the friendship of our peoples."[17]

The *second variant* for restructuring the Union has been proposed by the Baltic republics, and also by Georgia and Moldova. It calls for the establishment of independent or fully sovereign states, which would be associated in a single union on the model of the United Nations or the European Community. Lithuania has come closest to the realization of the goal of independence, at least at the level of policy, state symbols, and in its stance concerning the highest representative bodies of power.

The implementation of this variant, however, would not in fact result in the restructuring or reform of the federation, but rather would abolish it and replace it with an entirely new, and for the moment largely hypothetical, association of states. All the legal groundwork necessary for the implementation of this variant is already in place, and it gains legitimacy from the fact that it is based primarily on the right to self-determination, which is common to all democracies and widely acknowledged around the world. but there are at least two very important factors that have not been taken sufficiently into account by either of the opposing sides.

First, the right to self-determination, as it has been validated in numerous international legal documents and as it has been achieved in historical practice, has generally been understood not as the right of nations *qua* distinct ethnic communities (and it must be admitted that this is precisely how it is understood in the Soviet Union today, by our all-union legislators, our social scientist, and by the proponents of the national movement), but as a right that inheres in civil associations or in a people, using this term in the broad sense that relates to citizenship.

In other words, self-determination does not apply to the Estonians and the "Estonian nation," nor to the Lithuanians, and the "Lithuanian nation," nor to the Georgians and the "Georgian nation," but to the people of Estonia, the people of Lithuania, and the people of Georgia. These are not one and the same, although as a rule the majority, and in some cases even the overwhelming majority, of the population of these governmental entities will be made up of the representatives of the titular nationality. Let us look for a moment at the historical record. It was precisely on civic foundations that the people of France based their self-determination in the eighteenth century. Within the confines of France there were many diverse ethnic groups (including the French themselves, Bretons, Alsations, Corsicans, Catalonians, Walloons, Basques, and Flemings). The same civil basis for the nation was appealed to when the multiethnic population inhabiting England's North American colonies established a single national entity—the United States of America. The many peoples of Europe and Latin America who based their actions on their right to self-determination in the nineteenth century and the peoples of Asia and Africa who followed the same path in the twentieth century did so on the same civil basis.

Self-determination on strictly ethnic lines was impossible in the past and it is impossible today. The Soviet Union is no exception to this rule. Only the forcible, mass resettlement of millions of citizens could alter this state of affairs, but even were recourse to be had to such a distasteful expedient there would still be the problem of what to do with millions of people of mixed ancestry and ethnically mixed families.

As they approach their avowed goal, it appears that the proponents of secession in the Baltic are coming to realize both the danger and the dead-end logic of the narrowly construed, ethnically based interpretation of "the right of nations to self-determination." Not coincidentally, the basic phraseology of the leaders of national movements in these republics has changed over the last two years. There is much less talk now of "national statehood" as Estonian, Latvian, or Lithuanian statehood and of self-determination for Estonians, Latvians, and Lithuanians, and more talk of the self-determination of the peoples of these republics, a term that encompasses not only members of the "indigenous nations" but the citizens of all nationalities who live in these republics.

An analysis of the sovereignty declarations of a number of republics, which were enthusiastically approved by their respective Supreme Soviets during the summer of 1990, confirms the persistence of this contradiction. The authors of the majority of these texts could not avoid, and in some cases did not attempt to avoid, the inherent contradiction between the civil and the ethnic versions of sovereignty. In several instances they explicitly used both in defining the sovereign political community. In the Ukrainian and the Kazakh declarations, for example, the sovereign group was referred to as the "people of the Ukraine" and the "people of Kazakhstan" as well as the "Ukrainian nation" and the "Kazakh nation." In the declaration of the Russian Federation the relevant references were to the "multiethnic people of Russia" and "the peoples of Russia."

Second, the question of self-determination is not and cannot be solely within the competence of the republic's political authorities. In contemporary conditions this question should be resolved on a broad, democratic basis, preferably through the use of a general referendum among the citizens of the self-determining territory. Sometimes referenda have been held among the entire population of a state from which a new entity proposes to separate, or within which a new autonomous area is being established. Thus for example, the referendum on the question of self-determination for New Caledonia was conducted in 1988 among the entire population of France, a state that unquestionably ranks among the most democratic in the world.

Lithuanian and other Baltic leaders base their refusal to hold such a referendum on the illegality of the incorporation of these republics into the Soviet Union in 1940, but they are in fact depriving the current generation of citizens in these republics of the chance to make their own sovereign choice on the basis of legal procedures.

Concerning the law passed by the Supreme Soviet on April 3, 1990, "On the Procedure for Deciding Questions Pertaining to the Secession of Union Republics from the Soviet Union," this appears to have been designed in the same old "reactive" mold. It reduces the issue of self-determination to the question of separation from the union and limits its application to the fifteen union republics. Clearly secession from the federation should not be an easy process as such a decision would abruptly and fundamentally alter the character of the state and the fate of its citizens, but the procedures established in this legislation seem to be unnecessarily complicated and difficult to implement. Not only other union republics, but the autonomous areas within their borders, have been granted a form of veto over the decision.

The *third variant* for the reform of the federal system has been outlined, although not in any great detail, in the statements and platforms of the left-radical democratic forces of the center. It was most fully developed in the proposal of Academician Sakharov entitled "The Constitution of the United States of Europe and Asia." A more succinct expression of the same idea has appeared in the programmatic document of the "Interregional Group" of deputies and the former "Democratic Platform" of the Communist party.

In my view Andrei Sakharov, as a consistent supporter of both democratic principles and individual rights, was unable to overcome a number of profound contradictions in his vision of a Union of Soviet Republics of Europe and Asia. On the other hand, the first article of the draft constitution defines the union as "a voluntary association of sovereign republics (states) of Europe and Asia." On the other hand, he invokes in the second article the concept of "the people of the Union of Soviet Republics of Europe and Asia," that is, the "Soviet people." In the clauses dealing with freedom of movement, freedom to choose a place of residence, and other equal civil rights, Sakharov refers to these rights as inhering in the "citizens of the country." In acknowledging that "the fundamental and foremost right of every nation and republic is the right to self-determination," Sakharov seems to have confused two absolutely different concepts, that of the "nation" (which he understood as ethnic entity) and the "republic," without addressing the key question: who has the right to self-determination—the Kazakhs or the inhabitants of Kazakhstan, the Latvians or the residents of Latvia? This is all the more contradictory, as the very same text explicitly refers to the "nations (peoples)" in terms that identify those who reside in the territories of the republics as the owners of the land, the mineral wealth, and the water resources of the republics (states).[18]

Thus, the third variant suffers from the same problems identified in the discussion of the first and second variants, the confusion or substitution of the Soviet concepts of nation and state, of ethnic communities and civil societies. The main idea that distinguishes the third variant is its equalitarian vision of the right of nations to self-determination. It must be applied to all the peoples of the Soviet Union, the new republics must attain absolutely equal status with all the other union republics, and the existing hierarchy of national-state structures must be abolished.

Realizing the utter impossibility of creating a state composed of 128 union republics, proponents of this variant limit the number of possible national-state entities to 53, i.e., the present number of republics, autonomous oblasts and okrugs. But what of other peoples who might desire statehood or might desire autonomous status? The Ingush are now demanding the partition of the Checheno-Ingush Autonomous Soviet Socialist Republic into two separate republics, and the Crimean Tatars and Volga Germans are demanding the return both of their lands and the autonomous status they lost in the 1940s. The Gaguzi are similarly dissatisfied with their contemporary status within the confines of Moldova.

In conclusion, none of these three variants, nor their primary spokesmen, Gorbachev, Landsbergis, and Sakharov, has been able to go beyond the paradigm of nationalism. Similarly none of them can be implemented without hindering the process of democratization or without provoking a further intensification of interethnic and tension and conflict.

V

An alternative variant might have the following features:

In view of the enduring sociopolitical heterogeneity of the world, the dangerous military and strategic opposition of the great powers and their respective blocs as well as the global trends toward economic and political integration, the preservation of the integrity of the Soviet Union on the basis of a federative (or, in part, a confederative) structure is entirely justified and should not be seen as anomalous, unlike the historical situation at the beginning of the twentieth century. The "defeat of the reform process itself and a return to a more repressive and authoritarian pattern of political rule with unfortunate consequences, not only for the Soviet people, but for the entire international community" may be provoked, not only by "the use of harsh measures and repression against legitimate national movements," as Gail Lapidus believes, but also by an illegitimate leadership-formulated nationalism, that could provoke not only general economic and political chaos but also civil war.[19]

The historic destiny of our multiethnic state lies in the development of a civil society and in the assurance of equal rights for all peoples; on this basis they would be assured of a worthy place in the world community and could participate fully in modern international civilization while ensuring the preservation of all the riches of their cultural diversity. But this is possible only if the peoples themselves choose renewed federation, and do not prefer other variants of development. For this to take place it is necessary to declare the complete openness of the union, to guarantee that secession is a realizable option for any collectivity, and to conclude a new treaty that would specify the conditions for entry into the union, both for existing states and for any states that might be (re)established.

No matter how difficult it may be to overcome the official mentality and the clichés that have become firmly ingrained in the consciousness of the public, it would be most advisable to reject the absolutization of the principle of national (ethnic) statehood, which inevitably means the partitioning of peoples into their ethnic "quarters." The principle of "one people, one state" cannot be realized in the Soviet federation, just as it would be impossible to set up a governmental-administrative division along ethnic boundaries, or to divide territories between peoples or to categorize citizens as indigenous or nonindigenous. Statehood in and of itself will not guarantee economic prosperity, social and cultural well-being, or political rights and democratic freedoms, but rather will, with the preservation of the existing hierarchies of governmental units, lead to the further deterioration of the rights of citizens, minorities, and peoples who do not possess statehood.

Reforms in the realm of interethnic relations and governmental structures should be made along the following lines:

First, civil rights and freedoms should be expanded; this should include complete freedom of choice concerning national identity (i.e., individual national self-determination). The authorities must renounce the practice of officially designating nationality, including on passport documents. This legacy of Stalinism only divides Soviet citizens, places millions of people of mixed ancestry in a difficult position, and hinders the natural processes that draw people closer together and the mutual interaction of cultures. The state must not permit any laws or legal norms to be based on the nationality of the citizen—ethnically based laws inherently include elements of social racism. Legal norms and laws should take into account the cultural traditions and the particular interests of the inhabitants of republics, territories, or regions, but they must apply equally to all citizens who live there and must be enacted democratically. The all-union political structure, including the Soviet parliament, must be based above all on common civic and democratic principles. It must provide representation for its national constituents, but it must not become an "assembly of nations."

Second, there must be an expansion of rights in the area of national-cultural autonomy, special opportunities for population groups that live in territorially based communities, for urban communities, and individuals of any nationality to create their own associations and institutions, be they for social, religious, educational, political, or business purposes. This process must not be defined and controlled from above; it must reflect the citizens' desire and capacity for this type of self-organization on national foundations or in accordance with their national interests. Every community, and every people, whether large or small, should have the same right to its own cultural centers, schools, printed publications and other means of mass communication, and churches and other places of worship. In short, the state can and should promote the processes of national-cultural expression and self-determination.

Third, the reform of the state structure of the federation must include the elimination of the current hierarchy of national-state units and simultaneously expand the sovereignty of its component parts. It would be best to retain only one or two types of state-administrative units, to greatly reduce the differences in their prerogatives and to eliminate instances of collateral subordination. Some autonomous republics (the Tatar, Bashkir, Dagestan, and possibly the Chuvask, Mordovian, and Mari ASSRs) could become autonomous republics. Some purely artificial units could simply be dissolved. It will be necessary, however, to provide for the eventual formation of new, regional self-governing entities, especially in Russia.

Fourth, there must be measures that will ensure the specific interests of the small peoples of the North and Siberia and the preservation of important elements of their traditional life-style (reindeer breeding, hunting, and fishing). The existing autonomous okrugs, where these groups make up from 1.5 percent to 10 percent of the population, are obsolete; they do not protect the real rights and interests of these peoples and they have become an obstacle to their development. Instead of these okrugs it would be better to determine, with the participation of these peoples themselves, the territories over which they are currently dispersed and in which they are engaged in their traditional economic practices, and to secure in these reservations and territories their exclusive rights to the exploitation of the renewable and, in part, the nonrenewable resources. Provision must be made for compensation for the damages that have been inflicted on these peoples and their lands by the economic agencies of the state. The forms of self-government that will be instituted in these territories must be determined by the peoples themselves, secured through all-union legislation, and subordinated to all-union structures. No economic activity should take place in these territories without the consent of the local self-governing authorities.

Fifth, it is necessary to eliminate the injustices that have been perpetrated in connection with the deported peoples. They must be granted the right freely to choose their place of residence and the forms of their self-organization, and the state must compensate them as far as possible for the damages that have been inflicted. Those peoples who have been harmed by unreasonable economic decisions and the inappropriate exploitation of their natural resources have an equal right to be compensated by all-union economic agencies.

The preceding discussion may appear to suffer from the instrumentalistic thinking that has been characteristic of Soviet social science for so long, but it represents an attempt to go beyond the limits of "ivory tower" speculation. Societies are complex, self-regulating mechanisms, but under extreme internal and external pressure these mechanisms can become overloaded, producing unpredictable outcomes. Social science loses its credibility when it becomes the basis for attempts at "social engineering," but social theory remains one of the best guides for social practice.

NOTES

1. On this topic, see V. I. Kozlov, "Ethnos i gosudarstvo" (Ethnos and the state), and R. Koen, "Etnichnost' i gosudarstvo" (Ethnicity and the state), *Materialy sovetsko-amerikanskikh simpoziumov po izucheniiu etnichnosti* (Materials from Soviet-American symposia on the study of ethnicity) (Moscow, 1986).

2. On the concepts of "Russia" and "All-Russian," see N. M. Karamzin, "Rech' proiznesennaiia bv torzhestvenom sobranii imperatorskoi Rossiiskoi akademii," (Speech delivered at the grand meeting of the Imperial All-Russian Academy), *Literaturnaia kritika 1800-1820-kh gg.* (Literary criticism from 1800 to the 1820s) (Moscow, 1980), 36-47.

3. See *Konstitutsiia SSSR. Politiko-pravovoi kommentarii* (Constitution of the USSR: Political-legal commentary). (Moscow, 1982), 207-8.

4. *Argumenty i fakty* (Arguments and Facts), no. 39 (1989): 8.

5. Ch. M. Taksami, "Doklad na I s'ezde malochislennykh narodov Severa" (Report at the First Congress of Minorities of the North) (Moscow, March 30, 1990), 3.

6. *Sovetskaia Kul' tura* (Soviet culture), March 31, 1990.

7. V. A. Tishkov, "Assambleia natsii ili soiuznyi parlament?" *Sovetskaia etnografia*, no. 3 (1990) ["An Assembly of Nations or an All-Union Parliament?" *Journal of Soviet Nationalities*, vol. 1, no. 1 (Spring 1990).]

8. B. Anderson and B. Silver, *Demographic Sources of the Changing Ethnic Composition of the Soviet Union: Selected Tables and Figures*. November, 1989.

9. See René Lemarchand, "The Caucasus, Central Asia and Black Africa: Compartive Perspectives on Clientelism and Ethnicity" (unpublished manuscript).

10. A. Zingerman, "The Third World War," *Cultural Survival Quarterly.*

11. V. A. Tishkov, "Narody i gosudarstvo" (Peoples and the state) *Kommunist,* no. 1 (1989).

12. Zbigniew Brzezinski, "Post Communist Nationalism," *Foreign Affairs,* 68 (Winter 1989-90): 2.

13. E. Gellner, *Nations and Nationalism* (Oxford, 1989).

14. Brzezinski, "Post Communist Nationalism," 1.

15. *Time,* March 12, 1990, 52.

16. *Pravda,* February 13, 1990.

17. *Pravda,* April 11-12, 1990.

18. *Golos Izbiratelia* (The Voter's Voice), Informational Bulletin of the Moscow Voters' Union, no. 7.

19. Gail Lapidus, "Can Gorbechev Manage the Nationalities Crisis?" In *Can Gorbachev's Reforms Succeed?*, ed., G. Breslauer (Berkeley, 1990), 110.

12

Comparing Apples and Pears: Centralization, Decentralization, and Ethnic Policy in the Habsburg and Soviet Armies

István Deák

This very tentative comparative analysis has been inspired by this symposium on great power ethnic politics, and it is based, in part, on my own familiarity with the Habsburg army and, in part, on Teresa Rakowska-Harmstone's pathbreaking essays on ethnic policy in the Soviet army.

Needless to say, other authors, too, have dealt with the problems of centralization, decentralization, and ethnicity in the Habsburg army, foremost among them being Gunther E. Rothenberg in his classic, *The Army of Francis Joseph*. The names of many more such specialists can be found in my *Beyond Nationalism*. As for the Soviet army, Professor Rakowska-Harmstone's publications contain suggestions for further reading.[1]

In the following, I shall place primary emphasis on the Habsburg army, with only periodic attempts at comparing it to the Soviet armed forces. My goal is to show that while a consistent policy of ethnic neutrality and gradual decentralization enabled the Habsburg army to prolong its own existence, and thus also that of the multinational Dual Monarchy, increasing centralization and Great Russian/Slavic nationalism may well have contributed to the present crisis of the Soviet army and hence also to that of the Soviet empire.

This is not to belittle the terrible ethnic difficulties plaguing the former Habsburg Monarchy; it is to say only that, thanks in great part to its military policy, Austria-Hungary avoided dissolution until after the Central Powers had lost the Great War. Moreover, while the Habsburg army actually outlived the very state it defended, if only by a few weeks, in October-November 1918, the present crisis of the Soviet armed forces seems to be no less grave than that of the other Soviet institutions. In fact, the Soviet Union may well fall apart in peacetime.

Unification and centralization have always been on the agenda of continental states, whether absolutistic or constitutional, as indispensable props for a successful domestic and foreign policy. Ruling as they did over provinces of the most disparate origin, customs, and ethnic composition, the Habsburg and Romanov dynasties were particularly keen on devising principles and institutions that might facilitate the unification and centralization of their family possessions. The main weapons in this struggle were the principle of absolutism and the institution of a great bureaucracy coupled with a great standing army. Yet in 1867 the Habsburg dynasty finally and irrevocably abandoned its quest for absolute rule and for a centralized and unified administration. Instead, it reluctantly consented to constitutional government and territorial division. Whatever remained of political unity rested thereafter on the triple pillars of a common ruler, a common foreign policy, and the common or joint army.

In theory at least, the Romanov dynasty was in a far more favorable position than the House of Austria, if for no other reason than because the tsars were able to complement the principle of autocracy and the practice of bureaucratic centralism with their role as spiritual fathers of all true believers, and—in the age of nationalism—with their endorsement of Great Russian nationalism. Unlike Emperor-King Franz Joseph, the Russian tsars refused either to divide their possessions into two or more sovereign parts or to introduce genuine constitutionalism. What the Soviet regime inherited in 1917 was therefore a state without a real tradition of territorial autonomy, constitutional practice, or ethnic equality. The Bolshevik watchwords of proletarian internationalism and ethnic self-determination remained essentially slogans, altering little in the practices of centralization and Great Russian/Slavic domination. In fact, these practices reached their apogee under Stalin and his early successors. And even though there is today a dynamic popular movement for the federalization of the Soviet Union, President Gorbachev shows no more inclination to dismantle the centralized system than did his imperial and Bolshevik predecessors.

Let us now examine briefly the Habsburg experience with political centralization and decentralization, following it with an analysis of the ethnic policy of the Habsburg army and finally an attempt to compare it to the ethnic policy and practices of the Soviet army.

HABSBURG CENTRALIZATION AND DECENTRALIZATION

In hindsight it is clear that the attempts of the House of Austria to create a unified state were anything but successful. Indeed, only once during its very long existence, from about 1849 to 1860, did the Habsburg dynasty realize its goal of a unified and centralized empire, and even then the achievement was greatly complicated by the Emperor's simultaneous role as president of the German Confederacy, an assemblage of sovereign states marked by an almost total absence of political or economic unity. At all other times, the Habsburgs either struggled to achieve at least a semblance of unity among their numerous family possessions or, no less frequently, were forced to compromise, recognizing the "rights and liberties" of their several provinces and privileged estates.

The classic instrument of state power has always been a centrally trained, centrally paid, and centrally controlled bureaucracy, and yet, again with the exception of those few years in the 1850s, the administrative machinery of the Habsburg lands was none of these. In fact, the Habsburg family possessions could be easily divided into two basic categories: those in which the imperial bureaucracy was generally predominant, and those in which it exercised only a very limited authority. To the first category belonged the Austrian hereditary or crown lands, the lands of the Czech Crown, Dalmatia, the Adriatic Littoral, Bukovina and Galicia (but the latter only until the Compromise of 1867), and finally, the *Grenze* or military border (and that only until its dissolution in the 1870s). To the second category belonged those lands that generally provided their own civil service, namely, the Austrian Netherlands (until the loss of that province in the 1790s), Hungary, Transylvania, Croatia-Slavonia, and after 1867, Galicia. Until their transfer to Italy (in 1859 and 1866, respectively), Lombardy and Venetia occupied a middle position between the two groups, with a centrally appointed, but mainly locally recruited, Italian-speaking bureaucracy.

Nor would it be correct to speak of the gradual self-assertion, over time, of a centralized and unified imperial bureaucracy. Rather, that institution experienced a series of ups and downs, influenced by such factors as the shifting relations between the central power and the provinces, the determination and skills of a given ruler, the conditions prevailing in the individual kingdoms and lands, the international situation, and the *Zeitgeist* or prevailing ideology.[2] What Joseph II (1780-90) had achieved in terms of centralization was largely undone by his successor Leopold II (1790-92); what Francis I (1792-1835) and Metternich wove together was quickly unraveled by the revolutionary forces in 1848, and what Franz Joseph (1848-1916) and Interior Minister Baron Alexander Bach constructed in the 1850s was definitively torn asunder in the Compromise of 1867.[3] Hungary's own energetic and successful policy of bureaucratic centralization after 1867 must be seen as a sign not of the triumph but of the ultimate failure of Habsburg efforts toward centralization and unification.

To be sure, there were, from very early times, certain court offices, such as the chancelleries and the treasury, which could place an absolute claim on the entire civilian administration, but these central offices had to be reorganized again and again, and in 1867 they ceased to exist altogether. Thereafter, there were two constitutional governments, the Austrian and the Hungarian, each exercising its own authority over a state bureaucracy, and even then, the power of the government in the Austrian half of what had now become the Dual Monarchy was far from uncontested.

What ought to concern us here, therefore, is not the success or failure of Habsburg bureaucratic centralization, for its failure is beyond doubt, but rather, whether bureaucratic decentralization was an asset or a liability in the survival into the twentieth century of what was so often called the "Ramshackle Empire."

I, for one, believe that partial decentralization played a rather positive role in the relative longevity of the Monarchy, for it guaranteed, until 1848, that the privileges and power of the landed nobility over the peasants would not be fatally endangered. As for the period after 1867, the division of the Monarchy enabled a number of native elites to occupy command positions in their own provinces and kingdoms. Thus Hungarians constituted the administrative, and gradually even the economic leadership of Hungary; Germans played the same role in the Alpine provinces, Poles in Galicia, Croats in Croatia-Slavonia, Italians in Trieste and other parts of the Adriatic Littoral, and by the turn of the century, Czech speakers in Bohemia and Moravia. This, of course, left many Slovaks, Ruthenes, Slovenes, Serbs, Romanians, and Bohemian Germans utterly discontented, but their numbers, determination, and political power were never great enough to do more than annoy and occasionally infuriate the ruling national elites.

THE HABSBURG ARMY

If the imperial bureaucracy never, or hardly ever, held sway over the entire Habsburg realm, the same cannot be said of the army, which functioned as the monarchy's only true supranational institution. Its importance was ever upmost in the minds of the Habsburg rulers and their advisers, and indeed, its sense of importance grew in the age of nationalism. Witness the Habsburg war against Hungary in 1848-49, waged to force the latter to surrender its separate army and war ministry, or the predilection of the last great monarch for wearing a military uniform at all times and for seeing himself, above all, as first soldier of the realm. Witness, too, the desperate attempt of Franz Joseph, at a time of growing domestic disorder, to reassert the unity of the army in his famous (or notorious) Chłopy Army Order of September 16, 1903:

> My entire armed forces . . . are imbued with that spirit of unity and harmony which respects every national characteristic and is able to solve all antagonisms so as to utilize the individual qualities of each ethnic group for the benefit of all.[4]

As is well known, this seemingly harmless statement created a storm of indignation, especially in Hungary, since it flew in the face of the Hungarian view that theirs was not just one of many nationalities, but that Hungary, with its several ethnic groups, constituted a sovereign nation in equal partnership with Austria and its multiple ethnic groups. Worse still, the term "ethnic group" (*Volksstamm*) was translated into Hungarian as "tribal group" (*néptörzs*), an unforgivable insult in Hungarian eyes.

Let us now see how successful the Habsburgs were in centralizing and unifying their armed forces, and whether it was absolute centralization or partial decentralization that best served their interests.

The origins of the Habsburg dynastic army reach back to the sixteenth century, but only in the eighteenth century was the army organized into a coherent whole, and only in 1745 did Maria Theresia order her troops to display the black and yellow Habsburg colors, thereby separating her own "imperial-royal" forces from those of the rest of the Holy Roman Empire. Placed under the authority of a single Court War Council (in earlier times several such councils had functioned simultaneously), numbered consecutively, placed under a single disciplinary regulation, and equipped with distinctive uniforms as well as standardized weapons, Maria Theresia's regiments constituted a true dynastic army. Furthermore, the great Empress provided, or at least attempted to provide, for the systematic education and training of her officers. But even during her reign, the laws on conscription continued to vary, with the principle of voluntary enlistment preserved in such disparate lands as Hungary and the Tyrol; the commissioning and promotion of officers remained, to a large part, the preserve of regimental proprietors (*Regimentsinhaber*), and most important, the regiments were raised territorially, meaning that they preserved much of their provincial character. Hussar regiments existed only in the Hungarian lands; *Uhlan* (lancer) regiments were identified as distinctly Polish, and even infantry regiments bore such designations as Moravian, Croatian, Hungarian, or Lombardian.[5]

Because of the multiethnic composition of most kingdoms and lands, this diversity of territorial origin did not mean ethnic homogeneity except in a handful of regiments. Moreover, the officers and, to a lesser degree, the noncommissioned officers were posted to regiments irrespective of their ethnic and provincial origin. Finally, the Court War Council regularly dispatched the trained first and second battalions (*Linienbataillone*) of each regiment far from home base, less for purposes of "divide and rule" than for those of expediency. Still, the army's territorial organization was not without significance; nor was the army's concern for the ethnic peculiarities of the rank and file. Whereas German served as the language of command and service in all the regiments, officers and noncommissioned officers were obliged to communicate with their men in the language or, quite often, languages spoken by the latter. It was the army's distinctive territorial organization that enabled entire regiments of Lombardian, Venetian, and Hungarian origin to side with the revolutionaries in 1848-49. It is an open question, however, whether a nonterritorial organization would have served the Habsburg cause any better. One might well argue that the presence of disaffected Italian soldiers, for instance, in many more than the traditional eight "Italian" infantry regiments would have caused even greater confusion in Habsburg ranks during that crucial year. This way, at least, the loyalty of most other regiments could be trusted. Even units originating from Hungary and Transylvania proved reliable in 1848-49, provided they happened to be stationed outside of the Hungarian lands. In fact, many Hungarian and Transylvanian regiments were deeply divided: battalions and companies that found themselves in Hungary in 1848 ended up fighting in the Hungarian revolutionary army, and those outside, in the Austrian army.[6]

All in all, then, it seems to me that the dynasty was well served in 1848-49 by its traditional respect for the provincial and linguistic peculiarities of the troops. Without that supranational policy, it is rather likely that even more than the actual 10 percent of the officer corps and of the army's rank and file would have fought against the dynasty.

No doubt, the revolutions were a frightening experience for the Habsburg high command, and after the war, it set out to strengthen the unity of the army. Yet it could muster no more efficient measures than an even harsher discipline, the reorganization of some disloyal regiments, and the creation of a military police. The territorial organization remained unchanged, as did the army's respect for the languages spoken by the recruits.[7]

Finally, in 1868, the policy of centralization was reversed, and the armed forces were split into three, or, to be precise, three-and-a-half parts: a very large Common or Joint Army, which included the entire navy as well, two much smaller territorial defense forces or *Landwehre*, one Hungarian and the other "Austrian," and, finally, a Croatian defense force, or *Domobrantsvo*, which was, however, subordinated to the Hungarian *Landwehr* or *honvédség*. There was to be only one general staff, and only one chief of the general staff, with the latter acting as unofficial head of the entire armed forces, but the Common Minister of War was to have no authority over the two *Landwehre*, which were subordinated, in turn, to their respective national ministers of defense. Moreover, the ministers of defense were charged with recruitment and approvisioning even for the Joint Army.[8]

This marked the end of a unified Habsburg dynastic army, and it was duly perceived by most observers as the beginning of the end of the Habsburg Monarchy. "In no other country," said the conservative Field Marshal Archduke Albrecht, "are uniformity and dynastic soldierly spirit as vital. . . for only the dynasty and the army hold this divided monarchy together."[9]

Thereafter, further steps were taken toward the decentralization of the armed forces. In 1882, the territorial principle was strengthened by the decision that henceforth the monarchy's fifteen-and-a-half army corps would each draw its recruits from a specifically defined area, and that trained units would spend more and more time at or near their home base. In the ensuing decades, but especially after the turn of century, Franz Joseph made additional concessions to relentless Hungarian pressure, allowing Hungarian officers to transfer to Hungarian regiments of the Joint Army and tolerating the hoisting of the Hungarian flag next to the imperial one on Joint Army buildings in Hungary. He also ordered the compulsory teaching of the Hungarian language and the teaching of some other courses in Hungarian at all Joint Army military schools located in Hungary. Finally, in 1912, the two *Landwehre* were given their own artillery and other technical branches, making them the equals of the Joint Army. In fact, because of the generosity of their governments, Hungarian and Austrian *Landwehr* units were often better equipped during World War I than were Joint Army units. Indeed, on the eve of the war, few doubted that the Joint Army would eventually split into its Hungarian and Austrian halves, thereby hastening the final division of the monarchy.[10]

It is impossible today to tell whether or not this division would ultimately have taken place. When the Great War began in the summer of 1914, all the Monarchy's armies marched obediently to the front, and thereafter the two *Landwehre* and the Joint Army shared equally in the burden of the war. There is no evidence to show that the *Landwehre* were less loyal than the main army; on the contrary, some of their divisions were considered among the best of the entire armed forces. When disaffection set in, in 1917, and even more in 1918, Joint Army units proved no more reliable than *Landwehr* units. Indeed, in the last days of the war, some *Landwehr* regiments fought alongside the remaining Joint Army regiments in their final efforts to stop the advancing Italians. Only at the end of October, on the direct order of the Hungarian government, did Hungarian troops, both Joint Army and *honvéd*, begin to leave the Italian front to protect Hungarian lands against the advancing Romanians and Serbs.[11]

THE ETHNIC POLICIES OF THE HABSBURG AND THE SOVIET ARMY

The Habsburg Monarchy consisted of eleven major and a few other minor nationalities, an insignificant total when compared to the more than one hundred ethnic groups that make up the Soviet Union. And yet, because of the historically dominant position occupied in Russia and the Soviet Union by the Slavs, and among those, by the Great Russians, the Soviet nationality problem might, in theory at least, be expected to be less explosive than that of the defunct Habsburg Monarchy. Despite recent demographic advances by the non-Slavic peoples, Russian-speakers still account for just over one-half of the Soviet population, and Slavic speakers (Great Russians, Ukrainians, and Belorussians) for almost 70 percent. It is true, however, that because of the lower birth rate among the Slavs, and especially among the Russians, the ethnic composition of the cohort reaching draft age in the Soviet Union is more heavily weighted toward the ethnic minorities. In 1988, for instance, draft-age Russians constituted only 42.6 percent of the draft pool and all Slavs only 60.8 percent. Still, these figures pale in comparison to those in Austria-Hungary, where, in 1910, the Germans constituted only about 23.4 percent of the total population; the Hungarians, 19.6 percent; the Slavs, 45 percent; and the Italians, Romanians, and other minor ethnic groups, 12.3 percent. The ethnic distribution of the draft age cohort in Austria-Hungary did not differ significantly from that of the entire population.[12]

In brief then, whereas the "dominant" Slavs constitute about two-thirds of the Soviet population, the "dominant" Germans and Hungarians together constituted only about 43 percent of the Austro-Hungarian population.

Military statistics prove that the Habsburg army inducted young men irrespective of their ethnic origin. The slight variations on the theme in the Joint Army's rank and file (Germans, 25.2 percent; Hungarians, 23.1 percent; Slavs, 43.4 percent; Italians and Romanians, 8.3 percent in 1910) can be easily explained by pointing out that the army recognized fewer nationalities than did the civilian authorities who reported on the ethnic origin of the draftable population. In military statistics, members of the minor ethnic groups were thrust into one or another major nationality. This accounts for the difference between the "Romanians, Italians, and Others" (12.3 percent) in the civilian census reports, and the "Romanians and Italians" (8.3 percent) in the Joint Army's rank and file.

Differences could be found, however, in the ethnic distribution of the rank and file within the Habsburg army's several service branches, some of which were definitely more prestigious and thus more desirable than others. For example, German speakers were vastly overrepresented among the elite sharpshooters or *Jäger* (42.7 percent in 1911, as opposed to the general proportion of Germans among the rank and file, which was 24.8 percent in that year). Hungarian speakers were greatly overrepresented in the elegant cavalry (33.6 percent, as opposed to the general Hungarian representation among the rank and file, which was 23.3 percent in 1911). But Czechs and Poles, too, were overrepresented in the cavalry as were the Italians among the *Jäger*. All this is easily explained, however, by the disproportionate number of Hungarian, Bohemian, Moravian, and Galician cavalry regiments as well as by the fact that the *Jäger* regiments and independent battalions took their men mostly from the German- and Italian-speaking Tyrol and the other Alpine provinces. Clearly, tradition played a much greater role in the skewed ethnic distribution of the rank and file among the several branches of service than did national prejudice or other ethnic considerations.

As in all other armies, peasant recruits were primarily drafted into the infantry, which explains why "peasant" nations (i.e., nationalities lacking a large urban middle class or working class) such as the Romanians and Ruthenes were somewhat overrepresented in the infantry, whereas Germans and Czechs were overrepresented in the artillery and the technical branches. Finally, for purely geographic and professional reasons, there was a vast Croatian and Italian presence in the imperial and royal navy.

As Rakowska-Harmstone demonstrates, things are less simple within the Soviet armed forces, which comprise five basic services: strategic rocket forces, ground forces, air defense forces, air force, and navy. Add to these the KGB forces and the MVD troops, and you have a formidable force, amounting, in 1989, to 5.8 million men under arms. (Just before World War I, the Habsburg army numbered less than five hundred thousand enlisted men and noncommissioned officers in active service.) Unlike the Habsburg armed forces, in which active service normally lasted three years, the period of obligatory service in most branches of the Soviet armed forces has been, since 1968, two years. In the words of Rakowska-Harmstone:

> Information available indicates that there clearly is an "ethnic security map" in the Soviet Armed Forces, i.e. a pattern of distribution of ethnic manpower, which conforms to the perceptions of the dominant national group of how best to preserve its power. In the minds of the Soviet military high command this is synonymous with the need to maintain the military's traditional Russian ethnic character. The resulting ethnic pattern maximizes the presence of the Russian element in combat and elite formations as well as in the professional cadres, and consigns the most obvious *natsmeny* (a contraction for "national minorities," with a pejorative connotation) and other "untrustworthy" elements to less exposed or non-combatant branches of the service.[13]

What this means in practice is spelled out by two other experts on the Soviet military:

> Combat units [in the Soviet army] are staffed by a clear majority of soldiers from the Slavic nationalities, usually 80 percent or more. Noncombat units usually contain 70 to 90 percent or more non-Slavs, especially Central Asians and Caucasians. Non-Slavs who serve in combat units often are relegated to support roles, such as in the kitchen or in the warehouses.[14]

According to Rakowska-Harmstone, the KGB border troops are staffed almost exclusively by Russians. (In the Habsburg Monarchy, the border guards or *Grenzer* were made up of a vast majority of Croats and Serbs, and a minority of Transylvanian Romanians and Hungarian-speaking Szekelys.) Similarly, the Soviet strategic rocket forces, the air force and the navy are composed mostly of Slavs, with the non-Slavs—who account for aproximately 10 percent of their total manpower—being utilized mostly in support roles. The airborne units, too, are predominantly Russian. Only in the ground forces does the share of non-Russians amount to 20 percent, even in such combat formations as armor, artillery, and infantry. But these non-Russians are recruited mainly from among such people who are functionally integrated (i.e., virtually bilingual). Nonintegrated, unilingual ethnics, who comprise the great majority of Muslims but also a surprisingly large proportion of Georgians, Armenians, Ukrainians, and Belorussians, are generally relegated to the construction battalions. Note, however, the heavy Muslim coloration of the MVD troops, especially those charged with guarding the Soviet prisons.

Not that the Soviet military has always favored the Slavs! In 1924-25, for instance, there were three types of national formations: larger "national military divisions," smaller "ethnic units," and reserves organized in territorial divisions of the militia. The importance of national formations was deemphasized in the late 1920s and early 1930s, however, and they were abolished in the military reform of March 7, 1938. National military formations were briefly reinstated in World War II, but were again phased out after the war.

Today's Soviet army is, in theory, thoroughly integrated, its ethnic policy based on three fundamental rules: (1) that each military unit and subunit must be ethnically mixed; (2) that no soldier is to be stationed in his home area; and (3) that the language of the armed forces is exclusively Russian. Clearly then, a vast gulf separates the ethnic practices of the Soviet army and those of the Austro-Hungarian forces. After all, the Joint Army carefully distinguished between the language of command and service, which was German, and the language of instruction and communication with the men, which could be any one or more of the ten major languages spoken in the Monarchy. It is true, however, that the linguistic practices of the Hungarian *Landwehr* resembled those of the Soviet armed forces. In fact, the *honvédség* knew only one language, Hungarian, except for the Croatian units within the *honvédség*, which used Serbo-Croatian exclusively.

The question remains, of course, which of the two methods is more efficient. In the Austro-Hungarian Joint Army, recruits were expected to master only about eighty brief expressions in German. This might have sufficed in the nineteenth century when weapons, particularly those of the infantry, were relatively uncomplicated. But by the twentieth century, especially by the time of World War I, the Austro-Hungarian system had begun to falter. Among other things, hastily commissioned reserve officers were often totally unfamiliar with the languages spoken by their men. Nor did all the freshly commissioned officers speak German. But then, the situation is not necessarily better in the Soviet Union. In 1979, for instance, over 35 percent of the non-Russians—in absolute figures, almost 45 million people—did not speak Russian at all. This means that approximately one out of five young recruits was unfamiliar with Russian, the sole language used in the armed forces. A huge proportion of non-Russians serve in the construction battalions, thereby negating the principle of ethnic integration.

During World War I, ethnic disunity came to a head in the Habsburg army, especially after the high command had decided, whether rightly or wrongly, that some ethnic groups, such as the German-Austrians, Hungarians, Croats, Slovenes, and Bosnians, were more reliable than others. Units made up of these nationalities were systematically dispatched to the most exposed fronts, which in turn led to a vastly uneven ethnic (and social) distribution of battlefield casualties and to mutual recriminations.

The effectiveness of an army depends primarily on its career officers and noncommissioned officers. I have no data on the latter category, but ample information on the officers of the Habsburg army demonstrate that, with regard to the officers, the Habsburg high command was as "ethnically blind," at least in peacetime, as it was with regard to the rank and file. Students in military schools were recruited primarily from among the sons of soldiers and officials without the slightest concern for their ethnic origin (or their confessional allegiance). Freshly commissioned career officers were assigned to posts irrespective of the ethnic makeup of the unit. Honor students, or those with the best social connections, strove and often succeeded in getting into the more prestigious regiments, but the prestige of a regiment was mainly a function of such things as tradition, the social composition of the officer corps, and the educational level as well as reputed dynastic loyalty of the ethnic group constituting the bulk of the rank and file. These prestige units included such ethnically diverse formations as the Fourth Infantry Regiment whose men came from Vienna; the four *Kaiserjäger* regiments, whose rank and file was made up of Tyrolean Germans and Italians; the Seventh *Dragoner*, composed mainly of Czech cavalrymen; and the Seventh *Husaren*, consisting of Hungarian recruits.

It is true that in 1910, German speakers composed about 55 percent of the Habsburg career officer corps, and that, as a consequence, all other nationalities were grievously underrepresented (Slovaks, for instance, made up 4.3 percent of the Joint Army's rank and file, but only 0.4 percent of the career officer corps), but this, too, can be easily explained by the fact that some nationalities mustered a much larger educated stratum than other nationalities, and by the fact that educated young Slovaks, for instance, were much less likely to strive for a career in the Joint Army than young educated

Germans, Hungarians, or Croats. Moreover, even Germans from different regions of the Monarchy were most unevenly represented in the career officer corps. Whereas young German-Austrians from, say, the Salzburg province were hard to find at the military academies, youngsters from the German "Diaspora" in Bohemia, Moravia, Hungary, and Transylvania were enormously overrepresented.

Finally, all these considerations are of only minor importance when we take into account the fact that the vast majority (in some cases up to 90 percent) of the military students came from military and civil service families. The language of "everyday communication" (the basis of all Austrian statistics on ethnicity) in such service families was most likely to be German, yet their loyalty was generally not to the German nation but to the "Old Austrian" concept. These families had no nationality, unless one considers attachment to the House of Habsburg a form of nationalism. Besides, at least according to my own calculations, in 1900 over 16 percent of the career officers were of mixed ethnic origin.

The Austrian military statistician Wilhelm Winkler writes that, of the Dual Monarchy's actively serving generals on November 1, 1918, 166 can be considered German; 94, Hungarian; 64, Czech or Slovak; 25, South Slavic; 24, Polish; 9, Italian; 1, Romanian; and 4, classified "Other."[15] Winkler does not, however, recognize the phenomena of mixed nationality or no nationality, even though both were definitely quite common among the officers. During World War I, for instance, of the Monarchy's nine active field marshals, Friedrich, Eugen, and Joseph were Habsburg archdukes; Conrad was a German-Austrian; Böhm-Ermolli, born in Ancona, was part German, part Italian; Kövess and Rohr were Hungarian-born, but of German stock; Krobatin, born in Moravia, was a Czech; and Boroević, a South Slav.[16] Needless to say, all nine viewed themselves as "Austrians."

How different is the situation in the Soviet army! There, according to Rakowska-Harmstone, the career NCOs and warrant officers are mostly Slavs, as are the career officers. Even though no hard information is ever given on the ethnic composition of the Soviet officer corps, all Western estimates, based on an analysis of officers' names, agree that Slavs predominate, and that approximately 90 percent of the generals are Slavs. Moreover, the share of Slavs (and Russians) seems to have risen in the last twenty years. Of all the non-Slavic nationalities, only the Armenians and the Jews are overrepresented in the officer corps, which can be explained by the relatively high educational level of the two ethnic groups, and by their "disaggregation," meaning their tendency to live among other nationalities, especially among Russians.

CONCLUSION

It would be easy to marshal many arguments to show that more or perhaps even less centralization would have benefited the Habsburg Monarchy. A single, unified imperial bureaucracy might have provided for greater honesty and efficiency in administration as well as for a fairer treatment of the ethnic minorities. Conversely, a single, unified bureaucracy might have strengthened the government's absolutistic tendencies and might have hastened the alienation of the Hungarians, the most powerful nation in the Monarchy. A completely unified and centralized armed force might have allowed, after 1867, for a more efficient modernization, and it would certainly have prevented the unfair treatment of ethnic minorities in the Hungarian *Landwehr*, the only armed force within the Monarchy with a single language of command, service, and instruction, and with scarce respect for the languages spoken by its rank and file.

On the other hand, had Franz Joseph not granted the Hungarians their *honvédség*, by itself a rather modest concession, it is very likely that the Budapest parliament would never had ratified the Compromise. Finally, had the ruler not made further, rather symbolic concessions to Hungarian national pride, it is nearly certain that the Hungarian "Independence party" would have completely overwhelmed the pro-Compromise "Government party."

Perhaps the Czech nationalists were right in clamoring for their own national defense force, similar to that of the Hungarians and, to a lesser extent, the Croats. Conceivably too, this would have reversed the growing disloyalty of many Czechs and prevented their large-scale desertion in the first years of the Great War. But then, the setting up of a Czech national army had been repeatedly vetoed by the Hungarian government, and its realization might well have led to the secession of the Hungarians.

The conclusion seems inevitable: the partial decentralization of the administrative machinery and the less-than-perfect unity of the Habsburg armed forces were an inevitable consequence of the domestic political situation, and, in the final analysis, they served the dynasty surprisingly well. It is no less difficult to form a judgment of the policy of centralization, semi-integration, and ethnic prejudice practiced in the Soviet army. No doubt, modern military technology requires men able to understand not only a few words of command but also the intricacies of advanced weaponry and warfare. It is hard to conceive how a manageable program of instruction in contemporary military methods could be offered even in just the major languages spoken in the Soviet Union.

On the other hand, the experience of World War II proved the combat value of ethnically uniform military units, especially in the case of nationalities whose civilian population had suffered greatly from Stalinist terror, and among whom disaffection was rampant during the war. The particular heroism of the Nisei regiments of the U.S. army during World War II showed that, when formed into national units, young men were willing to fight even for such a country that had not hesitated to brutalize the soldiers' families. It might not be such a bad idea, after all, to segregate the members of particularly alienated nationalities into special units, provided that, when there, they are accorded the dignity and honor of full-fledged combat soldiers. This way, they are in a position to do their duty without "infecting" other soldiers. Nothing, however, excuses the segregation of soldiers into demeaning construction battalions. Such arrangements are inevitably perceived as punitive measures, and they can only lead to further alienation. Moreover, the brutal hazing to which recruits from the Baltic countries are regularly subjected in the integrated Soviet army undoubtedly contributes to the wish of Baltic peoples to secede outright from the Soviet Union. Finally, what kind of loyalty can be expected from soldiers who cannot even dream of a military career?

In view of the horrendous difficulties faced by today's unified and centralized Soviet bureaucracy and army, the less-than-ideal situation prevailing in the Habsburg Monarchy definitely appears as a lesser evil. When the dynasty fell, in 1918, it was not because its governing institutions had been insufficiently centralized, but because the Central Powers had lost the war. If the Soviet Union collapses, it might well happen because its governing institutions have been much too centralized, and because the Soviet army has failed to take into account the cultural and linguistic peculiarities of its soldiers.

NOTES

1. I refer here to my *Beyond Nationalism: A Social and Political History of the Habsburg Officer Corps, 1848-1918* (New York and Oxford, 1990) and to such works by Teresa Rakowska-Harmstone as "Nationalities and the Soviet Military," in eds. Lubomyr Hajda and Mark Beissinger *The Nationalities Factor in Soviet Politics and Society*, ("The John M. Olin Critical Issues Series, published in cooperation with the Harvard University Russian Research Center"; Boulder, San Francisco and Oxford, 1990), 72-93, and "'Brotherhood in Arms': The Ethnic Factor in the Soviet Armed Forces," in *Ethnic Armies: Polyethnic Armed Forces From the Time of the*

Habsburgs to the Age of the Superpowers, ed. N. F. Dreisziger (Waterloo, Ont., 1990), 123-57. In the same volume, see also my "The Ethnic Question in the Multinational Habsburg Army, 1848-1918," 21- 49. Finally, see Gunther E. Rothenberg, *The Army of Francis Joseph* (West Lafayette, Ind., 1976).

2. The most comprehensive recent work on the Habsburg administration is Adam Wandruszka and Peter Urbanitsch, eds., *Verwaltung und Rechtswesen*, vol. 2, *Die Habsburgermonarchie 1848-1918* (Vienna, 1975).

3. Two of the more important works on the Compromise of 1867 are Louis Eisenmann, *Le Compromis Austro-Hongrois de 1867. Etude sur le Dualisme* (1904; reprint, Academic International, n.p., 1971), and L'udovit Holotik, ed., *Der Österreichisch-ungarische Ausgleich 1867* (Bratislava, 1971).

4. Cited in Edmund von Glaise-Horstenau, *Franz Josephs Weggefährte. Das Leben des Generalstabschefs Grafen Beck* (Zurich-Leipzig-Vienna, 1930), 403.

5. On the pre-1848 history of the Habsburg army, see especially Oskar Regele, *Der österreichische Hofkriegsrat 1556-1848* (Vienna, 1949); Herbert St. Furlinger and Ludwig Jedlicka, eds., *Unser Heer. 300 Jahre österreichisches Soldatentum in Krieg und Frieden* (Vienna-Munich-Zurich, 1963), 1-251, and Johann Christoph Allmayer-Beck and Erich Lessing, *Das Heer unter dem Doppeladler 1718-1848* (Munich-Gutersloh-Vienna, 1981).

6. On the Habsburg army in the wars of 1848-49, see especially Rudolf Kiszling, *Die Revolution im Kaisertum Österreich 1848-1849*, 2 vols. (Vienna, 1948); István Deák, *The Lawful Revolution: Louis Kossuth and the Hungarians, 1848-1849* (New York, 1979), and Alan Sked, *The Survival of the Habsburg Empire: Radetzky, the Imperial Army, and the Class War, 1848* (London-New York, 1979).

7. The history of the Habsburg army in the period of absolutism is ably discussed in Antonio Schmidt-Brentano, *Die Armee in Österreich. Militar, Staat und Gesellschaft 1848-1867* (Boppard am Rhein, 1975).

8. The military side of the Compromise is discussed by, among others, Glaise-Horstenau, *Franz Josephs Weggefährte*, 132-152, and Deák, *Beyond Nationalism*, 53-60.

9. Cited in Heinrich v. Srbik, *Aus Österreichs Vergangenheit* (Salzburg, 1949), 145.

10. On Hungarian efforts to split the Common Army, see Deák, *Beyond Nationalism*, 65-71.

11. The most important work on the Habsburg army in World War I is Edmund von Glaise-Horstenau and Rudolf Kiszling, eds., *Österreich-Ungarns letzter Krieg 1914-1918*, 7 vols, with 10 supplements (Vienna, 1930-38).

12. Statistical data on the Soviet draft age cohort are in Rakowska-Harmstone, "Nationalities and the Soviet Military," 80. The data on Austria-Hungary were culled, in part, from *Statistische Rückblicke aus Österreich* (Vienna,

1913). Rather than encumbering these notes with lengthy references, I would like to assure the reader that all further statistics were culled either from Rakowska-Harmstone's essays or from my own *Beyond Nationalism*, and that they are based on such primary sources as census reports and the tremendously detailed *Militär-Statistisches Jahrbuch*, which appeared in Vienna between 1872 and 1912.

13. Rakowska-Harmstone, "Nationalities and the Soviet Military," 82.

14. Enders Wimbush and Alex Alexiev, "The Ethnic Factor in the Soviet Armed Forces" *Rand*, R-2787/1 (March 1982), v.

15. Wilhelm Winkler, *Das Anteil der nichtdeutschen Volksstämme an der 27 öst.-ung. Wehrmacht* (Vienna, 1919), 3.

16. See Georg Živkovi, *Heer und Flottenführer der Welt*, 2nd ed. (Vienna, 1980), 76, and Johann Weidlein, "Ungarische Offiziere donauschwäbischer Herkunft," unpublished manuscript, Kriegsarchiv Vienna, Brochure 1542.

13

Ethnic Politics in the Habsburg Monarchy and Successor States: Three "Answers" to the National Question

Dennison Rusinow

Nowhere else in the world has as much political and scholarly attention been paid to ethnonational diversity and fragmentation, and to their consequences in "the age of nationalism," as in East-Central Europe. Historically the region provided the first important testing ground for the diffusion of the Western European concept of the nation-state, intimately identified with nineteenth-century Western European definitions of "nation" and more recently with social scientists' attempts to identify the prerequisites for integrative "modernization,"[1] to lands where the ethnic map and the structure of traditional society render its application difficult and perhaps even inappropriate. In the process East-Central Europe, and especially the lands of the Habsburg Empire and its successor states, became the world's oldest laboratory for conscious efforts to solve "the national question"[2] in an ethnic shatterbelt, either by remaking the boundaries or the population of existing states to conform to the doctrine or by finding an alternative to it.

The authors and objects of these efforts were confronting a set of questions of general and continuing importance and dramatic contemporary salience for the Soviet Union and other multinational communities no longer legitimized and mobilized by Marxist-Leninist doctrine and socialist ideals. Is the nation-state in fact the only basis for a modern polity—that is, the only "truly legitimate" state and also the only way of achieving the kind of social integration as a self-aware and self-recognizing community that is necessary for orderly, self-sustaining social change and growth in a complex, differentiated modern society based on individual and institutional specialization? If it is not, what alternative to the nation could provide a basis for such community building as well as legitimacy? If it is, can a state or society ever become fully modern (or modernizing), as well as legitimate, if it contains numerically or otherwise significant national minorities? Moreover, how should such minorities be treated? Can ethnic diversity be tolerated or even encouraged, or does social modernization as well as the doctrine of the nation-state require its elimination through assimilation or other means?

In this chapter I will describe and seek to link two aspects of the history of "the national question" in the Habsburg Empire and its successor states that bear on these larger questions. Those who seek to answer contemporary versions of the same question in multinational ex-Communist states might also benefit from this examination.

In the first part I offer some observations on the social content of the national question in the Monarchy and the diverse nature and effects of what were, in effect, three different strategies to cope with it, discernible in the Empire's last half-century. These might be called the Austrian, the Hungarian, and the Austro-Hungarian models, although none was as consistent and as clearly defined as the label implies and all have been tried, with variations and rarely with attribution, in other times and places. These last include Russia and the Soviet Union, as well as several Habsburg successor states, where policies that arguably resemble the Hungarian model or variations on the Austrian model have both already been tried—would it be fanciful to suggest that Soviet policies have at times attempted to combine them?—and something resembling the Austro-Hungarian model may prove to be the only alternative to disintegration, with or without civil war, for the Soviet Union and Yugoslavia in the 1990s.

None of these strategies has eliminated ethnonational diversity (which only the Hungarian sought to do) or the problems it poses (which all three sought to do) in any of the states in which they have been tried. Nor have these strategies reduced diversity and attendant problems to a matter of peripheral minorities like those that still characterize most supposedly prototypical nation-states in Western Europe. Only changes in international boundaries and expulsions or migrations at the ends of two world wars have made nation-states (strictly defined as a state with a population very largely composed of members of one nation)[3] out of three of East-Central Europe's previously multinational ones.

However, Habsburg and post-Habsburg nationality policies and socio-economic transformations *have* significantly altered the magnitude, proportions, and social significance of this diversity. In the second part of this essay I consider one particular dimension of this process, which concerns the life chances of minorities, and the costs and benefits of heterogeneity or homogenization, in diverse circumstances. On the basis of case studies from the Monarchy and its successor states, I suggest a tentative typology of minority ethnic groups according to their potential, as determined by a cluster of five demographic, social, and attitudinal variables, for survival and/or inclusion in modernizing social change and a larger society. Contemporary Soviet and other analogues will easily come to mind.

My brief conclusions, drawn from both parts, are depressing for those who believe that ethnicity (and concomitant ethnonationalism) can somehow be eliminated, if it will not fade away by itself, but are perhaps overoptimistic in suggesting that an unsatisfying but viable formula for a multinational modus vivendi lurks in latter-day Habsburg history after all.

SOME OBSERVATIONS ON THE MONARCHY'S NATIONAL QUESTION

The ethnic map of East-Central Europe, especially in those lands that comprised the Habsburg Empire and Ottoman Europe at the beginning of the nineteenth century, is a patchwork in which the fragments are bewilderingly mixed, frequently minute, and often changeable, leading geographers to apply the graphic label "ethnic shatterbelt" to the region. Both the ethnic patchwork and the region's failure to produce enduring, stable, centralizing local states (of the kind that were forging the French, English, and some other Western European nations out of also diverse peoples since the later Middle Ages) were notoriously the consequences of its tortured history as Europe's southeastern marches, a buffer zone absorbing invasions and migrations that alternately depopulated and repopulated its plains and valleys in accordance with the whims and needs of foreign dynasties and tribes. Its peoples usually lived under the rule of aliens, in peripheries of multinational empires or ephemeral buffer states between them.

The arrival in this region of the originally Western European concept of the nation (usually defined as an ethnolinguistic group) as the only just basis for the organization of a secular modern state, and the awakening to its revolutionary potential by individuals and classes who were or felt themselves to be politically, economically, and/or socially aggrieved, equally notoriously created a serious "national question" in each of the multinational empires that then dominated the region. The national question was particularly acute for the Habsburg Monarchy, in which no one nation accounted for a majority or even a numerical predominance, and where the Habsburg Emperor and his ministers were the only rulers in Europe (unless one also counts the Ottoman Empire as European) who could not shift their claim to legitimacy from divine right or the dynastic principle to the will or consent of a national community. The latter-day history of the Habsburg Empire is therefore dominated by the national question and by experiments in the search for an alternative foundation for a modern state. The search was cut short by one of its incidental consequences, World War I.

One aspect of this familiar story that merits recapitulation here, despite its familiarity, concerns the social content of the national struggle in the Empire's last century.[4] In addition to its centrality in explaining the nature of the question and why it became so vital, this factor also provides an important basis for comparison and contrast with the national question in the Soviet Union (and the Ottoman Empire) and for an understanding of the post-Habsburg fortunes and misfortunes of the Empire's peoples.

In the Habsburg Empire in the early nineteenth century, and in many provinces as late as the early twentieth century, there was a rough but significant correlation between nationality and social status. There were urban nations and peasant nations (partly but not completely corresponding to what were also described as "historic" and "unhistoric" nations). Later there were middle-class nations and proletarian nations.

It is worth recalling that until the rapid growth of cities, usually only after 1850 and only sometimes associated with industrialization, the towns of the Empire were almost all German in language, culture, and (where such existed) national consciousness. The only significant exceptions were in Galicia and in the Habsburg possessions in northern Italy and Dalmatia, where ancient and distinguished Polish or Italian communes had not been created or repopulated by German merchant colonists in earlier centuries. The populations of these towns were not necessarily or predominantly ethnic Germans (or Poles or Italians) in origin, however. Their ancestors had usually come from the natural source for urban recruitment for each urban center, its surrounding countryside, which was usually Slav or Magyar or Romanian. But they had become townspeople in towns founded or restored by German-speaking merchants and artisans and in a German-ruled empire for which German was the language of government and commerce. So they had "become" German (or Polish or Italian) as a part of the process of their urbanization, "forgetting" their ethnic origin in a generation or two. To be urban was to be German or Polish or Italian.

The "national revival" of the peasant nations combined with the accelerated growth of towns characteristic of the nineteenth century, the beginnings of industrialization, and the spread of classic liberalism among the urban middle classes of the Monarchy to challenge this comfortable division. The process began after 1815 in Bohemia, soon to become the industrial center of the Empire, and reached even the still-traditional market towns of remote provinces like the Istrian hinterland and Bukovina by the end of the century. The transition to urban life-styles was made easier if the newcomers, in any case now far more numerous, listened to the teaching of poets and intellectuals of the romantic generation, who had already "rediscovered" their own identities in the peasant nations from which they had sprung, sung of their ancient glories, and preached the equality of their cultures and values with those of the "historic" nations. One could come to Prague or Brno and remain Czech, to Ljubljana or Trieste and remain Slovene, to Bratislava as a Slovak or to Cluj as a Romanian. The peasant became urban without losing his (peasant) national identity, and the German (or Italian or Polish) islands in a Slav or Romanian sea were overwhelmed one by one.

The acute phase of the national question in the Habsburg Empire, marked by growing competition and eventually bitter mutual hatred and incomprehension, was born of this phenomenon. It began as a reactive nationalism among the Germans of the threatened towns, who sought to defend jobs in the bureaucracy or monopolies in local business or the professions against pushy newcomers of alien tongue. The newcomers, inspired by their poets and intellectuals, those romantic generals who had at last found an army, responded with counteroffensive organizations of their own. The struggle was characterized, significantly, by the use of rival cultural institutions, which founded and financed ethnic schools, libraries, banks, marching bands, voluntary fire brigades, and alpine and youth clubs. The style was that of military warfare adapted to the cultural front, and at organizational headquarters "battle" maps were sometimes employed, on which front lines (language borders and ethnically besieged towns) and the disposition of "enemy" institutions were displayed as a basis for strategy. Political clubs and ethnic political parties followed, as the partial triumph of liberalism broadened the franchise enough to make them meaningful.

In many provinces ethnic groups could be identified with social classes on the land as well, with feudatories and large landowners belonging to one nation and peasants to another. German landowners were predominant in Slovene Carniola and Czech Bohemia, Magyars in Slovakia and much of

Croatia, Italians in Istria and parts of Dalmatia, Poles in Ukrainian Eastern Galicia, and so on. With the spread of literacy from the towns into the countryside in the last decades before World War I, the new nationalism at last flowed back toward its source among the peasantry of the peasant nations. The latter, learning to read and write in their native dialect, "discovered" their heretofore latent nationality and began, like their urban cousins, to identify social grievances with national grievances. The same phenomenon was repeated in the towns, where the new urban proletariat was usually of different nationality from the older, established capitalists. Demands for land reform, for a wider franchise, or for trade unions consequently became another battleground for ethnic conflict.

Thus the national question masked both a crisis of access and class warfare. In both cases tensions were increased by clashes between differing life-styles and value systems of the participant ethnic groups, formerly segregated by language borders or in separate villages but now rubbing shoulders uncomfortably in city streets and in the proliferating institutions of an industrializing, urbanizing society.

Frustrated desires for personal social mobility, an entrepreneur's, lawyer's, or bureaucrat's fear of competition for business or jobs, a capitalist's fear of organized labor and labor's resentment of the boss's power and prerogatives, the peasant's hatred of the great landowner and the landowner's fear of the peasantry, value clashes between old and newly urbanized, between secularist and clericalist and among Catholic, Protestant, and Orthodox worldviews—all were projected as clashes among nationalities, largely because in any locality the role players in each category could usually be identified with a particular ethnic group. Such a situation was not uniquely East-Central European: almost every society has its Ireland or its excluded minority. But the Habsburg Monarchy was unique in being totally composed of "Irelands" and ethnic minorities.

To understand fully the frustrating subjective difficulties encountered by every later attempted solution of minorities questions in East-Central Europe, one must understand the intensity of emotion that came to surround the question of nationality when every grievance, and perceived injustice was projected as a national issue. Characteristic of the resultant atmosphere in many parts of the Monarchy is the following description of one ethnically disputed corner of the Empire on the eve of World War I, the city of Trieste and the towns of Istria (Venezia Giulia), which urbanization was then in the process of converting from Italian into Slovene or Croat centers:

From this, in the years preceding the other world war, a growing disquiet in the Italian bourgeoisie of Venezia Giulia, an irritability and almost pathological hypertension of national sentiment, which even more than in the preceding decades became a daily atmosphere, almost obsessive in its fixation, in which the Italian of this region lived and to which all value judgments, all measures of merit were referred as to a single motive; the degree of national temperature displayed by each person became the criterion by which his honor and human dignity were judged; the Italian in his particularity took precedence over man in his universality. This hypertrophy of national passion was felt in everything, in social and personal relations, in taste, in judgments concerning the most ordinary matters, to which elsewhere no one would think of applying a national criterion of evaluation; this was reflected above all in the cultural climate, impregnated with national passion to the saturation point, to the point of suffocating any other extraneous germ or origin. . . . This is not simply the phenomenon of a frontier people, this is not the phenomenon of meeting points for diverse cultures, which modify one another, appease one another, and fuse; here it is the exasperation of wills which have chosen a single road, a single culture exalted and transfigured into a myth. As the Puritan asked himself in agony: "Are you saved?", so the antebellum Julian asked himself with the anxious hope of an intimate confirmation, "Are you sufficiently Italian?"[5]

Thus the Habsburg national question entered its critical phase.

ONE MONARCHY + TWO STATES = THREE STRATEGIES

One of the less-disputed clichés in Habsburg historiography identifies four "master nations" in the polyglot Empire's later history: the Germans and Magyars, undoubtedly, and the Poles and Italians, whom some demote to quasi-master nations. These nations are also widely held to have been more deeply infected with the nationalist virus by 1848, meaning that more of their members (or more members of their elites) had caught it, than the Empire's other nationalities. In the revolutions of 1848, or in their Galician rehearsal in 1846, the Magyars and Austria's Poles and Italians attempted to secede. The secession of most of the Monarchy's Italians, to join a new Italian nation-state that would soon be seeking to redeem the *Italiani irredenti* of Trento and Trieste, was consummated with the help of French and Prussian armies in 1859 and 1866. The Magyars' political class, largely synonymous with their large gentry class, exploited the second of these military defeats, which also ended Habsburg pretensions to primacy in Germany, to strike a deal with the Emperor for an autonomy that was tantamount to confederation.

The Polish ruling class consolidated its de facto autonomous control of Galicia. Except in Galicia the Monarchy's other "newly awakened" nationalities would henceforth confront two "master nations": the Germans and the Magyars.

These developments, between *Vormärz* and *Ausgleich*, set the stage and the parameters for the next act in the drama.

A proliferation of proposals for the resolution of the Monarchy's national question accompanied its growing intensity, urgency, and extension to include nationalities (the "unhistoric nations") and social classes (in the "historic nations" as well) that were latecomers to national consciousness. Most of these schemes never became more than blueprints or the stuff for later myths about what might have been. Others, like the "October Diploma" and "February Patent," were rescinded almost immediately. Three basic strategies, of which two were imposed by the Magyar political class and one by expediency, can be discerned in what actually happened. Like Franz Joseph's motivations and maneuvers in vacillating to and from the October Diploma and February Patent in 1860-61, each of the three also represented an attempt, in Berthold Sutter's words, "to solve the problem, which after as well as before [1860] consisted in finding a compromise between a strong central power, essential for the maintenance of Austria's Great Power status, and the desire for national development of the individual peoples."[6] Strikingly, the same words could be used to describe the way the present Soviet leadership, judged by its current policies and maneuvers, is defining the problem confronting the Soviet Union at the beginning of the 1990s.

The first derived from the constitutional nature and consequences of the Compromise of 1867 between the Emperor and the Magyars, whose demands for less than total secession he could not ignore after (and in the hope of avenging) Prussia's victory at Königgrätz. The result was de facto a loose confederation between the Kingdom of Hungary (including Croatia, Transylvania, and all other "historic" lands of the Holy Crown of Saint Stephen) and the Emperor's other possessions ("the lands represented in the [Vienna] Reichsrat").

After 1867 Hungary was in effect an independent state in all except foreign policy, defense, and some limits to its economic sovereignty that were less than those now being imposed on the twelve supposedly still sovereign member states of the European Community under the provisions of the Single European Act of 1986. Even in these areas the rulers of Hungary enjoyed equality with the Dual Monarchy's other half, and in practice often more than equality, through the system of delegations mandated by the Compromise.

The *Ausgleich* was an answer to the Magyar question that left other pieces of the Empire's national question (including even the German one) unanswered and in fact harder to resolve. Later attempts to extend this kind of solution to other nations or clusters of nations—as in the idea of "Trialism" in place of Dualism to accommodate the South Slavs—foundered on Magyar opposition and the difficulty of accommodating both South Slavs and Czechs either together or separately. For the Crown and the Magyars, however, the *Ausgleich* they had negotiated was a promising and on balance satisfactory "compromise between [the minimum of] a strong central power essential for the maintenance of Austria's Great Power status," which the leading faction in the Magyars' ruling class had now joined Franz Joseph in desiring, and at least the Magyars' "desire for national development." It was thus a formula that both the Crown (incarnate in Franz Joseph and the Imperial-Royal bureaucracy and army) and the Magyars could live with, although neither was entirely satisfied, and that others, like later advocates of Trialism, would consider worthy of adaptation to other parts (or indeed the whole) of the Monarchy.

The problem, of course, was that the Kingdom of Hungary was not a Magyar nation-state and that other potential candidates for equivalent status in a territorial confederation under Habsburg rule were also not national units. This was a problem because the idea of confederation, as a solution to the national question, carried an implicit assumption that the political boundaries of the confederated states would correspond, at least *in grosso modo*, to national boundaries. Everyone knew that this was not the case in Hungary or in most of the Monarchy's other "historic" units. This awareness led some to devise schemes for nonterritorial national autonomy, a secular and national Habsburg version of the Ottoman millet system. Others played with the map, vainly seeking to redesign the boundaries of historic units to correspond to national ones. In the context of a Dualism that could not be generalized into a Habsburg Confederation, these and the rest of the arsenal of hypothetical solutions to multinationalism—coercive or modernization-driven assimilation to a regionally dominant nation, cultural autonomy, legislated minority rights, or some combination of these—would now be considered, and sometimes attempted, within the parameters imposed by Dualism. The spotlight passes to the separate strategies, the Hungarian and Austrian.

The "Austro-Hungarian strategy" of confederation as an answer to the national question in a multinational state, a strategy thwarted of a more comprehensive test in the Habsburg lands, has nevertheless reappeared in later and contemporary times, and in the same and other places. It has done so as a ghost in interwar dreams of a Danubian or Balkan confederation and again, more recently, as an item actually on the agenda of solutions being canvassed for binational communities like Canada and Cyprus and multinational ones like Yugoslavia and the Soviet Union.[7]

The Hungarian strategy was straightforward and basically simple, despite complications imposed by the Nationalities Law of 1868, designed to protect non-Magyar cultures and participation, and efforts by some of its authors and their ideological progeny to take its provisions seriously. The rulers of Hungary after the *Ausgleich* sought to create a nation-state on the Western European model—a state for the Magyar (Hungarian) nation, which comprised less than half of the Kingdom's population. In this, but in Hungarian circumstances, they were not unlike their contemporaries in liberated and united Italy, who became fond of quoting Massimo d'Azeglio's "We have made Italy, now we must make Italians."[8] National community building, for the rulers of this state, could only be conceived through national assimilation of the non-Magyars (their Magyarization) and the exclusion from effective citizenship of those who resisted. The means they used to achieve this combination of assimilation and exclusion, although some were primarily or equally aimed at more efficient administration or communications through use of a single language, are well known.[9] Hungarian became the exclusive state language, despite provisions in the Nationalities Law of 1868 guaranteeing cultural (including linguistic) autonomy to minority districts. The use of local languages and customs in public life was gradually but ruthlessly suppressed. Local autonomy in Transylvania, with its Romanian majority, was finally liquidated, as it had temporarily been suppressed during the Hungarian revolution of 1848. The "historic state's right" of dependent Croatia was eroded, albeit with more difficulty, and major crises in relations with the Croats at the beginning of the twentieth century arose from the extension of the Hungarian language for official use into Croatia as well. The school system was Magyarized almost everywhere, and even the local German majority in the later Burgenland in Transdanubia, on the doorstep of Vienna, attended Magyar schools. The prospects of the Slovaks for survival as a nation were particularly bleak: they lacked the cultural and psychological support of fellow nationals organized in a nation-state of their own beyond Hungary's borders, such as the Romanians and Serbs enjoyed; they had no legal and traditional autonomy to defend them, as the Croats did; and their own "national awakening" was among the newest and consequently most traditionless in Central Europe.

Hungarian ethnic policy in the age of Dualism, which was to define the effective community as the Magyar nation and exclude all others, was not, however, racist. "Magyar" was defined culturally (or, as some have suggested, as a class concept), not genetically. Any Jew, German, Slovak, Romanian, Serb, or Croat could "become" a Magyar and so gain admittance to the community defined as nation, with as much social mobility and other perquisites of full citizenship as any lineal descendant of the Magyar horsemen of the tenth century.

This strategy was not without some apparent success. As István Déak has pointed out, citing recent Hungarian studies, between 2.5 and three million non-Magyars were assimilated ("became Magyars") between 1780 and 1914, about two million of them in the period between the censuses of 1850 and 1910. The 1780-1914 figure includes one million Germans, over 700,000 Jews, and 500,000 Slovaks.[10] William McCagg's studies of Hungary's Jewish nobles and geniuses and of the Jews of the entire Monarchy elaborate on Déak's brief summary of why Hungarian Jews (and Germans), predominantly urban populations, proved particularly susceptible to Magyarization.[11]

However, as Déak also noted, assimilation was an almost exclusively urban phenomenon. The countryside was barely touched by it. Moreover, an identical process and similar magnitudes of urban assimilation to local majority nations (German in Vienna, Czech in Prague, Slovene in Ljubljana, etc.) were being recorded in most other, non-Hungarian parts of the Monarchy. How much of this process in Hungary can therefore be attributed to the Magyars' nationality policies? How much should instead be traced to the imperatives of "modernization," which require learning the language and adapting to the culture that do or may provide access to jobs and opportunity (upward mobility) in modern sectors and a modernizing society?[12] In Hungary these went hand in hand and were mutually supportive, but similar results in "the chauvinist cities" of Cisleithania strongly suggest that state-mandated pressures to assimilate were contributory and facilitative (the latter because they ensured that education, where provided, would be in the langauge and culture of access rather than a language that inhibited mobility) rather than primary.

The same argument helps to explain the greater millions of non-Magyars, especially those who were also non-Jewish and non-German and usually nonurban, who did not avail themselves of the opportunity or succumb to the pressure to become Magyars. These were mostly of two kinds. The first, which included millions of Magyar as well as non-Magyar peasants, consisted of those who were content, or at least willing, to stay where they were—on the land and in villages and in the social status and categories these places offered. (The reasons might include lack of ambition, fear of change, pessimism about one's prospects or abilities, love of hearth, field, and traditional values, or all of these and more.) The second kind consisted of those whose frustrated hopes and ambitions, focused on the cultural barriers raised by the regime's policies and the Kingdom's alien, "chauvinistic" cities, led them to seek an alternative "at home" in their own culture and land—autonomous, independent, or joined to a nation-state of their own kind beyond the Monarchy's borders. Both categories inhibited the spread of modernization beyond its urban citadel by inhibiting the "cultural homogenization" that Ernest Gellner and others consider necessary to it. Both rejected assimilation and thus the extension of the Magyar nation to fill and fulfill the Magyar nation-state—although most of Hungary's rulers, content with less if they could continue to rule the whole, did not seem to mind and were very likely relieved. But the second category, growing in number and building the cultural and cooperative infrastructure of their own nationhoods and autonomist, separatist, or irredentist nationalisms, magnified Hungary's national question rather than diminishing it.[13] As a net result the Hungarian countryside, measured in terms of communes gained and lost by the Magyars, became less rather than more Magyar between 1867 and 1918.[14]

The Hungarian strategy of deliberate nation building through a combination of domination, assimilation, and exclusion was simply not feasible, and was never attempted, in the other half of the Dual Monarchy. The Emperor was German-speaking, as was much of the aristocracy. German was the language of the bureaucracy and army, and some of the Germans of the Austrian half of the monarchy sometimes dreamed of Germanizing the land on the Hungarian pattern; but for demographic, historic, and political reasons this was never possible. With its Czechs, Poles, Ukrainians, Slovenes, and Dalmatians, the Austrian half actually had a Slavic majority, but with interests and geographic distribution too diverse to permit effective cooperation or opposition to the Germanic tradition of the court.

With such an ethnic stalemate, the Austrian half of the Empire inevitably remained stubbornly non-national in an age of nationalism. It was ruled, as the historians' clichés have it, by playing the nationalities off against one another to preserve the power of the Crown and its ministers, who did their best to maintain a more-or-less balanced and equitable distribution of dissatisfaction among the more important nationalities.

For most of the participants in this game, it was always clear that this was a nonsolution and a temporary expedient. Surprisingly few of even the most fervent nationalists, however, favored a formal dissolution of their joint community into its ethnic components, until the course of World War I induced them to espouse such a policy. Instead, they devised ingenious schemes, most of them involving a federal solution, for restructuring and "democratizing" the Empire in a way that would grant effective local autonomy to some or all of the nationalities. In acting in this way they were motivated in part by a consciousness of the advantages of belonging to a larger state (and the disadvantages of a "Balkanization" of Central Europe), in part by the practical and political difficulties that would come with any attempt to draw ethnic frontiers in an ethnic patchwork, and in part by a kind of psychological rigidity or traditionalism: the dynastic conglomerate ruled by the Habsburgs had been around so long that a Central Europe without it was almost literally unthinkable.[15]

The failure of every plan to federalize the Austrian half of the Empire, and the key role of the Hungarians in frustrating the more hopeful of them, are well known. In ethnically mixed provinces, meanwhile, a generally agreed compromise, setting forth the rights of the ethnic communities and mutually satisfactory rules for their public interaction and cooperation, could sometimes be achieved, as was done in Moravia in the 1890s. More frequently, however, agreement was frustrated by an irreducible conflict between the "ethnic" and the "historic" principles, with a province's majority nationality insisting on its "right" to treat the "historic" province as its own national territory. The Czech majority used this argument against the German minority in "historic" Bohemia, and the German majority used it against the Slovene minority in "historic" Styria, with the minority in each case demanding administrative partition or national equality.

The failure to achieve an agreeable solution in places like Bohemia and Styria was further proof of the blind alley in which nineteenth-century European thinking about community definition found itself when the nation-state was generally accepted as the only legitimate focus of loyalty. Even when there was agreement to live together in a larger, multinational state, on the basis of administrative ethnic autonomy, the administrative units could only be thought of as sub-nation-states, within which a national definition of community must be applied. Given the ethnic map, such a conception could only reproduce in miniature, in almost every multinational province, the crisis of the multinational empire.

However, the Austrian strategy of improvisation and ad hoc "fire-fighting" responses to crises on the nationality front is no longer so widely regarded as the rarely mitigated and fateful failure portrayed by most first-generation, post-1918 historians, a failure that combined with Czech and South Slav nationalisms and separatists to make the disintegration of the Empire inevitable. Probably most historians now agree that the inevitability-of-disintegration thesis was usually based on *post hoc propter hoc* reasoning, or at best on a selective and often nationally prejudiced reading of the evidence. It is therefore arguable (and has been argued by those willing to indulge in might-have-been historiography) that the Austrians' supposed penchant for "muddling through," and thereby sometimes purposefully maintaining a balanced distribution of national grievances and tensions among the Empire's peoples, was not only a logical nonsolution for an unsolvable national question but enough to have assured the indefinite survival of the Habsburg's multinational state—if it had not been destroyed by the dynamics and outcome of World War I. This thesis also begs many questions, including the war as itself a product of the Monarchy's and the South Slavs' national questions. However, by calling into question the inevitability of the Monarchy's disintegration in the face of its multiple, conflicting nationalisms, it leaves open the question of whether "the Austrian strategy" could someday and somewhere (*ceteris non-paribus*) provide a sufficient, if never satisfactory, answer.

ETHNIC MINORITIES IN THE HABSBURG
SUCCESSOR STATES

The Balkan wars and World War I appeared to vindicate the concept of the nation-state for all of Europe. The former completed the "national liberation" of the subject peoples of European Turkey. The latter ended in victory for the Entente and the United States of America, whose war aims came to include "national self-determination"; in the replacement of the Habsburg Empire by what purported to be nation-states; and in the creation of other independent states for some of the non-Russian nations along the marchlands of the former Russian Empire—although all except Finland would be reabsorbed by the Soviet Union in the 1920s or in 1940.

With two exceptions, however, none of these states represented the kind of true national community, based on self-awareness of a common heritage, common interests, and common destiny, that was the ideal type of which the nationalist poets and politicians had dreamed—or even a less-than-ideal but still largely inclusive and effective national community like the Western European states that had provided the nationalists with their models. Some were assembled out of pieces of two or more former political entities, with widely differing historical experiences and levels of social development. Like the Italians after their national unification, these peoples soon discovered that common nationality (as in Greater Romania) or closely kindred nationhood (as in Czechoslovakia and Yugoslavia) does not necessarily produce common interests or value systems. Moreover, because the nation-state principle was now applied to the singularly inappropriate patchwork ethnic map of East-Central Europe, all of the new or enlarged states inherited sizable minorities, usually as intoxicated as the nations-of-state themselves with the effervescent spirit of new nationalism; two of them (Yugoslavia and Czechoslovakia) were officially multinational. So the national question persisted and came to dominate the interwar life of most of the successor states, as it had that of the empires they had replaced. It was resolved or simplified after World War II only where genocide, expulsions, or changed borders[16] resolved or simplified it.

In both chapters—the Habsburg and post-Habsburg—the "life chances" of these minorities,[17] measured in terms of their growth or shrinkage in official or estimated numbers, their social and economic development or stagnation, and intergenerational changes in their members' social and economic status, have been far from uniform. There are corresponding differences in the life chances of their individual members (the correspondence can be positive or negative, as noted below) and in the consequences for the stability (and prosperity) of the larger societies and states in which they live. The reasons for this variety are therefore triply worth examining.

It is clear that these differences are not only or even primarily a function of the presence or absence, and intensity, of official (state-sponsored) persecution, discrimination, or efforts to segregate or assimilate, all of which are at least as likely to strengthen communal solidarity and resistance as to weaken them. Nor are they primarily functions of the minority-friendly or nondiscriminatory policies of more benign governments like those of Austria after the Compromise of 1867 (de facto) and several successor states after 1919 (sometimes only de jure), which are different in principle and likely to have contrary effects. Protection and subsidization of a rural and "backward" or small minority can impair the life chances of its members, while enhancing that of the community, by inhibiting mobility and limiting their competence in the language and technology of the larger society "off the reservation." On the other hand, treating all citizens as equal may induce defections from a historically unequal minority by individuals hoping to escape the burden of that collective inequality. Other factors—demographic, social, and attitudinal—therefore appear to be more important, and may be easier to identify and aggregate, where the role of the state has been relatively or on balance neutral.

Case studies from the experience of the Habsburg Monarchy and its multinational successor states suggest a typology of minority ethnic and national communities in terms of their potential (a) to persist while joining a majority community in undergoing or participating in modernizing social changes; (b) to persist while being excluded from or opting out of modernization, thus remaining as significant nonmodern islands in a modernizing society; or (c) to be subject to a continuous "skimmed milk process" in which upwardly mobile members of each generation are assimilated into the dominating culture and nation, leaving a socially decapitated mass diminishing gradually in numbers as a politically and socially insignificant nonmodern island.

Which minority falls into which category appears to be determined primarily by five variables: (1) the numerical size (absolutely or relatively?) of the group; (2) its relative starting level of socioeconomic development and perceived status; (3) the extent to which the popularly understood values of "modernity" (urbanization, education, industrialization, specialization, mobility, mass communications, and the life-styles necessary to or determined by these phenomena) are internalized by members (or only leaders?) of the group; (4) the degree of official (state) and social toleration displayed by the majority community to minority individuals who aspire to upward mobility; and (5) the extent and intensity of the minority community's "national consciousness."

The following case studies, selected and summarized to illustrate this tentative matrix, could be extended and elaborated into a more meaningful test of the pertinence of these variables.[18]

Case A: The Croats of Austria's Burgenland, a part of the Kingdom of Hungary until Trianon. Until recently there were about 40,000 Croats. The community, settled since the Turkish war of the 1520s in villages of their own that are widely scattered among those of their German and a few Magyar neighbors, has persisted for more than four centuries far (by peasant measurement) from compactly Croatian territory. In their isolation they were virtually untouched by the Croatian nationalist movements of the nineteenth and twentieth centuries, and continued to speak a dialect close to the one their ancestors brought with them in the 1500s.

Still almost entirely peasant, these Croats stubbornly and triumphantly survived, in apparently undiminished numbers, both Hungarian efforts at Magyarization before 1918 and Nazi persecution from 1938 to 1945. Since that time Austrian governments and German-speaking Austrians, encouraged in liberality by the fact that geography precludes any Yugoslav irredentist challenge (in contrast to Carinthia), have treated their Croatian minority (in contrast to their Slovenian one) with no evidence of intolerance and little or no prejudice. The Croats enjoy full and modestly subsidized linguistic and cultural freedom. In their level of economic and social development Croat villagers are generally indistinguishable from their German neighbors, but there is of course no Croatian city or large town in Austria to serve as a pole of attraction for out-migration from their villages. Northern and central Burgenland, however, is now within commuter range of Vienna for those who wish to combine urban employment with weekends at home, while industrialization and other opportunities for employment have made rapid headway in many larger Burgenland towns (all German-Austrian in culture) since 1955.

For the first time the Croatian community is diminishing in numbers and significance as a self-conscious ethnic community. Most of their communal leaders support Croatian-language primary schools (with German as a compulsory foreign language and as the language of instruction in some courses at higher grades) but have refused offers of Croatian secondary schools, to the dismay of a very small minority of nationalists (mostly schoolteachers) among them. The reasons given are typified by the answer of a Croat village mayor in an interview I conducted in 1959: "I would defend myself, weapons in hand, if they again tried to prevent our listening to Croatian sermons in church or speaking Croatian in a café, but I do not want my children going to a Croatian secondary school. I want them to do well, which means a job in the city, and German is the language of those they must compete with there." Upwardly mobile young Croats, if they establish a family and weekend base in the village, remain bilingual and "bicultural"; if they move to Vienna or even to Wiener Neustadt, they become urban German-Austrian. Only the "pure" peasants remain "purely" Croatian, an "ethnically conscious" but apparently not "nationally conscious" skimmed-milk social stratum for whom both High German and modern literary Croatian are difficult foreign tongues.

Case B: The once at least 36,000 Italians of Istria, Rijeka (Fiume), and the Slovene Littoral in Yugoslavia. The story is similar to that of the Croats, with two distinctions. First, there are Italian secondary schools (required by international agreement through the "London Memorandum" that resolved the Trieste question in 1954), to which not only members of the Italian minority but also some Croats and Slovenes send their children. The second distinction would also appear to account for the popularity of Italian secondary education. The Italian minority's starting level of economic and cultural development, *as subjectively perceived by both Italians and Slavs*, was at least until recently considered higher than that of their Slav neighbors, and Italian culture has its (subjectively perceived) snob appeal. But ambitious products of these schools have no Italian university in Yugoslavia to go to, nor an Italian town or city in which to find scope for their ambitions. Except for a small number who may remain or return as teachers, local politicians, or managers of local (usually tourist) enterprises, the ambitious must either emigrate to Italy or out-migrate to Slovene or Croatian cities, where their starting cultural level and knowledge of an important foreign language and culture make it comparatively easy for them to hurdle language and cultural barriers to social mobility—and assimilation. The Italian minority, socially decapitated and with a low birthrate, decreases in absolute numbers from census to census: from 36,000 (probably an undercounting) in 1953 and 26,000 in 1961 to 15,000 "by nationality" and 19,000 "by mother tongue" in 1981.

Case C: The Vlachs of Yugoslavia's Dinaric highlands. This minority, so small that it no longer enjoys a separate listing in the census, speaks a Romance language and is presumed to be a remnant of the pre-Slavic, Romanized population of the Adriatic hinterland. They fascinate foreign anthropologists as practitioners of the dying art of transhumance. Because of their seminomadic life, it is difficult to get their children into school. They are nonparticipants in social change and seem likely to continue to be so, at least until that improbable or at least remote day when economic development or its infrastructure reaches their remote mountain homeland and makes their way of life impossible. They are a nonmodern island, but they do not matter except to curiosity-seeking anthropologists and themselves.

Case D: The South Tyrolese of Italy's province of Bozen-Bolzano. There were 220,000 of these German-speaking peasants, merchants, and aristocrats when they were left on the "wrong side" of the Italo-Austrian frontier by one of the Versailles-Saint Germain peacemakers' most notorious and flagrant violations of their own principles of national self-determination and ethnic frontiers. Their history since the Napoleonic Wars and Andreas Hofer's epic rebellion against the godless French and their Bavarian allies leaves little doubt concerning their national consciousness, although whether this should be defined as Roman Catholic German, Austrian, Tyrolese, or even South Tyrolese is debatable because it has been changeable over time and variable by social class.

Subjected to Fascist efforts at forced assimilation that were extraordinarily brutal by pre-Nazi standards, and reacting with a passionate and intolerant *German* nationalism that made good Nazis of many and acquiescent collaborators of most of the rest, they continued to demonstrate their sense of alienation from the Italian state throughout at least the first three decades of the postwar period, disdainfully rejecting every sign of post-Fascist Italian liberality as another subtle Italian nationalist trick. Most of them fervently believed that they were still the target of a deliberate policy of Italianization, although this was demonstrably no longer true. The evidence they cited included some significant items: Italian-built roads and hydroelectric plants designed as a diabolic infrastructure to permit the in-migration of more Italian capital and workers, who bring ugly Italian factories and industrial smog to replace the fruit orchards of the Etsch and Eisack valleys; mountainsides ruined by Italian villas and hotels (that many were German was usually overlooked) and the hideous high-voltage carriers of electrical current generated in Tyrolese mountains to serve Italian plains; Italian youth who made noise and love in unseemly fashion on respectable alps and sometimes seduced healthy Tyrolese youth into joining their urban, Latin debauchery; the ugliness of modern Italian high-rise subdivisions surrounding and suffocating handsome old German Gothic markettowns; and so on, and so on. If the list were examined[19] and those who presented it were questioned carefully, it would gradually become clear that what was objectionable was not primarily Italy, but the twentieth century, which was brought to these valleys by Italians because the South Tyrol happened to be in Italy when the impact of that century spread from the industrialized cities of the plains into the mountain valleys. The past history of ethnic tension and oppression, plus the presence of Italians who also identified modern with Italian and traditional idyllic-rural with Tyrolese, tended to reinforce this tendency to blame the Italians for things that were simultaneously imported and objectionable. Tyrolese Germanness was identified with a way of life that was no more typical of modern, urban Germany and Austria than of modern, urban Italy, but in defending this way of life against the twentieth century, the South Tyrolese imagined that they were defending *Deutschtum* against *Italianita*. In attempting to preserve their identity as a distinct ethnic community, they were also attempting to preserve an island of traditional values and life-styles against the unwanted encroachments of modernization. There was also, however, a minority within a minority that accepted the implications of modernizing social change at an early date, both for personal profit and because they have embraced the values of that kind of world. Significantly, in the 1950s and 1960s they were found primarily among businessmen who belonged to the Bozen Chamber of Commerce or among young South Tyrolese who left the University of Innsbruck, which they considered "square," to go to Italian universities they considered more "with it." Characteristically, both groups were impatient with the intense and xenophobic German nationalism as well as with the peasant provincialism of their compatriots, even while they were proud of their German national traditions and thought most Italians superficial and unreliable.

Having survived the onslaughts of Fascist Italianization and then of modernization (perceived as Italianization) with their ethnic community, national identity, and traditional values intact, the South Tyrolese were well positioned for the next and current phase. It had two roughly simultaneous foundations. The first was belated and foot-dragging Italian agreement, following years of intensified South Tyrolese nationalist agitation (initially including sporadic terrorism) and political maneuvering since 1959, to grant the Province of Bozen-Bolzano the extensive autonomy it had been promised and then craftily denied in 1947. The Tyrolese two-thirds majority in the province was transformed from a frustrated minority in the biprovincial Trentino-Alto Adige Autonomous Region (the gerrymandering device that had limited provincial autonomy since 1947) into masters of a wide range of public administration and policies—and a dominant position vis-à-vis their province's Italian minority. Second, by this time far more South Tyrolese, having tasted and liked the fruits of the economic and cultural changes they had previously resisted, were willing and even eager to compromise their "traditional way of life" and its values for more of the same.

With their little Alpine realm almost as autonomous as member states of the EC (including Italy), Italy's South Tyrolese minority became fully participant in modernization (for better or for worse) and in its own affairs—and inclined to bully the Italian minority in their midst.

Case E: The 427,000 Magyars (in 1981, but 500,000 in 1961) of the Vojvodina Autonomous Province (where they are 19 percent of the population) and of Slavonia and the Drava Valley of Yugoslavia. More numerous than one of Yugoslavia's nations-of-state (the Montenegrins), and the second most numerous of its non-Slavic "nationalities" (after the Albanians), the Magyar minority was and is represented in every social stratum, from peasants and unskilled workers to urban industrial and commercial managers, nationally known members of the cultural and technological intelligentsia, and successful members of the political elite. Their cultural and economic "starting levels" are generally considered to have been higher than those of any of the other ethnic groups of Vojvodina and Slavonia except the now-departed Germans and possibly the Slovaks, a judgment incorporated in the cliché that held that a stranger could promptly identify the ethnic character of each Vojvodina village by its position on a scale of relative prosperity, tidiness, and literacy that descended from German and Magyar or Slovak (I have heard them in both orders) to Serb and finally Romanian and gypsy. The Magyars are a majority in several large Vojvodina towns and share predominance (with Serbs) in the provincial capital, Novi Sad, the sixth largest Yugoslav city with a bilingual university and a distinguished bilingual cultural tradition. The districts in which they live are among the richest in the country in terms of gross national product, per capita income, productive agriculture and profitable industry, literacy, communications, and social services. Since the formation of Yugoslavia, they have suffered varying degrees of discrimination at different periods, apparently the result of a combination of ethnic envy on the part of politically superordinate peoples and sometimes well-founded doubts concerning the minority's loyalty and the strength of Hungarian irredentism. (Hungary, as a German satellite state, annexed much of this territory in 1941, and massacres of Serb populations in these districts at that time are not forgotten.) In the Titoist period, after Yugoslavia's break with Stalin awakened fears of Hungarian irredentism, the minority seems to have suffered a period of intensified police supervision and discrimination followed in the later 1950s by a period of special favoritism in comparison with other ethnic minorities, which may have been based on a policy of taming them by making life in Titoist Yugoslavia seem preferable to life in Stalinist Hungary.[20]

It has thus been perfectly possible for an ambitious member of the Magyar community to be upwardly mobile without losing his or her ethnic identity in the process. Such mobile members remain an effective part of the community from which they sprang, providing it with leadership or at least "going home" to it occasionally. They therefore act as a modernizing yeast among the stay-at-homes, spreading the values of "modern" life-styles. To be sure, retaining their ethnicity curtails their mobility, for they cannot easily move to Zagreb, Rijeka, or Ljubljana as Magyars. Neither, however, can a Macedonian or a Serbian (the latter with no *language* barrier to vault in Zagreb or Rijeka, merely barriers of life-styles and prejudice), so the horizons of the Magyar are roughly as wide as those of a member of a nation-of-state. The minority joins as fully in the processes and dividends of social modernization as any nationality in the country, but remains intact as an ethnic community.

Any lessons for the Soviet Union and other problematic multinational states derived from the experience of the national question and strategies to respond to it in the Austro-Hungarian Monarchy and its successor states seem on balance to be more negative than positive (more "don'ts" than "dos"). The multinational societies in question continued (and mostly continue) to be multinational, although with changing magnitudes and proportions. Their multinationality continues to pose problems for stability, community building or integration, and comprehensive social and economic modernization. Current events in the Soviet Union and Eastern Europe bear witness to the persistence of these problems, and to the failure of the three Habsburg strategies and their clones to resolve them.

The recent history of the nationalities question in East-Central Europe suggests, inter alia, that two frequent and superficially plausible answers or interpretations are in fact nonstarters.

When the roots of ethnic conflict and minorities problems are seen to be complex, and when one discovers that a passionately held sense of ethnic distinctiveness, interests, and grievances has assumed an independent and superordinate value reality for those who feel it (whether or not these were originally and "objectively" misperceptions of the real class, professional or personal nature of their interests or grievances), then one must reject the optimistic view of most Marxists and many others, who hold that more goods more equitably distributed, plus a more equitable share in the decision-making process (or an equitable deprivation of same!) will ipso facto lead to the disappearance of the problem.

Among other scholars and practitioners one also meets the view that, because this kind of ethnicity erects such formidable barriers to the kind of integrated and integrative social change once commonly called modernization, the only answer is that "ethnicity has got to go"[21]—presumably through some form of assimilation to a dominant or composite culture, for which American experience used to be cited as the best example. Again, Habsburg and other Central European experiences suggest that, with rare and particular exceptions (the "skimmed milk" phenomenon), this simply does not happen spontaneously, or as a result of partial modernization in other sectors, *once national "self"-consciousness has been achieved and is supported by historical-territorial claims*. It can therefore be made to happen only through the use of coercion in such measure that the state is trapped into dependence on an increasing use of force and appropriate authoritarian organization. However, these political means and forms are normally considered even more obstructive of modernization, as a whole, than the ethnic divisions they were invoked to liquidate.

Worse still, Habsburg and successor state history also suggests that coercive assimilation, along with its other disadvantages, simply does not work. I know of no European instance (although one may have escaped my attention somewhere) in which a minority that has achieved national self-consciousness in the age of nationalism has obliged its persecutors by disappearing. On the contrary, assimilative pressures have tended to stiffen the ethnic backbones of most target communities. The non-Magyars of pre-1914 Greater Hungary and the Tyrolese and South Slavs of Fascist Italy are examples. The Croats of the Burgenland, who defiantly survived both

Magyar and German assimilative pressures only to begin "disappearing" voluntarily under the most liberal ethnic policies they have ever enjoyed, are a revealing case that recalls why urban Jews and Germans were more susceptible to assimilation than other non-Magyars in Dualist Hungary. As Hitler realized, the only effective kinds of forced liquidation of a troublesome minority are genocide or expulsion.

If ethnicity will not go away, and if exclusion on the basis of community definition is rejected (on democratic principles, because the regime is aware of the total, *in*clusive nature of modernization, or for any other reason), what is to be done? As long as we accept, as most of humanity apparently does, that nationalism, and therefore the nation-state, are the only bases on which a fully legitimate and modern or modernizing political community can be built, the answer increasingly seems to be "Not much." Confederation (here called the Austro-Hungarian strategy) would appear to be feasible only when the units to be confederated are already reasonably homogeneous national as well as political-territorial communities, with a high degree of (national-) cultural self-confidence as possibly an additional prerequisite. Both criteria may be true of the current members of the European Community, or of most of them. They are not true of the ethnic map and the often manifestly insecure national-cultural self-confidence of most of East-Central and Eastern Europe. Here "not much" begins to sound rather like "the Austrian strategy" of ad hoc and often temporary improvisations. It is said that it worked quite well in Moravia and Bukovina; no group was excluded by its communal definition in the way the non-Magyars of Hungary were. The lands represented in the Reichsrat did not come apart until they were broken apart by military defeat and political maneuvers in the first "total war" since the Napoleonic ones that carried the doctrine of modern nationalism to these lands.

NOTES

1. Literature on this second aspect, increasingly prolific since the 1960s, ranges chronologically from pioneering works like those of Karl Deutsch in the 1950s and Kalman H. Silvert, ed., *Expectant Peoples: Nationalism and Development* (New York, 1963) to recent ones like Ernest Gellner, *Nations and Nationalism* (Oxford, 1983). Terms and concepts used or implied in this essay are drawn from both of these and others, probably too eclectically.
2. As posed by both basic meanings that Hugh Seton-Watson attributes to the term nationalism: as "a doctrine about the character, interests, rights and

duties of nations" and as "an organized political movement, designed to further the alleged aims and interests of nations" (in his *Nations and States* [London, 1977], 3).

3. How largely, as a percentage of total population, is another of the national question's many disputable definitional problems, with policy implications, that is of contemporary importance for countries like the United Kingdom and perhaps France (traditionally considered prototypical nation-states) but not for undeniably multinational ones like the Habsburg Empire and most of its successor states.

4. Studies that devote specific attention to this aspect for each nation throughout the Monarchy include Adam Wandruszka and Peter Urbanitsch, eds., *Die Völker des Reichs* (Vienna, 1980, the two-volume third part of the Austrian Commission for the History of the Austro-Hungarian Monarchy's monumental *Die Habsburger monarchie 1848-1918*); the older three-part *Austrian History Yearbook* III (1967), based on a major conference on the Monarchy's nations at the University of Indiana; and A. J. P. Taylor, *The Habsburg Monarchy, 1809-1918* (London, 1948) in which Chap. 2 ("The Peoples") is still one of the best brief summaries. See also István Deák, *Assimilation and Nationalism in East Central Europe During the Last Century of Habsburg Rule* (Pittsburgh, Pa., n. d.) especially the concluding sections subtitled "The 'Nationalism' of the Cities" and "The Chauvinistic City."

5. Ernesto Sestan, *Venezia Giulia, lineamenti di storia etnica e culturale* (Rome, 1947), 103; my translation. The author, a Triestine, is probably the most acute observer of history of ethnic conflict in his native region.

6. In Wandruszka and Urbanitsch, *Die Völker des Reichs*, 182.

7. It may also be discernible in the EC's Single European Act and the EC Commission's schemes for further political, monetary, and fiscal unification, but the EC is a case of movement from separate states, rather than from a previously unitary or federal one, toward confederation.

8. Quoted, inter alia, by Hugh Seton-Watson, *Nations and States* (London, 1977), 107.

9. The classic critical study, which was to affect previously sympathetic British (and also American) attitudes and policies regarding Hungary during and after World War I, is R. W. Seton-Watson, *Racial Problems in Hungary* (London, 1908).

10. In Deák, *Assimilation and Nationalism*, 8f.

11. William O. McCagg, Jr., *Jewish Nobles and Geniuses in Modern Hungary* (Boulder, Colo., 1972) and *A History of Habsburg Jews, 1670-1918* (Bloomington, Ind., 1989).

12. This is central to the explanation of cultural homogenization *and* nationalism in Gellner's *Nations and Nationalism*, passim.

13. Ibid., chap. 6, describes the kinds of boundaries and reactions to them that generate new nations and nationalisms and clearly has in mind (without saying so) the experiences described here.

14. Deák, *Assimilation and Nationalism*, 10.

15. This picture of reluctant separatists and eleventh-hour separatism, found in most standard works on the Empire's last decades and dissolution, is now virtually unchallenged.

16. Or, in the Austrian case and as argued (inter alia) by William T. Bluhm, *Building an Austrian Nation* (New Haven, Conn., 1973), by a new Austrian national consciousness and therefore nation and nation-state.

17. And of minority nations in the officially multinational states (Czechoslovakia and Yugoslavia before 1929 and after 1945).

18. The cases chosen are from on-site studies of the minorities in question, mostly in the 1960s and 1970s; the results have been reported or published, inter alia, in my "Letters from South Tyrol" (1959-62), "The Croats of the Burgenland" (1959), and "The Italians of Yugoslavia" (1963), all circulated as newsletters by the Institute of Current World Affairs (at that time in New York), and in a number of *Field Staff Reports* (New York and later Hanover, N.H.) published since 1963 by the American Universities Field Staff (later the Universities Field Staff International).

19. It is taken from an illustrated booklet, published in Bozen in the 1960s, which I have misplaced. South Tyrolese grievances included other items, such as discrimination in public employment or housing, which reflected either (or both) genuine residual discrimination or social problems requiring more sophisticated analysis than either they or the Italians usually undertake.

20. I put this two-phase view of Titoist policy toward the Magyar minority tentatively because, although I have often heard it described that way, no one that I know of has actually investigated the subject. The two phases may not have existed at all, and a study demonstrating this may have been done but escaped my notice.

21. The precise words, accompanied by a gesture of despair, were pronounced by a leading U.S. social scientist and theorist of modernization at a conference on nationalism and ethnicity in 1969, when he should have known better.

14

Between "Little International" and Great Power Politics: Austro-Marxism and Stalinism on the National Question

Helmut Konrad

In 1913 a man sat in the Schönbrunner Schloss-strasse in Vienna studying, at Lenin's behest, the problem of the national question and in particular the positions adopted by the Austrian Social Democrats on this question. The man's name was Joseph Stalin, and the book he wrote during these months was called "Marxism and the National Question."[1] It is no accident that this book was written in Vienna. For it is not so much a program for the nationalities policy of a future Soviet state as a critical discussion of Austro-Marxism. Stalin's plan for dealing with national problems within the Soviet Union, as it later became, was thus conceived at least partly as an antithesis to the Austrian positions.

That Stalinism was unable to provide a definitive solution to the national question became evident last year, if it had not been so before. Not one of the conflicts has really abated: on the contrary, the national question today has more explosive potential than ever. As late as September, 1989, the Central Committee in Moscow passed a resolution that invoked the peaceful development of interethnic relations within the Soviet Union as an inevitable consequence of the October Revolution;[2] but at the time of that resolution the reality was already quite different, and there have been further dramatic developments since then. While 48 percent of the Soviet Union's population are Russians and 14 percent Ukrainians, there are no fewer than a hundred other ethnic groups, and areas where ethnic and religious conflict lines coincide have become especially volatile, as the USSR's Muslim areas in particular (with a population, after all, of almost fifty million) showed so dramatically at the beginning of 1990.

Of course the failure of the nationalities policy based (though in a much modified form) on Stalin's ideas does not mean that its antithesis, the Austro-Marxist theory, would have stood the test of history. It was never given the chance to prove itself in practice, and it was too clearly designed for the specific situation of the Habsburg Monarchy to have been applicable to other areas of the world. It must be noted, however, that there were similarities as well as differences in the Austro-Marxist and Stalinist assessments of the national question, not least because both movements were products of the same intellectual tradition.

THE COMMON ROOTS

Except where the national question was based on older religious lines of conflict, it was a child of the nineteenth century.[3] As an idea it arose in the wake of the romantic movement, but it gained mass support only as a result of the Industrial Revolution. It was the mobility brought about by the emancipation of serfs, urbanization, and industrialization that turned the national question into an issue in which the masses too had an interest.

In the mechanistic worldview of Marxism two narrow viewpoints on nationalism became established. One view reduced it to nothing more than a "question of language"; in other words, the mother tongue was regarded as the sole criterion of membership of a nation. This turned the national question into a cultural phenomenon that Marxism was able to relegate to the domain of so-called superstructure, thus making it an issue of only secondary importance. Alternatively, nationalism was seen, because of the historical context of its origin, as a phenomenon belonging to a specific stage in the development of industrial society, the assumption being that it would automatically decline in importance as soon as the market ceased to be merely national and expanded to become a world market. This enabled the early theoreticians of the labor movement to regard national conflicts and sentiments as temporary phenomena that might be disregarded and would virtually resolve themselves.[4]

Moreover, Karl Marx and Friedrich Engels, in an odd curtailment of their own theories, judged the national question only in relation to the acceleration or slowing down of the processes of economic development. For this reason larger states were viewed a priori as being more advantageous, while the aspirations of smaller nations were all too easily dismissed as inimical to progress. Only this could lead to the formation of the theory of "nonhistoric nations,"[5] one of the "saddest"[6] chapters in the development of Marxism.

Engels based his distinction between "historic" and "nonhistoric" peoples on the difference between civilization and barbarism. By civilization he meant industry, capitalism, and the bourgeoisie. Feudalism, economic backwardness, and peasant culture counted as barbarism. This attitude to the peasantry had its due consequences not only in the 1848 revolution but in the whole history of the labor movement. Engels uses this distinction between historic and nonhistoric peoples to justify the oppression of "barbarians" by civilized peoples, thus indirectly also justifying colonialism.[7] This oppression is a historical necessity, as it is the only way in which the nonhistoric peoples can begin to be part of any political development at all.

This understanding of "progress" makes it justifiable, furthermore, "forcibly to crush many a delicate little nationflower"[8]—ruthlessly to implement a policy of assimilation. Here Marxism is in complete accord with the fundamental position of the liberal doctrine of free trade: the goal is the creation of large economic units, with the most favorable possible communications (i.e., one wholly dominant language).[9] This has been euphemistically called a *nationaler Flächenstaat*—meaning a large homogeneous national state—completely disregarding the ethnic minorities in Western Europe.

Another tradition also helped to shape the Marxist position on the national question. The intellectuals of the 1848 revolution were never able to free themselves from certain elements of German idealistic philosophy. They shared Herder's "illusion that social emancipation would render national conflicts superfluous,"[10] but they went further still and emphasized in *The Communist Manifesto* that even "nationality" itself would progressively disappear.[11] This tradition was continued and developed further in the naive cosmopolitanism of the young labor movement, epitomized by the creation of the world language, Esperanto. There is no mistaking the teleological element in this: here, as elsewhere, the pseudoreligious aspect of Marxism as a secularized doctrine of salvation is strongly present.

What emerges, then, is that there was no fully matured plan for the solution of the national question that the young labor movement could simply inherit. This newly formed political force had as its starting point only the few, contradictory, and fragmentary pieces of theory I have indicated in the writings of its ideological mentors, and was obliged to work out its own positions independently and in response to the concrete problems that presented themselves.

THE SPECIAL CHARACTERISTICS OF THE
HABSBURG MONARCHY

In this process it was, among the multinational states of the nineteenth century, the Habsburg Monarchy that had the key role. Only there had industrialization led to the formation of a working class that was numerically strong and soon also politically well organized, while no one nationality was strong enough to establish itself as the culturally dominant *Staatsnation*. In the large *Flächenstaaten* of Western Europe, language boundaries had largely adapted themselves to the frontiers drawn for reasons of power politics, and had thus created the preconditions for efficient communication systems, which in turn formed the basis for industrialization. In the Habsburg Empire such developments took place in a far more complex way.

An account of the Empire's national composition as a whole cannot really be included here. This discussion will focus on those aspects of it that enable a comparison to be made with Stalinism. The hope expressed by Friedrich Engels in 1848 that "the Austrian monarchy, that patchwork of territories amassed by inheritance and by theft, that organized muddle of ten languages and nations, that unplanned conglomeration of the most contradictory customs and laws,"[12] was at last beginning to fall apart, proved illusory. On the contrary, in the next seven decades it was the labor movement that was to become the strongest force, after the ruling house, the bureaucracy, and the military, cementing the multinational state together. Today the term Central Europe denotes, in essence, a region with identical or at least similar symbols of the ruling power (the same baroque churches, the same barracks, the same official buildings, and so on), which the present-day visitor sees with a sense of familiarity. But for the workers the Habsburg Empire meant more than merely suffering under the same scourge: this state was also the economic and living environment of an underprivileged section of the population that hoped that within this particular framework the dream of a future society without national prejudices could, as it were, be tested out in advance. The labor movement's "naive cosmopolitanism,"[13] expressed in the many documents of the movement's early phase, is characterized by a high degree of optimism that precisely in the multinational state it will be possible to demonstrate how tolerant the workers can be, in contrast to the other sections of society.

Even so, it was assumed without question at that time that the Austrian labor movement, which because of the different pace of industrialization in the individual regions of the Empire was a German-speaking movement with Czech sections, should take its lead from its larger and more fully developed sister party in the German states. At the party conference at Eisenach in 1869—three years after Königgrätz, when all hopes of a Pan-German solution, of a Germany including the Habsburg Monarchy, were buried—Austrian Social Democracy became, without any internal debate, an organization forming part of the German movement. It was only after the Franco-Prussian War that the labor movement accepted the separation of the Austrian from the German state—though it still regarded this as only a transient phenomenon, a point emphatically reiterated by Friedrich Engels shortly before his death.

In this first attempt to identify itself with Germany, the Austrian labor movement was not acting under the auspices of Prussian centralism of the kind advocated by Lassalle, nor, on the other hand, was it influenced by nationalist arguments of a more general kind: it was acting simply in what it saw as the interests of progress. In the second half of the nineteenth century the creation of large, unified economic areas with the simplest possible means of internal communication seemed to be what was required. In the eyes of the majority of the Austrian labor movement, the largest possible economic unit with the simplest means of communication was the area of Europe inhabited by German speakers. The idea was inspired, at this early stage, not by any emotional attachment to a "nation," but by the "rational" faith in progress prevalent in a period that, in Austria as elsewhere, saw the immense growth of capitalism. This attitude did, however, offer highly favorable conditions for the spread of nationalism among the working class.

However rationally these arguments were presented, there was bound to be opposition from non-German-speaking workers. Yet, all in all, conditions were such that there could have been a basis for discussion between workers of the different language groups. Although more than ten nationalities lived in the Habsburg Empire, the working class was made up almost wholly of Germans and Czechs, with some Italians and Slovenes. It was the relationship between Germans and Czechs that became the yardstick of tolerance and willingness to communicate among the nationalities, for the Slovenes were numerically of no great significance and the Italians were mostly engaged in types of work where they were wholly isolated and had almost no contact with members of other nationalities. They were employed, for instance, at brickworks that offered seasonal jobs to Italians in rural areas, and also in road and railway construction, where they moved with the work as it progressed and so stayed only briefly in any one place.[14]

Regional historical studies of the 1870s make it absolutely clear that at this stage there was no nationalism among the workers; on the contrary, it seemed to be taken for granted that the aim must be to fight, right across the language boundaries, for common social goals.[15] Also, the picture of the "privileged" German-speaking worker and the oppressed Czech worker is a considerable oversimplification. Of course Czechs who migrated to the Sudeten areas formed an industrial reserve force and suffered particularly harsh conditions. But when Czech workers moved to other parts of the Monarchy where the process of industrialization had only just begun, it was they, with their experience of industrial work, who generally became the foremen entrusted with the task of training the first generation of German workers. This can be shown to have happened in many industrial concerns in the provinces of Lower and Upper Austria, in the metal-processing industry, and also in the paper mills and the textile industry.[16] Thus national and social oppression did not necessarily go together, and this is why, even in the circumstances prevailing in the Habsburg Empire in the 1870s, no nationalism sprang up in the labor movement from within the Empire itself. That development took place only later, chiefly as a result of outside influences.

At the formation of the first workers' party in 1874 at Neudörfl—where, of course, discussion took place and minutes were recorded in several languages—on the national question there was a fundamental departure from the German model, however closely it was followed in other respects. That all the nations should have equal rights was not merely recognized as necessary: in the Neudörfl Program it was seen as "the sole guarantee of success."[17] By this formulation the German speakers' hitherto wholly un-questioned claim to leadership of the Austrian labor movement was lost. The party thus called into being was "the first internationalist, common organi-zation of workers in a multinational state."[18]

These promising beginnings were quickly undone by external influences: the Great Depression had halted the economic boom of the *Gründerzeit*, and in Germany, Bismarck's *Sozialistengesetz* (Socialists Act) had shown the means to an achievement Taaffe tried to emulate in Austria: the weakening of the labor movement by social reforms on the one hand and harsh political persecution on the other.

By the late 1880s, however, the character of nationalism in Austria, too, had changed. The ideology that had essentially run parallel with liberalism had become an aggressive, militaristic, and chauvinistic movement that served as a justification for oppression and discrimination.[19] As if in response to this, a more emotional form of nationalism grew up among the smaller Central European nationalities, or those that were not yet nation-states. Both these tendencies gained a foothold among the workers and undermined their cosmopolitanism.

It is understandable that the Austrian labor movement refounded by Victor Adler in 1889 could not at first find a remedy for this new nationalism. Adler therefore decided on a tactic of, as it were, overlaying this problem with other issues:[20] he pushed into the foreground common goals of great importance, such as the achievement of universal (male) suffrage, so that these should wholly dominate political debate and deny the national issue any room to develop. Adler himself bore the deep imprint of his own German-national political background. He had left Schönerer's movement only after it had included anti-Semitic points in its program.[21] His personal restraint with regard to the national question should therefore also be seen as a contribution to the lowering of tension. In the matter of theory he relied on Marxism's Keeper of the Holy Grail, Karl Kautsky. Kautsky himself had considerably pared down the already modest body of reflections by Marx and Engels on the national question, and recognized only the *Sprachnation* (the nation defined by language), which would lose all significance after the imminent collapse of the capitalist system. It was merely a matter of holding out until then.

Thus, while the Austrian labor movement, with desperate single-mindedness, discussed (and engaged in) the fight for universal suffrage, and on May Day carried banners bearing internationalist slogans, beneath the surface the multinational movement was breaking up into its national components. Adler's tactic was successful, then, only for a few years. By 1897 there was "no longer a common Austrian Social Democratic party, but a united party of Austrian Social Democrats made up of various nationalities."[22] The Czechs had by now formed their own section, completing a process of separation that was vigorously under way by 1893, when it became apparent how many Czech workers were going over to the "Young Czechs." The nationalistic slogans of that movement struck a chord with these workers, who saw themselves as belonging, in terms of both social and national status, to an underprivileged group, even though this was not always in fact the case. Only the federalization of the Social Democratic party gave Czech Social Democracy any chance of surviving at all.

Despite this development within its own ranks, it must nevertheless be acknowledged that the Social Democratic party in the Habsburg Empire was the only party that could claim to represent all the nationalities that made up the state. This meant that, paradoxical as it may sound, the Social Democratic party was, after the ruling house, the strongest force preserving the state during these years of powerful centrifugal tendencies. The much-quoted designation of it as the *k.k. Sozialdemokratie* (Imperial and Royal Social Democratic Party) therefore not only conveys criticism of a certain bourgeois tendency in the movement but also neatly describes the situation in which this party, which still saw itself as a revolutionary party, found itself in the two decades leading up to World War I. The breaking up of the Empire was at that time not only beyond the bounds of possibility, but also not desirable. This crucial premise was accepted also by the Austro-Marxists, who were to dominate the debate of the following years.

Once universal male suffrage had been achieved, in 1907 or more precisely the year before, the national issue occupied a prominent place on the agenda. Reconciliation with the state had been achieved, and the next problem to tackle was how to organize the coexistence of the nations within the multinational state. Within the borders of the Austrian half of the Empire lived about twenty-eight million people, of whom 35.5 percent claimed German as their mother tongue, 23 percent, Czech; 17.8 percent, Polish; 12.6 percent, Ruthenian; 4.5 percent, Slovene; 2.8 percent, Italian; and 1 percent, Rumanian.[23] A purely linguistic analysis of this kind takes no account of the Jews, who were also a factor in the complex of national issues but who, unlike their counterparts in Russia, did not play a separatist role within the labor movement.[24] The Jews in the Habsburg Monarchy, especially the intellectual elite (exactly according to the theories), opted for assimilation.

Naturally, the linguistic groups mentioned (whether these were to be equated with nationalities was, of course, one of the key issues in Austro-Marxist theory) had not all experienced industrialization to the same degree. Some, in particular the Czechs, already had a highly self-assured, educated bourgeoisie; others, most notably the Italians, looked to a neighboring state for their cultural identity. It was only these small sections of the population oriented to the outside that had a centrifugal effect on the Empire—and so of course (though this is often overlooked) did the Germans.

Austro-Marxist theory, as developed above all from 1907 onward, that is, from the first appearance of the monthly periodical *Der Kampf*,[25] had two outstanding characteristics. First, it was emphatically, indeed almost exclusively, concerned with the formation of a Social Democratic theory on the national question; and second, despite the multinational background, its exponents were predominantly German speakers. Not only that, but one cannot fail to recognize in it certain *deutschnational* elements.

The two leading theoreticians on the national question, who were, as holders of the most diverse offices of great influence on the course of twentieth-century Austrian history, were Karl Renner and Otto Bauer. While Bauer was concerned above all with the attempt to establish a definition of a "nation" in the context of the special characteristics of the Habsburg Empire, and to determine the consequences of such a definition for the policy of the workers' party, Karl Renner was giving thought to the practical reorganization of the Empire. Bauer was attempting to identify the essence of a nation, Renner to defuse the conflicts between the nationalities, though there was not such a rigid demarcation between the two as this implies. Nevertheless, it is appropriate here to concentrate on Bauer's development of theory and on Renner's application of theory to practical politics.

Without a doubt, the great historical significance of Bauer's theory lies in the fact that he rejected Kautsky's narrow view of the nation and instead saw the nation as an independent category that was not merely superstructural. "A nation is the totality of people bound together by a community of fate (*Schicksalsgemeinschaft*) into a community of character";[26] a nation is solidified, or "clotted," history.[27] In Bauer's theory, terms such as *Schicksal*—destiny or fate—and "history" no longer merely have cultural connotations. They are something more than language; they embrace communication in a broader sense, and of course they include territorial factors too. The experiencing of historical and political events does not necessarily happen only in linguistic or religious communities, but also in states.

Bauer believed that national characteristics would continue to exist even after a revolution. The workers could then participate in the national cultures, but even after a world revolution humanity would divide up into "autonomous national communities." Whereas Marx, Engels, and Kautsky saw national differences completely disappearing and world society developing a global language and culture, for Bauer culture is so closely interwoven with literature and history that it must form an independent category, the nation, which has validity quite apart from the question of society, and which ultimately cannot be fitted into political categories either.

Thus, although for Bauer a nation is defined by culture (*Kulturnation*) and the economic and territorial factor is secondary, the seventy-year-old Soviet state has in recent months afforded striking evidence that he was right. It is from that "clotted history" that the nationalities of the Soviet state draw their new self-assurance, and there is no link between this and the resolution of the social question that has been accomplished (successfully or not, but at any rate to the extent of abolishing private ownership of the means of production). Language, often regarded in Central Europe as the only criterion, is complemented by culture, tradition, and historical consciousness, thus forming the combination described by Bauer.

Renner's main concern, in view of the primary aim of preserving the Habsburg Empire as a political and thus also as an economic unit, was to make it possible for the nationalities to live together with as little conflict as possible. He saw no problem in equating nation with *Sprachnation* (nation defined by language), so retaining an exclusively cultural definition. For him as a pragmatist the question of whether in a future, postrevolutionary society there would still be national differences did not arise. His proposals were aimed at creating the best and most just state possible in whatever conditions prevailed at a given time. Only this made it possible for this enthusiastic advocate of the Habsburg Monarchy to become, twice in the twentieth century, the founding father of the Austrian Republic.

Although there are slight variations in Renner's attitude to the national question,[28] the characteristic tenor of his proposals is most clearly conveyed in a paragraph from a work published, under the pseudonym Rudolf Springer, in 1906, *Grundlagen und Entwicklungsziele der Österreichisch-Ungarischen Monarchie*:

> The territory of the state is everywhere divided up on a single basis: into provinces, districts, parishes. We, however, must survey the country twice, on different principles, we must trace two networks of lines on the map, an economic one and an ethnic one, we must make a division through the total number of holders of state office, separating national and political business, we must organize the population twice over, once on a national and once on a state basis.[29]

So in dealing with all matters of culture a different principle of classification from that of the state administration was to be applied. In a manner comparable to the organization of religious groups, the members of a nation, wherever they lived, were to be granted certain rights: the rights thus applied to a person, not to a territory. It was precisely this *Personalitätsprinzip* (principle of personality) (as distinct from the proposals of the Brünn Program) that was to become the key idea in the Austro-Marxist position on the nationalities issue. And, as we shall see, it was this idea that drew especially sharp criticism from Stalin, who saw the personality principle as a particularly clear indication of the weakness of Austro-Marxist theory.

Of course a contradiction is present when a movement capable on the one hand of developing a cogent theory of what constitutes a nation, and on the other of presenting such constructive proposals for the preservation of the multinational state, is unable to persuade its own members to fulfill its claim to be a "Little International."[30] It must be noted, however, that there were at least two special reasons for the separatism of the non-German-speaking labor movement. This was, first, a tactic it adopted in order to avoid losing all its workers to the nationalist parties with their strong emotional appeal. But it was also a reaction to the arrogant *deutschnational* stance of the elite, particularly the elite of the trade union movement, a stance that bore no relation to the theory that had been developed but was simply adopted unthinkingly.[31] This led to a curious dichotomy in the South Slav and Czech labor movements: up to World War I, its thinkers, prime among them Bohumír Šmeral,[32] were working intensively at the further development of the Austro-Marxist theory in close conjunction with Renner and Bauer, while the party organizations of which they were the leaders distanced themselves ever more noticeably from the all-Austrian party. Nevertheless, the Social Democratic party's role in the preservation of the Empire is one of its most salient features.

STALIN'S CRITIQUE OF AUSTRO-MARXISM

A notable characteristic of those Social Democratic parties, including the Russian one, that were late in becoming mass parties is that their adoption or development of theory rushes ahead of political reality in the country itself. The theory can develop without the corrective of concrete politics, and this is especially true of theories developed in exile. While the Austro-Marxists had had to take a rather hopelessly muddled situation as the starting point of their analyses, bolshevism was able to counter with the "pure doctrine" without, at least before World War I, having to descend to the lower levels where ideas had to stand up to reality.

Because of the later practical significance of Stalin as an individual in relation to the nationalities policy of the Soviet state, it is on him that we will focus here, though this is not to ignore the fact that Lenin and other Bolsheviks also took up positions on the national question. We will not enter here into the controversies about the authenticity of the texts.

In 1904 Stalin made his first contribution to the debate on the national question, in a short article that remains wholly within the tradition of Marx and Engels.[33] The national question, he says, merits attention only insofar as it may contribute to the raising of class consciousness. He claims that dialectical materialism has proved incontrovertibly that there is no such thing as a "national spirit."[34] Nationalism is relevant only when used as an instrument of the class struggle.

In 1913, in the longer work mentioned at the beginning of this essay, Stalin treats the question less simplistically. First he tries, as Otto Bauer had done, to define what constitutes a "nation." Language is of course one of the characteristic features of a nation, but Stalin adds the idea of territory to it, on the grounds that "living together for a long period is . . . impossible without a shared territory."[35] Alongside these there are the economic community and the culture. Accordingly, his definition reads: "A nation is a stable community of people created in the course of history, having come into being on the basis of shared language, territory, and economic life and of that psychological makeup that manifests itself in a community of culture."[36] One is immediately struck by a major difference between this and Austro-Marxist theory: Stalin's approach lays greater stress on the economic aspect, and his emphasis on this and on territory rules out Renner's personality principle. And indeed the very considerable intermingling of nationalities that in the Habsburg Empire resulted from the internal migration caused by industrialization was not a factor in the Russian situation. For Stalin there is nothing incalculable about nationalism; significantly, he accuses Bauer of making the nation into something mystically intangible and otherworldly.

One of the main points on which Austro-Marxism was criticized was its understanding of the right of self-determination. The traditions of the Empire, and the traditional *deutschnational* outlook that out of a sense of cultural mission wanted to preserve the Empire, were unfamiliar to Stalin, and his thinking went beyond the Habsburg Monarchy. Indeed, in 1913 it was still easy for Stalin's thinking to go beyond Russia, which was to lead to problems only a few years later. For Stalin in 1913 autonomy means that any nation "has the right to secede completely."[37] Under socialism in particular this aspect of the equal rights of all nations would pose no problems, given that even capitalist countries like Switzerland and the United States were able to minimize conflicts between nationalities. Thus a blind faith in progress marks Stalin's views in 1913 on the Caucasus, which today is a particularly volatile region:

> The national question in the Caucasus can be resolved only in the spirit of letting those nations and peoples that are latecomers become part of the general current of higher culture. . . . Regional autonomy for the Caucasus is acceptable precisely because it draws the late-coming nations into the general cultural development . . . propels them forward and facilitates their access to the benefits of higher culture. In contrast, national-cultural autonomy works in precisely the opposite

direction, for it leaves the nations encased in their old shells, holding them down at the lower levels of culture.[38]

Stalin's premise is, then, that the nations he describes as latecomers (that is, the less industrialized nations) will in any case not feel a need for separation, for they will "strain with all their might to ascend to higher levels of culture."[39] So once again technological and cultural progress mechanistically solves all problems, even if it is no longer explicitly stated that all national characteristics will disappear. Seen from the standpoint of this worldview, Austro-Marxism would inevitably appear idealistic and conservative, pusillanimous in its proposed solutions and not materialistic in its theory. And this criticism cannot be wholly brushed aside: neglect of the economic factor is indeed a weakness in the Austro-Marxist conceptions of the nation. Yet the twentieth century has amply demonstrated how small a part economic factors actually play in this context.

THE AUSTRIAN "SOLUTION" OF 1918/19: THE END OF CENTRAL EUROPE?

Although during World War I the Austrian labor movement was able to avoid a split, and this was of enormous significance for the history of the interwar years, the currents within it were perceptibly moving further apart, especially on the national issue. While Renner and the so-called rightists believed to the end in preserving the Habsburg Monarchy and cooperated loyally in the administration of the state, the "leftists" surrounding Otto Bauer chose a different path. Undoubtedly Bauer's period as a prisoner of war in Russia— he returned in 1917—played a part in this. At all events, in their Nationalities Program of 1917 the leftists recognized the right of nations to self-determination.[40] Although they had to express themselves cautiously because of censorship, they clearly envisaged a time when the Monarchy would have ceased to exist.

When the matter was decided, it was not decided by political programs, and not even, except in part, within the Habsburg Empire itself. The events of the war, the nationalities' (especially the Czechs') politicians in exile, and, last, the surge of nationalism bursting free from its bonds in the final weeks of the war were what finally led to post-1919 Austria's being left over as a mere "remnant."[41] The politicians assembled in the Paris suburbs did no more than acknowledge what had long since become a political reality.[42] The decisions on frontiers made at Versailles, Saint-Germain, and Trianon may be criticized for some instances where the final fixing of a borderline was unjust or at least unfortunate, but not for the breaking up of the Monarchy itself. And "Central Europe" was not broken up in Paris—no one will deny that in the interwar period Prague was at least as European as Vienna. The term Central Europe, used in a cultural sense, describes those regions whose eastern boundary marks the limit of the spread of Western European cultural traditions (the Reformation, the Renaissance, pluralistic democracy, etc.); the changes made in 1919 affected only the patterns of government and economic life, usually, in the short term, in the direction of greater democracy and more limited markets. Intellectually and culturally there was no real break in continuity: in Prague, "Austrian" literature (that is, literature in German) continued to be written, and nowhere was the old architecture deliberately destroyed.

It was only World War II that brought the traditions to an abrupt end, and created for the following decades a divided Europe with palpable incisions that suddenly placed a real distance between Vienna and Pressburg (Bratislava). "Central Europe" had up to 1933 been a concept of no real significance, since Prague at that time was—not only geographically—farther to the west than Vienna; but along this new dividing line a "Central Europe" came into being specifically in response to a need felt by the side that in 1945 had clearly come off worse. The fact that the region associated itself in a romantic fashion with the Habsburg Monarchy signifies no more than that politics need to be legitimized by history. But the area now described as "Central Europe" does not correspond even geographically to the old Empire. A region that includes Bosnia and Herzegovina, but not Silesia—what exactly is it supposed to represent in the present day?

At all events, for Renner, Bauer, and the other Austrian Social Democrats the decisive change took place in 1918. Suddenly invested with responsibility for the new, barely viable state, which, moreover, was largely homogeneous in terms of nationalities (despite the ethnic minorities, with whom the majority has an uneasy relationship to this day), they had other, more pressing problems to deal with. Before World War I the Austro-Marxists' strength had been that they responded to concrete political problems; after 1918 this same trait meant that the national question was necessarily pushed to the sidelines. To be sure, Bauer was an enthusiastic advocate of *Anschluss* with Germany, in the belief that this would accelerate progress toward socialism,[43] but the Social Democrats' political energies were fully absorbed by political conflicts within Austria. Austro-Marxism acquired a completely different political profile.[44] It was now most strongly identified with the discussion about the emergence of "New Men"[45] or about an integral socialism, a "third way."[46]

SOVIET NATIONALITIES POLICY IN PRACTICE

The events of 1917 meant that in Russia the nationalities policy conceived in theoretical terms could now be tested out in practice. What would the territorial principle, and the right of self-determination even to the point of secession, mean in the real world of politics?

The first retraction came even before the October Revolution. True, in May 1917 the Bolsheviks still emphasized the right of self-determination, but "the question of the right of nations to be free to secede must not be confused with the question of whether it is expedient for this or that nation to secede at this or that particular moment".[47] After Brest Litovsk this was expressed even more clearly: "The limited perspective of the Austrian Social Democrats of the type of Renner or Bauer is shown by the fact that they did not understand the indissoluble link between the national question and the issue of power."[48]

This was probably right during the phase of civil war and intervention. Under conditions of war, political independence was incompatible with military unity. A solution was found in the creation of Autonomous Soviet Socialist Republics (ASSRs), the first of which was set up in Turkestan in 1919. A commission was entrusted by the Central Committee with the "task of helping Turkestan to strengthen its state and party organs, to rebuild the economy, and to correct mistakes made in connection with the nationalities policy."[49]

In 1919 and 1920 a number of other republics were founded, namely, the Bashkir ASSR, the Tatar ASSR, the Kirgiz ASSR, and the Karelian ASSR, as well as a number of so-called autonomous regions. On December 29, 1920, the Russian Socialist Federative Soviet Republic and the Ukrainian Soviet Republic concluded a treaty of cooperation that united the military and economic People's Commissariats of the two signatories. Barely three weeks later Belorussia obtained a similar treaty.[50] Georgia swiftly followed. The Tenth Soviet Congress of December 1922 created the Union of Soviet Socialist Republics (USSR), consisting at that time of the Russian, Transcaucasian, Ukrainian, and Belorussian Soviet Republics (others joined later). With this development, and the constitution of 1923, which the individual republics adopted in 1924 by making appropriate changes in their own constitutions, the process of consolidation was largely complete. "In this way the proletariat has found in the Soviet system the key to the proper solution of the national question, and has found in it the way to organize a firmly united multinational state based on equal rights for the nationalities and their voluntary agreement."[51]

Statements were still made confirming the right of self-determination—even the "inalienable right to secession from Russia," in Stalin's words of 1920[52]—but the reality was that secession and the viability of the state were incompatible. Also involved were the vital interests of the mass of the people at the "center": "The interests of the masses of the people signify, however, that at the present stage of the revolution the demand for secession of the peripheral regions is wholly and utterly counterrevolutionary."[53] Since the autonomy of a cultural group—the outstanding instance of a demand for such autonomy being the program of the Jewish *Bund*[54]—was also ruled out, there remained only the concept of regional autonomy, which, although it did permit federative structures, was based on an association that was fixed and not to be called into question.

Stalin also modified his theory on these matters. He now accepted that the existence of different nations remained and would remain a fact, even after the revolution. "Allowing the schools, the law courts, the administration, the organs of state power to operate in the mother tongue is to realize in practice autonomy within the Soviet system, for this autonomy is nothing other than the sum of all these institutions clad in Ukrainian, Turkestani, Kirgizian, etc., forms."[55] Once again the nation is defined by language, and the problem of mobility is disregarded. Despite the wish for, and later massive encouragement of, the centralization of large-scale industries, Stalin believes that he can identify linguistic groups by geographical area. The rights of minorities, if one is not to limit autonomy to the realm of culture, must therefore be attached to a specific territory because only then can administration, etc., be included.

It is one of the chief flaws of the Soviet nationalities policy that rights are thus denied to all groups that have become minorities through migration. The implementation of the territorial principle has, right up to the present day, led in practice to the creation of a very complex state structure that has nevertheless been unable to deal successfully with this problem of migration. As well as the fifteen Union republics there are twenty autonomous republics, which are independent but lack the sovereignty in international law possessed by the Union republics. Within these there are a further eight autonomous regions and ten autonomous districts, which are wholly subject to the laws of whichever republic they are situated in and exist only to preserve the languages of the groups concerned.

Even 24 million out of the 137.4 million Russians do not live in their own republic.[56] The Jews' territory in Asia is practically useless to them, since they virtually all live in the European part of the Soviet Union. Only 2.7 million of the 4 million Armenians and 1.6 of the 6.3 million Tatars benefit from the protection of their own republics. About half of the members of the 100 smaller nations live outside the regions in which they would enjoy autonomy.[57] Everywhere, then, the territorial principle reveals its limitations. It is more effective than any personality principle in safeguarding the existence of a language and culture, but its lack of flexibility creates new problems. And it was and still is impossible to avoid the creation of a linguistic hierarchy; upward social mobility inevitably leads to bilingualism, especially among the smaller nationalities with no republics of their own.

Lenin, who in the early years of the Soviet state accepted Stalin's views on the national issue, thought that the principle of "internationalism before nationalism" solved the problems.[58] While his People's Commissar for Nationalities set up the structures for the strict application of the territorial principle, Lenin spoke of the primacy of the class struggle, saying, in other words, that the resolution of social conflicts in Soviet society must be given priority over that of national conflicts. This is almost an echo of the naive cosmopolitanism of the young European labor movement, and it stands in stark contrast to Stalinist policies, especially of course those of the later decades. The liquidation of the intelligentsia of the non-Russian nationalities, the resettlements, and the particular role played by anti-Semitism, because the Jews fitted least well into the rigid scheme, were all logical and brutal consequences of Stalin's theory when put into practice.

CONCLUSIONS

There was unfortunately no opportunity for the Austro-Marxists' proposals, which vacillated between pure personality principle and moderate territorial principles, to be put to the test in practice. From the vantage point of the last decade of the twentieth century, our verdict must probably be that the main strength of the Austro-Marxist approach to the national question lay in its analysis of the problem rather than in its practical proposals for the ordering of the coexistence of different nations within one state. All theories on what constitutes a nation, right up to those, certainly the most important, that approach the subject from the perspective of communication theory,[59] take Otto Bauer's analyses as their starting point. To have laid down such a foundation, by developing a category of "nation" beyond the merely linguistic and cultural sense, but without falling prey to a rigid, mechanistic, predominantly economic interpretation, was unquestionably an important contribution.

The Austro-Marxists' practical proposals are, in contrast, still strongly influenced by the understanding of the nation as a linguistic group. Moreover, had these proposals been implemented, the personality principle would have had the effect of accelerating assimilation; the pressure exerted by the majority in a given region (and by, as some of the Austro-Marxists would have it, the superior German culture) would have been stronger than in the Soviet model, in which a nation's territory formed a protective zone—if only, in some cases, in the manner of the "homelands" in South Africa. However, the theory behind these provisions by the Soviet state cannot exactly be classed as a milestone in the history of European thought.

After the disintegration of the Danubian Monarchy and the end of the Russian civil war, however, the national issues ceased to be of central concern to Social Democratic and Communist theoreticians. For Europe at least, at the end of World War I the time of fulfillment seemed to have arrived when the continent could be divided up on a national basis. In Eastern Europe "the collapse of four empires created a conglomeration of weak and inexperienced states,"[60] all formed in the name of the right of peoples to self-determination. But the drawing of the frontiers was not easy, for strategic, power-political, economic, historical, or simply practical factors were often the primary considerations. Furthermore, especially in the decades following industrialization, the lines separating nations (here in the sense of linguistic groups) had become increasingly blurred. With the "balkanization" of Eastern and Central Europe, sixty million people were liberated from foreign rule, but twenty million became new minorities[61] in the new states, a breeding ground for social and political unrest in the decades that followed. This is especially true of the German-speaking minorities who, more than others, suffered a lowering of their political, though usually not their social, status. They were ready to support revisionist movements that called into question the results of the Paris peace conferences, and among these groups elements of fascist ideology, that monstrously heightened form of nationalism, were able at an early date to find fertile soil.

Certainly exaggerated nationalism is not the only or even the central characteristic of the fascist movements of the interwar period. Nevertheless, it is an essential component, and is cited in all attempted definitions of fascism. Fascism would be unthinkable without an ideology of the "community" that enables sections of the population whose social position is threatened or who have already suffered a loss of social status to feel a sense of security and superiority (over other communities, i.e., nations or states).[62] That this process was inevitably accelerated to an extraordinary degree by the world economic crisis can hardly be doubted. That was one of the reasons why fascism attained a mass following and why left-wing internationalist attempts to oppose it were powerless. Internationalism—apart from some forms of naive cosmopolitanism—can on the whole be transmitted only by rational arguments, whereas nationalism and the "community" ideology were spread almost entirely by irrational, emotive means.

Because nationalism was being taken over by fascism, and because analysis of the causes of World War I pinpointed the role played by nationalism, the organized labor movement for some time suppressed nationalist ideas. Although there were two movements, in sharp competition with one another, which each had their own international organizations, both attached great importance to dissociating themselves from nationalist tendencies. The acute anti-Marxism that is characteristic of all fascist movements was to a large extent a hostile reaction to the international aspirations of the Social Democratic and Communist workers' movements ("the Jewish-Bolshevist world conspiracy").

The labor movement, by its distrust of nationalism, made it easy for fascism to appropriate a whole range of emotionally charged aspects of culture such as the study of one's native land, traditional customs, folksong, dance and so on, and was unable to offer effective alternatives.[63] It remained elitist, rational, and abstract, and was therefore bound to be defeated, at least outside the Soviet Union.

A change in Stalin's attitude toward the nationalities in the years of greatest threat helped Bolshevist Russia to succeed in its struggle for survival against National Socialism, but this does not prove that Stalin's theory was correct. Quite the contrary: whereas until a few years ago the national issue was considered to have been resolved reasonably satisfactorily, the events now taking place show that the problems had merely been overlaid with other things, not actually overcome.

The new nationalism in the Soviet Union corresponds to an awakening of nationalist tendencies in many parts of Europe.[64] The belief that nationalism was a nineteenth-century ideology and that modernization would make it less and less relevant is increasingly proving to be a fallacy. On this point Bauer's theory that national sentiment and the division of people into national groups would continue is borne out even in our present-day world of growing uniformity, in which McDonald's and Coca-Cola (and, equally, Sony, and higher culture) are beginning to iron out cultural differences. Given the speed of events in the last few months, however, any prognosis for the future, especially one by a historian (whose profession makes him more inclined to bet on yesterday's horseraces), would be pure charlatanry.

NOTES

1. Quotations from this work and others of Stalin's own writings are taken from J. W. Stalin, *Der Marxismus und die nationale und koloniale Frage* (Cologne, 1976). All translations are mine.
2. John Rettie, "The Decline and Fall of the Russian Empire?" *Guardian Weekly*, January 21, 1990 (a slightly abridged version of Rettie, "Vengeful Spirits of a Bitter Past," *Guardian*, January 16, 1990).
3. For a fuller account see Ernest Hanisch, *Der kranke Mann an der Donau. Marx und Engels über Österreich* (Vienna, 1978).
4. This point is clearly made in the best-known work, *The Communist Manifesto, Marx-Engels-Werke (MEW)* (Berlin, 1956), 4:459-593; see esp. 479.
5. Roman Rosdolsky, "Friedrich Engels und das Problem der 'geschichtslosen' Völker," *Archiv für Sozialgeschichte* (Hannover, 1964), 4:87-282.
6. Hanisch, *Der kranke Mann an der Donau*, 265.
7. Helmut Konrad, *Nationalismus und Internationalismus: Die österreichische Arbeiterbewegung vor dem Ersten Weltkrieg* (Vienna, 1976), 11.
8. *MEW*, 6:278f.
9. Hans Mommsen, "Sozialistische Arbeiterbewegung und nationale Frage in der Periode der I. und II. Internationale," *Internationale Tagung der Historiker der Arbeiterbewegung* (Eleventh Linz Conference, 1975) (Vienna, 1978), 263.
10. Ibid.
11. *MEW*, 4:479.
12. *MEW*, 4:504.
13. This expression, which has become a standard term in the subject literature, was first used by Otto Bauer in *Die Nationalitätenfrage und die Habsburgermonarchie*, 1st ed. (Vienna, 1907), 304.
14. On the situation of the Italians in Austria see Helmut Konrad, *Das Entstehen der Arbeiterklasse in Oberösterreich* (Vienna, 1981), 367-70.
15. Thus pamphlets were printed in two languages as a matter of course. At meetings speakers used their mother tongues. At party conferences in the early years there were interpreters. Several instances of this are cited in Herbert Steiner, *Die Arbeiterbewegung Österreichs, 1867-1889* (Vienna, 1964).
16. Konrad, *Oberösterreich*, 370ff.
17. Klaus Berchtold, ed., *Österreichische Parteiprogramme, 1868-1966* (Vienna, 1966), 116.
18. Herbert Steiner, "Der Neudörfler Parteitag und der Internationalismus." Conference paper given at Tagung der Internationalen Konferenz der

Historiker der Arbeiterbewegung (ITH; the International Conference of the Historians of the Labor Movement), in Neudörfl, 1974, 1.

19. Jochen Blaschke, ed. *Handbuch der westeuropäischen Regionalbewegungen* (Frankfurt am Main, 1980), 13.

20. Helmut Konrad, "Österreichische Arbeiterbewegung und nationale Frage im 19. Jahrhundert," *Sozialdemokratie und Habsburgerstaat*, ed. Wolfgang Maderthaner (Vienna, 1988), 126.

21. This had happened in the mid-1880s. Before this, as late as 1882, Adler had played a major part in formulating the Linz Program of the *Deutschnationalen*. See Berchtold, *Österreichische Parteiprogramme*, 195ff.

22. *Verhandlungen des sechsten österreichischen Sozialdemokratischen Parteitages, abgehalten zu Wien vom 6. bis einschließlich 12. Juni 1989* (Vienna, 1897), 125.

23. Peter Urbanitsch, "Die Deutschen in Österreich. Statistisch-deskriptiver Überblick," in *Die Habsburgermonarchie 1848-1918* (Vienna, 1980), vol. 3, *Die Völker des Reiches*, part 1. Percentage are taken from the table on p. 38.

24. John Bunzl, *Klassenkampf in der Diaspora: Zur Geschichte der jüdischen Arbeiterbewegung* (Vienna, 1975).

25. The editorial to the very first issue states explicitly that it is the special task of the Austrian Social Democrats to concern themselves with the national question. Otto Bauer, Adolf Braun, and Karl Renner, eds., *Der Kampf. Sozialdemokratische Monatsschrift*, (Vienna, 1908), 1:1.

26. Bauer, *Nationalitätenfrage*, 135.

27. Norbert Leser, *Zwischen Reformismus und Bolschewismus. Der Austromarxismus als Theorie und Praxis* (Vienna, 1968), 253.

28. Ernest Panzenböck, *Ein deutscher Traum. Die Anschlussidee und Anschlusspolitik bei Karl Renner und Otto Bauer* (Vienna, 1985), 28f.

29. Rudolf Springer [Karl Renner] *Grundlagen und Entwicklungsziele der Österreichisch-Ungarischen Monarchie* (Vienna, 1906), 208.

30. Raimund Löw, *Der Zerfall der "Kleinen Internationale". Nationalitätenkonflikte in der Arbeiterbewegung des alten Österreich (1889-1914)* (Vienna, 1984).

31. Konrad, *Nationalismus und Internationalismus*, 97ff.

32. See, for example, Bolumír Šmeral, "Die Sozialdemokratie und die nationale Frage." Paper given at the Ninth Conference of the Czechoslav Social Democratic Workers' party, Prague, September 4-8, 1909. Reprinted in Löw, *Zerfall der "Kleinen Internationale,"* 238-74. See also Zedenek Solle, "Die tschechische Sozialdemokratie zwischen Nationalismus und Internationalismus." In *Archiv für Sozialgeschichte*, (Hannover, 1969), vol. 9.

33. J. W. Stalin, "Welche Auffassung hat die Sozialdemokratie von der nationalen Frage?" In Stalin, *Der Marxismus*, 5-25.

34. Ibid., 23.

35. J. W. Stalin, "Marxismus und nationale Frage," ibid., 30.

36. Ibid., 32.

37. Ibid., 44.
38. Ibid., 79.
39. Ibid.
40. Otto Bauer, *Die österreichische Revolution* (Vienna, 1923).
41. The expression is Clemenceau's.
42. In the very last weeks of the war large parts of the Habsburg Monarchy were designated as belligerent states in opposition to the Central Powers. This made the work of the conference in the area of reparations, too, very complicated. See Manfred Bansleben, *Das österreichische Reparationsproblem auf der Pariser Friedenskonferenz* (Vienna, 1988).
43. Hanns Haas, "Otto Bauer und der Anschluss 1918/1919." In *Sozialdemokratie und "Anschluss". Historische Wurzeln—Anschluss 1918 und 1938—Nachwirkungen*, ed. Helmut Konrad (Vienna, 1978), 36-44.
44. Hans Hautmann, and Rudolf Kropf, *Die österreichische Arbeiterbewegung vom Vormärz bis 1945. Sozialökonomische Ursprünge ihrer Ideologie und Politik*, 3rd ed. (Vienna, 1978), 146ff.
45. Josef Weidenholzer, *Auf dem Weg zum "Neuen Menschen". Bildungs—und Kulturarbeit der österreichischen Sozialdemokratie in der Ersten Republik* (Vienna, 1981).
46. Otto Bauer, *Die illegale Partei* (Paris, 1939).
47. Resolution on the national question passed by the Seventh All-Russian Conference of the Russian Social Democratic Workers' party in April 1917. In Stalin, *Der Marxismus*, 365ff.
48. J. W. Stalin, "Der Oktoberumsturz und die nationale Frage" (1918). In Stalin, *Der Marxismus*, 111.
49. I. B. Berchin, *Geschichte der UdSSR, 1917-70* (Berlin [East], 1971), 201.
50. Ibid.
51. "Die nationalen Momente im Partei—und Staatsaufbau." Resolution passed by the Twelfth Party Conference of the Russian Communist party in April 1923. In Stalin, *Der Marxismus*, 386.
52. Ibid., 383.
53. J. W. Stalin, "Die Politik der Sowjetmacht in der nationalen Frage in Russland" (1920). In Stalin, *Der Marxismus*, 115.
54. On the history of the *Bund* see Arye Gelbard, *Der jüdische Arbeiter-Bund Russlands im Revolutionsjahr 1917* (Vienna, 1982). See also Bunzl, *Klassenkampf in der Diaspora*.
55. J. W. Stalin, "Die Politik der Sowjetmacht in der nationalen Frage in Russland" (1920). In Stalin, *Der Marxismus*, 120.
56. Helen L. Krag, "Vielvölkerstaat Sowjetunion." In *Wiener Tagebuch* 11 (1989): 24.
57. Ibid.
58. Ibid., 23.
59. See the studies by K. W. Deutsch, which are also cogently summarized in Hans Mommsen and Albrecht Martiny, "Nationalismus, National-

itätenfrage." In *Sowjetsystem und demokratische Gesellschaft* (Freiburg, 1971), 4:623-950.

60. K. R. Stadler, *The Birth of the Austrian Republic, 1918-1921* (Leiden, 1966), 8 (German edition, *Hypothek auf die Zukunft. Entstehung der österreichischen Republik, 1918-1921* [Vienna, 1968], 10).

61. Ibid., 17/17.

62. Reinhard Kuehnel, *Formen bürgerlicher Herrschaft. Liberalismus-Faschismus* (Reinbek bei Hamburg, 1971), 85f.

63. Helmut Konrad, "Nationalismus. Eine 'bürgerliche' Ideologie?" In *Ideologien im Bezugsfeld von Geschichte und Gesellschaft*, ed. Anton Pelinka (Innsbruck, 1981), 225.

64. On the regional movements see *Handbuch der westeuropäischen Regionalbewegungen*.

REFLECTIONS ON NATIONALISM AND EMPIRE

15

Main Themes—A Commentary

Teresa Rakowska-Harmstone

I

Two major themes have dominated the symposium: the emergence of modern nationalism and its immediate and inevitable corollary, the decline and disintegration of the imperial structures within which the new nations had appeared. Manifestations of nationalism have taken many forms. But its impact was felt with equal force by traditional dynastic and colonial empires, such as Austria-Hungary and imperial Russia, and by a modern imperial system based on universalistic ideological appeal, such as the Soviet Union.

There is no agreement among specialists on the definition of what constitutes nationalism, although there is no question that the phenomenon is instantly identifiable when it appears. But there is a consensus that two components—one subjective and another objective—are essential for nationalism to exist. The subjective component is a set of beliefs that assumes that a nation is a community into which a segment of the human race is naturally divided. If division into nations is a part of natural law, then a nation is the only valid source of political power, and loyalty to it overrides all other competing loyalties. It inevitably follows, therefore, that a community's destiny is fulfilled only when its nationhood converges with a statehood or, in other words, when it emerges into the international arena as a sovereign nation-state. Nationalism is thus the only true source of political legitimacy.

Because it depends on a set of beliefs, the subjective aspect of nationalism generates a high emotional quotient, which makes it an ideal instrument for political mobilization. Based on a sense of a common identity, a collective "we" excludes all others who are seen as an alien "they." The formation of this identity is stimulated by competition with other groups and is strongly reinforced by the presence (and perceptions) of foreign rule and oppression or an external threat. Ultimately the sense of a common nationhood rests on a belief in a common destiny, inclusive of a common past and a common future, the perception which is usually, but not necessarily, based on a set of objective circumstances.

The subjective component, essential for purposes of political legitimation, has been identified as modern nationalism's core doctrine. But it builds on particular characteristics specific to a given group, which constitute the necessary objective component, identified in turn as accretions.[1] The latter comprise primarily the group's cultural characteristics such as the language, forms of artistic expression, symbols, customs, and "way of life," as well as an accumulated historical memory.[2] The dynamics of interaction between the subjective perceptions and objective characteristics have been essential for the emergence of modern nationalism. Ultimately, an ideal of a nation-state becomes a goal of a nation's aspirations and an embodiment of its final destiny.

An ideal of a nation-state articulated by an ethnic community in a multiethnic state creates an obvious conflict of political loyalties. Very few states are in fact homogeneous, and the withholding of political loyalty to the state by the groups within that are seeking independent political expression has been a major source of instability in the late nineteenth and twentieth centuries. The conflict is particularly acute in the state systems whose political legitimacy rests on principles other than nationalism. This has been the case in the three empires under review here. The Habsburg Empire was built on a dynastic principle. The colonial expansion of the Russian Empire was justified by the Russians' civilizing mission. The legitimacy of the Soviet Union has rested on an ideological assumption that loyalty to a class historically overrides loyalty to a nation.

The perception of a common identity by an ethnocultural group does not automatically equate with full-blown nationalism. Rather, the latter develops gradually. Students of ethnicity suggest at least three basic stages in the evolution of an ethnic group into a nation: self-identification; internal cohesion as an ethnic community; and separatism, which demands independent statehood.[3]

The stage of self-identification is reached when an ethnocultural group acquires a sense of its own identity, through the development of its language and other cultural markers. Internal cohesion grows in response to challenges and competition from other groups. The second stage is marked by the emergence of ethnic elites who formulate and articulate the community's particular demands, seek satisfaction of these demands from central authorities, and mobilize members of their community in support of these demands. One keen observer of the ethnic scene noted that social demands generated on an ethnic base are strategically more efficacious in a modern state, particularly a welfare state, than demands generated by other causes, because ethnic demands have higher affective value and are potentially more explosive.[4] Such demands are still seen as an expression of ethnic rather than nationalist movements. Particular ethnic political loyalties are formed at this stage, but they are still compatible with overarching political loyalty to a common state. Each community pursues its own advantage in competition with others within the existing state structures in a process best described as ethnic politics.

The third and final stage, separatism, is reached when the loyalty to a particular ethnic community becomes incompatible with the loyalty to the state of which it is a part. Ethnicity becomes nationalism when the group demands the establishment of its own sovereign national state. By withholding their political loyalty from the existing state structure, members of the group deny the state its political legitimacy, and preclude any relationship between their community and the state, except on the basis of full equality and independence. Separatism requires the existence of a compact territorial base of national settlement, a requirement that is not essential for the pursuit of ethnic politics.

The stages of development in national self-assertion are well illustrated in this volume. Miroslav Hroch convincingly analyzes the crucial importance of language for the self-identification of ethnic groups in Austria-Hungary and in the Russian/Soviet empires, and for the development of their ethnic cohesion. John-Paul Himka charts the evolution from ethnicity to nationalism in the Habsburg Empire and in the Soviet Union, and Paul Magocsi discusses the transition, among the Ukrainians of Galicia, from the stage of multiple loyalties, to that of an exclusive loyalty to the ideal of a sovereign Ukraine.

Stages of development may vary widely for particular ethnic communities in a multiethnic state at a given point in time. This was true of the two historical empires under discussion here, and it is the case in the Soviet Union today. The nationalism of the three Baltic states (Lithuania, Latvia, and

Estonia), as well as that of the Romanians of Bessarabia, now known as the Moldavians, predated their incorporation by the Soviet state, and similar and more ancient claims can be made on behalf of the Armenians and the Georgians. Ethnic politics of other union republic nations, and of other ethnic minorities, came into the open in the period of the post-Stalin thaw. Ethnic politics became an important variable in the struggle for political power among Stalin's successors.[5] In the five years since the ascendancy to the Soviet leadership of Mikhail Gorbachev, the so-called "national problem" has emerged as the key threat—next to the economic crisis—to the preservation of the Soviet Union and to the maintenance of Gorbachev's leadership.

As of February 1991 the demands of union republic nations ranged from proclamations of independence by the three Baltic republics, Armenia, Georgia and Moldova (Moldavia), to the statements of "sovereignty" by the remaining nine republics, including that of the Russians who form the core of the union. In current Soviet usage "sovereignty" has come to mean a transitional position on a continuum from ethnicity to nationalism, but a position that approaches nationalism. As defined in the declarations of the Supreme Soviets of the nine republics (genuinely elected for the first time), "sovereignty" allows for the preservation of the union, but strictly on the basis of a transfer of power *from* the republics *to* the federal government. The declarations leave no doubt that it is the nationhood of each of the republics rather than the All-Union state that is the source of political legitimacy, an interpretation that makes the disintegration of the Soviet Union as a centralized state all but inevitable.

But the process is by no means complete, even as the momentum accelerates. The Russians, Ukrainians and Belorussians have yet to consolidate their full national identity. Southeastern Moslem republics lag even further behind on the continuum in that they press for far-reaching autonomy, but are obviously not ready to strike out on their own. One should remember also that substantial ethnic minorities—immigrant as well as indigenous—are present in all of the republics. The Russian Soviet Federated Socialist Republic (RSFSR) is itself formally a federal entity, with one-fifth of its population of non-Russian ethnic origin. Most of the Soviet minorities now seem to have moved from the stage of self-identification to that of ethnic cohesion.

As the union republics have carved out for themselves a substantial autonomy and are pressing for more, ethnic politics have come to the fore in their own domestic arena. One needs only to mention immigrant Russian minorities in non-Russian republics, the notorious conflict between the

Armenians and Azerbaijani over the Nagorno-Karabakh enclave, the Abkhazians and Ossetians in Georgia, or the Gagauz in Moldavia. In the RSFSR also the autonomous republic (ASSR) nations such as the Tatars, the Bashkirs, and the Yakuts are becoming restive. The potential for political gain for the center through the manipulation of lesser nationalisms has not escaped the attention of Gorbachev's government.

II

A number of factors contributed to the rise of nationalism. This summary cannot begin to review the origins of the concept and its importance and development as a dominant world ideology. But it is relevant to remember that it originated in Europe in the wake of the French Revolution, which had replaced the outdated concepts governing human association under ancien régime with new principles. The Revolution's holy trinity of *liberté, égalité, fraternité* was taken throughout Europe and into imperial Russia by the armies of Napoleon and contributed to the erosion of the ruling myths and to the breakdown of boundaries between the various populations of the two empires. These boundaries were undermined also by industrialization, which moved the people from closed traditional peasant societies into new urban and industrial centers. The accompanying development of education and communications stimulated the sense of self-identity among ethnocultural communities and led to a new emphasis on the development of their languages and other cultural attributes. Opportunities that opened up with economic development led to new socioeconomic differentiation and new competition in the marketplace, the competition in which each group sought support and protection among their traditional kith and kin, both in their traditional setting and in its new urban and industrial counterparts.

New conditions created a new focus for each group's sense of ethnic cohesion. Political expectations were stimulated by the new ideas. As the old principles of political organization were eroded, the ideas of liberty and equality served to direct each group's efforts toward the maximization of its own role, status, and advantages. Interacting in a multiethnic setting, the perception of each community's standing was influenced by the relative position of the others. The perceived inequalities as well as the rising expectations made the communities' newly developing (or revalidated) sense of identity the basis, first, for cultural, then for social, economic, and political demands, inaugurating a new era of ethnic politics. Ethnic elites, formed as the result of changing social and economic conditions, came to be the spokespersons for the demands, and a vital element in their articulation and implementation (see Dennison Rusinow's chapter in this volume).

The idea of fraternal unity, on the other hand, proved irrelevant to the new surging sense of ethnic consciousness, even as it provided the impetus, along with the idea of equality, for the development of the other dominant new ideology, socialism. In the struggle between the two, and as the twentieth century comes to a close, nationalism appears to be the winner in the battle for humanity's primary allegiance.

In Western Europe and in the Habsburg Empire, the first wave of instability brought about by new nationalism was felt in the "Spring of the Peoples" of 1848. The reverberations in the Russian Empire were still weak then. But as the century progressed, ethnic politics increasingly moved on toward nationalism, not only in the case of the "historical" nations, such as the Hungarians and the Poles, but very much in the case of the "new" ones, such as the Czechs and the Ukrainians. In the cataclysm of World War I nationalism was the key factor in the disintegration of the two empires; in Russia it was also a major component in the October Revolution. But as the Bolsheviks took over the Revolution and consolidated the new Soviet state, it came to be subordinated again to a new unity based on class Principle, in a triumph of rival socialist ideology. Nationalist manifestations were suppressed, and the proponents of nationalist ideas were liquidated.

Nonetheless the historical process of the reemergence of ethnic politics and its maturation into nationalism was repeated in the Soviet Union as soon as the suppression eased off. Although the setting was different, the constraints more formidable, and the stimuli more differentiated and in some ways more effective, the same two key conditions that stimulated the growth of nationalism in Austria-Hungary and in tsarist Russia were also instrumental in its development in the Soviet Union. These were the impact of modernization and social and economic change—stimulated this time by policies directed from above—and an emergence of powerful ethnic elites within the Soviet power structure, acting as the advocates of new nationalisms.[6]

It is interesting to note that Lenin and early modernization theorists both assumed that the process of modernization and economic development, and the resulting destruction of traditional societies, would also result in the destruction of traditional ethnocultural divisions, and thus would mean an adoption, in a modern setting, of uniform modern values. Lenin saw it as the process of internationalization, which began under mature capitalism and was to be continued under socialism, in the course of which the loyalty to a class worldwide would supersede loyalty to a nation. Both were proved wrong because the transition from the traditional to a modern setting has in fact resulted in "nationalization" of traditional ethnicity. In both cases the theory has to be revised. In the Soviet case the survival of nationalism was explained by a persistence, in each ethnic community, of a core perception of a national *etnos* that survives through all stages of historical development. It was explained also by dialectical progression, as the need of each nation to fulfill its historical destiny by consolidating its nationhood. The latter point is similar to Daniel Bell's perception that nations are driven by historical energies to seek a place on the stage of history.[7]

Central state policies have been of major importance in the development of nationalism, especially in the case of policies that brought results the opposite of those intended. Each of the three imperial systems attempted to deal with the ethnic factor in its own way. Austria-Hungary's "dualism" relegated lesser nations to subordinate status; imperial Russia followed an assimilation policy, aiming to submerge non-Russians into a culturally Russian whole.[8] The Soviet Union developed an elaborate formal hierarchy of national units governed *de facto* by a unitary and avowedly supranational Communist party. All three failed to resolve the national problem, perhaps because each carried the seeds of its own delegitimation, as Motyl argues in this volume, by tacitly favoring the hegemonial nation: the Germans in Austria-Hungary and the Russians in imperial Russia and the Soviet Union. This denied others access to political power and undermined the very legitimacy of the imperial systems.

III

This brings us to the second major theme, that of imperial disintegration. As I have noted, each of the three imperial systems has failed in its stated aim of developing a supranational common identity, a failure that eroded the systems' legitimacy and created a vacuum that was to be filled by new nationalisms. The use of coercion was a poor and ineffective substitute, serving only to reinforce the nationalism of the oppressed. The imperatives of system maintenance took priority over officially stated goals. The substitution (goal-transfer culture in Chalmers Johnson's definition)[9] was particularly glaring in the case of the Soviet Union where the need to maintain the political status quo excluded meaningful reforms, until Gorbachev's desperate gamble. The latter's reforms, now in partial retreat, have in fact destroyed the system but so far have failed to provide a new one that would be acceptable to the country's national constituencies.

The failure of integration had many features in common in all three imperial systems. None was able to develop a common identity that would override new burgeoning political loyalties based in particular nationalisms. All failed in developing policies that would neutralize and counteract nationalist claims. Instead, the policies instituted to achieve that aim boomeranged by perpetuating inequalities, inflaming nationalist tensions, and stimulating nationalist demands. Nationalist elites were given the form but not the substance of political power and progressively became more militant. Last but not least, each imperial system ultimately proved unable to perform the basic political, economic, and social functions required by the citizens. The two historical ones collapsed by becoming involved in a war that acted as the catalyst in exploding accumulated historical grievances and failed policies. The modern one is folding under the weight of its own ineptitude and the systemic flaw that precludes accommodation to change.

Crane Brinton's seminal analysis of the causes of four great revolutions does not explicitly treat nationalism. But it highlights the reasons for the disintegration of "our" three empires, even though only one of them (so far) also underwent a great revolution.[10] Brinton suggests that revolutions came, not when the oppressive characteristics of the regimes were at their peak, but when they were in decline, with the need for reform recognized and the will to repress largely lost. He also notes that the impetus for change in each case was provided by newly emerged prosperous elites, which had no access to political power but were economically and socially too important to be ignored. Both these points are valid for an analysis of national disintegration of imperial multiethnic states.

The most important of Brinton's insights, however, concerns the dynamics of revolutionary development. The demands of the new elites, he tells us, were initially moderate, but, as the old regimes were reluctant to respond, the demands became increasingly more radical, acquiring an accelerating momentum of their own. Thus, even as concessions were eventually made, they were far too late for accomodation as new, more radical demands had already been formulated. The resulting dynamics of interaction can best be described as snowballing toward disintegration. This kind of snowballing has been characteristic also of the disintegration of "our" imperial systems. The snowball effect is unmistakably present in the current Soviet situation, which seems to be accelerating out of control. In all cases there was also a loss of will to repress, and a loss of fear by and consequently a marked increase in the militancy of the dissident elites.

In the modern era the snowball effect has been greatly enhanced by the effectiveness of the technology of communications, as seen in the speed of mobilization of ethnic consciousness not only in the interaction between the center and the periphery but also across political boundaries. In comparing the historical with the Soviet case, the symposium's discussions have centered largely on the internal dynamics of mobilization of national consciousness within the USSR. But the process has affected both the "outer" and the "inner" Soviet empire, with the momentum of nationalism gathering up and exploding first in East-Central Europe thence it has spread to Soviet western borderlands. The "outer" empire was established by the Soviet Union after World War II on the same supranational class-mobilizing principle that formed the basis for the creation of the Soviet Union after World War I. But it comprises the familiar peoples of the old Habsburg and Romanov domains, and once again the use of force, the imposition of foreign rule, and the failure of the mobilizing myth to develop legitimacy fanned the fires of nationalism. Looking at the events from the perspective of the "Lands in Between," there is historical justice in the events unfolding in the last decade of this century, because the myth of "internationalism" that had been imposed on the region is now being rolled back eastward and replaced by a tide of nationalism.

NOTES

1. See A. D. Smith, *Theories of Nationalism* (New York, 1971), 171.
2. It may be relevant to note here that in the case of many Third World postcolonial states, especially in Africa, the accretions were reduced to a minimum, with the impetus for decolonization having been provided mainly by an idea, based on little else than a collective belief in a given community, that they constituted a nation. See Rupert Emerson's classic study, *From Empire to Nation: The Rise to Self-Assertion of Asian and African Peoples* (Cambridge, Mass., 1960). But the problem inherent in the coexistence of a number of different ethnocultural communities within these new nations inevitably came to the fore later, as the competition between them led to demands for self-assertion by each. This phenomenon has been perhaps the most important source of political instability in the Third World, repeating processes that affected East-Central Europe in the early twentieth century, and which are now at work within the inner (the Soviet Union) and outer (the Bloc) Soviet empire.
3. See Smith, *Theories*, and Paul R. Bass, "Ethnicity and Nationality Formation," *Ethnicity* 33 (September, 1976).
4. Nathan Glazer, "Introduction," in *Ethnicity: Theory and Experience*, ed. N. Glazer and P. Moynihan (Cambridge, Mass., 1975).
5. See my "Dialectics of Nationalism in the USSR," *Problems of Communism*, 23 (May-June 1974).

6. For a detailed discussion of the conditions that facilitated the emergence of ethnic nationalism in the Soviet Union see my "Dialectics of Nationalism." See also my "Chicken Coming Home to Roost; A Perspective on Soviet Ethnic Relations," in *The "National Question" in the Soviet Union*, ed., John Jaworsky (Waterloo, Ont., 1991), forthcoming.

7. Daniel Bell, "Ethnicity and Social Change" in Glazer and Moynihan, *Ethnicity*. For a discussion of this point see my "Nationalities Question" in *The Soviet Union: Looking to the 1980's*, ed., Robert Wesson (Stanford, Calif., and Millwood, N.Y., 1978).

8. The very name for the country—Rossiya—and an adjective, rossiiskii, indicate a multiethnic entity, but an entity mobilized on the basis of the Russian language and culture. The terms describing ethnically Great Russian equivalents were Rus' and russkii. In translation both appear as "Russia" and "Russian."

9. Chalmers Johnson, "Comparing Communist Nations," in *Change in Communist Systems*, ed., Chalmers Johnson (Stanford, Calif., 1970), 1-34.

10. Crane Brinton, *The Anatomy of a Revolution* (New York, 1938).

16

Reflections on Great Power Ethnic Politics

Walter Leitsch

Many interesting contributions to the meeting gave the participants a chance to broaden and deepen their knowledge of Habsburg and Soviet history. This was a pleasant surprise to me, since in the beginning the topic of the meeting had seemed rather curious to me as a historian. There is an essential difference between the two empires: Only one of them fully belongs to the historians because it does not exist any more. The other exists and—what could not but profoundly influence the outlook of the participants—has in our times considerable troubles as a multinational state. This is, however, not really a historical but a political problem. The outcome is open. The historians had better not meddle into affairs like this.

There was another phenomenon that made me feel uneasy and that is that any such comparison makes us commit the sin of anachronism: One of the two empires crumbled, whereas the other was created. They existed in two different periods. Even had their political philosophies been closer, a comparison would be a doubtful undertaking. The difference of time is always and everywhere also a difference of principles and mentalities (John-Paul Himka, Valery Tishkov, and Miroslav Hroch touched this point).

For a scholar a comparison like this seems to contradict the principles one is used to observing in one's work. However, does a person earning a living as a historian stop being a curious person asking strange questions? Those who ask strange questions often allow us to understand things better. Historians should never give up and try to act as normal persons. I think that after this meeting we all understood some of the problems of the Habsburg Empire and the Soviet Union better than we did when we arrived in Minneapolis. What conclusions can be drawn from such a comparison? Should Austria-Hungary serve as a paradigm for methods of breaking up multinational empires? Should we study the tactics the nineteenth-century politicians devised to prolong the existence of the multinational Habsburg state? I do not believe that Soviet politicians need lectures in "muddling through." I think they master this art brilliantly and they are not really in need of enriching their knowledge in political strategy by studying what Taaffe did or rather what he did *not* do.

In trying to understand what has been going on in Eastern Europe in the last several years there seems to be a dividing line between the lands. I think that one of the characteristics may be traced back to the times before 1918. Franz Joseph is not one my favorite heroes of Austrian history. He had, however, one political quality that had a beneficial impact upon the development of his empire: He tolerated activities and developments he did not approve of; more often than not, he did not even understand them. There is, I think, a certain tradition of Habsburg ruling methods that survives up to our days. In Poland, Czechoslovakia, Hungary, Croatia, and Slovenia even Communist politicians time and again tolerated the activities of dissident groups, although they disapproved of their ideas and aims and were in many cases unable to understand them. Thus alternatives to Communist rule have been built up and the transition to a multiparty system of government can be mastered with less hardship than in other parts of Eastern Europe that have no such tradition of a limited political laissez-faire. One should, of course, not overestimate the merits of Franz Joseph for developments in the years 1989 and 1990. There are many more elements in the tradition of these nations that contributed to their recent achievements.

After listening with great attention and profit to the speeches and discussions I had the feeling that there were six problems that have not received sufficient attention. This is quite understandable: Two topics as complex as the nationality troubles in the Habsburg and Soviet empires cannot be discussed exhaustively in just two days. I shall try to describe these six issues briefly.

1. People have to move around and work wherever their capacities are needed. In multinational states this leads to an inextricable mixture of population and to various forms of assimilation, that is, to a complex set of sociopolitical attitudes. The authorities have to work hard to keep order in such a society. Development in the past 150 years shows, however, that these

problems can be mastered whenever there is enough goodwill and political skill. The borders that had existed in earlier centuries between these nations were blurred by their cohabitation in one state. In East-Central Europe there were regions with a nationally mixed population since the Middle Ages. The economic development and increased mobility of the population speeded up this mixture in the nineteenth century. German and later Czech skilled labor, as well as Ruthenian, Slovak, and Polish cheap unskilled labor, migrated to rapidly developing new industrial centers just as Russian skilled labor moved to Central Asia and Russian skilled and unskilled labor to the Baltic lands in later decades.

Political commentators living in other countries and observing from a great distance the troubles between nations living in a multinational empire often considered the territorial dismemberment of the empire along national boundaries as the best of all possible solutions. But was it really a good solution? For the successor states in the interwar period, only the losers had relatively little trouble with nationality issues. All the others inherited the difficulties that had contributed so much to the dissolution of the empire. Only the roles were in some cases exchanged: Those who had been suppressed—or at least felt like it—were now the suppressors, and vice versa. The total quantity of happiness and unhappiness in the region did not decrease or increase considerably; only the distribution of it changed.

As to this issue, the parallels are evident. The difference in attitude, living conditions, and political standing between the Germans in Bohemia in 1920 and the Russians in Latvia in 1990 is primarily one of history: Germans had lived in Bohemia for many centuries, but most of the Russians now living in Latvia were not born there. As to the rest the situation is similar: Being in the future possibly no more part of the "ruling" nation the Russians might consider leaving Latvia, which they had considered their home for many years. But where should they go? Home to Russia? Is this really "going home"? To create clear borders between nations, drastic measures were taken during and after World War II. They caused enormous hardship to one generation, but liberated the children and grandchildren from the troubles caused by the cohabitation of people speaking different languages. Does anyone have the right to sacrifice the happiness of one generation for the benefit of posterity?

On the other hand the mixture of language groups has been culturally fruitful, and there is good reason to believe that the clear-cut separation of them will make us poorer. This is speculation, however. The militant hatred against the Slovenes has by no means raised the intellectual level of the German-speaking Carinthians—just the contrary. On the other side competition between Czechs and Germans in Bohemia worked wonders in culture before 1914. Nationality conflicts often accelerate the cultural development, but they do not have this effect always and everywhere.

Empires may be broken up in the name of nationalism, but nationalists cannot offer solutions for the problems of cohabitation of different national groups living together in one territory. The contented and the discontented might change roles, but there is always the risk that in the final account this turns out to be rather a loss. States with an extremely severe control of all spheres of life may for a while create the impression of having defeated national hatred, but (as they lack these qualities themselves) they cannot improve mutual understanding and tolerance.

2. Few contributors speak about the principal differences in the demographic structure of the two empires. These differences deserve more attention. In 1910 the Hungarians and Germans constituted together slightly more than 44 percent (23.9 percent Germans, 20.2 percent Hungarians) of the total population of the Habsburg Empire; Slavs made up almost half of it. Repeated efforts to mobilize the Slavs for joint actions were seldom successful, but caused great apprehension among the Germans and Hungarians. There were several underprivileged peoples that spoke similar languages. United they were numerically stronger than the privileged. These, the *Staatsnationen*, did not live in harmony and in some years before 1914 it looked as if they disagreed about almost everything. In the divided empire the two *Staatsnationen* had very different weight in their own parts. The Hungarians—growing in percentage (1880, 41.2; 1900, 45.4)—still were a minority (48.1 percent) in their own part in 1910, if we include Croatia-Slavonia (without Croatia-Slavonia, 54.5 percent in 1910). The percentage of Germans in the Cisleithanian part of the Empire—which, however, was not called German as the other was called Hungarian—declined (1880, 36.8 percent, 1900, 36.1) and dropped to nearly one third (1910, 35.6) before the great war.

The demographic structure of the Soviet Union—as of the Russian Empire—is very different. If the calculations based upon the results of the first and only census ever carried out in the Russian Empire (1897) are correct, the Russians were about as numerous as the Germans and Hungarians together (viz. 44.3 percent), but in second and third place we find the Ukrainians and the White Russians, who are closely related to the Russians. Their languages do not differ very much, so they can communicate without learning the other languages. In Soviet times the Russians passed the 50 percent mark in all censuses. But what counts more is that before and after 1917 the three East Slavic nations together made up more than two thirds of the total population. On the other hand most of the other nations—with the exception of those living in Central Asia—are divided by language and tradition. Even those who have a common background speak entirely different languages, and others who have related languages have different cultural traditions.

I remember that in the 1930s, when I was a boy, many adults thought Austria was too small to survive. The dismemberment of the Habsburg Empire produced a number of small states. In the case of Russia or the Soviet Union the situation is principally different. If all the republics of the Soviet Union were to become sovereign states, the Russian republic would be left with more than half of the population, most of the territory, and most of the raw materials for industrial development. Compared to the dismemberment of the Austro-Hungarian Empire the dismemberment of the Soviet Union would produce an entirely different political system: For all the peripheral regions of the Soviet Union that might be transformed into sovereign states, Russia would remain the big and mighty neighbor, the chief problem of their foreign relations.

3. In this conference the relationship between center and periphery (Alexander J. Motyl); the importance of the constitutions of the lands as an element of order (István Deák) and the advantages and disadvantages of centralism (Sergei Romanenko) were discussed. Politicians in both empires could not but act on the ground prepared by previous generations. Beginning in the time of Maria Theresa the particularism of the lands in political life was systematically reduced, sometimes with more vigor, sometimes with more respect for traditions. The historical lands, however, continued to play an important role as an element of the political order. At all times new rules could gain full force only when accepted by all constituent parts of the Empire. Bargaining had to be developed into a refined art to preserve the unity in diversity.

Most of those who touched this problem did so in the context of the Habsburg Empire. Finland is an interesting, but unimportant, exception. In the Russian Empire bargaining was not a necessity; the center was strong enough simply to give orders. In the fifteenth century there existed a well-developed regionalism that was destroyed in the sixteenth century. When Catherine II tried to create noble institutions at the regional level, she evidently had in mind the *adelige Landestände* of Central Europe. No such institutions developed in Russia. The nobles had no ties to a specific region. When asked, where he comes from, a noble would call himself a *tambovskii pomeshchik*, a landowner from Tambov. It is hard to translate this into German—*der Gutsbesitzer von Tambov* sounds strange. The same difficulty arises when the term *ein steirischer Edelmann*, a noble from Styria, is to be translated into Russian. The political upper class in the Habsburg Monarchy had grown up with the regional diversity of Styria, Moravia, Tyrol, and so on, and easily accepted the Empire as a conglomeration of particular regions. The Russian-speaking upper class of the Romanov Empire never experienced regionalism. Peter the Great and Alexander I acted against the Russian tradition when creating autonomous regions, which for the Russian bureaucrats, and not just for the conservatives among them, represented a transitional stage on the way to full incorporation. Their tradition of administration and political order was purely centralist. Why should they accept regional autonomy for the nations living in the border regions?

The organization of the Bolshevik party, too, was highly centralist. It fit into the Russian tradition and brought no break at all. The federal order of the Soviet Union was to a great degree only an ornamentation on the facade; the house behind it was highly centralized in character. Many of the problems of our days would not exist had the central administration in the Soviet Union shown more understanding for federal solutions. These are, however, alien to the mind of a Russian functionary. On the other hand, we should not forget that tolerance for local traditions did not prevent the dissolution of the Habsburg Monarchy and that the principles were not always the same in the two halves of the Monarchy.

4. Almost all peoples of the Habsburg Monarchy had in common the century-old tradition of Latin culture. It is true that they spoke different languages, but they had common roots in art, architecture, music, and life-styles. This shared background created a common cultural atmosphere, which in recent years has become a favorite topic of historians and politicians. This *spirito mitteleuropeo* made communication easier, brought about a balance between diversity and unity, and produced common cultural qualities.

Political authorities intervened to a greater extent in cultural life in the Russian Empire and with much more serious consequences in the Soviet empire. To a certain extent they distorted the culture, but even under these adverse conditions the quality of culture life remained high. However, all attempts to unify it failed. The differences among the Eastern Slavs are not significant, but they are distinct in comparison to all the others. The background of the Estonians and Latvians is German, of the Lithuanians it is Polish. The peoples living south of the Caucasus Mountains show great differences in tradition and culture. These differences are smaller in the large plain of Central Asia. In both regions the native cultures are, however, extremely different from the Russian one. Unification in Soviet terms remained superficial. These peoples not only speak their own languages, they live in completely different worlds. They have much more trouble understanding each other than did the subjects of Franz Joseph two generations earlier.

In the sphere of tradition and culture, too, the difference in size has a negative effect. The Russians with few exceptions considered these small peoples with their own traditions as picturesque ornaments to their own cultural life, whereas the small ones sealed themselves off from the Russian influence out of fear of the tremendous weight of the giant master. In this and other regards the Soviet Union is much more a colonial empire than was the Habsburg Empire.

5. The specific problems of the Hungarians, Czechs, South Slavs, Ukrainians, and Jews were analyzed during the conference, but the problems of other nations were not discussed. For two reasons I especially missed a discussion of the problems of the Poles. First, they lived in both the Romanov and Habsburg empires. This gives the historian a good chance for a comparison of the ethnic policies of the two empires. Second, the Poles fared rather well in the Habsburg Empire by cooperating with the center. They were able to build up a well-functioning autonomy in Galicia. The imperial administration agreed to a "deal" primarily to make the Reichsrat function and strengthen the loyalty of the population in a border region, which was of strategic importance for the Empire.

The Poles, having been rather unruly in the hundred years before this cooperation with Vienna began in the 1860s, had a disproportionately large share in the central administration and were reliable and loyal subjects of the emperor. This was a problem much discussed by contemporaries and historians: The Poles were loyal to the Polish nation, which was divided into three parts and lived in three empires, and at the same time they were loyal to the Empire. This double loyalty was bedeviled by militant nationalists and in general by all those who subscribed to a totalitarian ideology. Double loyalty is often considered by historians as something not quite clean and decent. These historians—to be consistent—tend to condemn multinational empires, since they could function in the nineteenth century only with the help of double loyalty.

All those who practiced double loyalty time and again suffered from inner conflicts. But these conflicts contributed to a more conscious life and forced people to refine their political philosophies in the same way that any conflicts of loyalty contribute to a person's maturation. One is loyal to one's parents, to one's teachers (I hope so!), to one's school, firm and colleagues; one can combine loyalty to one's spouse and one's friends.

I think it is time to appreciate the positive qualities of a well-developed and well-balanced multiple loyalty—to one's house, town, province, and country. As a European I like to see Europeans being also loyal to their continent. Why should there not be an empire between country and continent? This is—I have to admit—not in vogue in our day, but our ancestors should not be blamed for their multiple loyalties.

6. The economic problems were discussed only at the very end of this meeting. Many historians manage to see everywhere and always nothing but economic problems. They might have been astonished—to say the least—about the behavior of colleagues who have lost touch with reality. This obsession with problems of economy is, however, a relatively modern phenomenon. In the community of historians the Marxists were those who pushed this development most vigorously. They were, however, well within a general trend. In the times of the Habsburg Empire the educated opinion leaders and the population in general paid much less attention to economic development. They did not believe that a government was able to steer the economy; they did not make the government responsible for solving economic difficulties as people do in our time. It would have been one of those anachronisms I mentioned earlier, if too much attention had been paid to the economic and social side of the nationality troubles before World War I. The economists are right when they argue that the Habsburg Monarchy was an asset and should not have been dismembered. Most of those interested in politics in the beginning of the century might have agreed with their arguments, but they would not have attributed to them as much importance as people do today. The Marxists were an exception, but the split of their party into separate national units demonstrates, better than anything else, that the public was more interested in national separation than in economic prosperity.

Today things are different. The public is interested in economic problems and does make the government responsible for their prosperity. Recently I told a representative of a small Soviet nation: "Most of the Austrians, although living in a prosperous country five times bigger than your republic, think that their prosperity can only be safeguarded in a big economic region, and that is why they are in favor of joining the European Economic Community. Why does your small nation want to give up the advantages it enjoys being part of the huge Soviet market?" His answer was: "But this is not an economy, it is a mess."

The Habsburg Empire was economically successful. It fell apart. People did not care so much for the economic implications. Most certainly one of the important arguments of the small Soviet nations for separation from the

Union is its failure to build up a prosperous economy. As to the second part of the general topic of this meeting, economic arguments would have deserved more attention.

LIST OF CONTRIBUTORS

ERHARD BUSEK - Vice Chancellor of Austria and the Austrian Federal Minister of Science and Research.

ISTVÁN DEÁK - Professor of History (Columbia University, New York).

DAVID F. GOOD - Director Center for Austrian Studies and Professor of History (University of Minnesota, Twin Cities).

JOHN-PAUL HIMKA - Associate Professor of History (University of Alberta, Edmonton).

MIROSLAV HROCH - Professor of History (Charles University, Prague).

TOFIK M. ISLAMOV - Researcher (Institute of Slavic and Balkan Studies, USSR Academy of Sciences, Moscow), Lecturer (Moscow State University).

HELMUT KONRAD - Chair of Department of Contemporary History and Professor of Contemporary History (Karl Franzens-University of Graz).

WALTER LEITSCH - Director Institute for East and Southeast European Research (University of Vienna), Lecturer (Institute of European Studies, Vienna).

PAUL ROBERT MAGOCSI - Chair of Ukrainian Studies, Professor of History, and Professor of Political Science, (University of Toronto).

WILLIAM O. MCCAGG, JR. - Professor of History (Michigan State University).

ALEXANDER J. MOTYL - Assistant Professor of Political Science (Columbia University, New York).

TERESA RAKOWSKA-HARMSTONE - Professor of Political Science (Carleton University, Ottawa).

SERGEI A. ROMANENKO - Research Associate (Institute of Slavic and Balkan Studies, Academy of Sciences, Moscow).

RICHARD L. RUDOLPH - Professor of History (University of Minnesota, Twin Cities).

DENNISON RUSINOW - Professor, Russian and East European Studies Center and Department of History (University of Pittsburgh).

HENRYK SZLAJFER - Professor, Institute of History (Academy of Sciences, Warsaw)

VALERY A. TISHKOV - Director Institute of Ethnology (Academy of Sciences, Moscow).

INDEX